Library of
Davidson College

SOCIAL PSYCHOLOGY AND THE STUDY OF DEVIANT BEHAVIOR

Andrew John Pavlos

Copyright © 1979 by

University Press of America, Inc.™

4710 Auth Place, S.E., Washington, D.C. 20023

All rights reserved
Printed in the United States of America

ISBN: 0-8191-0664-X

301.6
P338s

Library of Congress Catalog Card Number: 78-65426

81-130

To Charlotte, Ricky and Anthony

Pavlos

About the Author

Andrew J. Pavlos, Ph.D., the author, is Associate Professor of Social Psychology at George Williams College. He has read and published research in experimental social psychology and has had extensive research and teaching experience with special interests in attribution theory, philosophy of science, and research methods.

ACKNOWLEDGEMENTS

Colleagues and countless students enrolled in my devivant behavior classes have influenced significantly the efforts that produced this book. I thank them collectively because they are indeed too numerous to thank individually. And, finally to my wife Charlotte Altizer Pavlos goes my gratitude and affection for turning handwriting into typescript. She is a warm friend and a loving wife.

CONTENTS

Chapter 1: <u>Deviant Behavior</u>: <u>Perspectives</u> <u>and</u> <u>Problems</u> <u>of</u> <u>Definition</u>

Introduction..............................1
The Sociology of Deviancy..................4
Sociology and the Symbolic Interactionist
  Perspective...........................5
Deviance as Norm Violation............... 6
Labeling Theory and Norm Violation:
  What's Wrong With Labeling Theory?......9
Deviance and Role Theory................ 17
Role Theory and Its Relationship to
  Deviant Subculture....................22
The Deviation Hypothesis: A Psychologi-
  cal Perspective.......................24
The Social Psychology of Deviance........26
Difference Theory: Does Difference Make
  a Difference?.........................27
Deviance, Problems with Definitions......30
Summary and Conclusions..................34

Chapter 2: <u>Social</u> <u>Learning</u>, <u>Exchange</u> <u>Theory</u>, <u>and</u> <u>Deviant</u> <u>Behavior</u>

Introduction............................39
Social Learning: A Model for Deviant
  Behavior..............................40
Observational Learning and Deviancy......42
Delay of Gratification and Modeling......51
Reinforcement Theory and Deviant
  Behavior..............................53
Social Exchange Theory and Deviant
  Behavior..............................58
Social Exchange and the Reward-Cost
  Model for Deviant Behavior............63
Summary and Conclusions..................68

Chapter 3: <u>Social</u> <u>Influence</u> <u>and</u> <u>The</u> <u>Deviation</u> <u>Process</u>

Introduction: Conformity and Compliance.71
Group Influence: More on Conformity and
  Compliance............................71
Early Research on Conformity and
  Deviation.............................75
Status, Conformity, and Deviation........85
Being Different Makes a Difference.......87

i

	Self-Esteem, Conformity, and Deviation...95
	Objective Self-Awareness, Deviance, and Conformity..............................96
	Groupthink and Conformity................98
	Then, Why Do People Conform: Social Comparison Theory?....................100
	Obediance as Deviance?...................101
	Deindividuation and Deviance............106
	What About Those Who Witness Deviant Behavior?............................112
	Deviance In The Dark: Another Case of Deindividuation.......................114
	Summary and Conclusions.................115
Chapter 4:	Deviancy: <u>Negative</u> <u>Attitudes</u>, <u>Stereotypes</u> <u>and</u> <u>Social</u> <u>Stigma</u>
	The Attitude-Behavior Consistency Problem.............................117
	Then, Do Attitudes Cause Behavior?......118
	Dissonance and Deviant Behavior.........122
	Does Behavior Cause Attitudes: The Forced Compliance Paradigm............125
	Deviance As Fun: The Case of Sufficient Justification......................129
	Self-Perception and Dissonance Theory...130
	Deviance and the Overly Sufficient Justification Hypothesis..............134
	Defensive Projection: Still Another Case of Dissonance....................136
	Deviance as Reactance...................138
	Negative Stereotype and Impressions: How to Tell a Deviant When You See One................................141
	Physical Appearence as a Source of Deviance............................145
	Ugly People Get Ripped Off More Than Beautiful People......................147
	Obesity and Deviance: "I Don't Love Her (Him) She's (He's) Too Fat For Me"...............................149
	If You Smell Bad I Don't Like You: Body Odor and Deviance...............151
	The Case of Bumper Stickers and The Cops................................153
	Seeking Help For Deviant Behavior Stigma and Rejection..................157
	What About People Who Talk About Their Deviancy: Self-Disclosure and Deviant Behavior......................159

	Summary..............................160
Chapter 5:	**The Attribution Perspective: Inferring Deviant Traits and Motives**
	Deviancy: Traits or Situations, or Both?.............................164
	The Medical Model: Myth or Reality?....166
	Attribution Theory: How We Come to Explain Deviant Behavior...............167
	Kelley's Attribution Theory and The Problem of Causality...................174
	A Comparison of the Jones-Davis and Kelley Attribution Theories............179
	Deviant Behavior and the Actor-Observer Hypothesis............................180
	More Research on the Actor-Observer Hypothesis............................183
	Watergate: Observers and Actor's Perception............................184
	Attributions to Others For the Responsibility or Blame for Their Deviant Acts...........................191
	Defensive Attribution or Just World?....192
	Self-Attributions: Coming to Find Out That You're Deviant....................195
	Misattribution As Self-Labeled Deviancy................................198
	Self-Attributions From Longstanding Deviant Behaviors......................200
	Negative Consequences of Making Attributions...........................201
	Community-Based Attributions For Deviant Behavior.......................208
	Attribution Theory: Unique or Just Warmed-Over Labeling Theory?..........210
	Summary and Conclusions..................219
Chapter 6:	**Personality: The Search For The Deviant Individual**
	Deviance and Personality: Some Problems of Definition.........................223
	Traits and Their Relationship To Behavior...............................228
	Deviant Behavior and Personality: Problems of Measurement................233
	Are Machiavellians Deviant?.............237
	What About the Development Aspects of Machiavellianism?......................243

iii

The Need For Social Approval and
  Social Desirability...................245
The Authoritarian Personality,
  Dogmatism, and Deviancy..............246
Locus of Control and Its Relationship
  to Deviancy..........................250
Self-Concept and Self-Esteem: Their
  Development and Relationship to
  Deviancy.............................255
How Stable is One's Self-Concept?......256
Self-Esteem and Social Influence.......258
Self-Esteem and Acceptance or
  Rejection of Deviant Others..........263
Summary and Conclusions................266

Chapter 7: The Social Psychology of Deviant Behavior: Research Methods and Problems

Introduction: The Nature of Deviant
  Behavior Research....................270
Laboratory Experiments.................272
Going Outside the Laboratory: Field
  Experimentation......................275
The Problem of Internal and External
  Validity.............................278
Sources of Research Bias...............281
Research Ethics For Deviant Behavior
  Experimentation......................283
Are Those Who Study Deviants,
  Deviant?.............................286
Correlational Methods..................290
Observational Methods: A Basic
  Research Paradigm....................292
Survey Research........................296
Measurement: Social Psychologists
  Assess Deviant Behavior..............298
Self-Report Measures...................299
Some Problems With Self-Report
  Measures.............................301
Then Why Not Do Longitudinal Research?.302
Summary and Conclusions................302
References.............................307
Author Index...........................342
Subject Index..........................348

PREFACE

A central theme has guided the focus and organization of this book: to present a social psychological perspective of the major areas of concern of deviance; to show how this perspective might be employed to obtain an understanding of some of the major causes of deviant behavior; and to show how contemporary psychological social psychologists can produce meaningful research by extending and elucidating some of the more well-established principles of social influence gleamed from research. This perspective has had its origin in the observation that the study of deviance is as yet a fragmented area embodied here and there in theory and research in social psychology. To this end the text itself is an attempt to ameliorate this condition.

This book is divided into seven chapters, each elaborating on a major theme. The first chapter deals with the problem of defining deviant behavior and outlines some of the major theoretical concerns for deviancy. The second chapter examines the proposition that reinforcements shape and maintain anti-social behavior. It is also maintained that deviant social models can and do have harmful influences on peoples' behavior. And, finally the chapter utilizes concepts from exchange theory to elaborate on a reward-cost model for deviancy. Classical and current research on conformity and obedience are employed in chapter three to describe conforming and deviating behaviors. Chapter four seeks to understand the relationship between deviant behavior and deviant attitudes. Here a number of stereotypes about deviants are examined and the negative impact on the deviant actor is noted. Next, attribution principles are used to deal with the problem of how people explain the causes for their own and others' deviant actions. Then, chapter six focuses on the relationship between personality and deviancy. And, finally in chapter seven the reader is exposed to some of the more important research methods and problems faced by deviant behavior investigators.

CHAPTER 1: DEVIANT BEHAVIOR: PERSPECTIVES AND PROBLEMS OF DEFINITION

INTRODUCTION

The study of the social influence processes is burgeoning---compelling questions are being asked and actively researched. What, then, can be said about the relative merits of research into the study of social determinants of deviant behavior? Actually what we know is that during recent years the area of deviancy has become one of the fields of social behavior which has been given only peripheral attention by psychological social psychologists (see Baron & Byrne, 1977). Why is this so? Perhaps the best way to answer this question is to note that a perusal of recent social psychological literature shows that it is necessary to understand how and why people conform to the existing norms; it also seems necessary to understand why some people on more than occasion do not conform (or comply) to the norms and in this way their behavior gives rise to the label of "deviancy; an area studied primarily by sociologists and not generally by social psychologists.

Then, a fuller understanding of the complete spectrum of social behavior requires not only that social psychologists examine the so-called normative behaviors, but also that they examine deviant or nonnormative behavior as well. And if we do focus on deviant behavior we are likely to be puzzled by the nonnormative behavior of some people, but this is not too difficult to understand because the attempt to comprehend deviant behavior is one of the oldest concerns of social scientists.

Being a group member can have a wide variety of effects on a person's social behavior. Then, the empirical question posed in one form is quite simple: "Does a person's deviant actions result from the influence of others or is it the result of interaction with others or indeed is deviant behavior some kind of individually motivated behavior?" And finally does deviant behavior have its origin in so-called inherited or learned traits?

Now it is not to be supposed that simple answers may be offered for these pressing questions for the causes of deviant actions because they are indeed complex social phenomena; they entail more than the individual engaged in a specific set of nonnormative behaviors. Both the deviant actor and an analysis of other people's reactions to the "deviant" takes place in an extremely complex social context. In addition, it is indisputably true that negative deviancy is likely to have a number of serious consequences for those persons whose actions are labeled deviant. Hence, there seems to be little question that nonnormative behaviors are important determinants of the negative evaluations a person elicits from others. Their importance lies in the observation that deviant behavior generally places the actor at a distinctly disadvantageous position vis-a-vis the behavioral outcomes obtained from other people.

It now seems appropriate to discuss, of course in general terms, some of the reasons for deviant behavior. First off we should note that the empirical study of deviancy is not really a form of social behavior studied in the 1970s; people have been violating the social norms from the very beginning and no doubt people have attempted to understand such behavior from the time of early history. Hence, it should come as little surprise that the number of popular and scholarly perspectives that have been brought to bear on the interpretation of deviancy seems to have been limited only by the breadth of man's imagination. However, despite the undeniable diversity of the many perspectives, they all must focus on at least one thing in common; an actor's observable norm-violating behavior. In addition, any theory that pretends to account for the occurrence of deviancy must be able to explain why one person's norm-violating behavior is labeled deviant while still another individual's norm-violating behavior is not.

On a more particular level we should ask: "What is the process of becoming deviant and what impact does a person's deviancy have on others?" What we are suggesting by this question is that the study of deviance should include both the actor's deviant behavior and the reactions of other people to the deviant. Before we can attempt to answer these questions we need to know why people violate social norms in the first place and why only certain kinds of norm violation leads to social disapproval. On the other hand we need to know why norm violation leads to social disapproval under certain conditions while in still other situations it does not. We need to know how and why a person can be induced to do things likely to violate the norms of one group while at the same time this very same behavior compliments the norms of still another group?

Clearly then, what we are suggesting is that under certain conditions a person's behavior can be viewed as deviant while under still different circumstances the very same or similar behavior may be viewed as normative. And, still why do some persons, who are confronted with situations where others conform to the judgments of the majority, also conform to the group's judgments even where these judgments are erronious or have a negative connotation for the individual group member.

These questions about deviancy are indeed complex. There is good reason to suspect, however, that the scope and deversity of deviant behavior, of course, may be difficult to connect with any one theory and to any one set of research efforts. That is, even the dedicated researcher is likely to find that particular theoretical nuances provide too little or perhaps even too much jargon to carry forth into situations requiring pragmatic and/or empirical statements about deviancy (see Kuhn, 1962).

On a more specific level, sociologists, and to a greater extent social psychologists, who have studied deviancy, have drawn broadly from the social influence work. And sociologists in particular have employed labeling theory derived from the social interactionist perspective. Here deviancy is accounted for in terms of labels formulated by those people having a great deal of social power. We will have a great deal to say about labeling theory, however, in general, as we have noted, all theories of deviancy seem to be in general agreement when they claim for deviancy to occur a group's social norms must be violated. At this point we begin to describe deviant behavior. Most researchers seem also to agree that the person's behavior in everyday social interaction is regulated by the norms and values that are part of the person's culture. However, a person must violate not just any norm but an important norm or at least an important norm for the group and then people seem to take notice that something is "not just right."

Once having said this, it may be difficult to decide, for example, whether or not a person is really considered deviant because we may not know how representative the behavior in question is for that person without first knowing the many different forces (variables) that have influenced the individual's behavior (see Jones & Davis, 1965).

Finally, it seems obvious to point out that in order to evaluate deviant behavior we must know something about some of the many theories employed to account for deviancy. To this extent sociologists and social psychologists have offered many different explanations for deviancy and at this juncture it seems only logical for us to examine some of the more important assumptions made by sociologists and social psychologists about deviant behavior. Then, how do we know when someone is deviant from the perspective of the sociologist?

THE SOCIOLOGY OF DEVIANCY

On a general level the sociologist is likely to focus on a social system and its social structure. Then the sociologist attempts to relate these general dimensions of society to patterns of social behavior. On a more particular level, the sociologist, who is interested in deviancy, may employ an analysis of the institutional effects on deviant behavior and here a stress is placed on deviant roles and/or norms assumed to regulate normative and nonnormative behavior. In this context it is noted that each social institution differentiates special kinds of norms for the regulation of people's behavior. For example, the public school system, as a social institution, tends to regulate students' behavior through formally or informally acknowledged rules. That is, students are expected to study, take examinations, and attend classes, while on the other hand they are expected not to smoke pot in school, strike teachers or to disrupt school activities. In other words, rules or norms prescribe how people in various roles should or should not behave. In addition, negative and positive sanctions are employed by a group to increase the likelihood that conformity and not deviation to its norms will take place.

Hence, from a sociological level of analysis it is suggested that the regulation of behavior takes place through the application of society's social norms. In addition sociologists associate rates of crime, alcholism, and drug addiction with such factors as social economic status, urban-rural differences, educational level, religious affiliation, etc. They study the norms and social roles along with the social institutions and make observations relative to the rates and kinds of deviancies observed. And for the sociologist, on the simplest level, norms and social roles are the smallest units of analysis used to explain patterns of deviant behavior.

SOCIOLOGY AND THE SYMBOLIC INTERACTIONIST PERSPECTIVE

From the symbolic interactionist perspective deviance is understood by assuming that the deviant individual does not necessarily hold to the dominant values of the culture, and also the person fails to behave according to the prescribed rules for action. Accordingly, the basic assumption made is that people are able to arrive at a consensus of meaning for the symbols they use to define the values of a culture through social interaction. Hence, the acts of rape, threft, deception, and so on, are not considered bad only to the extent that they are culturally defined as bad. In addition, a person, who is labeled as a deviant in one society could at the same time be behaving in a nondeviant manner in still another culture because such behavior may be consistent with the values of that culture. Deviance, then, results when people do not adhere to the existing definitions of a particular society's norms.

Taken in this sense, norms are defined as the "general expectations that people will act or behave in prescribed ways." When a person's reference group has reached consensus as to the definitions of its values, and have defined its norms, failure of the individual to act in accordance with the norms, or to hold the acceped values, leads to the disapproval of the group member and consequently the person is labeled deviant. For example, the educational system provides students with definitions of what is "appropriate" behavior and what is "good" and what is "bad." Since the educational system provides these definitions for behavior there are behaviors that are unacceptable and there are behaviors that are acceptable, good or bad, and so on. In addition, education has consequences for the individual's life. Accordingly, the person whose behavior does not reflect the educational values or whose behavior is nonnormative would in effect be violating value definitions which are held by the educational institution in that society and as a result the person is highly likely to be defined or labeled as a deviant actor.

At this juncture comes "labeling theory" and suggests that there is a relationship between symbolic interactionism and labeling. For example, Edwin M. Lemert (1951, 1972) makes the distinction between _primary_ and _secondary_ deviation and he then goes on to show how value definitions operate when people label an act as deviant. For example, primary deviation occurs when people violate norms regulating everyday behavior or when people fail to conform to the expectations of others. On the other hand secondary deviation takes place when the person defines himself or herself as deviant and subsequently takes a deviant role such as the role of criminal or what Becker (1963) calls "career" deviant. Taken in this sense, any act can be defined (or labeled) as deviant. This is so because an act which is viewed as uncommon or socially undesirable, relative to the norms of a particular group or culture, is subject to labeling.

We began our discussion of the sociology of deviancy with the observation that there are several major ways to view deviancy. In this respect, John W. Kinch (1973), a sociologist, tells us that there are at least three ways a sociologist may classify the study of deviancy: Deviant behavior as norm violation, deviant role enactment, and deviant subculture. We have already said something about the concept of norm violation and we will again examine this concept, however, next time in more detail.

DEVIANCY AS NORM VIOLATION

As we have suggested, no doubt, the most prevalent conception of deviancy is that deviant behavior is a persistent form of norm violation. However,

Darrell J. Steffensmeier and Robert M. Terry are quick to point out the ambiguity inherent in this conception of deviancy and they suggest that the concept of norm violation is compounded by the fact that: "Norms are frequently dealt with by behavioral scientists as rules that exist out there and which are used as the orienting perspectives by the actor in determining his course of action" (1975, p. 3). Hence, when the researcher employs one act of norms as a standard to judge norm deviating behavior, the researcher is likely to overlook the fact that the violation of a particular norm may require that the norm violator follow the prescriptions for yet another set of norms. Hence, when the researcher subscribes to the norm-violation perspective of deviancy her value judgments must guide her conception of deviance because in this case violating a norm or norms valued by the majority or a dominate group places the researcher in the boundary conditions of the dominate group.

What, then determines whether a person will conform or deviate from the norms of a particular group, or as a matter of fact to society in general? And how are we to employ the concept norm violation when we attempt to explain deviant behavior? Before we attempt an answer to this question we should note that on the most general level the problem of conformity or deviation to societial norms has been explained by the concept social control, which is defined as "those characteristics of a society that insure that its members will conform to the norms of that society."

There still remains the question of what do we mean by social control and how does this help us to explain norm violation? First we should note that Paul F. Secord and Carl W. Backman list five functions of social control:

1. They shape behavior in the direction of shared values or desirable states of affairs.

2. They vary in the degree to which they are functionally related to important values.

3. They are enforced by the behavior of other persons.

4. They vary in how widely they are shared;

they may be societywide, or they may belong to groups of varying sizes, even as small as two person groups.

5. They vary in the range of permissible behavior, some norms set more stringent limits on behavior than others (1974, p. 410).

Then, on a more particular level, conformity and deviation share some basic psychological processes in common; both depend on an "awareness" of the group's norms. In this respect, a methologically sound conception of the norm violation perspective of deviancy would at the very least require that we regard norms as rules for behaving whose violation is a matter of degree and whose *importance* to the group vary on one or more dimensions. This view of deviant behavior, then, would require that the importance of norms as regulators of behavior and the degree to which violation has occurred must be scaled before the norm violation conception of deviancy can adequately be researched and eventually assessed (see Stevens, 1973).

Implicit in the concept of norm violation is the idea that the violator is more or less dissatisfied with the group's norms. Hence, the source of a person's reasons (motivations) for violating a particular group's norms varies greatly. For example, the person may come to expect that rewards may be low for conformity and that high costs are incurred in conforming to a group's norms (see Thibaut & Kelley, 1959). And some people may not obtain a satisfactory level of reward-cost outcomes by conforming to the norms and they may attempt to change the normative structure of the group or a person may even change his behavior to increase his outcomes or the person may leave the group and seek out a different means to satisfy personal goals and needs.

What we are suggesting is that a wide variety of actions, depending on the nature of the group, can be taken by members of a group toward a member who violates its important norms. In this regard people are not entirely self-sufficient and capable of obtaining their major goals without the social support of other people. And, of course, members of a group do not always have complementary or incompatible goals, however, we do know that not all persons who violate the norms of a group are labeled deviant by the group's members. That is, the attribution of deviant to an actor and the labeling of behavior as deviant are, of course, not always preconditions for deviancy; deviations from the norms must first take place. Then, in this case it is the values and norms of the group, rather than some intrinsic aspect of the person's behavior (like traits), that lead to the negative attribution of deviancy. Because the labeling of a group member as a deviant often means that the "deviant" will be mistreated by group members the person may attempt to justify her deviant actions (see Freedman & Doob, 1968).

LABELING THEORY AND NORM VIOLATION: WHAT'S WRONG WITH LABELING THEORY?

By now it should be clear, of course, that the normative approach to deviancy attempts to explain deviant behavior as the consequence of norm violation. The concept <u>norm</u> refers to the expectations people hold concerning how they and others should or should not behave. In this regard some norms are more or less stable while still other norms change because the expected behaviors of people change from time to time. Thibaut and Kelley (1959) tell us that norms operate in interpersonal situations and tend to control the actor's behavior. Hence, a group employs sanctions in order to enforce its normative standards for behavior. From this perspective it follows that when an individual departs from the norms of a group he is subject to punishment (disapproval) from other members of the group. And, in this way, then, members of a group adhere to the group's norms in order to avoid possible negative consequences and at the same time to obtain rewards for socially approved behaviors.

This is not the whole story, people behave in accordance with the group's norms and when they "do things the correct way" they are able to define social reality while at the same time they reduce their uncertainty (see Jones & Gerard, 1967). That is, when people are confronted with ambiguous or uncertain situations, they tend to rely on the norms of the group to evaluate the situation, and hence, conformity to a group's norms can be seen as having its source in the norms for behavior or the rules that tend to set standards for appropriate actions. Then, at a later time external pressures are said to be less important and norms eventually become internalized. Individual differences in the adherence to the group's norms are assumed to result from differences in the individual's "internalization of the controlling norms."

Now labeling theory stresses the reactions of others to the norm violator by first noting that a person must violate an important norm for the group. As a consequence others are likely to define the norm violator as deviant. In a sense, then, the process of becoming deviant, according to labeling theory, is said to take place as the person is labeled deviant and there is public acknowledgement that the individual has violated the norms of society or the norms of a particular group.

As the result of being labeled deviant, the "deviant" person has acquired a different public identity. And, depending on the nature of the violation, the individual is accorded the role of homosexual, criminal, drug addict and the like. Now, according to Howard S. Becker (1963) the attribution of the status of deviant person is highly likely to determine the kinds of socially undesirable "traits" or characteristics others assign to the deviant. Finally the attribution of deviant tends to mask all other alternative views of the person and the likely result is a self-fulfilling prophecy. And, at this point the deviant may seek out similar deviants who, of course, are sometimes organized into deviant subcultures (see Becker, 1963; Lemert, 1967; Matza, 1969).

Then, the labeling perspective suggests that deviance is not originally a characteristic of the person or is it created by the individual's behavior *per se*: deviance has its origin in a group's definition of the individual's deviation from its norms and the group's negative reaction to the norm violator. At this point we should also take notice that strictly speaking people attribute the deviant label to only certain behaviors and to only certain people--those whose status is generally low relative to others. Here the label makes the person deviant and in time a selffulfilling prophecy is realized, and according to Edwin M. Schur (1965), the status of secondary deviance is said to take place. For example, Becker notes that:

> Social groups create deviance;....deviance is
> the consequence of the application by others of
> rules and sanctions to an "offender." The
> deviant is one to whom that label has success-
> fully been applied; deviant behavior is be-
> havior that people so label (1963, p. 9).

Another arena in which labeling has been applied is noted both by Scheff (1966) and by Szasz (1961). They suggest that when psychiatric symptoms become labeled the labels are essentially stated as violations of the social norms. Once public labeling has occurred the person who is so labeled is likely to take the role of the mentally ill person. Then, as a consequence, the label is said to engender a stigma from social control agents who are at the same time likely to exsert pressure on the person to change her behavior. Hence, in the broadest sense, the labeling perspective of deviancy suggest that we focus on the impact that labeling has on the actor. Then, an important question to ask is: how does it feel to be a norm violator who is labeled deviant? Of course, this depends on how the group feels about the violator and the importance of the norm(s) that has been violated to the group and also the importance of the behavior to the norm violator. In this respect, Leigh Marlowe tells us that:

> It may be somewhat threatening to perceive one-
> self as different from one's fellows. To some
> degree, the opposite may also be true: to be so
> conforming as to be indistinguishable from
> everyone else is also threatening to one's
> identity. The solution is to believe we conform
> because the norm/expectation/standard is right.
> It is the abstract rightness then, that produces
> our conformity, not our desire to avoid being
> different. If the individual finds himself at
> some psychosocial distance from the expectations,
> the level of stress may be quite incapacitating,
> and he may not be able to perceive accurately
> what he is doing. His response will not be
> adaptive. Individuals vary in their ability to
> resist stress, so that individual-group discre-
> pancy that might be upsetting to one person
> might not have as marked effect on another. In
> any event, the situation is usually noxious and
> often has spreading effects. The individual may

be less confident about where he stands with
regard to other items, as well. Taking the easy
way out of the dilemma and conforming to expectations may make the erstwhile deviant a fervent
convert to the group norm (1975, p. 160).

Then, in these instances, who is deviant and what
impact being labeled deviant has on the individual
depends on how the person responds to others evaluations of the specific norm-violating behavior.

Since much of human behavior is socially determined, either deliberately or inadvertently, through
the processes of social learning it makes sense to
ask: "How do sociologists of the labeling perspective
account for deviant behavior without direct reference
to the specifics of social learning theory?" In the
broadest sense, it seems unnecessary to insist that
deviant behavior is merely socially defined behavior.
This approach does not take into account social
models for deviant behavior nor does labeling theory
take into account the many ways society has to control deviant behavior (see Akers, 1977). In addition, labeling theory has not attempted to explain
why or how labeling theory is related to nondeviant
behavior. Are there separate processes at work for
labeling deviant and nondeviant actions or as seems
to be the case does labeling theory direct its focus
only on deviant behavior? The theory does not
explain how and why deviant behavior occurs in the
first place other than to note that a norm violation
has taken place and then the norm violator may or
may not be labeled deviant.

During the 1960s labeling theory became the
major sociological approach to deviance and this
theory still engrosses much of the attention of those
sociologists who identify with the labeling perspective. Among the major tenets of the theory the
following appear to be the most obvious: (1)
behavior in and of itself is neither "good" or "bad";
(2) a person is in a state of becoming deviant when
by social definition or labeling those persons or
agencies in power, such as judges, psychiatrists,
psychologists, the police, social workers, etc,
define the person as deviant; (3) We all conform and
deviate from the norms during our lives, however
when a person is "caught" in the act of deviating
sufficiently often, labeling of such behavior as
deviant is likely to take place; (4) those persons of

lower social economic class or lower status are more likely to be labeled deviant (e.g., poor blacks, poor whites, homosexuals, etc); and finally (5) labeling a person deviant changes the person's self-image to be more congruent with the label. That is, the person comes to see himself as different and then comes to accept or reject those who have labeled him deviant.

In contrast to the more traditionally psychologically-oriented perspectives of deviancy (e.g., theories that stress traits and other internal causes), the focus of labeling theory is on the observers of deviancy not on internal states or internal causes for the actor's behavior; it is the observer that determines whether or not a person's actions are labeled deviant. And as we have noted, those in power are said to create the conditions that produce the deviant (see Becker, 1963).

A final point we should make is that the labeling perspective is ideologically in opposition to a psychological trait view of deviance. That is, labeling theory suggests that the labeling of "deviant" confers a quality of deviance and the person reacts to the label. It then seems a fair question to ask: "What do we know about the implications of a deviant label other than deviant labels are descriptive accounts of observations for social roles or characteristics of those who violate the norms?" There is little in the labeling perspective to rule out the notion that personal traits (deviant traits) do not in fact determine a given portion of the variance for deviant behavior. The fact that a person must first appear to others different before labeling is said to take place raises some unsettling questions about why people violate social norms in the first place. People who have killed, raped or stolen things from others have violated the norms and accordingly, the question raised is what caused these behaviors. Are such persons different from most of us? The fundamental proposition of labeling theory is that powerful person create deviance by creating the norms used to evaluate behavior, for example, judges, the police, parole officers, psychologists, and psychiatrists create deviancy through labels. In this regard, the labeling perspective has been severely criticized for denying that deviants do harm to others. For example, Alvin Gouldner (1968) has repeatedly noted that too much stress has been placed on the role of the deviant as a victim and he notes that there is an attempt to glamorize the "underdog" subculture of deviancy.

From the labeling perspective the person who violates the norms (or engages in deviant behavior) must be caught. What if the person is successful in concealing her deviancy? In this case the focus should be to the actor, however, the focus is on the outside observer who by definition is not aware of the actor's private behavior. How do we correct this obvious shortcoming of labeling theory? Do we investigate the background of the deviant and look for the causes for people's violations of the norms or do we study how people come to label deviant behavior? Hence, labeling theory poses a serious methological problem--it seems untestable in its present form.

What about the private actions or thoughts of people? According to labeling theory only public actions seem to count. That is, the person must be caught or publically observed deviating and then the processes of labeling and stigmatizing occur. Hence, rather than focus on the act itself, labeling theory takes into account the social reactions of others to the "deviant" person.

Researchers have been quick to point out that socioeconomic class and ethnic and racial factors may not be the all important or necessary aspects of deviancy relative to our criminal justice processes (as is assumed by the labeling perspective). For example, Chiricos and Waldo (1975) report that the seriousness of an offense, and whether or not the person has committed a previous offense, is likely to be more important for deviance than either socioeconomic class or race. In addition, it appears that many deviant behaviors are not distributed evenly in any given lower socioeconomic population, as is suggested by labeling theory (see Wellford, 1975).

We should also note that Walter R. Grove (1970) tells us that labeling theory cannot be applied to the so-called mental illnesses without serious difficulties. For example, Grove notes that if all people who commit acts that are congruent to the public's image of mental illness, as is assumed by labeling theory, how are we to explain those who seem to suffer from serious neurophysiological, metabolic or psychological factors? In such cases it is the inability of the person to cope with the demands of society that leads the individual to take the mentally ill role and not the fact that the person is caught publically acting different and then labeled as deviant or mentally ill (see Grove, 1970; Grove & Howell, 1974).

One of the most serious criticisms of labeling theory is offered by Jack P. Gibbs (1966). Gibbs notes that labeling theory is underconceptualized and is not a fully-developed theory of deviance afterall. Such questions as: (1) "Why does the incidence of a particular act vary from one population to the next?" (2) "Why do some persons commit the act while others do not?" and (3) "Why is the act in question considered deviant and/or criminal in some societies but not in others?" Gibbs tells us that these questions remain unanswered.

Since labeling theory posits that deviant identity is in fact the end product of labeling, Sharon Guten (1978) notes that psychologists and sociologists alike have failed to formulate an empirically sound theory tracing the process of deviant identity. The investigation of deviant identity is important because variations in people's identities could in fact have differential behavioral consequences for the actor, as seems to be the case for sex and gender identity, ethnic identity, and identity as a mental patient.

A number of writers have specifically addressed the question of whether or not labeling a person as deviant is channeled into a deviant identity (e.g., Becker, 1963; Schur, 1971), but Guten tells us that these writers have not in fact gone beyond symbolic interactionism to incorporate and assess the reactions of the audience to labeling as well as the person so labeled.

A very different approach to the study of deviant identity is taken by Stuart Valins and Richard E. Nisbett (1972) in their application of attribution theory to the development and treatment of so-called emotional disorders. For example, the patient who has identified herself as "crazy" or "homosexual" is allowed to reattribute the causes of these behaviors to situational factors where in fact the patient initially assumed the deviancy was caused by psychological traits and/or genetics. We will have more to say about attribution theory and deviancy later on.

Let us suppose that we have said enough about what the labeling perspective of deviance is and end our evaluation very shortly. First, as we have attempted to show, labeling theory puts forth the basic assumption that deviance is created by the label <u>deviant</u> and then the labeling perspective suggests the relevance of researching social definitions for the labeling of deviancy as well as doing research into the process by which "deviant" behavior gets labeled. In this regard, we are asked to examine how the powerful groups decide what is deviant behavior and how the labeling of nonnormative actions takes place. We are also told that we should study those who yield and those who resist being defined as deviant. An underlying assumption is that the norm violator has broken the rules that are important to powerful persons, and we are asked to study the consequences for the norm violator.

There is something obviously evasive when we rule motives out in assessing why people do deviant acts like murder and other forms of crimes. It is also a manacing delimitation of the concept deviant when we do not consider culpability, responsibility, and individual differences when we attempt to understand deviant behavior, as seems to be the case with labeling theory. It seems superficial to suppose that only labels create deviancy and that deviancy cannot take place unless a public "awareness" has occurred. Not doing deviant acts in public may still involve a decision to act every bit as "deviant" as deciding to act in a deviant manner in public. For example, if I decide to torment animals in private, knowing what the consequences will be if I am found out is deviant surely as if I had done the very same thing in public and was found out and labeled deviant.

It appears that labeling theory does not account for the totality of deviance. However, it does seem more correct to say that labeling theory makes us "aware" of the impact of labeling behavior as "good" or "bad," but the human responsibility countenance has been removed from our understanding of deviancy. At best this perspective stresses mainly the view that powerful others decide whether or not we become deviant. Therefore, we will suggest, in a later chapter, an alternative to labeling theory--attribution theory.

Finally, Hogan, DeSoto, and Solano, in a recent review and evaluation of the labeling perspective, note that Murphy (1976) claims that:

> There are three conclusions that one can draw from the evidence for or against labeling theory. First, the more extreme claims of labeling theory regarding mental illness are empirically unsubstantiated. Second, some of the diagnostic categories assessed by the MMPI (i.e., anxiety, schizoid thinking, depression) refer to properties of actors that, if not real, are at least recognized in a wide variety of cultures. Third, to the degree that disorders such as alcoholism are interpreted as constructs of the therapists rather than as problems of the client, labeling theory will tend to increase rather than ameliorate the level of human suffering in the modern world (1977, p. 261).

DEVIANCE AND ROLE THEORY

Since we have discussed the labeling perspective we will now turn to still another sociological perspective--role theory.

First, a frequent shibboleth for the concept "deviant role" is that it is related to the concept norm violation. This is so because a person who is labeled deviant is said to engage in deviant acts, and in turn these deviant behaviors are interrelated to specific kinds of deviant roles. For example, the person who is labeled an alcoholic will be expected by others to consume excessive amounts of alcohol, however, the person will also be expected to neglect his or her family, work, and to be careless in dress and behavior.

Much like labeling theory, whether or not a negative and deviant role is chosen or is imposed on the person, according to role theory, the consequence is said to dehumanize the individual and, of course, more particularly the person is viewed in negative terms (see Turner, 1972). And like labeling theory, the perspective deviant role, when applied to norm violation, raises the question of conformity and deviation to the norms of society in general or a certain group in particular. This is so because norms relate to aspects of the person's relationship to others. For example, the plain hard logic of it is that social norms are said to perscribe the kinds of behaviors judged as appropriate or as inappropriate relative to a particular role relationship to other people. And relationships that extend over relatively long periods of time tend to become more or less stable, and norms for appropriate behavior are likely to become more or less explicit. In this respect, Thibaut and Kelley (1959) suggest that a group's norms emerge because they tend to reduce the costs for a group's members while at the same time adherence to the norms increases one's rewards. Thibaut and Kelley define a norm as a "behavioral rule that is accepted at least to some degree by both members of the dyad" (p. 129). They note that as a consequence the concept norm is deduced from the fact that there exists some degree of regularity in the behavior of a group's members.

Consider the profound implications of this aspect of Thibaut and Kelley's exchange theory. Where a person has violated a norm other members of the group are likely to incur costs (dissatisfactions), and they are highly likely to appeal to a rule or norm as a way to reestablish the role relationship on a more or less equal basis. In addition, the group is highly likely to view the norm violator's (the deviant's) behavior as costly to the maintance of the group's goals.

A further understanding of the relationship of role theory to deviancy can be gained by examining some additional aspects of role theory. First, we should note that Theordore R. Sarbin and Vernon L. Allen (1968) have observed that role theory is derived from the language of the theater, and that in more recent times the concept "role" has been viewed as a metaphor applied to expected patterns of social interaction. That is, the relationship a person has to others is said to prescribe certain appropriate behaviors. For example, the college professor is expected to depart certain knowledge to students and students are in turn expected to reflect this acquired knowledge on classroom tests. When this does not happen the professor or the student is said to be "out of role." For example, not all professors or all students assume roles with equal degrees of involvement (see Sarbin, 1966). In some cases a person is highly committed to her role and is unable to conceive of any other role. On the other hand a person may find his role dissatisfying and may in fact seek out other more rewarding roles or perhaps live with the dissatisfaction and focus on those rewards that are likely to emerge from the person's present role.

In a most general sense, role theory suggests that we start from observable events (behavior) and then predict that certain kinds of prescribed role behaviors will be enacted (see Biddle & Thomas, 1966).

Role theory does not offer a unified set of constructs, however, its application to a wide variety of research areas has been noted by Marvin E. Shaw and Philip R. Costanzo:

> Role theory is a body of knowledge and principles which at one and the same time constitutes an orientation, a group of theories, loosely linked networks of hypotheses, isolated constructs about human functioning in a social context, and a language system which pervades nearly every social scientist's vocabulary.... Roles as the basic data within this "theoretical system" have been considered from many viewpoints: learning, cognitive, field-theoretical, sociocultural, and dynamic points of view. As such role theory seems to be more of a subject matter than a theoretical framework (1970, p. 326).

Then, an important question at this point is just how are deviant roles enacted in the first place? It should be noted that we have discussed role theory in its more general context, and most importantly our present task is to relate role theory to deviant behavior. It is clear that role theory deals with matters which are of central importance to the understanding of deviancy: What is less clear is whether or not role theory can be translated into an account of deviancy and still be free from ambiguity. Then, how does in fact role theory attempt to account for conformity and more paricularly deviance? Shaw and Costanzo suggest that:

> Conformity is the correspondence between an individual's performance and the other's performance or between his performance and the prescriptions for his performance. It is important to note that the conformigy process is based upon both the similarity between the prescription or norms and the resultant behavior, and the degree to which the prescription determines the conforming performance. Conformity behavior in response to the normative prescriptions that one holds for himself or the prescriptions that another holds for him constitutes a very important functional concept in role theory. Thus, conformity or the lack of it (i.e., deviancy) is implied by the degree of correspondence between the role expectations for and role performance of a given role occupant (1970, p. 343).

However, despite societal attempts to enforce role conformity such attempts are not always "successful." For example, homosexuals are now demanding that other people accord them equal status and equal advantages in the various occupational roles to heterosexuals. However, it is likely that most people will continue to respond with attempts to demonstrate homosexual unequality. What then is the effect of negative reactions to homosexuals? Does it invariably lead to a loss in self-esteem and an acceptance of unequality? That is, are homosexuals likely to accept a low image of themselves? None of these are easy questions to answer. One would suspect that homosexuals as a group are unlikely to accept this low image of themselves and they are unlikely to change their sex-orientation role to that of heterosexuality.

Apart from such isolated instances as the above, how does role theory attempt to account for stability and change in deviant and nondeviant role enactment? Lemert (1972) tells us that a person who violates the normative prescriptions for roles is made a victim of others, and is defined as deviant. Then, as a consequence the person may enact the role of deviant when no alternative behavior at the time seems available.

While early formations of deviance attributed nonnormative behavior to personal characteristics of the actors and/or social disorganization variables, Edwin M. Shur (1971), in accordance with role theory, suggests that through the process of deviant role identity the deviant person gets "caught up in" the role of the deviant. In considering this process, Shur postulates the concept "role engulfment." Role engulfment is in effect the reaction of people to the person who assumes a deviant role. As role engulfment increases the end result is a tendency for the deviant actor to define himself as others define him. And finally then, the deviant person finds it increasingly difficult to view herself as nondeviant. Shur suggests that the central problem here is one of "validating one's identity" and he asks: "What kinds of events (or what kinds of information acquired by others) are particularly likely to precipitate or to accelerate the process of role engulfment?" Shur suggests that when an individual has been stigmatized as a deviant "the community expects him to live up to his reputation." Role engulfment prevents the person from altering the situation and the person's image (and role) is unlikely to change. The person who is an ex-drug addict or ex-convict or ex-mental patient is likely to encounter some very difficult and serious problems in convincing others that she is "no longer like that."

Clearly this analysis of deviancy suggests that there is a relationship between role theory and labeling theory. For this reason we now return to the question of what are the most important contributions of role theory to the understanding of deviancy? The advantage of this perspective would suggest that such roles as "delinquent" or "homosexual" are products of behaviors perceived by people to be behaviors that explain delinquency or homosexuality. Briefly, the role perspective attempts to explain deviancy as deviant behavior expected to take place in a more or less predicted way when people assign the role of deviant to an actor. The perceived behavior indicates the type of person people expect. This, of course, is said to lead to deviant self-perceptions and self-categorizations, and influences the specific role the person will continue to play when he attempts to behave in ways consistent with the role prescriptions for deviancy.

The role theory perspective for deviance seems to avoid the problem of psychological traits as causes of deviant behavior by viewing enduring deviant characteristics as aspects of the person's roles. Hence, whereas the concept deviant role refers to certain relative uniformities in deviant behavior of different persons said to occupy the same role or deviant classification, so-called deviant traits, postulated by trait psychologists for deviancy, refers to the seemingly uniform patterns of deviant behavior of the individual.

ROLE THEORY AND ITS RELATIONSHIP TO DEVIANT SUBCULTURE

For purposes of extending role theory, we will consider a related perspective for deviant behavior--deviant subculture. According to this perspectives John W. Kinch notes that:

> In a society such as ours, there is likely to be great variation, both in norms and behavior. Occasionally we find within the larger society a subsociety whose norms seem to be patterned to counter the norms of the larger society, if not with deliberate intent at least with little regard for the predominant norm structure. The deviant who is part of a subculture differs from the deviant role concept in that he is conforming to norms that are expected, or even demanded, of him by the other members of his group but that violate the norms of the larger society. The lower-class gang delinquent provides an excellent example of this type of deviance (1973, p. 216).

Then, deviant subcultures are variations within the more general patterns of the social order where there is identification with the group's special norms for behavior. In this regard, Mack notes that:

> Normative standards vary by social class, by ethnic group, by degree of urbanization, and by region. It is proper to enter a store, sit

down on the counter, and offer a chew of tobacco to the clerk. A group-shared expectation in a company store patronized by sharecroppers in rural Arkansas may be a violation of the norms in a Park Avenue gift shop catering to wealthy New Yorkers. Taking a hubcap from an automobile in a lower class slum area is stealing; taking a piece of the wronght-iron picket fence (much more expensive than hubcaps) from in front of your neighbor's fraternity house at a college is only a high-spirited prank. In this case, class position determines what is or is not criminal (1967, p. 157).

Now that we have said something about deviant subculture let's put the variables together. Obviously, different subcultures entail different role prescriptions for deviant and nondeviant behaviors. In this respect, Robert B. Edgerton, an anthropologist, has observed that people from widely diverse subcultures and cultures deviate: They murder, steal, rob and rape, and offended people react negatively. Then, an important question we should consider is: "What do we know, on a very general level, about deviant roles as these roles are involved across different social classes and social orders?" Edgerton tells us that:

> The most incontestable conclusion that can be reached with regard to deviant behavior is that societies differ significantly in the amount and type of deviance that occurs within them. Thus, if one wants to understand a deviant act--how it came about, what its consequences will be and whether it is likely to recur one must first understand the culture of the society in which it occurs. This is not only true for an understanding of a single deviant act in any given society, it is equally true of a class of deviance, such as suicide, invarious societies (1976, Pp. 76-77).

There is one final issue which is raised by the subculture and cross-cultural perspective of deviance: What other reactions take place toward deviant behavior other than rejection of the deviant person? Robert A. Scott (1977) tells us that it is difficult for a society to deny or normalize persistent forms of deviancy, however, in some cases a society may attempt to transform a deviancy into so-called normal dimensions. For example, Scott notes that Robert Edgerton (1964) shows how this has taken place with the case of the hermaphrodite. Of course, the hermaphrodite poses a special problem because the intersexed person defies the social differentiation between male and female. Scott notes that in some cases a society may surgically bring the person into line with the social definition of male or female. However, this is not always the case. Scott tells us that Edgerton has observed that the:

> Navaho offer the hermaphrodite a high status in their community. An intersexed person is believed to be a supernaturally designated custodian of wealth, and the family that gives birth to such a child will have its future wealth assured. Special care is taken of such children and they are accorded unusual respect and reverence (1977, p. 228).

And finally, Scott (1977) notes that in some cultures psychotherapy is often used to change a person's behavior and to make the person "more normal" or to prevent further deviations from normal patterns of behavior.

THE DEVIATION HYPOTHESIS: A PSYCHOLOGICAL PERSPECTIVE

As can be gathered from the preceding pages, the sociological level of analysis is today the dominant social scientific theme in deviant behavior theory and "research." As we have noted, the basic assumptions of this level of analysis are (1) the labeling of deviant acts (2) due to the violation of important norms, and (3) the enactment of deviant roles, all of which have negative consequences for the deviant actor.

At the present time, there is no doubt that psychologists do not play a dominate role in understanding deviancy. They have tended to focus on what is generally labeled abnormal behavior or psychopathology. In general, the study of deviancy has been treated as part of the conformity-deviation literature, a topic filimiar to psychological social psychologists.

The frequent occurrence of deviant acts by a

relatively small number of persons has for many years led social scientists to look for general forms of deviancy. Of course, an important question to ask of any theory of deviancy is whether deviancy is highly specific or are there identifiable general patterns of deviancy characteristic of certain persons and not others?

Suppose that we observe an individual going nude in public places, can we use this behavior as our guide to infer that this very same person is likely to engage in additional deviant acts or is this behavior highly specific. Irwin A. Berg (1955, 1957, 1961), a psychologist, has formulated what he calls the <u>deviation hypothesis</u> which is based on the assumption that experience suggests that some people seem to be much more consistent than others, and as a result make it much easier for us to predict their behavior. Berg tells us that the general idea here is that when a person gives deviant responses to noncritical stimuli such behavior is likely to accompany general patterns of behavior characteristic of the person's everyday life. Hence, Berg answers the question: "Does deviancy generalize across situations or is it highly specific" by indicating that:

> Deviant response patterns tend to be general; hence those deviant behavior patterns which are significant for abnormality (atypicalners) and thus regarded as symptoms (earmarks or signs) are associated with other deviant response patterns which are in noncritical areas of behavior which are not regarded as symptoms of personality aberration (nor as symptoms, signs, or earmarks) 1961, p. 355.

Berg cites laboratory research which tends to demonstrate that deviance tends to be general; if deviance occurs in one segment of the individual's behavior (noncritical area) it is highly likely that we might expect deviance to occur in certain other segments of the person's behavior (critical areas). The most important word here, however, is "generalization." But, generalizations of deviancy are not always instances beyond the experiences upon which they are based. For example, Berg elicited deviant responses through the use of unstructured stimuli (e.g., the autokinetic phenomenon, meaningless sounds, abstract designs, etc.) where the deviant responses of subjects were identified and scaled. Not surprisingly, Berg's deviation hypothesis, then, proposes that some persons may be "predisposed" toward a form of deviation so that when they deviate on one occasion, and in one area of their lives, they are likely to deviate in still others aspects.

Although one can extrapolate from Berg's hypothesis and predict that consistency (or lack of it) exists in the "real world," there are no studies that have focused on the deviation hypothesis in a broad social context. However we should note that there are a number of factors that make it difficult to apply Berg's hypothesis to general forms of deviant behavior. For example, the deviation hypothesis seems to characterize extreme forms of deviance (e.g., psychotics and criminals), and Berg's research results do not seem to fit well with other forms of less extreme deviancy like political radicals, drug addicts, and homosexuals (see Berg & Bass, 1971). This line of reasoning suggests that deviant behavior may or may not be general and the author suggests that situational factors have not been assessed relative to the deviation hypothesis. Situational variable are likely to play a major role in deviant behavior (see Mischel, 1976).

THE SOCIAL PSYCHOLOGY OF DEVIANCE

As the reader may have guessed, the study of deviant behavior reaches a point of extreme complexity when we attempt to understand the many causes or reasons why people are labeled deviant. But how does social psychology enter the scene? How then is a social psychological level of analysis of deviancy different from the sociological theories or indeed Berg's psychological model? First, the social psychologist is unlikely to focus on individual patterns of deviant behavior (e.g., the murder, etc.). The focus shifts from the individual to the social influence processess (e.g., conformity-deviation, obedience, etc.). Unlike, the sociologist, the social psychologist is less likely to stress social structure or social institutions as the major source of variance for deviant behavior.

Psychologists who have studied deviant behavior have arrived at different conclusions for deviant behavior and they have more generally covered such behaviors under the rubric of "abnormal psychology" or "psychopathology," where, of course, the focus has been on the psychodynamics of the individual or personality patterns or traits, and they are likely to view forms of deviant behavior as individually motivated or determined (see Davison & Neale, 1974).

Now, in order to illustrate a social psychological perspective for deviant behavior let us examine Freedman and Doob's (1968) difference theory.

DIFFERENCE THEORY: DOES DIFFERENCE MAKE A DIFFERENCE?

A fairly straightforward view of deviant behavior is gleamed from a series of experiments carried out by Jonathan Freedman and Anthony Doob (1968). In order to determine how people react to those who are different (deviant), Freedman and Doob used the results of a series of bogus personality tests to make some subjects feel different or deviant and still others nondeviant. Those subjects, who were led to believe that they scored at the lower end of several personality scales (the deviants), were asked which subjects they wanted to work with on laboratory tasks. It was found that deviants chose to work with other deviants more often then nondeviants. This findings tends to support Goffman's view of stigma. That is, deviants are said to attempt to "manage their impressions" in such a way as to avoid detection by others._ They do this by choosing to associate with other deviants rather than with their nondeviant counterparts.

Freedman and Doob found that when deviants are given the chance to hurt others (i.e., give electric shock to others), they choose to hurt similar deviants rather than hurt nondeviants, or as a matter of fact deviants who are different than themselves. It was also found that when deviants are directly faced (public behavior) with a request they complied more than did nondeviants especially when the request cam came from a_nondeviant. On the other hand, in private, deviants complied significantly less than nondeviants. Freedman and Doob suggest that:

> These results indicate that the effect of
> deviancy on social influence depends on the

specific situation and type of influence being exerted. We suggested that deviants are influenced less than nondeviants in most situations, but that deviants also avoid appearing different in public. When there is little or no direct intereaction or when responses are private, deviants succumb less to social influence. The more contact there is, the more dominant the avoidance tendency becomes, and the more they give in to the influence attempt (1968, p. 150).

At this point a fair question to ask is: "How does a person arrive at a deviant status?" There are, of course, many possible sources of influences, so many that we need to seek out some of the more general steps in becoming deviant. In this respect experience suggests that by choice or by circumstance deviance may entail the formation of a deviant identity and may be encouraged by membership in a deviant subculture or group. Then, perhaps one of the most important questions we should ask of social psychologists is : "How does a person become a deviant?," and we should ask: "What happens if an individual does indeed assume membership in a deviant group?" In this case John and Susan Darley have suggested that we might explain deviancy through a series of "choice points":

1. A person discovers that he is in disagreement with the majority on some important issue, and his disagreement becomes apparent to the group because he chooses to make it so or because he cannot avoid making it so.

2. He either chooses not to, or is not able to bring his views into agreement with the group, and the group begins to treat him negatively, i.e., to reject him, or to criticize his values.

3. For several reasons, he now seeks out a group that shares his opinions. The reasons might include the following: to find safety in numbers; to provide revalidation and social support for his challenged opinions, and to fill interpersonal needs for which a group is necessary, e.g., friendship, prestige.

4. A group composed primarily of people who have been through steps 1 to 3 is a highly cohesive one. That is, it shapes its individual members' views on many issues and behaviors, not only the ones that initially led the members to join the group. A highly cohesive groups are especially likely to reject and exclude members who deviate from the group consensus.

5. This kind of group, however, can provide the social support necessary to allow its members to face whatever inevitable chalenges they receive when they must confront and intereact with the majority culture. Although an individual's deviant beliefs are maintained by his own choice, these beliefs are heavily supported by his group of fellow deviants (1973, p. 22).

Now that we have shown that there are many perspectives for understanding deviancy our next task is to conclude with a definition of deviancy. The perspectives we have reviewed propose to explain the origin of deviant behavior. In this respect we have shown that the concept deviancy has replaced "older views." For example, Patricke Johns Heine tells us that:

> It may be observed that in the language of deviation, all current theoretical quanderies are set adrift. The deviant has replaced the criminal character and delinquent personality of yesterday; he is wayward in strictly statistical terms, permitting us to take cognizance of changing norms. But he can also be defined in role terms (outsiders), or formal structural terms (nonconformity to institutional requirements). What is called deviant includes all categories traditionally included in criminal codes (con man, hobo, addict, embezzler, tax dodger, and the usual felonies). Technically, "deviant" sounds less morally censorious and has the advantage of seeming neutrality (1971, Pp. 127-128).

Finally in concluding this section it is noted that in our daily lives the clearest notion of what seems deviant sometimes is inferred from violations of our written laws, however, Walker and Argyle

1964) carried out a survey and then an experiment in order to ascertain whether people are more likely to believe certain behavior immoral when they also view the same behavior as illegal than when they view the behavior as legal. The legal-illegal dimension had a nonsignificant effect on the deviant categories of drunkenness, littering, and use of obscene language. On the other hand, the deviant category of prostitution had the opposite effect. That is, when prostitution was viewed as illegal it was not viewed as more or less negative than when it was perceived as legal.

DEVIANCE, PROBLEMS WITH DEFINITIONS

We have considered some of the major explanations, related to the social psychology of deviant behavior, provided by researchers of deviancy---norm violation, labeling theory, role theory, deviant subculture, the deviation hypothesis, and difference theory---for how people become deviant. The elusive nature of the perspectives covered necessitates that we carefully formulate a definition for deviant behavior. First it should be noted that rapid changes in our views of what constitutes deviant behavior have taken place during the last decade or two. This requires that we consider definitions that do not restrict deviancy to behaviors that are time bound nor that fit only one perspective and not others. For example, no doubt, many behaviors that were once thought to be "perversions" have now turned out to be fairly common behaviors (see Gibbons & Jones, 1975).

The reader should also remember that when writers describe characteristics of different deviants they do not mean to imply that all deviants are the same. Deviants, no doubt, are as varied and differ as much as their nondeviant counterparts. Therefore, it would be a simple task if it were possible to say that a person is "normal" or "deviant," through the simplicity of definition. Unfortunately, such is not the case. Identifying what is meant by deviant becomes even more difficult because norms for behaving change over time and definitions for what is deviant also change (see Yankelovitch, 1974). The problem of defining deviant behavior is sometimes simplified when theorists refer to deviant behavior as a unitary or unidemensional phenomenon (see Freedman & Doob, 1968). In this regard, Ronald L. Akers notes that "attempts to set up absolute or universal categories of behavior that are inherently deviant have largely failed: (1973, p. 7). Akers suggests that in some cases people may do more than others expect of them and in a sense are labeled deviant. For example, the industrial worker who produces more than is expected may threaten the production norm for fellow union members. Actually, Akers is quick to point out that this form of behavior is more than likely to be rewarded or at least under most conditions than punished and should in this case appropriately be called <u>approved</u> <u>deviation</u>. On the other hand, Akers indicates that:

> ...More specifically, attention is directed primarily to instances of <u>disapproved</u> <u>deviant</u> <u>behavior</u> <u>which</u> <u>are</u> <u>considered</u> <u>serious</u> <u>enough</u> <u>to</u> <u>warrant</u> <u>major</u> <u>societal</u> <u>effort</u> <u>to</u> <u>control</u> <u>them</u> <u>through</u> <u>the</u> <u>application</u> <u>of</u> <u>strong</u> <u>negative</u> <u>sanctions</u> (1973, p. 7).

Interestingly enough, the concept deviant turns out to be even more complex than we first suspected. For example, Frank R. Scarpitti and Paul T. McFarlane suggest that:

> Social deviance..., may include acts, attributes, or beliefs. It is not confined to "deviant behavior" since there are also human conditions which evoke evaluative judgments and reactions by observers. <u>Deviant</u> <u>acts</u> are overt behaviors which may be evaluated negatively, e.g., crime, homosexuality, suicide; or positively, e.g., heroism, working exceptionally hard. Deviant attributes are characteristics, usually physical, which influence the way in which the possessor is evaluated and responded to by others. These may range from extreme beauty or exceptual intelligence to being depolitical, mute, blind, or exceptional in height. Deviant beliefs are ideas, often religious or political, to which one subscribes and which tend to influence the ways in which others interact with one who is perceived as holding these types of beliefs. Such beliefs may include those of social idealists and extreme moralists as well at the convictions of

religious zealots or political nihilists. In each case, the social deviance must be known to, and elicit a social sanction from, an observer--one who bases his sanction on his evaluation of the deviance as either good or bad (1975, Pp. 7-8).

Then, the definition of deviancy turns out to be a major problem for those who research deviant behavior. First, we must, of course, reject some common sense views that equate deviance with moral judgment and instead focus on the behavior or actions of people who deviate from the normative expections of society in general or specific groups. What seems to be important, then, is that all perspectives for deviant behavior suggest that deviancy must entail norm violation. Taken in this context, deviance can either lead to negative or positive reactions from others. And this raises another question: "Are there both positive and negative forms of deviance?" In this regard, Scarpitti and MaFarlane (1975) suggest that both negative and positive forms of deviance need to be considered for a balanced perspective. In addition, any attempt to establish criteria for deviancy must take into account society's double standards for many behaviors, for example sexual behavior and aggression relative to male and female roles in our culture.

What then are the most important differentiations of deviant and nondeviant behavior? First we know that deviant and conforming behavior are the kinds of behaviors that emerge through patterns of social interaction. That is, deviant behavior is the response to social influence attempts. No doubt most of us conform most of the time; we also deviate from the norms on occasion. Some of us more than others. Clearly, then, much of the social psychological literature on conformity-deviation has relevance for such instances.

Then, as definitions of deviance go one would surely expect that any single definition would entail obvious limitations when applied to an attempt to account for all instances of deviancy. With this caution set forth we will offer a definition of deviance which assumes that deviant behavior produces negative reactions and evaluations from a particular group and/or the larger society. Along with Edward Sagarin and Fred Montanino (1977) we shall note that two general forms of deviancy emerge: <u>involuntary</u> and <u>voluntary</u>. Sagarin and Montanino suggest that a person's "freedom to make decisions" is likely to lead to an acceptance of the responsibility for the consequences for one's deviant actions; however not all persons can freely chose to engage in deviant actions or possess deviant characteristics or not and the end result is still a negative evaluation or reaction from others. In such cases the term <u>involuntary deviance</u> is employed. For example, those who are physically handicapped or psychotic seem not to be responsible for their condition. On the other hand, in cases where a person is perceived to have had freedom of choice to engage or not to engage in deviant actions, the term <u>voluntary deviance</u> is suggested. For example, criminals, prostitutes, drug addicts, etc. Then, again, according to Montanino and Sagarin, what is considered voluntary or involuntary deviance is based on the degree of responsibility or freedom of choice a person is perceived to have had in choosing a deviant role or deviant behavior. In both cases the deviant "incites negative social reaction or negative evaluation from significant others or significant portions of society" (1977, Pp. 14-15).

Whether or not we consider deviancy a form of voluntary or involuntary action there seems to be general agreement that certain behaviors are unacceptable and therefore are generally prohibited. Essentially, unacceptable behavior is that which substantially violates the social norms. More difficult is the issue of whether irresponsibility or unforeseeability of the consequences of one's actions should be or is in fact generally excused by most observers of deviant behavior. Variations on this theme have been considered, but an absolute solution to this problem is not now available. Then, should we move toward a view of deviant behavior where little or no negative labeling is said to go on? This view would suggest that changing our practices which create the labels we use may only create new or different labels and only set different standards for labeling deviant actions. This implies that norms or standards for defining norm violation cannot easily be changed without considering a philosophy that takes into account the impact of labeling on the norm violator and society in general. Then, for reasons that will be examined in detail, norms used to judge human behavior are often essentially value statements. And to understand how norms contribute to the definition of deviant behavior, it is necessary to examine the nature and purpose of the norms we use to evaluate behavior. Of course, this enterprise is beyond the scope of this book. Nevertheless, we should note that the issue is not new, philosophers and social scientists have struggled with these very same issues. It is in this context that we began the serious task of crafting a social psychology of deviant behavior, but first a viabile part of this endeavor requires that we offer a tenative definition of deviancy. And if we successfully circumvent the problem of ambiguity our definition should be sensitive to the complexities of the problem.

Now, finally here is our definition. Deviance involves the perception of an actor's verbal or nonverbal behaviors, or physical characteristics, which are at variance with the norms of the actors social comparison groups or the larger society. The actor is accorded the status of deviant when the group or greater society attempts to explain the cause or causes for the norm violation by either inferring that the violation is or was due to either personal attributes (dispositional) of the norm violator (e.g., deviant traits) or that the violation was a response to situational pressures or both personal and situational pressures are assumed to have caused the actor's norm violating behavior.

SUMMARY AND CONCLUSIONS

We have seen that there are many ways to examine deviant behavior, however, any one perspective does not tell the whole story about deviancy. Given that there are wide differences among the many perspectives, you might wonder whether a major focus has been uncovered in our short review of these approaches to studying deviance. Then, how do we explain that people come to deviate from the more expected behaviors or deviate from the more socially desired behaviors? We have found out this is not a simple question. Yet the picture is not entirely bleak. First, our choice of explanation is, no doubt, influenced by our beliefs about the major determinants of human behavior. If, for example, we suspect that psychological traits or innate factors are the major sources of variance for deviant behavior, we are unlikely to examine the complex social factors said to determine deviant patterns of behavior. On the other hand, if we suspect that social factors are more important than biological entities, then we are likely to focus on social determinants of deviant behavior. Then, in many ways, we are only at the crossroads of what constitutes the nature of deviant behavior. Nonetheless, let us offer a few suggestions on how we might compare the different views of deviancy. The several perspectives on deviance we have discussed can be pitted aginst each other and compared in terms of how they deal with the following questions:

1. What is the source of an actor's deviancy?

2. How is deviancy sustained over time?

3. What impact does deviancy have on the actor?

4. Are deviant persons psychologically different from their nondeviant counterparts?

First, the perspectives discussed in the present chapter seem to emphasize, despite their variations on the theme of deviancy, certain common factors. One of these is the view that the actor has to violate an important norm. What this suggests is that there is a focus first of all on observed behavior. Another feature common to the perspectives is the view that deviant actions often have a negative consequence for the actor (or at least if the actor persists in violating the norms). And still another general characteristic of deviancy is that people will generally attempt to explain why they think the actor has deviated from the norms, and they will use dispositional (e.g., traits) or situational factors or both to explain deviant patterns of behavior.

Having said this let us proceed to comment on the different perspectives. First, labeling theory accepts the proposition that deviant behavior is the product of social interaction between those persons who define and enforce the norms on the one hand, and the norm violator, who violates the norms on the other. Then, according to this perspective deviance is not a characteristic of the person, but that of a particular norm-breaking act. There is a heavy emphasis on public recognition that a norm has been violated. Hence, the origin of deviancy is said to come from "outside" the person, and labeling theory makes a sharp distinction between primary and secondary deviance. Primary deviance is in effect the norm-violating activity that gets labeled by powerful persons. Secondary deviance results from continued and sustained norm-violation which results in negative consequences for the violator. Finally deviant identity takes place.

According to labeling theory normviolating behavior apart from the negative reaction it ensues from others is not different in origin from non-normative behavior. Then, the labeling or interactionalist perspective of deviant behavior stresses the institutionalization of the labeling process, and deviancy is not viewed as an inherent characteristic of the person's behavior per se but comes about because there are socially shared definitions (labels or typifications) which are employed by those individuals who define and impose socially approved standards for society's actors. Then, deviants are not necessarily "sick" or "unhealthy" psychologically nor do they necessarily possess the traits assigned to them by observers. Then, in short, deviancy is created by social definition or labeling.

Role theory suggests that deviant behavior is reflected in the person's roles, and in turn it is claimed that deviancy serves to define the paricular role enacted. Then, role theory suggests that deviant behavior is closely interrelated to the kind of identity accorded the actor. According to role theory there is the assumption that institutional pressures "force" the individual into a role enactment appropriate to the person's deviant or norm-breaking behavior. Hence, in this instance, both the behaviors that deviates from the norms and the evaluations of these behaviors define who is deviant and who is not. And while certain roles are viewed as more preferable, when a person deviates from the expectations for her role the consequence of deviation is the "forced entry" into a new and different role identity, which of course, is highly likely to be an entry into a deviant life style.

Since role theory does not postulate psychological traits, the focus is on characteristics of the role. And, deviancy is defined as those role characteristics of actors who play or take deviant roles. Hence, there is said to be an assumed identity with the deviant role enacted by the individual. In this sense, role theory is related to labeling theory.

The psychological or "deviation hypothesis" posits that there are general forms of deviancy and that some persons more than others are predisposed (have traits) toward deviancy. When a person deviates in one way the very same individual is said to be more likely to deviate in other ways. Hence, the deviation hypothesis suggests that deviants are special kinds of norm violators in that they have special kinds of characteristics that force then to violate the group's norms in the first place. The assumption here is that they are unable to cope rationally with the demands imposed on them by society. Then, norm violation is one consequence of those persons who have personality defects. And, the major problem here is to identify "deviant-prone" persons. This, then, would be done through psychological tests and personality evaluation.

Unlike labeling theory or role theory, the deviation hypothesis does not lead us to conclude that the source of deviancy lies outside the person. Yet in spite of its neglect of social factors, the deviation hypothesis would have it that general patterns of deviancy can be identified. Here one word of caution is in order, in adopting this perspective research suggests that this view seems to fit only the extreme forms of deviancy like the psychoses and the more violent forms of criminal behavior. It does less well in accounting for lesser forms of deviancy like political radicals and those who hold deviant religious beliefs.

And, finally there are undoubtedly the more social psychological levels of analyses of deviancy. For example, difference theory states that deviancy is a universal attribute, and whenever an individual is negatively different from others by virtue of a physical characteristic or assumed personality "trait" or behavior, then for the sake of definition the person is in fact deviant. Of course, virtually any characteristic can in effect be deviant if this characteristic is not shared by members of a particular group or by a signficant number of people in the social order who compose the individual's social comparison group.

How, then, does difference theory account for the impact of being deviant (different) has on the individual? Deviants are mistreated and they have good reason to worry about the negative treatment they receive from nondeviants. They also are likely to avoid being treated negatively and conform publically and they are likely to deviate only privately. Other things being equal, the person remains a deviant unless the characteristic which lead to deviancy in the first place changes. In short, what difference theory suggests is that as long as there remains a difference being different is in effect being deviant.

Accepting for the moment the proposition that we have said enough about the different perspectives, let us now turn to the general relationship between social learning, exchange theory, and deviant behavior.

CHAPTER 2: SOCIAL LEARNING, EXCHANGE THEORY, AND DEVIANT BEHAVIOR

INTRODUCTION

One of the first questions commonly asked social psychologists about human behavior is whether social behavior is due to heredity or learning or both? Applied to the study of deviancy this question is generally translated into: "Are people born deviant?" or "Do people learn their patterns of deviant behavior from others?" That is, is there a sound basis for believing that an exposure to deviant social models can in fact elicit similar behavior in children and adults?

First, when deviant behavior takes place it is frequently suggested by the lay person that such "deplorable" behavior occurred because people seem to possess a so-called "natural tendency" to deviate from acceptable norms. This concept of deviant behavior is not new, and as a matter of fact William McDougall, who in 1908 wrote one of the first American textbooks about social psychology, "suggested that people have "instincts that lead to cruelty toward other humans." However, subsequently it was found, that this view of deviancy was misleading and in more recent years social psychologists have tried to understand social behavior not as an instinct or unlearned behavior but mainly as the result of social learning, either deliberately or unintentional through an exposure to social models (see Miller & Dollard, 1941).

A recent impetus giving a genetic view of deviance has been the finding that an extra male chromosone found in a few males is related to aggression frequently observed in persons jailed for violent crimes.

Chromosones are the carriers of the genes of heredity and males and females have forty-six chromosones in twenty-three pairs. Without going into the complexities of genetics, very simply the sex of the indivdual is determined by the X and Y chromosone: The normal female cell has two X chromosones (XX) and the normal male one X and one Y chromosone (XY). However, the cells of a small percentage of males have two Y chromosones and one X chromosone (XYY). How then is the male with XYY chromosone arrangement different from the XY male. Jacobs, Brunton, and Melville (1965) have shown that the XYY chromosone pattern is more common among those males imprisoned for violent crimes. They describe the XYY "syndrome" as consisting of three general characteristics: (1) excessive height, (2) violent behavior, and (3) mental retardation. Recent research has shown that the rate of XYY abnormality is about one in a thousand for infant and adult males and more than fifteen times greater in the case of prison inmates (see Jarvik, Klodin, & Matsuyama, 1973). However, it has also been shown that crimes of violence are generally committed by XY males rather than by XYY males and that an extra Y chromosone does not necessarily relate to violent behavior. In addition, Price and Whatmore (1967) suggest that most prisoners who are "XYY's" have not been arrested for the major violent crimes, and as a matter of fact are much more likely to commit crimes such as robbery, forgerery, and the like.

Bandura (1973), from a social learning perspective, notes that "XYY's" are large for their peer group and he suggests that social factors may have been responsible for their excessive aggression during adolesence. That is, they are more likely to be exposed to aggressive models at an earlier age than their "XY" counterparts.

If we set aside inmate views of deviance the central argument is that deviant behaviors are preponderantly the result of social learning. Taken in this context, we will argue that deviant behavior is learned much the same way as any other form of social behavior, that is, through the principles of reinforcement (rewards and punishments) and/or through social imitation and modeling (see Bandura, 1969, 1973).

SOCIAL LEARNING: A MODEL FOR DEVIANT BEHAVIOR

An exposure to the deviant actions of models and the rewards or punishments the model experiences can serve to either weaken or strengthen an observer's inhibitions against engaging in similar deviant acts. That is, observing another person trangress or violate a particular rule or norm can in fact serve to elicit norm-violating behavior in observers. In such cases we refer to the influence of social models as either inhibitory or disinhibitory contingent upon whether the model violates a norm or indeed behaves according to the normative demands of the situation. In addition, the presence of one or more norm-violating models may facilitate the spread of norm-violating actions in such instances as collective violence and deviant behavior often observed in delinquent gangs.

Albert Bandura (1969, 1973, 1977), a Stanford University psychologist, whose research has contributed much to our understanding of social behavior, tells us that social modeling can influence the observer through three different processes. First, new patterns of behavior can be acquired through modeling other's behaviors and the models don't even have to be real-life models because research has demonstrated that children do indeed imitate aggressive behavior through an exposure to animated cartoon characters (see Bandura, Ross & Ross, 1963). Second, social models may act to strengthen or to weaken previously learned prohibitions or inhibitions for deviant behavior depending of course, on whether the model is rewarded or punished for certain behaviors. And, third, the behavior of models may serve to stimulate or to facilitate similar behaviors in observers through <u>vicarious conditioning</u> or through the observer's own "imagination." Such behaviors are then displayed in the absence of the social model, at a later time.

So we can see that one of the major contributions to the study of deviancy is social learning theory's stress on the employment of differential reinforces for deviant behavior. However, the specific behavior that elicits reward from one group (or person) frequently elicits punishment from still another group. And, as a result people come to show vast differences in their behavior relative to any one group or any one situation. Then, how is it that when a person observes deviant behavior enacted (via a social model) and go unpunished the individual observer is likely to model his behavior after the deviant actor. While on the other hand, because a person observes deviant behavior punished the observer is less likely to model her behavior after the deviant social model. Before we attempt an answer to these complex questions we should note that the other side of the coin is the fact that we often attempt to control deviant behavior once it results from modeling and/or reinforcement. Parke (1970) tells us that punishment is widely used as a child-rearing technique, however, he suggests that its effect is mainly suppressive. But, he does show that mild forms of punishment seem to be most effective in reducing deviant behavior, if indeed punishment occurs at the outset of a child's deviant actions because deviant behavior generally entails instrumental responses which lead to positive outcomes. In addition, if punishment is administered long after a deviant act has taken place, confusion as to its purpose is likely to lessen its effect (other than suppress on).

What then is the effect of punishment and affection? Parke (1970) notes that punishment followed by an "excessive" display of affection toward a child, who has violated a rule (or norm), may actually strengthen the deviant behavior, hence the timing of reward and punishment seem to be important determinants of deviant behavior, especially in children.

OBSERVATIONAL LEARNING AND DEVIANCY

At this point it is necessary to reintroduce a major theoretical assumption, mainly, derived from observational learning research. Since researchers have often noted that observational learning can take place without obvious rewards, it makes sense to ask: "Why is it that deviant behavior can take place when a person observes deviant behavior and later suddenly engages in such behavior in still a different situation?" Such learning can be very difficult to understand, however, Bandura (1977) tells us that during the time that a person is exposed to cues emitted by a social model such cues seem to elicit in the observer "perceptual responses or images, and the observer attaches verbal labels to these stimuli." For example, Bandura (1965) had children observe a film where the model emitted aggressive behavior. In one of the conditions the model was rewarded for aggression; in a second condition the model was punished for the very same behavior; and in still a third condition aggressive behavior had no consequences for the model. Bandura, then placed the children in a situation where they could reproduce the model's behavior.

Now, what about the results? Boys imitated the model more than girls, however, those children who observed the model being punished showed significantly less imitation of the model than where the model was rewarded or where there was no consequence forthcoming for the model's deviant behavior.

Next, Bandura asked all of the children to reproduce the model's behavior and this time he offered them attractive incentives for doing so. The children reproduced the model's behaviors, even though they had previously seen the model punished for aggression. In such cases Bandura suggests that children who observe a model's responses, and at the same time experience an emotional arousal, (through contiguity) are conditioned to images related to the model's responses. Then, at the same time, as children observe a model they verbalized the model's behavior.

It is probably safe to conclude that such type of deviant behaviors as stealing, lying, and aggression, can be accounted for through the application of social learning theory. We have noted that Bandura (1969) has demonstrated that children do learn highly specific behaviors by observing these behavior performed by others (social models). He has suggested, as we have already indicated, that the observer attaches verbal labels to the social model's behavior. These representational responses serve as mediational cues and later on become discriminative stimili for behavior that more or less matches the previously observed model's aggressive or deviant behavior.

Bandura suggests that both inhibitory and dis-inhibitory behaviors can occur as a function of observing a social model's deviant responses. For example, Walters and Parke (1964) have demonstrated that when children observes a peer model punished for playing with prohibited toys, the children's propensity for deviant behavior is decreased. On the other hand, Bandura, Ross, and Ross (1963) have shown that when a peer's (model) aggressive behavior goes unpunished, this increases the likelihood that observers will at a later time engage in deviant or aggressive behavior.

Research reported by Walters and Parke (1964) entailed a procedure where young children (boys) were shown a film where an adult female told a young boy that he should not play with toys left on a nearby table. The female asked the child to remain seated in a chair placed near a table. Then she left and the child played with the prohibited toys for about two minutes. For a model-rewarded condition, the final part of the film showed the female return to the room where the child was left and sit by the child, hand the child toys and then interact with the child in an affectionate manner. For subjects in the model-punished condition, the end of the film showed the female return to the room and take the toy from the child, shake the child, and sit the child down in a chair. In contrast, those assigned to the no-consequence condition the film ended when the child played with the toys for two minutes; hence, the female did not reenter the room. After the subject viewed one of the three films, he was shown toys identical to those with which the model had played. At this point the researcher left the room after handing the child a book to read and remained outside the room and observed and recorded the latency of the first deviant response made by each of the children; the number of times a toy was touched or played with, and the duration of the deviance. Children in a fourth condition did not see a film and were treated in the same way as children assigned to the film condition.

Walters and Parke found that subjects in the model-rewarded condition did not differ significantly from those in the no-consequences condition on any of the three measures used for deviant behavior. Subjects in both the model-rewarded and the no-consequences condition differed on the three measures used for deviant behavior. Subjects in both the model-rewarded and the no-consequences condition deviated quicker, more often, and for longer periods of time than did subjects in the model-punished and no-film condition (control).

Bandura explains the inhibitory and disinhibitory effects of modeling as a function of <u>vicarious reinforcement</u>. That is, the observer of deviant behavior tends to "vicariously experience" the reward or punishment delivered to the social model. In this respect Marvin E. Shaw and Philip R. Costanzo note that Bandura gives four reasons for the importance of vicarious reinforcement in producing inhibitory or disinhibitory effects in the behavior of observers:

1. It provides the observer with information about the probility of attaining reinforcement through the emission of certain specified responses.

2. It provides the observer with knowledge about the stimuli in the field and helps to direct his attention to these stimuli.

3. It provides the observer with a display of the incentives which he might receive for performing a given act.

4. It provides the opportunity to view the affective reactions of the model to receiving a given reinforcement (that is, it provides pleasure and pain cues to the observer), 1970, p. 66.

Given that vicarious reinforcement acts to inhibit or facilitate the occurence of deviant behaviors, Walters, Leat, and Mezei (1963) have demonstrated that an exposure to the trangressions of a social model can markedly decrease an observer's inhibitions against deviant behavior. Walters et al. set a probition for children so they would be unlikely to play with attractive toys and then the researchers exposed the children to films where a child (a social model) was either rewarded or punished by his mother for violating a similar prohibition. Next, the researcher left the experimental room and recorded the latency and frequency with which the boy violated the imposed restriction against playing with the forbidden toys. A control group was left along and the child was told not to play with the toys and, of course, the child did not observe the transgression film.

Walters et al. found that children who had observed the film, where the social model was rewarded for violating the experimenter's rule, disobeyed the rule not to play with the toys quicker and more often than did children who saw the film in which the model was verbally punished. The control group differed significantly from the experimental groups.

So, what does Walters *et al*. research suggest? For one thing a social learning perspective of deviant behavior, shows that an exposure to a norm violator, who is rewarded for the violation, weakens the observer's inhibitions against an explicitly stated norm or rule. That is, where children are exposed to a norm violator they may acquire new or different forms of behavior(e.g., deviant) without overtly displaying such actions in the presence of the norm-violating model. Consider the profound implications of these findings for deviant behavior: Deviancy is learned and evidence indicates that social models play an important role in its development.

Now then let us turn to the question of learning without reinforcement. Consider, for example, in everyday situations people are often exposed to social models who neither seem to be rewarded nor punished for their deviant actions. Since reinforcement theories have stressed that learning occurs only in the presence of rewards or punishments, how do we account for such learning without appealing to reinforcement explanations?

Bandura (1969, 1973) has demonstrated that imitative learning can and does take place without the presence of reinforcers. Apparently people do observe social models and at a later time reproduce the behavior observed without the benefits of rewards. For example, Liefert and Baron (1972) showed young boys and girls (ages 5-9) either an excerpt taken from the TV program the "Untouchables" (aggressive-program condition) or they showed excerpts taken from a national TV sports program (nonaggressive condition).

After the child saw one of the two films, he was taken to a second room and seated in front of a panel with two buttons labeled "hurt" and "help" A white "ready" light signaled and then the child was told that another child, located in still another room, would play a game to win a prize and that each time the signal occurred the child could either help by pushing the "help" button, or hurt the child by pressing the "hurt" button. Actually, there was no other child in the next room, and, or course, no one was hurt during the experiment. The child was left alone and the "ready" signal was illuminated twenty times.

Results showed that children who had viewed the aggressive film pressed the "hurt" button significantly more often than did those who had witnessed the nonaggressive TV excerpt. Liebert and Baron did not find significant differences between boys and girls in either condition.

But what about the generalizability of the above findings? We have seen that reinforcement need not be involved in order to demonstrate the learning of deviant behavior. That is, reinforcement may not affect the initial acquisition of a response or set of responses, however, the performance of that response may at a later point be affected by reinforcement. For example, Bandura and McDonald (1963) carried out a study dealing with children's moral judgments and they demonstrated that reinforcement is not necessary for moral judgment to be learned. Hence, children who displayed different moral evaluations of "right" and "wrong" were studied. One group of children was classified as immature or what Bandura and McDonald labeled an objective-responsibility orientation. These kind of children judge their actions on the basis of the harm or damage done to others. A second group of children was classified as more mature or having a subjective-responsibility orientation. Children so labeled consider the seriousness of their actions along with a perpetrator's intentions in carrying out an act when they judge the nature of moral behavior.

Responsibility orientations were measured by asking the children to judge which of a set of actions is "naughtier." For example, "Who did the naughtier thing---Johnny, when he accidentally dropped and broke a whole tray of glasses while trying to help his mother, or Jimmy, who broke one glass while trying to steal cookies from the cupboard?" A child who is oriented objectively would be expected to assign greater blame to Johnny, who broke the "whole tray of glasses," whereas a child who is oriented subjectively would be expected to assign more responsibility to Jimmy because Jimmy intended to steal the cookies.

Bandura and McDonald assigned their subjects to one of three conditions. In a model-reinforced-child-reinforced condition, both the model and the child were rewarded for making moral judgments inconsistent with the child's moral orientation. In the model-reinforced-child-not-reinforced condition, only the model was rewarded. Finally, in the no-model-present-child-reinforced condition, there was of course, no model, however, the child was rewarded for behavior contrary to the child's moral orientation. Finally, each child made moral judgments in the absence of a social model.

Results showed that in both the presence of a social model and where the child was isolated, children's moral judgments were contrary to their own moral orientation but consistent with the moral judgments of the model. On the other hand, reinforcing a child for moral judgments contrary to the child's moral orientation had little or no effect on the child's moral judgments.

Given that we can generalize from Bandura and McDonald's study, what implications are there for deviant behavior? We may sepulate that children can be induced to behave contrary to their moral orientation where they are exposed to social models. For example, children can be induced to lie or cheat in school on the basis of social modeling. Again, the evidence is only suggestive; but it seems logical to assume that social models for deviant behavior can influence a child's behavior for better or for worse.

In yet another experiment, Bandura (1965a) demonstrated that reinforcement is not necessary for the learning of deviant behavior, but it does affect performance. Nursery-school children watched a TV program where an adult model aggressed against a lifesize inflated plastic Bobo doll. Bobo was hit by the model in the nose, on the head with a hammer and kicked and then pelted with rubber balls. These actions were accompanied by verbalizations such as "Sockeroo stay down" and "Take that," "Bang," and the like.

The film depicted three kinds of endings. A model-rewarded condition showed a second adult enter the room and proclaim the "champion" and he gave the model candy and soft drinks. In the no-consequences condition, the model was neither rewarded nor punished. In a third condition, model-punished, the model was scolded, denounced and actually spanked.

Then children were taken into a room that contained toys (including Bobo). The child was left "alone" to play with the toys while the researcher observed and recorded the child's aggressive responses. Results showed that the no-consequences and model-rewarded conditions did not differ significantly but these two conditions did lead to significantly more aggressive responses than did the condition where the model was punished for aggression (attacking Bobo). Since the experimenters had offered treats for each aggressive response that the child could have performed, this condition reduced all the differences among the three conditions. That is, the model-punished subjects now showed as much aggression as did the children in the other conditions. Hence, observing the model get punished did not result in a failure to learn. Neither the direct nor the vicarious rewards seemed to be necessary for learning, but once the aggressive responses had been learned, the performance of these responses depended on rewards.

Then, can an exposure to deviant behavior serve to elicit similar behavior from observers? The best information on this point seems to suggest that this is indeed the case (e.g., Bandura & Ross, & Ross, 1963; Bandura & Walters, 1963; Bandura, 1969; Walters & Parke, 1964), however, criticism of modeling research suggests that behavior like hitting Bobo is not really the kind of behavior likely to take place in the "real world." Nevertheless, what seems important here is that Bandura and his associates have demonstrated how deviant behavior is likely to occur in the "real world." For example, there are, no doubt, many situations where people are likely to engage in norm-violating behavior and they do not do so, no doubt, because they have observed others punished for such actions. On the other hand, these very same persons, who are likely to be otherwise inhibited in the presence of a social model who is punished for deviant actions, may in the presence of a norm violator themselves violate the norms. For example, Ladd Wheeler (1966) sug-

that socially deviant behavior may in fact
among people, once it is previously learned,
conditions of <u>behavioral contagion</u> such as
...ds of behaviors involved in collective vio-
...r even in such situations where large scale
...ions of traffic laws take place. In such
instances a person's restraints against norm
violation is likely to be reduced when the person
observes that other people have "gotten away" with
their norm-violating behaviors. And, when a group
contains a number of disinhibited members, modeling
of antisocial or deviant behavior will sometimes
result and it is here that deviant models have a
powerful effect on others' behavior. In this
regard, Diener, Dineen, Endresen, Beaman, and Fraser (1975) sent groups of eight subjects into a
large room containing wads of newspaper, styrofoam
bats and other such materials to use on a would-be
pacifist, who was awaiting mistreatment. However,
before the subjects were allowed to "beat the
pacifist," they were shown a movie. In a nonaggressive film a person was shown walking around the room
and carrying on a conversation with the pacifist,
whereas in an aggressive-film condition the person
was shown beating the pacifist by hitting and club-
bing him. The researchers varied the subjects'
feelings of personal responsibility for their actions so that in one condition subjects were told
that they were responsible for their own behavior
at all times. In another condition subjects were
told that the researcher would take full responsibility for anything that might happen during the
study. The experimenters also manipulated subjects'
"expectations." Some of the subjects were informed
that the experiment was in reality a game, while
still other subjects were told that the experiment
dealt with human aggression. Of course, in the
aggressive-modeling condition the denial of responsibility on the part of subjects and the would be
game arrangement was expected to lead to a greater
degree of aggression directed toward the pacifist.

Diener <u>et al</u>. found that the greatest effect
was due to modeling. That is, subjects who viewed
the aggressive movie displayed significantly more
aggression toward the pacifist than did subjects
who viewed the nonaggressive movie. In addition,
those subjects who had viewed the aggressive model
and, who were made to feel responsible for their
actions, were more aggressive then subjects who saw

the nonaggressive model and who felt responsible for their behavior.

Then, being with other people can lead to deviant behavior where responsibility for one's action is shared and where models for deviant behavior are present. But what impact do the observers of deviant behavior have on the deviant's behavior? In order to answer this question, Richard Borden (1975) carried out an experiment where he asked male subjects to interact with a confederate of the experimenter during which time the two argued over the level of shock that the confederate should receive. While the argument was underway the subjects were observed by either a male or a female who was required to sit quietly and was asked not to intervene.

Results showed that Borden's subjects were significantly more aggressive where a male was watching them than if a female was observing the heated argument. Next, the male or female observer left the room and the subject's level of aggression was recorded by the experimenter. As a consequence, subjects who had been observed by a male showed a significant decrease in aggression, whereas subjects who had been observed by a female showed a non-significant reduction in their level of aggression.

Because observational learning seems to have wide range implications for deviant behavior, we have suggested conditions which might help us understand how deviant behavior is learned in the first place. We have suggested that the presence of a norm-violating model may affect the observer of norm violation through modeling. Unfortunately, there are apparent reasons to suspect that there is more to learning deviant behavior than mere observation of deviant behavior. For this reason we now turn to some additional observations derived from social learning theory.

DELAY OF GRATIFICATION AND MODELING

This brings us to a consideration of the impact that delay of gratification is likely to have on deviant behavior. As you are already aware, social models have been found to have important influences on deviant actions of observers. It should be apparent by now that modeling can have inhibiting or disinhibiting effects. In this regard the ability to delay present rewards in order to obtain larger rewards at a later time seems to have important implications for deviant behavior. Without being able to do so would in effect make it difficult for the individual or society to focus on long-range goals. Hence, it seems logical that an exposure to social models (parents or peers), who show a preference for either the more immediate or relatively delayed rewards, should have an important influence on one's own behavior. For example, Bandura and Mischel (1965) exposed children to either a social model who was immediately rewarded or whose reward was delayed. Bandura and Mischel expected, and found, that children in the immediate reward condition took the smaller but immediate reward (prizes), whereas children in the delayed gratification condition choose the larger but future reward.

In an earlier paper, Mischel (1961) reports that there is a high correlation between delinquency and the inability to inhibit needs for immediate gratification. Mischel tells us that he has found that delinquent children prefer an immediate small prize to a future prize which is more valuable. Nondelinquent children, on the other hand, seem to prefer the more valuable delayed prize to the immediate but smaller prize.

Additional evidence for the existence of delay of gratification and deviant behavior comes from an experiment reported by Stumphauzer (1972). He carried out an investigation where he first determined whether male prison inmates held preferences for small immediate or large delayed rewards. Subjects were asked to choose between a number of pairs of rewards where one was small but immediate and the other larger and delayed. Next, Stumphauzer exposed or did not expose his subjects to a peer model. The model always chose the large delayed reward.

It was found that when subjects subsequently made their own choices (on different items), those exposed to the social model showed a significant increase in preference for delayed rewards over immediate rewards. In addition, when these same subjects were retested four weeks later, they still preferred the delayed larger reward. This finding demonstrates that social modeling can reverse a well-established pattern of a self-indulgent behavior which is, no doubt, an important aspect of many deviant patterns of behavior (see Mischel, 1976).

You might expect that young adult prison inmates, like those used as subjects in Stumphauzer's research (1972), who observed an older inmate delay his rewards, are likely to have an impact on still other inmates and the consequence may be one of better self-control. Mischel suggests that this is indeed the case.

REINFORCEMENT THEORY AND DEVIANT BEHAVIOR

Reinforcement "theories" of learning like B.B. Skinner's operant conditioning view, indicate that for learning (deviant or nondeviant behavior) to take place responses must first be emitted and then followed by reinforcement. During early phases of learning Skinner proposes that a method of successive approximations or shaping takes place. In other words those responses that increasingly come close to those desired are reinforced and finally the desired performance takes place. For example, when a parent wishes to teach a child how to eat with "proper" utensils, the parent could in fact reward the child for holding a knife or fork or spoon and then later on the child would be rewarded only for the "correct" or appropriate use of these utensils. It is in this way that very simple responses are combined to form more complex responses.

Ronald L. Akers (1973, 1977), a sociologist from the University of Iowa, has attempted to bridge the gap between a sociological theory of deviancy (Edwin H. Sutherland's differential association theory) and Skinner's radical behaviorism and he has shown the relevance of behavioral psychology for the learning of deviant behavior. That is, Akers assumes that deviance is learned when people acquire deviant beliefs rather than nondeviant or conforming beliefs. The type of learning, according to this view, differs from nondeviant behavior only in what is learned rather than how behavior is learned. More specifically, Akers tells us that deviant behavior is learned according to the principles of operant conditioning. For example, Akers notes that:

The primary learning mechanism in social behavior is operant (instrumental) conditioning, in which behavior is shaped by the stimuli which follow or are consequences of the behavior. Behavior is strengthened through reward (positive reinforcement) and (negative reinforcement) or weakened (punished) by aversive stimuli (positive punishment) and lack of reward (negative punishment). Whether deviant behavior or conforming behavior occurs and persists depends on past and present rewards or punishment for the behavior and the rewards and punishment attached to alternative behavior (differential reinforcement). In addition to learning acts, a person also learns definitions which evaluate the acts as good or bad. These definitions are themselves verbal behavior (vocal and subvocal) which can be directly reinforced and which also function as discriminative (cue) stimuli for other behavior. The more a person defines behavior as a positive good or at least as justified, the more likely he is to engage in it . A person participates in deviant activity then to the extent that it has been differentially reinforced over conforming behavior or defined as more desirable then conforming alternatives, or at least justified (1973, Pp. 287-288).

From this line of reasoning, it is only a simple step from the principles of reinforcement theory to an explanation of how deviant behavior is acquired. That is, acquiring deviant behavior, the individual learns specific ways to express deviant beliefs, attitudes and behavior. This brings us to the crux of Aker's theory; there is little if any difference in how deviant actions are learned from that of non-deviant behavior. Then, in a very general sense, Akers' major assumption is that a person is more likely to engage in deviant behavior if she has learned, through operant condition, that deviant behavior is more rewarding than not engaging in deviant actions. Hence, Akers, along with Burgess, (see Burgess & Akers, 1966), has formulated seven principles, more or less consistent with operant conditioning principles, in their attempt to account for deviancy:

    1. Deviant behavior is learned according to the principles of operant conditioning.

2. Deviant behavior is learned both in non-social situations that are reinforcing or discriminating, and through that social intereaction in which the behavior of other persons is reinforcing or discriminating for such behavior.

3. The principle part of the learning of deviant behavior occurs in those groups which comprise or control the individual's major source of reinforcements.

4. The learning of deviant behavior, including specific techniques, attitudes and avoidance procedures, is a function of the effective and available reinforcers and the existing reinforcement contingencies.

5. The specific class of behavior learned and its frequency of occurrence are a function of the effective and available reinforcers, and the deviant or nondeviant direction of the norms rules, and definitions which in the past have accompanied the reinforcement.

6. The probability that a person will commit deviant behavior is increased in the presence of normative statements, definitions, and verbalizations which, in the process of differential reinforcement of such behavior over conforming behavior, have acquired discriminative value.

7. The strength of deviant behavior is a direct function of the amount, frequency, and probability of its reinforcement. The modalities of association with deviant patterns are important insofar as they affect the source, amount, and scheduling of reinforcement (1977, Pp. 42-43).

Akers notes that the object in much of the application of operant conditioning has been reflected in the area of the self-control of deviant behaviors that produces aversive or negative consequences, such as disapproval from others. The existence of negatively evaluated behaviors must in fact have negative consequences for the actor because, according to operant conditioning if this is not the case then there exist no contingency of reinforcement through which the person can develope self-control. For example, if a person should fail to conform to the norms of a particular group, and nonconformity to the group's norms does not lead to disapproval from the group, deviant behavior is said to be rewarding in itself and the person is likely to continue to deviate from the group's norms. Hence, if deviant behavior is followed by negative consequences, the likelihood of the emission of such behavior should in fact decrease.

The outcome of deviant behavior, then, has either positive or negative consequences. That is deviant behavior has positive effects when reward or reinforcement follows the behavior and negative effects when punishment is the outcome of deviant behavior.

Then, it seems only logical to suspect that punishing people for deviant behavior or even threatening to do so could in fact prevent persons from engaging in deviant activities. As a matter of fact most societies have established varying degrees of severe punishment for the more extreme forms of deviant behavior such as rape, murder, and assault on a person. However, as we now know punishment has not always been found to deter deviant behavior. For example, research has shown that the threat of punishment for aggression has, at least in several recent experiments, been found to increase rather than decrease subjects' tendencies to aggress or attack a victim (see Wilson and Rogers, 1975). And, it has also been observed that those who punish others for their aggressive actions may indeed serve as powerful models for aggression themselves (see Bandura, 1969). Another serious limitation is that the effects of punishment are only short lived and that later on following the use of punishment an individual may indeed engage in even more deviant actions, for example, physical aggression (see Bandura, 1969).

To gain some idea how rewards or reinforcements might affect deviant behavior, Harris, Wolf, and Baer (1964) have shown that negative behavior can be established inadvertently through reinforcement. Harris and his coworkers first noted the existing contingencies of reinforcement for children and then they asked the child's teacher to alter the behavior of the child through the administration of specific reinforcements and the withholding of other reinforcement unwittingly given to the child in the past. In addition, teachers were told to withhold disapproval for certain deviant behaviors. Alternative normative behaviors were rewarded throught the teacher's approval (reward). In this case the child's behavior changed from deviant to nondeviant.

Harris and his associates did not stop here, they carried the procedure further in order to ascertain whether extinguished deviant behavior would recur: They asked the teacher to reinforce the previously extinguished behavior. And, of course, a return to the original reinforcement did in fact lead to a recurrence of the deviant behavior. Finally, the teacher reinforced the child's normative behaviors and then the teacher gradually decreased the reinforcement. In this way the child's normative behavior was not dependent upon reinforcement. The authors report that the original deviant behavior did not reoccur.

We have, then, noted several ways in which reinforcement theory attempts to account for deviancy, but to view deviance simply as reinforced behavior can be quite misleading. Such a view undermines the role that cognitive factors play. A cognitive account of deviancy suggests that violating the rules is more rewarding than conforming, however, people first must violate the rules in order to judge rule-violating behavior as more rewarding than non-rule-violating behavior. What then might lead a person to violate norms in the first place? Do the sources of deviance lie within the norm-violator's personality? If this is the case, then, does society shape the person's personality and as a result do norm violating actions compliment the personality "needs" of the deviant person. In other words, do we locate the sources of deviance outside or inside the individual or in the parameters of the person's immediate social environment? Or do we, as labeling theorists tells us, concentrate primarily on the social processes of defining deviancy?

Finally, in contrast to social learning theory, reinforcement theory suggest that the deviant engages in rule-breaking behavior because such behavior is rewarding. All that is required is that we focus on the reinfocement for deviancy. This suggests that we identify the rewards for deviant behavior and attempt to control them or induce the rule-breaker to engage in non-rule-breaking behaviors and reward the individual accordingly. Future research on deviancy might well examine the specific rewards for conformity and deviation. It would appear that the deviant's behavior is not necessarily controlled by rewards obtained through legitimate means. Then, we might ask: "To what extent does the person seek illegitimate means to rewards (ends) and to what extent can the individual be induced to seek more legitimate means?" These are not simple questions, however, to more fully understand deviant behavior requires that we focus on this problem. Finally, it is tempting to lay the problem of reinforcement theory aside and argue for an alternative and compelling version of deviant behavior---exchange theory.

SOCIAL EXCHANGE THEORY AND DEVIANT BEHAVIOR

To the learning theorist deviancy is the result of reinforcement. Then deviant behavior is acquired in the same way as any other learned behavior. More important, the principles of reinforcement are said to be involved in the maintance of deviant actions once such behavior is learned. On the other hand, social learning theory suggest that reinforcement may not be necessary and that people learn from observing social models without the consequences of reinforcement. Modeling of deviant behavior may show up later on or after the person has beee exposed to a social model and, the individual may continue to reproduce the model's behavior for a long time even in the seeming absence of reinforcement.

Having said this, what then are some other applications of learning theory to deviant behavior? Perhaps one of the most important extensions of learning principles to the study of deviancy is that of social exchange theory. And we should note that perhaps no other area of social psychology has been responsible for bridging the apparent hiatus between reinforcement theory and the cognitive approaches to social behavior than has exchange theory. For example, John W. Thibaut and Harold H. Kelley (1959) explain why people interact with one another by first postulating that the rewards (satisfactions) people obtain and the costs (dissatisfactions) people incur while interacting with other people are in themselves determinants of social interaction.

Thibaut and Kelley tell us that we are unlikely to continue interacting with other people unless our rewards exceed our costs in doing so (or at least in the long run). In order to account for the relative value of rewards, Thibaut and Kelley introduce the concept <u>comparison level</u> (CL). Then, accordingly, people are said to compare their <u>residual outcomes</u> (their rewards minus their costs in an interaction) obtained in a given dyadic interaction in their past with outcomes (rewards minus costs) likely to be obtained in the present or outcomes that they anticipate for their future interactions. In this way individuals are said to employ a subjective standard (CL) or value in comparing their past rewards with their past costs relative to particular classes of social interactions.

Thibiaut and Kelly do not stop here but they take us a step further and introduce the concept <u>comparison level of alternatives</u> (CLalt). In this way Thibaut and Kelley are able to account for alternatives interactions that the person is likely to consider. Alternative interactions may or may not yield outcomes either with a greater or a lesser value than those that the person is now receiving in her present situation (CL). On a more general level, a person's CLalt is "a subjective standard that the person uses in judging possible outcomes in one social interaction in comparison to the expected or anticipated outcomes in other alternative interactions." The more promising an alternative relationship (CLalt) seems at the moment, the more likely the person is to consider leaving a present interaction or relationship and to engage in an alternative relationship. What this implies is that the person is likely to terminate a current relationship where his CL yields outcomes less than what might be anticipated in an alternative relationship(s).

Now that we have considered some of the major assumptions of exchange theory, it is now time to return to the problem at hand. As the reader will recall we suggested earlier that under certain conditions a person may find deviant behavior more rewarding than nondeviant behavior. In such cases we should hasten to add that an individual is likely to come to value deviant behavior more if the person's CL for satisfaction (reward) is high while at the same time the person's CLalt is low. On the other hand, if the rewards a person anticipates for deviant behavior drops lower than his CLalt, the person may consider leaving a present interaction (where deviant behavior does not pay off) and seek out alternative nondeviant relationships where, of course, the potential for satisfaction is assumed to be greater. Of course, people do not always consider alternative relationships, and in such cases they are likely to maintain non-rewarding interactions. But not for long.

Thibaut and Kelley assess status, relative to conformity and deviation, by suggesting that in newly formed groups, where all members of the group wish to be accepted by others, those who are least certain of being accepted will tend to conform the most and will continue to do so as long as their status is low and they desire to improve their position or status. On the other hand, Thibaut and Kelley say that high status persons have the most counterpower and they are the most effective in defending themselves against punishment for their deviations from the group's norms. An individual's counterpower is defined as "his or her value to the group, which may be used by the person to make the group's power unusable."

What Thibaut and Kelley are suggesting is that people will conform to the group's norms as long as they seek social approval and are not certain that social approval is forthcoming. However, once the group has assigned persons, more or less on a permenent basis, to low status, whether they have failed to conform or not, they are likely to devalue the group and they are likely to seek alternative group membership and rewards; at this point the group has little or no control over the person. In addition, Thibaut and Kelley observe that group members, who are not convinced that the group will reward them for conformity are unlikely to conform and in effect they may find deviation rewarding.

Yet another variation on the exchange view of deviancy is proposed by George C. Homans (1961,

1974). He assesses conformity, in relation to social status, by postulating that people seek and find social approval for conformity or nonconformity (or deviation) and to induce its group members to conform to the group's norms. Homans suggests that:

> Much depends, then, on the degree to which the conformers monopolize social rewards and thus are able to deny them to deviates. If there is even one other member who will also hold out against the group, and thus provide for a deviate an alternative source of social reward, including support for his opinions. The evidence suggests that the deviate is apt to remain one. He becomes what we shall call a <u>holdout</u>. Though it be misery to be a deviate, companionship in misery helps preserve deviance (1974, Pp. 105-106).

Homans (1974) tells us that those who deviate from the group's norms in similar ways tend to hold similar values and to have similar backgrounds. An example is the person who tends to violate output or production norms in factory settings. Homans suggests that these "rate busters " tend to come from rural areas, are Protestants and their ancestors came from northwestern Europe. In addition, "rate busters" place high value on hard work and material rewards gleamed from hard work. This background, of course, makes it difficult to restrict their production to fit normative expectations for output. Hence, Homan claims that: "similar background... is often found in similar deviation. But what is cause can become effect. Persons who were not similar in behavior to begin with are apt to become so if they persist in their deviation. Their rejection by the rest makes them more dependent on one another for social rewards" (1974, p. 107).

What then happens when a person continues to deviate? Those who conform to the group's norms began to punish the deviate more and more severely. However, when the group has punished the deviate as much as it can and has failed to make the deviate conform, the group has in effect lost its control over the deviate. In this case the deviate is likely to become angry, giving the deviate more and more reason to remain deviant. Of course, this is more likely if the punishment is viewed as unfair or unjust. In this respect Homans tells us that the deviant may seek out alternative group membership and Homans tells us "What men feel to be justice or injustice makes a difference to their conformity or deviance: (1974, P. 107).

According to Homans how does conformity and deviation first take place? Homans suggests that social approval is rewarding and that social approval or social disapproval is used by members of a group to induce its members to conform to the group's norms. However, not all of a group's members conform. In such cases deviant behavior is likely to be more rewarding (or less costly) than conforming behavior.

The status level of a group's members is related to conformity to the group's norms. When group members are divided into three status levels, high, middles, and lows---middles, in general, are found to be the most conforming, whereas highs confrom most to the central norms of the group relative to the group's goals. Highs also deviate from the less important norms, whereas lows conform less to all kinds of group norms. Homans tells us that this is so because highs tend to be responsible for the group's most valued actives or scarce resources. In a sense, then, highs can more easily deviate from the lesser valued norms because other members of the group allow them to deviate. This in effect is "a small price to pay for the valued activities afforded to the group by highs." Highs have what might be called extra sources of social approval not available to lows or middles. In fact, the highs' deviations may serve as a source of deviation for lower-status persons seeking approval from high-status individuals. On the other hand, middles have little to gain and much to lose from deviating from the group's norms. Lows can deviate without risk of social approval and the group has little control over its members who are assigned low status. In general, the rewards a person tends to receive are <u>conguent</u> with the status of the person as are his costs. In other words, a state of <u>distributive justice</u> is said to exist and in this case Homans suggests:

> The question for distributive justice is whether what a man gets, his reward, is in line with what he gives in social exchange. If, it is in line, the condition of distributive justice is realized (1974, p. 211).

Distributive injustice is said to exist when a person "perceives that other people of similar investments obtain greater rewards and/or less costs."

SOCIAL EXCHANGE AND THE REWARD-COST MODEL FOR DEVIANT BEHAVIOR

How then do we begin to account for deviant behavior through the application of exchange theory? First certain features of exchange theory suggest that reinforcement theory has considerable potential for explaining deviant behavior. But to pursue these matters would require a somewhat detailed account of exchange theory, which we have tried to do, before we can afford to recognize that rewards and punishments (costs) are involved in the process of social exchange. The reader should know that the application of exchange theory to the study of deviance has had its most effective use through a series of studies carried out by Irving M. Piliavin and his associates (Briar & Piliavin, 1965; Piliavin, Vadum, & Hardyck, 1976, Piliavin, Hardyck, & Vadum, 1968).

Since exchange theory postulates that people tend to maximize their rewards in a relationship, exchange theory notes that people also tend to maximize rewards at minimum costs. With this observation, Piliavin and his associates have postulated a reward-cost model for deviant behavior which suggests that everyone of us is at one time or another capable of engaging in deviant behavior. Then, what seems to deter or inhibit a person? Piliavin et al. suggest that when we subjectively experience greater costs associated with deviant actions and higher rewards with conforming behavior we are likely to be inhibited and therefore not likely to engage in deviant behavior. That is, deviant behavior is said to have its origin in interpersonal situations where people assess their reward-cost outcomes for conformity or nonconformity to the group's norms and where the person concludes that deviant behavior yields more rewards than costs. The person at this point is more likely to engage in deviant behavior.

Once they reasoned that people tend to seek rewards and avoid punishments, Piliavin, Hardyck, and Vadum (1968) decided to carry out research in order to test their reward-cost model for deviancy. In choosing a research strategy they employed high school students (males) as subjects and set up a study where they examined the effects of personal costs for deviance (cheating) in terms of monetary gain.

Since the authors found (in a previous study) that high-cost delinquent males show a lesser tendency to engage in crime than low-cost delinquent males, they decided to use scales they had previously used to measure the potential deviation costs for their subjects (see Briar and Piliavin, 1965). These scales were found to be significantly correlated with subjects' self-reports for criminal behavior, police apprehension of delinquent behavior, and subjects' actual police arrest records.

Since Piliavin et al. observed that the direction of causation could not be established for their earlier study, they then designed an experiment by selecting subjects from their survey sample and they assigned their subjects to a high-cost or low-cost condition and to a delinquent or to a nondelinquent condition on the basis of subjects' past self-report classifications.

The subjects were given booklets and told to note the number of times a sequence of letters appeared on each page. They were promised $.50 per page and then they were given the opportunity to cheat, of course, after the experimenter left the experimental room.

As expected, Piliavin et al. found that low-cost boys cheated for monetary gain significantly more often than did high-cost boys. Additional results tended to support earlier findings. That is, high-cost boys were less likely to report delinquent behavior and to have official police records than low-cost boys.

These findings clearly tend to support the reward-cost model and suggest that exchange theory can be successfully applied to the analysis of deviant behavior. As a matter of fact, Piliavin et al. suggest that their reward-cost formulation of delinquency has implications for the prevention and control of juvenile delinquency. That is, they suggest that we should increase the costs for engaging in delinquent behavior and reward nondelinquent actions or behavior that compliments the social norm.

What the findings of Piliavin et al. clearly indicate is the crucial role of rewards and costs in affecting a person's likelihood for deviation from nonmative patterns of behavior, especially where the individual enters an ongoing situation with a past history of norm violation. The subjects used in the research were males with a history of delinquency.

And more recently support for the reward-cost model is reported by Dennis E. Michael and his associates (Michael, Penner, & Brookmire, 1978). They found that subjects who indicated that they would "keep money they found" actually made lower cost estimates for their potential anti-social behavior than those who said they would in fact return the money to its owner. In addition, the "anti-social" subjects tended to score higher on Spielberger, O'Hagen, and Kling's (1977) Sociopathy Scale than subjects who indicated that they would return the lost item.

One question not addressed in the above research is how do we account for the process of emergent deviant behavior. The question here is how deviant behavior can be group-based (i.e., where the individual initially prefers nondeviant behavior and where such behavior has low reward value). How then does this sort of situation induce the person to a full-blown pattern of deviancy as the only recourse open to realize higher rewards than costs?

If we press the issue a bit more the answer to our question may be found in what Jones and Gerard (1967) tells us. That is, they have suggested that there are several ways people can increase their rewards through the process of increasing their degree of power in a social relationship. For example, the individual can come to see a higher reward value for deviant behavior than nondeviant behavior. The person can also minimize the rewards other members give them for conforming or the cost incurred for deviation and come to hence find deviant behavior highly rewarding. Then, understandably deviant behavior can be extremely rewarding in situations where its costs are minimal or in situations where the ability of others to punish deviant behavior is weak or absent. Hence, the nature of the situation undoubtedly has an important effect on whether an individual will find deviancy more or less costly than nondeviant actions.

Thus far we have looked at exchange theory and have found it instructive in attempting to account for deviancy. And, having discussed some of the major tenets of this theory we come full circle, and we have eskewed some of the shortcomings of exchange theory. We have also noted its advantage as an extension of reinforcement theory. Besides being an extension of behaviorism exchange theory has stimulated relevant research in deviancy, however, exchange theory does not tell the whole story. Then, clearly exchange theory pits the profit motive (gleamed from microeconomics) against a loss in profit and we are lead to believe that deviants are like most of us when they go out searching for rewards; they are said to avoid costs. There is an obvious failure of exchange theory to relate observed deviant behavior to the personal and unique characteristics of the individual deviant. However, despite its overwhelming shortcomings, exchange theory does tell us how the potential deviant can be won over to the norms of a deviant subculture or group. That is, if the outcomes (profits) the potential deviant receives from a current relationship drops lower than his comparison level (CL) for alternative relationships (CLalt), the person will leave the current relationship and seek out an alternative interaction where profits seem higher (e.g., a deviant relationship). On the other hand, if the profit from a current relationship is more satisfying than the person's comparison level (CL), the individual will tend to more or less be satisfied with her current relationship (to be a relationship entailing deviant behavior or nondeviant behavior). Then, to the extent that a deviant group's members are able to control the individual member's rewards and costs, they in effect are said to have either <u>fate control</u> or <u>behavior control</u> over the individual member's outcomes.

Hence, by broading their concept of outcome, Thibaut and Kelley have explained how groups can indeed induce its members to leave or remain in the group. And, we can conjecture that rewards or costs for deviant behavior stems from members of the individuals group or the greater society.

You may guess from our presentation of the exchange theory perspective of deviancy that both this perspective and reinforcement theory make some common assumptions. Before we comment on what these might be let us first note what then are the prospects for an exchange theory of deviance.

According to exchange theory how does deviancy develope? Obviously a person's reference groups control many highly desirable rewards not otherwise readily accessible to the individual. Another prominent source of group influence is the person's "need" for defining social reality and for affiliation. Then, by comparing one's rewards with other similar persons (deviant or nondeviant) one can come to anticipate the likely rewards and costs for emitting certain kinds of behaviors. And, the individual may therefore come to adopt behaviors that increase the likelihood of rewards and decrease the probability of costs. Then, the discrepancies between the person's perceptions of desirable rewards and undesirable costs for engaging in deviant behaviors may in fact induce the person to behave as though she believes that when deviant behavior is similar to that of other group members' behaviors in fact they are shared vicariously by both the person and other group members.

Needless to say, it should be obvious from our earlier discussion of exchange theory that the individual may in fact adopt deviant behavior patterns in order to increase the similarity between himself and the group. This process may be aided by other group members through their ability to reward deviant behavior or to make deviant behavior less costly for the individual. Furthermore, one's perception of similarity to the group's standards for behavior may indeed become more firmly entrenched over time and the attractiveness that alternative behaviors have for the person are lessened. Then, in an effort to maintain a more or less desirable reward-cost outcome, the individual finds deviancy intrinsically rewarding. And, it should be added that the person, particularly the deviant who becomes highly similar to other members of the group, may become motivated to develope attitudes and beliefs about "outsiders" or nondeviants which become increasingly more negative. This change that occurs, for the most part, may be gradual or abrupt, however, the very nature of these changes may increase the difficulty of maintaining a perception of the self as clearly defined and consistent with the greater society's definition of what is socially desirable. In short, it is hardly surprising, then, that when the individual is confronted with people who do not share his self definition, negative attitudes are likely to be expressed towards such persons.

SUMMARY AND CONCLUSIONS

Unformturately, people who are rewarded for the more negative forms of deviancy no doubt are expressing their values about the desirability of particular forms of deviant behavior. For example, the value placed on television violence. In effect what we have stressed is that the learning of deviant behavior does not take place in a vacuum, but in situations where others provide reinforcements and/or social models for deviant actions.

Some students of deviant behavior argue that reinforcement is always necessary for learning deviant behavior (e.g., Akers, 1973, 1977), whereas, others feel that reinforcement is not a necessary condition for learning but effects motivation and performance once deviant behavior is learned (Bandura, 1977). In effect those that argue for a reinforcement position have stressed that when rewards follow a deviant response there is an increase in the likelihood that deviant response will take place the next time a reward is present and the particular deviant response has preceeded the reward.

Meanwhile, Bandura (1969, 1977) has shown that observational learning has important implications for deviant behavior. He has found that people are more likely to imitate the behaviors of high status social models, as well as models who are similar to the person themselves, rather than dissimilar. For example, a person is more likely to pay attention to the behavior of their peers than to those who are highly dissimilar to themselves. And, because Bandura has found that reward is not a necessary condition for imitation, then modeling one's behavior after deviant social models can indeed take place through an observation of such models.

Needless to say, a person can learn to inhibit or display deviant behavior, subsequent to modeling, depending on whether or not a model is observed to be punished or rewarded for deviant behavior. That is, the learning of deviant or nondeviant behavior by observers can be strengthened or weakened (inhibitory or disinhibitory effects) depending on what happens when a model deviates from a rule or norm.

It appears, then, in other words, that the social-learning perspective has had some success in accounting for complex forms of social behavior like deviancy. We can now suggest that people can learn to seek out particular cues in the behaviors of social models which seem to proscribe "how to and how not to behave." Then, from what we have said so far, social learning has some important heuristic implications, however, what is called for in research designed to assess the more general principles of social learning and their relationship to specific forms of deviant behavior in the "real world." In addition, sociologists have argued that there are social and cultural differences that emerge when we assess the values and attitudes people hold toward deviant behavior. Then, all in all, a particular society's values, no doubt, restricts the alternatives open to its individual members, and as such increase or decrease the likelihood of deviance in general or as a matter of fact particular forms of deviancy. Social learning theory needs to address these issues if we are to understand how social modeling of deviant behavior operates in different subcultures and across different cultures. But for the present we have to be satisfied with what we have gleamed from social learning theory. Guided by current social learning principles we have been able to trace the development of deviant behavior.

When we turn to exchange theory an ask "how do we account for deviant behavior?" it is hardly surprising that we are told that people tend to maximize their rewards at minimum costs. Then, just as postulated by reinforcement theory, deviant behavior is said to be shaped by rewards and punishments (costs). However, we are told that a group typically rewards some behaviors more than others. For example Thibaut and Kelley (1959) suggest that compliance to a norm tends to make interaction less costly. It tends to facilitate certain goals of the group. And, we should also note that the problems of exchange theory poses some of the same problems faced by other "behavioral" versions of deviant behavior (e.g., Skinner radical behaviorism), when they attempt to account for complex social behavior.

Then, comes exchange theory and the concepts comparison level (CL) and comparison level for alternatives (CLalt). We are introduced to a cognitive element in the scene. When present and alternative interactions are pited against each other the more rewarding actions win out to the more costly behaviors.

And, in effect, the person is said to adopt behaviors that do not seem to incur high costs in the long run. As an interaction proceeds the individual comes to place greater stress on personal goal-seeking activities in such a way that deviant behavior may eventually serve to maximize rewards at lower costs. This link between the deviant's private reward-cost outcomes and the person's concern with other members of a group is controlled, or at least to some extent, by the potential of group members to threaten the individual's positive outcomes. If the person should forsake his present rewards, then he must be motivated to seek more attractive alternative reward-cost outcomes. So it appears that, at least to a certain extent, the potential deviant is attempting to behave according to the principles of reinforcements. Deviance, then, comes about because of the disenchantment with relatively low rewards for nondeviant actions and seemingly higher rewards for emitting deviant behavior.

In concluding this chapter on social learning and exchange theory, we should point out that learning views are central to the concern of social psychologists, and this same observation holds true no less for the study of deviant behavior. Then, it seems only logical that an adequate description of deviancy requires that we keep on examining its social influences, including the implications of social learning and reinforcement theory for deviant behavior.

CHAPTER 3: SOCIAL INFLUENCE AND THE DEVIATION PROCESS

INTRODUCTION: CONFORMITY AND COMPLIANCE

One might guess that conformity and deviation have little in common. Actually social psychologists who have studied conformity suppose that individuality and deviancy stem from the opportunities for uniqueness in a complex society such as ours. Then, from a social psychological perspective conformity and deviation, as we suggested in the previous chapter, implies that the individual group member meets the group's normative expectations or does not and when deviation does in fact take place normative controls are made implicit or explicit to the individual. That is, in effect when we claim that people conform to the norms we also imply that there is indeed some form of social control or pressure brought to bear on the group's members.

What, then, do we mean when we refer to conformity? According to one definition conformity is a noticeable change in one's beliefs or behavior toward the norms of a group due to real or imagined group pressure (see Kiesler & Kiesler, 1969). As a matter of fact, Charles A. Kiesler (1969) tells us that there are no less than three different common uses of the concept conformity: (1) an actual change in a person's attitudes and beliefs due to group pressure; (2) going along with a group; and (3) a disposition or personality trait. Kiesler goes on to note that we can distinguish between two types of change that are due to group pressure: When we conform on the basis of public behavior Kiesler uses the label compliance, whereas when we conform in terms of attitude change, Kiesler notes that this is in effect private acceptance. And, private acceptance is said to involve the process of internalization, and it is very similar to what social psychologists call attitude change (see Kelman, 1958).

GROUP INFLUENCE: MORE ON CONFORMITY AND COMPLIANCE

Then, again, what do we mean when we refer to conformity or compliance or in fact deviation?

First, uniformity of behavior in a group does not by necessity suggest that members of a particular group are conforming to the group's norms, or does it? Actually, conformity generally is assumed to have taken place when people yield to group pressures to accept the group standard. That is, conformity suggests that an individual group member would not behave as he or she has without an "awareness" of pressure from the group to do so (see Kiesler & Kiesler, 1969, p. 2). And it is here that Stephen Worchel and Joel Cooper, cite an example of conformity which illustrates the effect of group pressure:

> In the My Lai incident, the reports of many of the 25 soldiers who took part in the massacre of Vietnamese civilians indicated that they experienced a great deal of conflict between their own beliefs and the pressures from the group. A soldier reported: "I knew it was wrong. I was sick at the sight of the slaughter and begged God to forgive me as I shot into the trenches." Many of the GIs did not believe their actions were right, and they probably would not have acted as they did if they had been along. Thus one pressure acting on the soldier was his feelings that he should not murder the civilians. On the other hand, there was also pressure from the group and the group leaders for the soldier to shoot into the trenches of civilians: "What was I to do? The orders were to shoot and guys all around me had opened fire" (1976, p. 319).

In essence, group pressure is likely to lead a person to view reality in much the same way as other members of their group. Having said this, now let us return to our earlier question and attempt to differentiate conformity from compliance. First, we have noted that, social psychologists have shown that there are at least two types of general social influence processes: (1) compliance which refers to the overt or public actions which results when a person's behavior is like the behavior of other members of the group. That is, where the person "goes along with the group without privately agreeing with the group," and (2) conformity or private acceptance refers to "changes in a person's attitudes or beliefs in the direction of the group's attitudes or beliefs." However, compliance (public behavior) and conformity (public behavior) are likely to have very different implications for the understanding of deviant behavior. For example, the person who outwardly complies with the group but does not privately accept the group's standards (norms) to judge its member's behavior may conceal his deviancy from the group (see Freedman & Doob, 1968). But, how then can public compliance be changed into private acceptance (or attitude change)?

Let us turn to John and Susan Darley (1973) and see how they employ cognitive dissonance theory to the present problem. Then, according to dissonance theory, what happens to an individual who publicly holds a position with which she does not privately agree? If the person is pressured into taking a descrepant position, because the group has exerted a great deal of pressure on him to do so, the individual may later on be faced with the question "why did I agree with the group when I felt differently then they?" In such cases, Darley and Darley suggest two "explanations" open to the person who complies: <u>external justification</u> and <u>internal determinants</u>. For example, if the individual concludes that going along with the group was necessary because there was no other choice, then, the person is likely to believe that others would also have done the very same thing under similar circumstances. Then, in a sense, the person feels that he has complied due to excessive "external pressures" to do so. Internal determinants refers to reasons for behavior which "lie within" the person and have caused the person to behave as she has. For example, the person who has complied in the face of group pressure may later on conclude that he was really not doing anything inconsistent after all. In this regard Darley and Darley ask the question:

> But what determines how a person decides whether his public compliance was the result of external justification or of internal determinants? (1973, p. 14).

They answer this question and suggest that:

> ...the person thinks of himself as someone who is independent and true to his own opinions. Such a person will experience considerable dissonance when he gives a public opinion counter to his private attitude. If the group pressure on him were strong, however he can quite easily

resolve his dissonance by pointing to the external compliance pressure that were brought to bear. For instance, consider the romantic case: "I spoke against what I believe. Why did I do that?---because they would have kidnapped my children, taken my job, and beaten my wife if I would have done otherwise!" (1973, Pp. 14-15).

So far we have been discussing how a person decides whether her behavior was due to external or internal factors. What about situations where compliance pressures decrease and the person finds it quite difficult to justify certain behaviors on the bases of group pressure alone? In such cases external justification is unlikely to provide the individual with sufficient reasons for the public behavior in the first place. Then, Darley and Darley suggest that "the person is likely to resolve the dissonance by deciding that there must have been internal determinants for his behavior" (p. 15).

Now, suppose that a person finds himself in a situation where he is induced to tell a lie. When this happens, the individual may become upset because he may have an image of himself as an honest and truthful person. How then is the person likely to allay the dissonance between his self image of an honest person and the act of lying? Then, in effect what factors seem to contribute to a person's acceptance of a lie as the truth?

An experiment was conducted by Leon Festinger and J. Merrill Carlsmith (1959), where subjects were asked to perform a boring task (spool packing) and then the researchers stated that they had an assistant who did not show up for the research and they asked the subject to help by lying to the next subject to the effect that the spool-packing task was in fact very interesting. The subject was promised either $1.00 (low-incentive condition) or $20.00 (high-incentive condition) for telling the lie. In addition, the subject was asked to "remain on call" in the event that the subject was needed to help the experimenters out at a later time.

As Festinger and Carlsmith had predicted, subjects who had lied for the small incentive "reduced" their dissonance more by persuading themselves that the boring task was really interesting (internal justification). On the other hand, subjects who lied for the larger incentive externally justified their actions by coming to believe that the task was still boring and, no doubt, justified the lying on the basis of the incentive.

Additional evidence shows that when subjects are given the task of convincing their peers that a boring task is indeed really not boring, if they are led to believe that they have succeeded, as opposed to failed in their task, just as in the Festinger-Carlsmith study, only subjects in a low-incentive condition, who thought they had succeeded in the task, showed dissonance reduction by claiming that the boring task was indeed interesting (see Cooper & Worchel, 1970).

Cooper and Worchel's (1970) study illustrates the need to take into account the individual's evaluation of her own behavior as a source of dissonance reduction. And now that we have finally concluded that the degree to which a person complies or conforms to the expectations of others depends on a number of variables, let us next consider some of the more traditional-research into conformity and compliance.

EARLY RESEARCH ON CONFORMITY AND DEVIATION

One of the first experimental approaches to the study of conformity was carried out by Muzafer Sherif (1935, 1936). Sherif took advantage of a well-known perceptual technique labeled the autokinetic phenomenon. If, for example, a person focuses on a stationary light in a dark room, the light soon appears to move. In Sherif's studies he brought subjects into a darkened room and showed them a small light, and as expected his subjects soon reported that the light had moved. Later the subject found that she was confronted with a group of the experimenter's confederates, who this time gave bogus estimates of how much the light appeared to move. And, of course, their judgments were descrepant from those of the subject. Hence, the measure of conformity is the degree to which the subject shifts her estimate of the lights apparent movement to match those of the confederates.

Sherif found that his subjects' estimates of movement was profoundly affected by the presence of others. Now, Sherif asked his subjects, who had made judgments of the lights movement with the experimenter's confederates, to return the next day to make private rather than public judgments. What Sherif found was that the influence of the confederates was still apparent. As a matter of fact, more recent research shows that this change persist as long as one year after subjects have been exposed to incorrect judgments (see Rohrer, Baron, Hoffman, & Swander, 1954).

Then, some years after Sherif's original studies, Solomon Asch (1951) noted that Sherif's subjects were confronted with a highly ambigious situation (a stationary light in a darkened room) and for this reason he decided to study conformity in a situation where the stimulus conditions were almost devoid of ambiguity. Hence, he developed a method where a subject is taken into an experimental room and is introduced to "other subjects." The experimenter, then enters the room and informs those present that they are to take part in an experiment concerned with visual perception. At this juncture the experimenter shows the subjects two large cards. One card contains a single line, and the other card has three lines labeled A, B, and C. The single line is about 10 inches long, and while line A in 8 3/4 inches long, B is 10 inches long, and C in 8 inches in length. Next, the experimenter tells the subjects that they should match the single line with the line of equal length from the card with three lines. Then, after all others (i.e., the confederates) had made their estimates, the subject was asked to match the line. Subjects continued to estimate the correct match and each time the subject was the last to judge the lines.

Finally, the experimenter shows the subject a 3-inch line and three additional lines where A is 3 3/4 inches long, B 4 1/4 inches long, and C 3 inches in length. The subject can easily observe that line C is the correct match. Then, suddenly the first subject claims that line A is a match for the single line. At this piint the subject begins to wonder "whats wrong" and then another subject suggests that line A is correct. Then, after all seven subjects reports "incorrectly" the naive subject's turn comes.

What does the subject do? Of course, Asch's paradigm is different than Sherif procedure: There are no correct answers in Sherif's experiment and the degree to which movement is seen by any subject varies greatly from subject to subject. What Asch found was that his subjects conformed to the group's incorrect judgments over one third of the trials. This took place even when the naive subject knew full well that the group was "dead wrong." And, of course, Asch was surprised to find that his subjects had conformed since he originally predicted that people will not conform to group judgments when in fact they know that their own judgments are correct and the group's judgments are wrong.

Asch's findings are particularly relevant for the study of deviant behavior. For example, Asch (1956) found that a single deviant can have an important impact on the conformity of other group members. Hence, on the average members of the group conformed about thirty-five percent of the trials when in fact they were confronted with a group decision on the line judgment task. On the other hand, when the group was faced with members where all but one of them concurred with the group decision, conformity of the group dropped to about nine percent.

Of course, Asch's findings suggest that when one lone deviant exists in a group, the group's decisions or judgments can indeed become significantly altered. Why should this be the case? Stephen Worchel and Joel Cooper tell us that:

> From the group's point of view, allowing one deviant to exist can be very dangerous, since it could result in other members taking deviant stands. In view of the influence of normative and informational pressures, it can be argued that the addition of one deviant should not strongly affect an individual's conformity if he is responding to informational influence. A group of ten people all agreeing on a point should provide a great deal more information about what is correct than a group of nine people who hold this view, plus one dissenter. However, if normative pressure is responsible for the conformity, when the subject sees one other person deviate from the group and "gets away with it," this should reduce the normative pressure and reduce his fear of being rejected if he to deviates. If, on the other hand, he sees the deviant being severely punished by the group, he will think twice before he decides to violate the group's norms. This suggests that

a group that relies on normative influence to obtain conformity will persecute a deviant, while one that relies on informational pressure will not (1976, Pp. 328-329).

In everyday situations people are likely to be influenced by several sources. For example, Deutch, and Gerard (1955) tell us there is a difference between _normative_ and _informational_ social influence (a distinction also made by Kelley, 1952). Normative influence is said to take place when an individual's conformity stems from the person's reaction to the evaluation from others, whereas informational influence occurs when a person regards others as a credible source.

Deutsch and Gerard tell us that normative influence tends to be high under conditions where others hold scarce resources (e.g., social approval) that the individual would like; and where the person is willing to expore whether or not their expectations are being met. Hence, normative influence tends to operate to increase the salience of social power and it leads to conformity.

Then what is really important here is that the person believes that his behavior is being monitored by others. Hence, if the person should believe that her behavior is being monitored, normative social influence should increase conformity, whereas if this is not the case deviancy is more likely to occur. Then, the person must believe that others will provide rewards for conformity and/or punishments for deviancy or nonconformity.

To illustrate the above process, then, it is perhaps appropriate that we show evidence that people do in fact conform to avoid disapproval or punishment from other group members and also they conform to gain social approval or scarce rewards. Jones, Gergen and Jones (1963) had ROTC cadets work in pairs, with one member higher in status than the other. Half of the subjects were informed that they should try to be compatible and the other half of the subjects were told that the study was concerned with how people get acquainted with one another. Then, the subjects exchanged information and a measure of subjects' conformity to the other group member's opinions was taken.

Results of the study showed that there was significantly more conformity in the compatibility condition, more conformity by low-status persons, and it was found that the patterns of conformity differed for the different conditions. That is, high-status subjects conformed least on the important issues, and low-status subjects conformed most on the important issues.

Overall, it seems apparent that people do conform for social approval. On the other hand for normative social influence to become operative, people must believe that they will be rejected by the group because of their deviant behavior. Actually, evidence does exist which suggests that deviants are indeed rejected under these conditions (see Allen, 1965; Schachter, 1951). And, indeed under these conditions deviates do come to <u>expect</u> that they will be rejected by the group (see Gerard & Rotter, 1961). On the other hand, Allen (1965), has shown that when a group has rejected a deviate, there is less subsequent conformity by other members of the group than when the group has not rejected the deviate. Finally, as we have shown, subjects lead to believe that they are deviant actually do conform less than do nondeviates at least in private situations (see Freedman & Doob, 1968).

Now, let us return to Asch's research and comment on some of its limitations. Here we should note that Allen and Levine (1968, 1969) have challenged Asch's research and they have shown that extreme cases of deviancy do not always reduce conformity in the group. They had a simulated subject deviate in one of two different ways from the unpopular views of three other simulated subjects on two different occasions, opinion statements (e.g., "Most young people get too much education."), and on a visual perception task. In a social support condition, the deviate gave acceptable or popular answers, whereas in the extreme deviate condition, the deviate gave extremely unpopular answers compared to the majority, who gave erroneous answers. In an unanimous condition, all simulated subjects gave the same unacceptable or unpopular answers.

Allen and Levin (in two different experiments) showed that subjects conformed less in the social support than in the unanimous conditions on both the opinion and visual perception tasks. On the other hand, and consistent with Asch's line judgment task, the extreme deviate reduced conformity significantly. Meanwhile, on the opinion statements, the extreme deviate did not reduce conformity.

Of course, what Allen and Levine's findings suggest is that Asch's claim that "mere dissent" reduces conformity on a visual perception task, is not supported in cases where opinions are involved instead of a perceptual task.

In view of the above research, we will examine additional evidence gleamed from a study carried out by Levine, Saxe, and Ranelli (1974). Levine *et al*. investigated the effect of extreme dissent and social support on both visual perception and opinion items under both normative and informational conditions. In the normative condition subjects were pressured to avoid group punishment. That is, subjects were led to believe that agreement among group members was necessary to obtain reward and that group members would have the choice to punish those who failed to go along with the group. In the informational pressure condition subjects were made to avoid punishment by giving the "correct" answers to questions. In an additional condition, no mention was made of punishment for not going along with the group, and subjects were next exposed to a social supporter who deviated from an erroneous majority by giving acceptable answers or to an extreme deviate who gave very unpopular answers even more so than the majority of the group, or as a matter of fact a unanimous group.

Leven *et al*. found that under both normative and informational conditions, both social support and extreme dissent reduced conformity on visual tasks, whereas on opinion items only social support reduced conformity. Then, in effect a social supporter reduced conformity on both visual and opinion items, whereas the extreme deviate produced a reduced degree of conformity on only the visual task. This finding is, of course, consistent with Asch's research.

So far we have demonstrated that social support for erroneous views, and extreme deviations from the majority are about equally effective in reducing the degree of conformity in a group. Then, does social support for one's views lead to resistance to group pressures? Two general factors have been noted to increase resistance to group pressures: The social supporter's skill in increasing a person's confidence in his own position or <u>assessor</u> <u>utility</u>, and, the social supporter's skill in reducing other's fear that the group will punish deviations from the group or <u>ally</u> <u>utility</u>.

Allen and Levine (1971) created two different social supporters, who gave the same answers but differed in terms of the adequacy of their sources of information. In an invalid condition the experimenter's confederate wore thick eyeglasses to give the impression of poor vision. And the confederate stated that he had difficulty seeing the stimuli. He actually failed an easy "visual test." In a valid social support condition, the same confederate did not wear eyeglasses and he did not claim that he could not do the task.

Results showed that the valid and invalid social supporters reduced the group's level of conformity. Also, the valid social supporter reduced conformity significantly more than the invalid social supporter. Of course, these results support the "assessor utility" hypothesis, which suggests that a social supporter's skill in judging stimuli is an important determinant of conformity reduction.

In an earlier study, Allen (1966) carried out an experiment where his subjects were led to believe that their views on an important topic did not agree with the group's opinion. Also, some of the subjects were told that they were the sole dissenter, whereas other subjects were told that another group member agreed with them. Subjects were then asked: "Whom do you think the majority will vote to eliminate from the group?" Results suggested that fewer subjects expected that they would be rejected when they deviated with a partner then when they deviated alone. Hence, Allen's findings support the view that the presence of a social supporter can reduce a deviating person's expectations for group punishment. Once more we can see that the presence or absence of others who support the group's judment can make a difference in conformity or deviation.

More recent research Ross, Bierbrauer, and Hoffman (1976) suggest that subjects in the Asch experiment are faced with the dilemma where the correct judgments are a matter of objective reality, while at the same time "other subjects" give judgments that are obviously incorrect. Under these conditions the subject is in conflict between what is perceived and what a peer group reports. As a result uncertainty and discomfort lead the subject to attempt to explain the situation to herself. What if the subject should disagree with the group? Others might think the subject is stupid, deviant or incompetent. Then, one way to avoid potential criticism from the group is to conform (or comply) to the group's standards.

Ross et al. (1976) reasoned that when people disagree with others they are likely to make attributions about the motives of others. Then, why does a person hold an opinion or make judgments which are unrealistic? When we make such attributions we begin to "understand" why others appear to be different from ourselves. In order to assess this hypothesis, Ross et al. designed an experiment where some subjects were exposed to a regular Asch paradigm and there was no reasonable explanation for the incorrect responses given by the group members. Still other subjects (confederates) were told that they could earn extra points for particular responses. In this way an explanation was provided for the incorrect responses given by others. Another group of subjects were given instructions to take a risk for extra points or "play it safe." As Ross et al. had predicted, conformity was higher in the typical Asch situation than in the other conditions. When subjects attributed others' responses to different payoffs there was less influence from others and, of course, the subjects conformed less.

The findings of Ross et al.'s research, their implications, and their relationship to deviancy are far reaching. Then, in effect we have found out that conformity is greatest when the individual can find no adequate explanation for the group's incorrect judgments (deviant responses), and when a rational explanation is available conformity decreases.

If it be granted, then, that we need reasons to conform to the norms of a group, does the timing of social support for deviant actions or beliefs make a difference? To put the question another way, when most members of a group disagree with an individual member is the person more likely to feel greater support if an ally initially supports the deviant or only later offers support?

In order to put this question to a hard test, Morris and Miller (1975) conducted an experiment where groups of five subjects were used and they made judgments about the number of dots shown briefly on slides. On six critical trials the subject was faced with an incorrect answer by the majority and then the subject responded. Morris and Miller used three conditions: All four of the others were incorrect, the subject was confronted with one dissenting group member who either made responses before the incorrect three or after them.

Contrary to their prediction, Morris and Miller found that conformity on the critical trials was greater in the condition where there was total agreement among the other four group members, and the social support from one other person was found to reduce instead of increase conformity. Then, it appears clear from Morris and Miller's research that the least conformity takes place when a deviant partner makes deviant responses first not last. What this seems to suggest is that a deviant cohort who gives early support provides the deviant with immediate validation for nonnormative judgments and this seems to take place before the deviant begins to doubt his own judgments.

Other researchers have used variations on the theme of dissent. For example, Thomas Moriarty (1974) asked the question: "Assuming a minority-majority situation arises, under what conditions will the minority individual feel deviant?" In order to look for an answer to this question Moriarty created his own deviance and he did so in a laboratory setting. In this case each subject found out that during the exchange of opinions about political and social issues that they were not in agreement with the majority of others present in the situation. One member of the group consistently agreed with the person's opinions and as such provided social support for deviance. In addition, and in order to evaluate the effects of stigma, the minority was derogated in half of the cases. And, in order to assess the effects of "secret deviance," the subject either proclaimed his (the subjects were all males) opinions publicly or simply listened to the opinions of the other group members. Then, the group rated first impressions of each other (attraction measure), and the subject was paired with one of the members in a "disguised test of susceptibility to social influence."

In effect the subject took part in what was alledgely an auditory acuity test (they judged the number of clicks they heard over headphones over a series of trials). After each trial the subject announced his judgment. The pairing of the subject and a confederate was done in such a way as to match the subject with a fellow minority or former majority group member. In both cases, the judgments of the confederates were identical; they systematically overestimated the number of clicks on eleven of the twelve trials. Moriarty asked his subjects: "On those occasions when there was disagreement did you experience, even for just a brief moment, a desire to change your opinion, to make it more like the other's?"

Moriarty found that twenty-seven of the eighty subjects reported a desire to change. Nineteen of the twenty-seven (70 percent), who indicated that they wanted to change, were from the stigma conditions ($p<.01$). Of the eighty subjects, thirteen (16 percent) did in fact make one or more changes on the initial opinion questionnaire after they exchanged opinions with other group members. Eleven of the thirteen were in the stigma conditions ($p<.04$). This finding suggests that when opinion exchange takes place, it does so as a result of minority derogation.

Then, when the opinion exchange was concluded, each subject indicated how much he liked his fellow minority member and the four majority group members. A comparison was, then, made of subjects' ratings of minority and majority members.

Moriarty found that the ratings of the fellow minority member was only moderate (14-18), whereas, ratings for the majority members (11.3) was toward the neutral end of the scale ($p<.01$). This finding suggests that the subjects liked their fellow minority group members and viewed the majority with neutrality.

Finally, Moriarty assessed the subject's liking of their fellow minority member (in order to evaluate the effects of stigma on liking) and found that stigma had a significant effect on liking for their fellow minority member. That is, where the minority members were derogated by the majority, attraction between them was lowered. In addition, it was found that liking for the fellow minority member was greater in the public than in the "secret" (or private) conditions.

STATUS, CONFORMITY AND DEVIATION

Can we find other dimensions to the conformity-deviation spectrum? What about people who start out not accepting the norms of the group? In this case when a person does in fact reject the influence attempts of other group members, social psychologists refer to the process of anticonformity or counterconformity. For example, if an individual should decide not to respect the authority vested in the role of her employer, and in effect she does not conform to the demands required of other employees, we are essentially referring to a case of anticonformity. However, the individual must resist the influence attempts of her employer, and she may do just the opposite from what is expected of other employees.

Then if we accept the proposition that the definition of deviant behavior comes initially from the group itself, and that group members do indeed influence its members into conformity or deviation, how is it that some group members can deviate more than others? In this case Edwin P. Hollander (1958, 1964) has suggested that conformity and nonconformity (deviancy) are not fixed to norms applicable to all members of a group. Indeed, what Hollander is suggesting is that deviance depends on how an actor is perceived by other members of the group. And in this case Hollander tells us that idiosyncrosy credits accumulate. These are "positive impressions of a person held by other members of a group." Actually credits represent accorded status which has the potential to produce nonconformity and on occasion innovation. These credits are said to accumulate when the person conforms to the group and/or has other sources of "positive impressions," such as competence which is highly valued by the group. And here is the punch line: A person's credit balance offers the individual greater latitude for deviancy; persons with high status have a greater chance to deviate without serious consequences.

In a test of Hollander's "credit theory," Alvarez (1968) assigned ten men to a group. Nine of these men were "actual subjects" and the tenth a confederate of the experimenter, who was either assigned the role of "coordinator" or "fellow worker." The group was given the task of "generating creative ideas for greeting cards." In addition, the confederate behaved in a deviant way (e.g., by violating the task instructions given to the group). The confederate deviated at first forty percent of the time and then sixty percent, and finally eighty percent of the time. Then, in order to induce "successful" or "unsuccessful" treatment conditions, at this point in the study half of the subjects were told that their work was "very good" whereas the others were informed that it was "not of the caliber expected." Then, finally after each "work period," subjects gave their evaluation of each other in terms of the individual's value to the group by completing an "esteem measure."

As he had predicted, Alvarez found that for the same "deviant acts," the higher status person lost status at a slower rate than the lower status person. In fact this was the case only for the "successful" groups. Where the "organizational" groups were "unsuccessful," the results were just the opposite. Hence, with a record of deviations which have resulted in "successes" for the group the high status person becomes highly valued and a lack of "success" gives the deviator a negative evaluation and, of course, subtracts credit.

But as so much of real life is based on less structured situations it becomes important that we look at status and nonconforming behavior from a different perspective. In this regard, Lefkewitz, Blake, and Mouton (1955) have shown how status affects conformity and deviation. They observed that pedesrians will indeed violate a traffic signal light more often when someone else violates it with them or before them. In addition, they found significantly more traffic signal light violations when the violator was dressed to represent a high-status person reather than a low-status individual.

Not surprisingly, high-status persons are likely to induce others to violate the norms more so than low-status individuals, especially where people seem to be highly motivated. For example, Kimbrell and Blake (1958) report research on norm violation where drinking of water was prohibited. That is, a subject and a confederate of the experimenter was asked to wait outside of an experimental room until they called the subject to take part in "ongoing research." During a short waiting period the confederate drank or did not drink from the water fountain over which a sign was hung stating "Do not use." Before being asked to wait in the hall, the subject and the confederate were either given crackers treated with hot sauce, untreated crackers, or nothing at all. As expected, results showed that the greater the motivation to drink, the greater the number of subjects who did in fact drink; and, for our present purposes, the deviation of a high status confederate produced a significant increase in the number of subjects who also deviated.

BEING DIFFERENT MAKES A DIFFERENCE

Sociologists have noted two very general characteristics of deviance: an actual or imagined difference from the majority and being devalued or stigmatized for being different (see Becker, 1963; Clinard, 1963; Goffman, 1963). In our society a formidable obstacle faced by many people is their obvious difference from others. And many apparently well-meaning persons have stigmatized those who are different. Furthermore, the process of stigmatization may have long-range implications for those devalued. We have already noted, in chapter one, that Jonathan Freedman and Anthony Doob (1968) have stressed that difference is indeed a major determinant for deviance.

Once again we will return to Freedman and Doob's view of conformity and deviation. Freedman and Doob report a series of experiments where they have attempted to experimentally focus on the implications of deviance (being different) for the person's own behavior as well as how other people treat the deviant. One important point to make here is that Freedman and Doob, in order to control for some of the obvious difficulties faced by many deviant behavior researchers, defined deviance simply as "one who is indeed different from others."

Then, for normative influence to have an important impact on the individual, the person must somehow feel that he will be or has been rejected by the group for not conforming to the group's norms or expectations. In this regard, we have shown that deviates are indeed likely to be rejected and that they come to expect rejection by the group (see Gerard & Rotter, 1961; Schachter, 1951).

Now, Freedman and Doob's examination of deviance begins with the application of falsified personality tests, used to make some subjects feel deviant (different), and others nondeviant or "normal." That is, subjects took five tests and after each test they were given false feedback and finally a summary sheet of all of the test results. Then, in effect feedback was made either private (only the subject knew the results) or public (all subjects knew the results of both their own as well as others personality scale results.)

Employing this basic experimental procedure a number of studies were carried out to determine the effects of being deviant (different). Freedman and Doob summarize the results of several experiments as follows:

1. When their deviancy is not publicly known, deviants will attempt to avoid close contact with others. When their deviancy is public knowledge, they will not do this.

2. Deviants prefer to associate with other deviants rather than with nondeviants. This may hold even when the other deviants are different from them.

3. Given the opportunity to aggress against a previously chosen individual, deviants choose to hurt a deviant who is similar to them less than they do a nondeviant or a different deviant.

4. When asked to choose someone to receive electric shock, there are big differences between deviants and nondeviants. The deviants select nondeviants more than deviants, whereas nondeviants have the opposite preference. In contrast, when the choice is for someone to receive a reward, all of this is reversed--with deviants picking other deviants and nondeviants picking other nondeviants (1968, Pp. 148-149).

Some additional results from Freedman and Doob's research, which bears on conformity and compliance, are noted:

1. In face-to-face situations, with responses

public, there was no overall effect on deviancy. When normative responses are presented on a questionnaire and subjects respond privately, deviants conform less than do nondeviants.

2. Deviants are influenced more (attitude change) by communications from peers than by an authority, whereas, nondeviants had the opposite preference.

3. With direct confrontation, deviants complied more than did nondeviants...with no direct confrontation, deviants complied less than nondeviants (1968, p. 150).

In order to extend the "difference hypothesis," Anthony N. Doob and Barbara Payne Ecker (1970) conducted a field experiment where 121 housewives were asked either to complete a 79-item questionnaire and return it by mail or to take part in a 15-20 minute personal interview. Since research shows that people generally do not feel comfortable when interacting with physically handicapped persons, Doob and Ecker had the person making the request wear a black eyepatch or no eyepatch was worn.

Results showed that in the questionnaire condition, compliance was significantly greater where the person wore an eyepatch, whereas in the interview condition, the eyepatch had little effect on compliance.

How do we explain these seemingly conflicting results? First whenever compliance does not involve future face-to-face interaction, a stigmatized individual (a person wearing an eyepatch) is more likely to obtain compliance than a nonstigmatized individual. In this respect Doob and Ecker suggest that the subjects could have felt sorry for the handicapped researcher while at the same time they felt uncomfortable interacting with the experimenter. The net result, then, was that the housewifes complied with the request to complete the questionnaire, but somehow could not comply with the request for a prolonged interview. Then, in effect the subjects avoided any prolonged interaction with the deviant interviewer.

In order to demonstrate that groups do in fact

reject their nonconforming members, Stanley Schachter (1951) set up an experiment where he used naive subjects and a confederate planted in each group. The group was given the task of discussing how to work with a juvenile delinquent named Johnny Rocco. In one condition the deviant confederate consistently disagreed with the group's judgment about how to work with Rocco. In a second condition a confederate slider begin by disagreeing with the group's decision but then switched to a position where he conformed to the group's norm. In still a third condition, a confederate (the model) agreed with most members of the group. In addition, Schachter manipulated the cohesiveness of the group by suggesting that half of the group would be working on attractive tasks (high cohesive condition), and the other half were led to believe they would be working on unattractive tasks (low cohesive condition). Then at the completion of their discussion about the Johnny Rocco case, all subjects were asked to rate how much they like other members of the group and they were asked to nominate group members to take part in additional functions of the group.

Schachter found that the group at first reacted to the deviant by directing a great deal of its communication and attention to him (norm-sending) in an apparent attempt to get the deviant to conform (or comply). Then, finally the group "gave up" on the deviant and rejected him. The deviant was consistently given the negative tasks. The rejection of the deviate was strongest in the highly cohesive groups. On the other hand, the slider, who began by deviating from the group, but later on switched to a conforming pattern, was liked significantly more than the mode, who consistently agreed with the group's judgments.

So far we have learned that the prepondance of research on conformity is directed at the conformer and not the deviant, however Schachter's study, just as Freedman and Doob's (1968) research, demonstrates that the deviant is likely to be rejected by the group and in the case of Freedman and Doob's research the deviant is often singled out for aggression by nondeviant members of the group. Nor is this all, replications of Schachter's (1951) study has obtained similar results for subjects in Belgium, France, Holland, Germany, Norway, and Sweden (see Schachter, Nuttin, Demonchaux, Mancorps, Osmer,

Duijker, Romnetveit, & Israel, 1954).

Of course, the central concern of this chapter is to specify some of the more important determinants of group-based deviance. In this respect, Dittes and Kelley (1956) report a study where their subjects were made to feel that they were only marginally accepted by other members of their group. And, it was suggested to them that there was the possibility of becoming more or less completely accepted. Under such conditions it was found that a high degree of conformity to the group's norms took place both publicly and privately, whereas, those subjects who had only a very low degree of acceptance, and who also perceived the likelihood of being rejected by other group members, conformed very close to the group's norms publicly, but deviated from the norms privately.

Then, clearly, researchers have very different ways of explaining conforming and nonconforming behavior. With this view in mind, Jones, Davis, and Gergen (1961) asked their subjects to make judgments about the traits of a person who either had complied with or deviated from role expectations during an employment interview. In one condition, an individual (an experimenter's confederate) was interviewed for the position of submariner. The subjects heard the interviewee being told that a successful submariner should like being with people (affiliative) and should conform and be able to function in a small space with other people. The confederate was then interviewed for the job. He presented himself as either affiliative and conforming (consistent with the job description) or as nonaffiliative and nonconforming (a deviation from the job description). In the second condition, the confederate was interviewed for a position as an astronaut. A successful astronaut was described as independent and able to make decisions or somewhat nonconforming. The confederate presented himself as either (nonaffiliative and nonconforming) or as (affiliative and conforming).

Then, after the job interview was completed, the subject responded to questions about what the confederate was really like. As the authors had predicted, when the job interviewee deviated from the role expectations, the subjects made more extreme dispositional attributions than when the confederate complied with the role expectations. That is, when the confederate presented himself as affiliative, subjects assumed that the interviewee was really more affiliative than when his behavior deviated from the required job description. When the behavior was consistent and the confederate behaved nonaffiliatively, subjects inferred that the interviewee was less affiliative when his behavior deviated from role requirements then when it was in role. Hence, deviant behavior led to more extreme dispositional attributions than complying behavior. An additional finding showed that subjects placed more confidence in their judgments when the confederate's behavior was deviant than when it was conforming. What this suggests is that out-of-role behavior seems to be more attributionally informative than is in-role behavior especially when we attempt to understand the causes for a person's action.

We will return to this assumption in a later chapter, meanwhile it has been observed that when people are exposed to information inconsistent with their attitudes, they either change their attitudes to become consistent with the information or distort or reject the information (see Abelson, Aronson, McGuire, Newcomb, Rosenburg, & Tannenbaum, 1968). For example, in a test of the cognitive consistency model, Silverman (1971) reasoned that the events surrounding the Senator Edward Kennedy Chappaquiddick incident and the publicity given to this event would induce many people to change their attitudes about Kennedy. Silverman describes the Kennedy incident as follows:

> Prior to the incident in question Senator Kennedy was a generally esteemed personal and political figure, considered to be one of the leading candidates for the Democratic presidential nomination in 1972. On the night of July 19, 1969, the Senator was present at a party on a small island off Edgarton, Massachusetts, attended by five other men; four, like Kennedy, married, and six single girls: At about 11:15 p.m. he drove off a bridge on a country road into a pond about 10 feet deep, with one of the girls in his car. Senator Kennedy rescued himself. The girl perished. The Senator did not, however, report the accident to authorities until about 10 a.m. the following day. He claimed that he had made several unsuccessful attempts to find the car, then walked back to the cottage where

the party was held (there were several lighted houses with telephones along the way), and informed two of his associates of the event. He attributed his delay in informing the police to 'shock' and 'exhaustion.' According to his own and witnesses' reports, he made one trip back to his hotel in Edgarton at about 2 a.m. and then back to the island before returning again to Edgarton to make his report.

The Senator was tried for leaving the scene of an accident, pleaded guilty, and received a 2-month suspended sentence. After the trial he addressed the public and asked for their judgment by mail as to whether he should retain his Senate seat, which he did (1971, p. 172).

Silverman focused on a sample of those who changed and those who did not change their attitudes toward Kennedy after the incident. Nonchangers tended, in contrast to changers, to be more positive toward Kennedy as a political figure, to be less willing to state that the sentence given him was two lenient, to be less willing to agree that the same circumstances of an ordinary citizen would have resulted in more severe treatment, and more were in favor of Kennedy keeping his position in the Senate.

A.P. MacDonald jr., and Ranjit K. Majumber (1973) have critized Silverman's study on the grounds that his results were "not statistically significant, or marginally so" (p. 133). Because of these serious limitations for Silverman's study, MacDonald and Majumder took advantage of another naturally occurring event to test the cognitive consistency model-- the Senator Eagleton incident. These researchers noted that:

> In July, 1972, subsequent to his being offically designed as the Democratic Vice Presidential Nominee, it became public knowledge that Senator Thomas Eagleton had been a mental patient on more than one occasion. Concern was expressed regarding his ability to withstand the stress of the office of the Vice President of the United States, the ethics of his remaining silent about his having been a mental patient, and so on. Additionally, it was claimed but later unsupported, that Senator Eagleton had more than once been arrested for driving while

intoxicated (1973, p. 134).

In order to test their hypothesis the authors recruited 225 subjects from the student union of West Virginia University, shopping centers, grounds of the University, private homes, and from various departments of the University. They collected data two days prior to the withdraw of Senator Eagleton from the Democratic ticket. Subjects were asked to report (on a questionnaire) on how favorable they felt toward Senator Eagleton <u>before</u> and <u>after</u> learning that he had been a mental patient.

Responses from 195 (87%) subjects showed that they were very favorable, favorable, or neutral toward Eagleton prior to learning that he had been a mental patient. Twenty-seven of the 195 subjects (14%) changed to an unfavorable position and 168 (86%) still remained favorable or neutral after learning about the Senator's past mental hospital record. In addition, of the 107 respondents (48%) who had held very favorable or favorable beliefs before the Eagleton incident, 83 (76%) did not change their beliefs, whereas, 14 (13%) changed to a neutral position, and 10 (9%) shifted to an unfavorable position. It was observed that those initially neutral (39%) were still likely to be neutral after the incident (31%). As was expected, of those subjects who were initially unfavorable toward Eagleton (30%) twenty-eight remained unfavorable after learning of the Senator's status.

MacDonald and Majumder's results, in general support the cognitive-consistency model for attitudes and are consistent with Silverman's (1971) study of the Kennedy incident. That is, 84 percent of those who did not change believed that Senator Eagleton should not withdraw from the Democratic ticket, whereas 85 percent of those who changed stated that he should withdraw. MacDonald and Majumder conclude that:

> The studies are similar in that they each deal with a naturally occurring event that involves a political figure. The two figures (Kennedy and Eagleton) themselves, however, have dissimilar images. Kennedy and his family were considerably better known by the public, and the incidents had little or nothing in common. Though Silverman's sample was drawn entirely from

the university, the sample of the present study included university and nonuniversity people. From the point of view of difference between the two studies, the congruence of results is striking and offers promise concerning the utility of this kind of research (1973, p. 143).

What do these studies tell us about people who stigmatize others? Simply that our attitudes toward those who deviate determine how we are likely to feel about the deviate after it is found out that he violated the group's norms.

SELF-ESTEEM, CONFORMITY, AND DEVIATION

When a person is led to believe that she is deviant or different from others her self-esteem is likely to decrease and she is less likely to conform. For example, D.J. Stang (1972) found that subjects who were asked to judge a series of visual stimuli conformed less where they scored higher on a paper-and-pencil measure of self-esteem. In other words, the higher the person's self-esteem, the less conformity to the judgments of others took place.

More recently, Steele (1975) reports a study where he predicted that name calling would reduce a person's self-esteem and subsequently increase the individual's compliance. An alledged representative of a polling institute called and insulted subjects with such comments as, "Isn't it accurate to describe you as predominantly self-oriented and apathetic about the welfare of others?" Still other subjects were told that they were "concerned, cooperative, and helpful"; and still a third group did not receive a telephone call (control group). Then, a second experimenter called two days later and made a request for help in obtaining information for a proposed neighborhood food cooperative. Of the subjects who were insulted, 93 percent were willing to help, whereas only 46 percent of those who were not called complied. Of those subjects given a positive message, 65 percent were willing to help. Steele (1975) tells us that people will comply if their self-esteem can be increased in the process of complying.

In still another study, Filter and Gross (1975) administered a battery of personality tests to subjects and then gave them false feedback as to how they compared with a large normative sample of other college students. Under one condition subjects were told that their test results were extremely deviant. A partner of the subject (actually a confederate) either knew or did not know about the subject's deviant test scores. Then, the confederate asked the subject to assist in writing letters for an undergraduate committee to improve education. The measure for compliance consisted of the number of letters the subject agreed to write.

As the researchers had predicted, subjects told that they were deviant agreed to write about twice as many letters as subjects who were led to believe that they were "normal." In addition compliance was greater when the subject's deviancy was not revealed to the confederate. In effect subjects seemed to comply in order to convince their partner that they were not deviant.

Finally, Darley, Moriarty, and Darley (1974) have shown that persons (subjects) who were lead to believe they were deviant in a conformity experiment later on were more likely to conform in a second "experiment" dealing with conformity. This suggests that being made to feel deviant can indeed lead to subsequent conformity. And research has also shown that people who believe that they are in fact deviants are more likely to comply to a request than non-deviants even though their deviancy is not known by other people (Filter & Gross, 1975).

OBJECTIVE SELF-AWARENESS, DEVIANCE, AND CONFORMITY

S. Duval and Robert A. Wicklund (1972) have proposed a theory they have labeled objective self-awareness which states that:

> Conscious attention is viewed as diehotomous, having the property of being directed either toward the self or toward the environment. The direction of attention is guided by events that force attention inward, such as reflections of the self, and events that pull attention outward, such as distracting stimuli outside the self. Under objective self-awareness the person will experience either negative or positive affect, depending on whether attention is directed toward a negative or positive discrepancy (Wicklund, 1975, p. 237).

In a test of objective self-awareness theory, Duval (1976) told subjects that their answers on a number of attitude measures were like those of 95 percent, 50 percent, or 5 percent of a group consisting of 10,000 persons who were said to have completed the same scales. Next, the subjects took part in a conformity study where half of the subjects saw a live image of themselves on a closed circuit TV monitor. Those subjects lead to believe that they possessed unusual attitudes (deviants), and who saw themselves on TV, tended to conform more than those who did not see themselves on TV

What implications are there for deviant behavior from Duval's study? First, many people who deviate may in fact not focus on themselves and in effect fail to conform. However, those that just happen to become "aware" or their own deviant behavior may become motivated to bring their behavior in line with others because there is a heightened recognition that their behavior is different. Then, in effect, the person becomes "an audience to their own performance." Why then should a person's attention to the self be critical for deviant as well as conforming behavior? First, the individual may come to find out that others are "correct" when they describe the person as different. Second, the person may in fact find out that being deviant is not really bad and not become motivated to change, however the odds are on the side of change because we are likely to become critical of ourselves. As a matter of fact John H. Harvey and William P. Smith speculate that:

> First, in conjuction with observing the outcome, individuals focus on themselves and that they are "imperfect beings." When the outcome is negative individuals may reduce objective self-awareness by attributing responsibility to themselves; they may infer that negative outcomes are most often caused by people with faults--like themselves. If the outcome is positive, individuals may reduce objective self-awareness by attributing responsibility to themselves; the positivity of the outcome may stimulate them to infer that they really do not have that many imperfections (in other words they may think that they are the kind of person who could have done something that turned out well) 1977, p. 52.

GROUPTHINK AND CONFORMITY

In our discussion of conformity we stressed the importance of pressures by the group to bring about uniformity of opinions and behaviors of its members. There are cases when a group member experiences strong feelings of <u>esprit de corps</u> and loyalty to its members and the desire for uniformity may curtail the desire to logically and realistically consider alternative courses of action especially where difficult solutions to pressing problems require quick and direct solutions.

Irving Janis (1972), of Yale University, has studied how Presidents of The United States have faced important group decisions and he suggests that the greater the feeling of <u>esprit de corps</u> among advisers to a President, the less likely the group will help make decisions which reflect independent and critical thinking. Janis uses the concept "groupthink" to refer to the "deterioration of mental efficiency, reality testing, and moral judgment that results from in-group pressures" (1972, p. 9).

Janis characterizes groupthink as: (1) the illusion that the group is invulnerable, (2) collective efforts are made to rationalize and discount negative information, (3) there is a tendency to ignore ethical or moral consequences of group decision, (4) stereotyped views of other groups develop, (5) there are active pressure to change the views of any deviant member, (6) self-censorship of deviations from apparent group consensus takes place, (7) a shared illusion of unanimity develops, and (8) there is an emergence of "mindguards" where individuals take it upon themselves to guard the group against information not in accord with the group consensus.

When groups show the above characteristics it is highly unlikely that efficient decision making will take place. Instead group decisions known as <u>fiascoes</u> are likely to occur. For example, Janis traces the impact of groupthink on the Bay of Pigs, the Korean War, Pearl Harbor and the escalation of the Vietnam War, and concludes that in all of these cases defective group decisions resulted in the failure of group members to express minority opinions (or deviant opinions), and a state of "pluralistic ignorance" took place. That is, each of the group's members who disagrees with the preferred decision of the group believes that no other member of the group also disagrees. Of course, unless the leader of the decision-making group encourages minority opinion, the illusion of uniformity of opinion goes unchallenged. There is a restriction placed on alternatives. The desire for consensus leads to selective perception and valid alternative information is inhibited.

Since Janis based his groupthink hypothesis upon ex post facto analyses of historical documents, dealing with several significant political and military decisions, Matie L. Flowers (1977) designed a laboratory experiment where college students were presented with a crises problem to solve. And since Janis had postulated that the variables of leadership behavior, group cohesiveness, and norms for group-decision making interact in a crisis to produce the condition of groupthink, Flowers decided to test the effects of two of the three variables--leadership style and group cohesiveness--on possible solutions to the crisis (a public school related problem). Group cohesiveness was either arranged to be high or low and the groups had leaders displaying either non-directive (open) or directive (closed) leadership styles.

The open-leadership style produced significantly more solutions and subjects used more available facts than did subjects in the groups with "closed" leaders regardless of the level of cohesiveness of the group. Hence, there emerged no support for Janis' assumption that cohesiveness is an important factor, however, partial confirmation of Janis' hypothesis that groups with open leaders produce more solutions to a crisis, and use more information in doing so than closed leaders, supports Janis' original hypothesis in a nonpolitical context. Finally, Flowers suggests that "a revision of Janis' theory may be justified, one which would eliminate cohesiveness as a critical variable" (p. 895).

Since the theme of this section has been the concern of conformity and deviation it is often claimed that conformity and deviation both have negative and positive implications for the individual. With this note it seems appropriate to cite what one team of researchers have concluded about conformity. Hence, Walker and Heynes tell us that:

If one wishes to produce conformity for good or
evil, the formula is clear. Manage to arouse a
need or needs that are important to the individual or the group. Offer a goal which is appropriate to the need or needs. Make sure that
conformity is instrumental to the achievement of
the goal and that the goal is as large and as
certain as possible. Apply the goal or reward
at every opportunity. Try to prevent the object
of your efforts from obtaining an uncontrolled
education. Choose a setting that is ambiguous.
Do everything possible to see that the individual has little or no confidence in his position.
Do everything possible to make the norm which
you set appear highly valued and attractive.
Set it at a level not too far initially from the
starting point of the individual or group and
move it gradually toward the behavior you wish
to produce. Be absolutely certain you know what
you want and that you are willing to pay an
enourmous price in human quality, for whether
the individual or the group is aware of it or
not, the result will be CONFORMITY (1967, p. 98).

THEN, WHY DO PEOPLE CONFORM: SOCIAL COMPARISON THEORY?

In any case the source of conformity is located
in the social setting, as is also the case with
deviancy. But conformity and deviation is more than
that: It is the product of the individual and the
group. Because people must depend on others, especially in an ever-changing society, they often compare
their own views of the world with those of others.
As a matter of fact, Leon Festinger (1954) some years
ago proposed a theory of social comparison which has
proven helpful in explaining how conformity and
deviation are likely to take place. Festinger tells
us that we all have a basic drive to evaluate our
opinions, attitudes and behaviors against those who
are similar to ourselves. Hence, through the process of information seeking we are said to look for
evidence to define social reality because this is at
the time more important to us than is physical
reality. Then, when we go out looking for definitions
of social reality we are likely to find that some of
our opinions, attitudes, and behavior are "out of
line" with those of our peers. And, for most of our
opinions, attitudes, and behaviors there is little or
no objective or nonsocial way to evaluate them, as is

the case with physical reality, and so we turn to others to define the socially desirable dimensions of our world.

Then, what happens when we find out that our views of the world are deviant or in fact "far out?" One possible solution to the problem is to change so that we bring our views in line with our peers. However, if we should compare ourselves with those who do in fact hold deviant views of the world, there is a chance that our opinions could indeed become deviant. It follows, then, that people will seek out others whenever they are uncertain as to the "correctness" of their own views. Then, one obvious implication of Festinger's theory is that our confidence can be threatened when we find that others are "different," and this condition in itself can create uncertainty and conformity is more likely to take place. Having said this let us now turn to the study of obedience.

OBEDIENCE AS DEVIANCE?

While on the faculty of Yale University Stanley Milgram planned to research the degree to which people obey authority figures because he wished to compare Americans with the Nazis of Hitler's Third Reich. Milgram reasoned that during World War II Nazis were different than Americans because he assumed that only the Nazis were willing to kill countless numbers of people under the guise of political expediency (Milgram, 1963, 1965, 1974).

Perhaps you might reason that only a Lieutenant William Calley, an Adolf Hitler or an Adolf Eichman could inflict cruel and extreme punishment on innocent people. Before you dismiss this question as merely academic, imagine that you find yourself in a situation where you are told (as an experimental subject) that you are to participate in a learning experiment and that you have been designated as the teacher and that another "subject" is the learner. The experimenter then goes on to explain that you should use punishment in order to teach a series of pairs of words to the learner. In this case you are ordered to administer varying levels of electric shock to the learner by pressing a series of lever switches. Of course, you are told that punishment should only be given to the learner (who is said to have a "bad heart") when the learner fails to acquire the required task or makes an error. You are then shown an apparatus which has thirty lever switches connected to a shock generator. Each of the thirty switches is labeled in 15-volt increments ranging from 15 to 450 volts. Throughout the "learning task" the experimenter insists that you increase the level of shock each time the learner does not respond correctly.

You probably consider it impossible for you (or for most people) to punish someone for such a trivial thing as not learning a simple task fast enough. As a matter of fact when Milgram asked psychiatrists to predict the outcome of his research they were confident that only a fraction of one percent would obey, however, almost two-thirds of Milgram's subjects complied to the experimenter's demands for obedience. That is, where subjects delivered what they probably thought was a highly dangerous level of electric shock to the learner; 450 volts.

From this basic experimental paradigm, Milgram created several different conditions, for example, variations in the amount of feedback from the learner (victim), and proximity between the "teacher" and the learner. Milgram's subjects did not obey to the same degree when the experimenter placed himself at a greater distance from the subject. When the experimenter placed himself close to the subject he was able to get the subject to obey (deliver shock) contrary to the subject's overt protestations or the seeming unwillingness of the learner-victim to continue on in the research.

Since Milgram's research yielded unexpected results what may we conclude from this research? Would you consider Milgram's subjects deviant or are they just "ordinary persons?" That is, can we conclude that Milgram's research demonstrates a wide-scale potentality for people to show "twisted and sadistic" behavior? Perhaps not! On the contrary what Milgram's research does show is the crucial role of authority in affecting the behavior of people in ongoing situations. Once a person is induced to engage in seemingly deviant behavior it no doubt becomes difficult to disengage the person from such behavior. And once people engage deviant behavior, especially deviant behavior that is authority based, such behavior can have serious consequences. What comes to mind, then, are such activities as the

Watergate scandal and the My Lai massacre. Hence, Milgram's research underscores for deviance the need for researchers to consider the emergent qualities of deviant actions. Such questions come to mind as "who is deviant, the subject, the experimenter, or both?" Actually, Martin T. Orne and his associates (see Orne & Holland, 1968; O'Leary, Willis & Tomich, 1969) have argued that the Milgram paradigm lacks plausibility in that Milgram's subjects were not given very good reasons for shocking the "learner," and that they were merely responding to the <u>demand characteristics</u> of the situation. And subsequent research, at first blush, seemed to substantiate Orne's claim. For example, O'Leary, Willis and Tomich (1969) did in fact obtain data contrary to what might be expected from the Milgram obedience paradigm. Subjects led to believe that they had delivered electric shock at only 10 percent of the value indicated on the lever switches and told the "real purpose" of the research did not in fact display the high level of obedience one would predict from Milgram's research.

Later research, carried out by Charles L. Sheridan and Richard G. King, has attempted to answer Orne's criticism that demand characteristics operated in Milgram's studies. In this case Sheridan and King employed a seemingly more authentic situation than Milgram; they used a "cute, fluffy puppy dog" instead of a human "learner-victim." Subjects delivered shocks that produced "running, howling, and yelping." Results of Sheridan and King's research are very similar to the results obtained by Milgram. For this reason these authors conclude that Milgram's results hold under conditions of "high plausibility" (Sheridan & King, 1972).

All in all Milgram's experiments have provided us with a striking example of destructive over obedience to authority. And the act of obedience is a seeming paradox because serious actions may be committed out of a sense of duty. Considering the issue of obedience and wrongdoing in an authority context this raises the question of whether or not Milgram's finding have application to other social orders? Apparently the answer to this question is yes because cross cultural studies have shown that in Germany (Mantell, 1971), Australia (Kilham & Mann, 1974), and Jordan (Shanab & Yahya, 1977) results similar to those of Milgram's studies have been reported. As a matter of fact, Mitri E. Shanab and Khawla A. Yahya (1977) found that Jordanian children (ages 6-16) obeyed a female authority figure (experimenter) much the same as Milgram's subjects. That is, 73 percent of Shanab and Yahya's subjects continued to deliver shocks to the end of the shock scale where in fact the researchers used Milgram's research paradigm. Undoubtedly the importance of this study is that children from a nonwestern culture showed not only the obedience effect, but in point of fact over-obedience to an authority figure.

Then, if we extrapulate from Milgram's obedience research the conclusion seems clear, deviant behavior may result from the respectability people seem to accord to persons who occupy authority positions. If this reasoning is correct then those who are sensitive to authority cues are also more likely to harm (or perhaps kill) others in obedience to authority. But you might ask: "Are there individual differences in obedience or is obedience related to the level of moral development of those who are asked to harm others?" At this point let us turn to Lawrence Kohlberg of Harvard University and ask what he has learned about moral development and obedience.

First, Kohlberg proposes that there are six stages of moral development which takes place as human development proceeds from infancy to adulthood. The development from one stage to another stage of moral development is said to depend on corresponding changes in a person's cognitive development and organization. And moral development is said to be invariant, however fixation or arrestation may occur at any stage of moral development (see Kohlberg, 1970).

In effect we would expect that as the degree of an individual's moral development reaches higher levels (stages) there should be less likelihood that the person will obey an experimenter's request to harm others. In other words what we are suggesting is that the order to obey and the degree of obedience obtained is contingent upon the level of moral development of the person who is asked to harm another person. Actually, Kohlberg attempted to answer this question and he reports research where he did find that 75 percent of his subjects, classified as having reached stage six (the highest level of moral development), did in fact refuse to obey the experimenter's demands to harm another person. On the other hand, only 13 percent of Kohlberg's subjects, who were found at lower levels of moral development refused to carry out the experimenter's request to harm another individual.

On the basis of what we have presented so far, you have probably formed a fairly clear conception of the conditions under which obedience is likely to take place. You no doubt have asked yourself: "Did this same kind of blind obedience to authority contribute to the My Lai massacre?" As a matter of fact, Kelman and Lawrence report results from a national survey of Americans (those over 18 years of age), taken just prior to Lieutenant Calley's trial, where respondents were presented with a hypothetical situation and they were asked "whether most soldiers should, when given orders, shoot all person (i.e., women, old men, and children) suspected of supporting the enemy?" Sixty-seven percent of the national sample replied that they thought most people would or should in fact carry out such orders. Fifty-one percent indicated that they themselves would shoot "the enemy under these conditions." And additional data showed that 58 percent actually disapproved of Calley's trial (see Kelman & Lawrence, 1972).

Finally, when we consider all of the negative consequences of over obedience it seems hard to believe that most people would be willing to carry out orders under conditions where authority figures demand that they do so. Fortunately, as is the case with most human behavior there are exceptions to the rule. For example, H.A. Tilker (1970) has shown that when individuals are informed that they are totally responsible for the welfare of a person being shocked (the victim) with painful amounts of electricity, they not only disobey the experimenter but they disrupted the experiment. Some of Tilker's subjects, who were in fact told that they were responsible for the "learner," threatened the experimenter if the experiment was not stopped, and Tilker tells us that one of his subjects even attempted to wreck the shock apparatus!

Now that we have concluded that deviance does take place when people are following orders, a reasonable contrast to obedience is the possibility that the condition of anonymity also produces deviant behavior. Then, the section that follows deals with <u>deindividuation</u> where deviance comes about when there is a loss of personal identity and individuality, and the end result is reflected in a lowering of restraints for prohibited or deviant behavior. Let us now consider how deindividuation is related to our major concern: deviant behavior which is group-based.

DEINDIVIDUATION AND DEVIANCE

Why do people sometimes engage in deviant behavior when with others and not when alone? It has been suggested that people seem to lose their sense of personal identity and responsibility for their actions when with others and consequently engage in antisocial behavior. As a matter of fact LeBon (1896) was one of the first observers to note that people in crowds change their behavior in such a way as to lose their self-control and therefore engage in what he labeled "savage behavior." Hence, emotions were assumed to be aroused in the presence of others and violent and mass destructive behavior was said to occur without "reason." LeBon said that people who are aroused or agitated become highly suggestible and they assume little or no responsibility for their own deviant actions. LeBon reasoned that people lose their sense of individuality and the group functions as one what LeBon called the "group mind."

LeBon's <u>The Crowd</u> had an impact on social thinkers who attempted to explain deviant behavior in groups, however, recent research on deviant behavior carried out by Philip G. Zimbardo (1969), suggests that deviant behavior is facilitated by the presence of others and he challenges LeBon's concept of "group mind." In this way Zimbardo has identified a number of situational variables. For example, the feeling of being unidentifiable to those in authority positions and anonymity are said to reduce the liklihood that the deviant will be singled out for punishment. In addition, the presence of others tends to produce a feeling of "shared responsibility" and also provides social models for deviant behavior because there is an increase in arousal among those present. Hence, people seem to develop present-time orientations and past behaviors seem to be of little consequence. The <u>deindividuated</u> person becomes absorbed in his actions. Internal controls are lessened and individuals tend to act spontaneously. Then, in effect the threshold for deviance is lowered.

Zimbardo (1969) initially designed research to test his model of deindividuation by creating a situation where he assigned females to either anonymous or non-anonymous conditions. Subjects in the anonymous condition wore large lab coats and hoods which covered their heads and thus their identity was concealed. On the other hand, non-anonymous subjects wore large name tags and, of course, they were fully identifiable to others. All subjects were assigned the task of shocking another person "as part of a study concerned with learning."

Zimbardo's findings supported the hypothesized effects for anonymity. That is the anonymous subjects delivered shocks that lasted twice as long as those delivered by subjects assigned to the non-anonymous condition. In a sense, then, deindividuated subjects became insensitive to their victims. In addition, the non-anonymous subjects tended to shock their victims longer when they didn't like the female victim whereas anonymous subjects showed little difference in shock duration regardless whether they liked or disliked their victim.

Zimbardo introduced a condition where he ran his anonymous and non-anonymous subjects individually rather than in groups. He found, contrary to his predictions, that anonymous subjects delivered significantly less instead of more shock to the victim. Zimbardo tells us that in this case "the individual has no group support and is made to feel self-conscious" (1969, p. 279).

More recently, Diener, Westford, Dineen, and Fraser (1973) devised a situations where group members interacted with their victims, as well as with other subjects. Punishment was delivered directly by each subject and the victim was described as a pacifist, who wished to have his nonviolent beliefs assessed by the subjects. That is, the victim took the role of an antiwar sit-demonstrator and the subject took the role of a heckler. Subjects were told that they could harass the pacifist verbally or they could use balls of paper, rubber bands sponge rubber bricks, picket signs, pistols that shot plastic pellets, and foam rubber swords to "beat the pacifist." Diener et al.'s findings tend to support Zimbardo's deindividuation model. That is, in the anonymity conditions there was an increase in aggression in the subject-alone conditions.

How do we explain these differences? Let us turn to some recent research for an answer. Since deindividuation theory predicts that people found in conditions of high anonymity will in fact experience greater deindividuation than conditions of low anonymity, Dale O. Jorgenson and Fred O. Dukes (1976) hypothesized that subjects in high-density settings or in large social aggregates should report feelings of deindividuation and consequently act in a less inhibited manner than subjects found in lower-density settings or in smaller social aggrates. Jorgenson and Dukes also predicted, contrary to Zimbardo's deindividuation model, that members of interacting social groups would experience less deindividuation and act more inhibited than solitary individuals.

Results supported the authors' modified version of Zimbardo's deindividuation model. That is, subjects who were part of a large aggregate behaved in a less inhibited manner and also reported more deindividuated feelings relative to those who were part of smaller aggregates. Of course, these results are consistent with Zimbardo's theory. On the other hand, members of interacting groups behaved in a more inhibited manner and reported more individuated feelings than solitary individuals. Jorgenson and Dukes suggest that:

>...Simply being a member of a face-to-face interacting group may in itself produce no deindividuation; the occurrence of deindividuation in such groups may depend on the presence of several conditions (e.g., the consumption of alcohol) or may vary as a function of the type of group, the group's goal, and their activities (1976, p. 28).

Then, we have just observed that Zimbardo's model depends on feelings of anonymity and it is suggested that the number of persons present has an impact on deindividuation. Next, let us consider another variable---arousal. Recently, Edward Diener (1976) investigated three of Zimbardo's major deindividuation variables: group presence, anonymity, and arousal. He assessed the effects of these variables on subjects' level of aggression and feelings of deindividuation. In this experiment only arousal was found to produce a significant increase in subjects' aggression, whereas group presence actually led to a decrease in aggression. Finally, anonymity had little effect on aggression. Diener used a postsession assessment of deindividuation and found that only aroused subjects showed deindividuation changes.

Now, what else can be said about the effects of deindividuation on deviant behavior? This time we turn to more "realistic" situations and in particular examine deviance as it takes place in more or less "natural settings." For example, in order to evaluate "interpersonal dynamics in a prison setting," Craig Haney, Curtis Banks, and Philip Zimbardo (1973) created their own prison in which subjects role-played prisoners and guards in a mock prison setting. Like Zimbardo's other studies he was interested in whether or not deindividuation can in fact produce deviant behavior.

Haney and his associates asked undergraduate Stanford University males to take part in a "two-week psychological study," and they were promised $15.00 for each day of the experiment. The subjects were actually told that they were going to take part in a simulated prison study, and they were given prescreened psychological tests in order to "weed out any males who might have psychological problems." Following this one half of the twenty-four subjects were randomly assigned to a prisoner condition and the remaining half were assigned to be guards.

Those subjects who were assigned to the prisoner condition were actually arrested at their homes by local police and were taken, without an explanation, to a city jail, where in fact they were blindfolded, fingerprinted, and placed behind bars. Subsequently they were taken by the researchers from the city jail to a simulated prison, located in the basement on Stanford University. At this point the "prisoners" were searched, stripped naked and given prisoner clothes to wear. Finally, a heavy chain was locked around their ankles.

Haney et al. gave their "guards" khaki uniforms and nightsticks, and reflecting sunglasses to conceal their eyes. "Guards" were told to "do what they felt necessary in order to maintain law and order."

As the initial day came and passed the "guards" began to assert their authority, but by the time the second day arrived the "guards" actually rebelled. At this point the "prisoners" barricaded themselves in cells, took off their clothing and heckled the "guards." Then the "guards" responded and attempted to "break" the "prisoners" solidarity. The guards, on an arbitrary basis, gave special privileges to some "prisoners." Then as time passed the "prisoners" became increasingly more accepting of their incarceration. Finally, by the end of the sixth day the study was terminated, and then Haney et al. put the subjects through a series of encounter-group situations in order to "undo" any negative influence from having taking part in the study.

In many of the studies reported, researchers have deliberately deceived subjects and they have concealed the "true purpose" of their research. Unforturnately, subjects do react to the experimental situation by responding to the cues which seem to convey the experimenter's hypothesis to the subject (see Orne, 1962). In this regard, Philip Zimbardo's Stanford Prison "experiment" has not gone unchallenged. For example, Banuazizi and Movahedi (1975) suggest that Zimbardo's subjects were volunteers who were well aware that they were taking part in a psychological study. They suggested that the subjects' actual behavior could have very likely been do to their knowledge of how "real prisoners" and "prison guards" react to each other. Hence, Banuazizi and Movahedi suggest that demand characteristics could have operated where the subjects were "aware" of the experimenters' hypotheses.

First, in answer to Banuazizi and Movahedi's criticisms of Zimbardo's research it must be kept in mind that while demand characteristics may have operated in the prison study, applying this analysis to Zimbardo's research must first be checked out through experimentation before we can conclude that demand actually can account for Zimbardo's findings.

Next, when we turn to "real life" situations things are not nearly as simple as they sometimes appear to be at first blush. This is so because the "real world" is indeed complex. And, since we have already noted that conditions of anonymity are likely to increase uninhibited negative behaviors (or deviant actions) we should also note that Zimbardo

(1970) has suggested that people who live in large urban areas are more likely to feel more deindividuated than are their counterparts who reside in more rural areas because they are no doubt more uninhibited than their country counterparts.

Then, in an extension of the deindividuation model, Zimbardo (1970) left a ten-year-old automobile, without license plates and with the hood up, on a busy New York City street. He also left a car in the same condition on a street in Palo Alto, California. Researchers observed what took place for sixty-four hours. The car left on the street in New York was vandalized and stripped within ten minutes of the investigators' departure, and after thirty-six hours the car was "totalled." On the other hand, the car left in Palo Alto was not disturbed during the observation period.

These results tend to support Zimbardo's hypothesis. But what about deviance in children? Are children different than college students or middle-aged adults? Can they be influenced by conditions of anonymity? In order to answer these questions let us turn to a field study carried out by Fraser, Keiem, Diener, and Beaman (1972).

Fraser et. al. (1975) wished to study the effects of a group on otherwise "law-abiding children." They chose a natural setting---trick-or-treat on Halloween night--and provided students an opportunity to steal candy and money. The researchers were mainly interested in the size of the group (1 to 7) and whether the children's identity was anonymous or not. At homes located in the Seattle area, tables were set up with small candy bars and pennies and nickels placed in small bowls. While the children were observed through a peephole an anonymous condition was created by having the children wear costumes, however half of the students were asked to identify themselves before the researcher left the child alone. Fraser and his associates found that the 1300 children actually stole extra candy or money. There were more transgressions where children were in groups than when they were alone, and greater stealing took place by anonymous children than by those who had revealed their names to the researchers. As a result of their research the authors suggest that perhaps higher crime rates, especially in large urban areas, may be a function of anonymity and group size.

WHAT ABOUT THOSE WHO WITNESS DEVIANT BEHAVIOR?

What happens when several persons witness a crime? Logic would have it that intervention would be increased because together people are more likely to physically overcome the criminal and hence help bring the offender to justice. Not so claim Bibb Latané and John M. Darley (1970), who have noted that when there are several bystanders (or witnesses) to a crime, the danger to anyone of the witnesses is lessened and so is the likelihood lessened for anyone of the bystanders to report the crime or to intervene as they witness a theft taking place.

Latané and Darley created their own theft situation ("the hand in the till"). College freshmen (males) were asked to volunteer for a one-hour interview. When the subject arrived for the study an accomplice of the experimenter also arrived and a receptionist announced that subjects would be interviewed. She apologized for the lateness of the interview, picked up an envelope and took out several large bills and payed subjects their two dollars for their research participation. She then put the remainder of the money back in the envelope and she left the room, ostensibly to answer a phone call. Moments after the receptionist left the room the accomplice (the thief) blatantly took money from the envelope and returned to his seat. Then, the receptionist returned giving the subject an opportunity to report the crime. The subject was either alone or with another subject when the theft took place.

The results of this study showed that individuals are less likely to report a theft when with another person than when alone. As a matter of fact many subjects reported that they had not noticed the crime when in fact the blatant clumsiness with which the crime was carried out made it almost impossible for subjects to witness the crime and not remember that they had done so.

Latané and Darley carried out a second study in a discount beer store located in Suffern, New York. Singly or in a pair "robbers" (confederates of the experimenter) entered the store and asked "what is the most expensive imported beer that you carry?" The cashier replied, "Lowenbrau. I'll go back and check how much we have." At this point the robbers picked up a case of beer near the front of the store and said: "they'll never miss this."

The robberies were staged when there was either one or two customers in the store. Results showed that subjects were more likely to report the theft if they were the sole witness to the theft. In addition, sex of the bystander had little or no effect on reporting the crime.

Although Latané and Darley's research does indeed suggest that crime (or other forms of negative deviance) may in fact go unreported in situations where we least suspect this to happen what about situations where people are actually threatened if they should consider violating a norm or rule? In this regard it has often been observed that under some conditions proffered threats may actually increase rather than decrease the incidence of deviant behavior. For example, James W. Pennebaker and Deborah Yates Sanders (1976) placed large placards in toilet stalls in men's restrooms at a large southwestern university. The signs cnnstituted either a high treat or a low threat to students' freedom to write on the walls. In addition, these two levels of threat were ascribed to either a high authority or to a low authority. The dependent measure consisted of all graffiti inscribed on the placards or the walls for a prescribed time interval.

The authors did an analysis of the mean number of graffiti inscribed on placard and on the walls per two-hour intervals. Pennebaker and Sanders found that the high threat acribed to a high-level authority actually produced significantly more graffiti on the walls than when the threat was attributed to a low-level authority.

Pennebaker and Sanders view psychological reactance as the "mediating variable," and suggest that:

> ...Threatening signs concerning shoplifting may be extremely effective in public sections of a store where a person could be seen purloining merchandise. However, in dark corners or unattended dressing rooms the same high threat could actually facilitate the incidence of shoplifting. In the future, psychologists must separate the conditions under which legal threats from legiti-

mate authorities arouse reactance and produce defiance from those situations where threats are accepted and compliance results (1976, p. 267).

DEVIANCE IN THE DARK: ANOTHER CASE OF DEINDIVIDUATION

Now that we have shown that people may react to threats by violating the rules set down by authority figures. What about situations where people are with strangers and they do not expect to meet them on subsequent occasions? In this respect, Gergen, Gergen, and Barton (1973) have demonstrated a more or less "positive" form of deviance said to result from deindividuation. Males and females were left in a room under conditons of either normal lighting or total darkness. All of the subjects were strangers and they were individually told that they would not encounter others other than in the experimental room. And, of course, subjects in the dark room were assured of anonymity.

Gergen et al. found that compared to the subjects left in the lighted room those left in the dark room spent little time talking, and almost 90 percent of those in the dark room touched at least one person "intentionally" and actually a large number hugged and embraced another individual. Almost none of the subjects in the lighted room touched another person. Those in the dark-room reported feelings of joy, wantonness, and freedom, whereas when subjects were left in the lighted room, after being informed that they would be introduced to each other, they were less likely to touch or "feel close to others." Gergen et.al. concluded that a condition of anonymity tends to influence whatever behavior is most prominant at the time---deviant or nondeviant.

Finally, if we can generalize from research reported in this section it seems likely that many of the norms for social interaction sometimes "break down" when people encounter others who are deviating in "darkened places," and we can suggest that people react to their surroundings with a "loss of self-control" and lowered restraints against antisocial behavior. Then, behavior under these conditions is more extreme than is behavior that results from social influence in more ordinary situations. As a matter of fact in recent days we have experienced a seeming increase in antisocial behavior such as rape, murder, and vandalism especially where conditions of anonymity are increased. Then, one can only speculate whether there is a growing sense of deindividuation as restraints against antisocial actions are weakened. For example, when the "lights went out" in July, 1977 in New York City, wide-scale vandalism resulted. Then, an important question for students of deviant behavior is "why did this happen? Does Zimbardo's deindividuation model help us to better understand such situations? An answer to this pressing question must depend on subsequent research carried out in natural settings.

SUMMARY AND CONCLUSIONS

The major stress in this chapter is that pressures that give rise to deviant behavior take place when people attempt to maintain or to increase their reward-cost outcomes by complying or cnnforming to a group's norms. Hence, our discussion has been mainly concerned with norms and the conformity-deviation processes. And we have found out that those who do not conform or comply to the norms or refuse to obey are labeled deviants and they generally elicit negative reactions from others. That is, a group will attempt to bring the deviant in line with the group's position. But those who persist in their deviant behaviors are likely to find themselves rejected by the group. However, the person must first, as well as the group, have an awareness of the normative expectations if group pressures are to contribute to this process. And, deviants who believe that they are different from others can also resist attempts to influence their behaviors. Information on how one is different from others comes from finding this out from group members. And, to the extent to which a deviant is responsibe to the influence by others depends on the person's relationship to other group members, whether or not the individual anticipates future interaction, how resistent the person is in changing her deviance, and, of course, the kind of deviance.

We also suggested that people seek evidence for the correctness of their opinions and behaviors. And, an opinion or behavior is correct or normative to the extent that it is supported by the group. Hence, we become more confident that our beliefs are in fact correct if others share the _same_ or similar beliefs or engage in similar behaviors. When one finds out that he is indeed different the person can either change or seek out other people who support his beliefs. And, the deviant who finds that others' beliefs are similar allows herself to be influenced much more than the deviant who is dissimilar from other group members. Hence, being labeled a deviant has serious consequences for the individual's present as well as future behavior.

    Finally we have observed that the authority vested in those who order people to obey and inflict harm on others has its roots in the institutional context of a society that encourages obedience to those in positions of power. And some institutional settings are more than others conducive to deviance because they seem to foster feelings of lowered personal responsibility for others' welfare. Hence, as Zimbardo notes, the brutality reported in prisons and mental hospitals probably is more a function of the situation than predispositions for aggression and brutality of guards or attendants. Hence, where personal anonymity and diffussion of responsibility are present, deindividuation results and deviance is likely to take place especially when people are with others who engage in mass forms of violence and other forms of collective deviancy.

CHAPTER 4: DEVIANCY: NEGATIVE ATTITUDES, STEREOTYPES AND SOCIAL STIGMA

THE ATTITUDE-BEHAVIOR CONSISTENCY PROBLEM

In an earlier chapter we noted that deviancy involves not only deviant behavior but also the actor's deviant beliefs and attitudes. Then, what is meant by the concept <u>attitude?</u> Robert A. Baron and Donn Byrne (1977) tell us that an attitude is a "relatively enduring organization of feelings, beliefs, and behavior tendencies toward other persons, groups, ideas, or objects" (p. 98). What this suggests is that pressures toward uniformity may operate directly on members of a group to bring not only their behavior in line with the group's norms but also their beliefs and attitudes. If this is so do group members always behave in ways that are consistent with their attitudes and beliefs? One might imagine that individuals who hold deviant attitudes are also more likely to display deviant behaviors more or less consistent with their deviant attitudes. For example, if a person should believe that "everyone ought to take advantage of others and exploit their weakness," then would this very same person openly support the efforts of organized crime to sell hard drugs to young people? In order to answer this question we must first ask an additional question: "Are attitudes directly linked to specific behavioral actions?" Before we attempt an answer to these two questions we should note that the behavior-attitude-consistency question seems to have important implications for the study of deviance. Why is this so? For one thing it is crucial that we understand how deviant behavior affects a person's attitudes and conversely how deviant attitudes influence behavior. In this instance what we are asking is: "Do deviant attitudes have motivational characteristics that direct an individual's behavior?" To put the question in still another way: "Do deviant attitudes and beliefs determine deviant behavior?" Also, "does the mere enactment of deviant behavior culminate in deviant attitudes, or are there other factors that operate to prevent this from happening?"

As logical as the above questions seem, research

into the attitude-behavior consistency issue is far from conclusive. As a matter of fact some recent reviews of the literature suggest that the relationship between attitudes and behavior is at best weak (see Wicker, 1969, 1971), whereas other reviewers do suggest that attitudes and behavior are at least moderately related (see Calder & Ross, 1973; Fishbein, 1972). For example, Bobby J. Calder and Michael Ross conclude that:

> It was hypothesized that attitudes cause behavior and behavior causes attitudes. These two propositions belong on the level of measurement, however, research findings are stated in correlational rather than causal terms. Research indicates only whether attitudes and behavior vary together, not whether one produces the other. Demonstrations of association provide evidence for theoretical causality, but the actual proof or disproof of causality is never possible.
>
> Does the research support our theoretical propositions? Consider the first proposition: Attitudes cause behavior. When standard attitude scaling techniques and multiple-act behavior scores were used, attitude tended to be a moderately accurate predictor of behavior....The second proposition stated that behavior causes attitudes. This proposition has received support. The dissonance and self-perception literatures indicate that behavior does affect attitudes. Once agin, however, it is clear that a simple relationship does not exist. Behavior interacts with situational factors to determine attitudes (1973, p. 30).

THEN, DO ATTITUDES CAUSE BEHAVIOR?

Now that we have observed that for a number of reasons people behave in ways which are sometimes inconsistent with their attitudes, we should ask "can it be demonstrated that research shows that attitudes can in fact influence a person's actions?" First, early research on this problem seemed to indicate that there is indeed a gap between one's attitudes and actions. For example, La Piere (1934) carried out a study to investigate the relationship of attitudes and behavior during a time when anti-Chinese attitudes were prevalent in the United States. La Piere took a Chinese couple with him on a tour of the United States and stopped at over 250 hotels and restaurants. Only in one case did the couple receive treatment anything like discrimination. Then, some time after La Piere returned from his travels he wrote each of the 250 proprietors and asked them whether they would accept members of the "Chinese race." Despite the fact that they had already accommodated the Chinese couple, more than 90 percent stated that they were against serving Chinese people.

We should note that as convincing as La Piere's study seems it poses the question that those persons who serviced the couple may well have been different individuals from those who answered La Piere's questionnaires (Dillehay, 1973). More recent research, carried out without the serious problems faced by La Piere, also shows that there is a gap between attitudes and behavior. For example, Lawrence Wrightsman (1969) had graduate students check automobiles in Tennessee parking lots during the 1968 Presidential compaign. He found that cars which had bumper stickers favoring George Wallace's law-and-order position were less likely to have complied to a then recent law which required people to obtain an automobile tax stamp than were supporters of Nixon and Humphrey. Of course, Wrightsman's study demonstrates that the relationship between people's attitudes and their "law abiding" behavior is indeed weak.

Then, as we have noted the concept attitude as a reliable predictor of behavior does not always allow us to predict that a given action will follow. For example, do people who dislike their employer "rip off" the company they work for because they dislike the mangement. If we should find that this is indeed not the case with most employees who hold negative attitudes toward management, then the assumed weak link between an employee's attitudes and his behavior may be due to several other variables. In other words it may simply mean that we have not taken into account the many other variables related to "ripping off the company." For example, a person's attitudes are likely to vary in intensity and may not be salient to the individual holding a weak negative attitude. Or as a matter of fact the person may hold the belief that "stealing is bad, no matter what form it may take."

One other possible reason for the low attitude-behavior relationship is that not liking management may be a highly general attitude, whereas stealing from the company is an extremely specific form of behavior. And, as a result the deviant behavior may have little or no relationship to the person's negative attitude toward management. In other words it seems unlikely that we can predict highly specific behavior from a general attitudinal measure.

Is it just possible, then, that the postulated relationship between an attitude (measured by scales) and overt behavior would in fact be higher if we measured more specific attitudes and correlated these attitudes with the deviant behavior in question? In order to answer this question Rokeach and Kliejunas (1972) measured how often college students cut their classes, their attitudes toward the professor teaching their classes, and student's attitudes toward attending classes. They also asked how important these attitudes were for students relative to their grades. Rokeach and Kliejunas found that the average of the different attitude measures, weighted for their relative importance, was indeed a significantly better predictor of class cutting behavior than either of the attitudes measures taken alone.

The major interest of Rokeach and Kliejunas' study is the effect of <u>attitude importance</u> for the understanding of the attitude-behavior problem. Of course, there remains the question of "why" subjects should cut class in the first place? In order to answer these kinds of questions, Martin Fishbein (Fishbein, 1967; Fishbein & Azjen, 1975) has proposed a two-process model where behavior is said to be a function of behavioral intentions, and the individual's intentions in turn are said to have their origin in the person's attitudes toward her behavior, as well as normative beliefs about what other people believe is "correct" and "incorrect" behavior for the situation.

Behavioral intentions are important for the attitude-behavior problem for at least two reasons. First, the person's deviant actions can often be predicted from a knowledge of the individual's behavioral intentions, and we can therefore assess how a person plans to behave. Secondly, when we know about how a person plans to behave we can surmise how deviant public action is anchored to a person's private responses such as, the individual's values, motives and attitudes.

Then, it would appear that the attitude-behavior-causal sequence has important implications for the study of deviant behavior. This is so because we need to know how deviant attitudes (private factors) can affect public behavior. And, we need to know under what conditions do changes in a person's attitudes reflect changes in behavior. For example, Gerrard (1968) tells us that members of the serpent-handling religion of West Virginia take the Bible literally and as a result employ deadly poisonous snakes in their elaborate religious services. What if a snake handler should get bitten while performing religious rites? In this case the members of the serpent-handling religion are likely to view recovery from snakebite as an example of the "Lord's miracle," and in case the person dies this is seen as an omen that "the Lord had to show scoffers how dangerous snakes really are." And, in addition, death by snakebite is viewed as a "means to enter God's throne."

　　What may we conclude from this example of attitude-behavior consistency? How is it that the snake handler's behavior seems to have its origin in religious beliefs? One answer to this question suggests that the snake handler's beliefs are highly likely to stem from a high commitment to certain religious views. However, this is not the whole story. The snake handler has group support for his religious beliefs and as such may be resistent to change in face of discrepant information. In addition, no doubt, we are dealing with a highly specific belief ("the belief that God controls what His creatures do"), and it is not surprising that a highly specific form of behavior seems to be correlated (snake handling) with the persons religious beliefs. On the other hand were we to predict the snake handling behavior from a general measure of religious attitudes, the story may be quite different: Little or no correlation is likely to hold.

　　In the same vein, we also find that peoples' attitudes may correlate with their behavior depending, of course, on the "distance" people are from the source of their attitudes. For example, it has often been observed that the perception of social injustice depends on how remote a person is from the locus of injustice. In this respect, Myron Rothbart (1973) examined the "liberal distance function" or the hypothesis which states that "the extent of favorable sentiment attitude toward social reform will increase in proportion to the distance between the population and the locus of reform" (p. 244).

Rothbart conducted two attitude surveys. One dealt with attitudes toward a prison live-out (half-way house) program and the other attitudes toward a public housing project. In order to assess the proposed relationship between physical distance and so-called liberal attitudes, three different groups of subjects, varying in distance from a half-way house for convicts, were asked to complete a questionnaire used to measure the subjects' attitudes toward the live-out program and their attitudes toward penology.

Results from the first survey indicated that favorability of attitudes toward the half-way house program tended to increase with distance from the live-out center. This finding is interesting since the results were not significantly influenced by differences in subjects degree of liberalness in attitude toward live-out programs and penology.

In a second study, Rothbart assessed attitudes of people who lived varying distances from the project site of a proposed federally subsidized housing project for low-income families (located in Eugene, Oregon). Results showed, as predicted, that the respondents perceived the need for low-income public housing, however, they did not want such a project next door to them. In addition, those living closest to the proposed site opposed the project the most. Then, it would appear that how "close" people are to an attitude object determines, in part, how they are likely to react toward the attitude object in question.

DISSONANCE AND DEVIANT BEHAVIOR

Before we go on and discuss the role of deviant behavior as a source of deviant attitudes let us first attempt to show how cognitive dissonance is related to the problem at hand. First, what is dissonance theory? The theory was formally introduced by Leon Festinger (1957) when he claimed that people just don't like cognitive inconsistencies and consequently they attempt to avoid or reduce it. More specifically, dissonance theory assesses the relationship between two or more cognitions (i.e., beliefs, knowledge, or opinions about oneself or the environment or other persons). Festinger tells us that there are two general kinds of relationships: consonant and dissonant. A state of consonance is said to exist when one cognition follows from or is implied by another. For example, if a person believes that she is an honest individual and at the same time she does not accept money from the Internal Revenue Service as an overpayment on personal income taxes, then a consonant relationship exist between her self-concept of being an "honest person." Dissonance, on the other hand, is said to exist if one cognition follows from or is implied by the opposite of the other cognition. For example, to use the case again of a person who believes that he is honest and this time the person does in fact take money from the IRS which is not due. This time a dissonant relationship exists between the person's self-concept of "honest" and the individual's "dishonest" behavior.

Then, in effect, dissonance is assumed to be an aversive state and people are said to avoid or reduce a state of dissonance. How does the person do this? Consider the case where a person believes that all homosexuals are "effeminate," but then learns that one of his favorite football players is indeed a homosexual. One way to reduce the dissonance would be to disregard the belief that all homosexuals are "effeminate." Still another way to reduce dissonance is to reinterpret his view of football players so that his view supports the concept of homosexual. For example, the person could conclude that most football players are not homosexuals and only a few homosexuals "pass" and become outstanding football players. Yet still another possibility would be to add new beliefs of cognitions that tend to support one of the person's dissonant cognitions. That is, the individual could in fact point out that the very best football players are not homosexuals and in this way one homosexual does not destroy the person's belief in football heros.

Several studies in the area of free-choice behavior and forced compliance tend generally to support dissonance predictions. For example, it has been found that once a person has made a choice the assumed undesirable qualities of the chosen alternative and the assumed desirable qualities of the rejected alternative tends to produce dissonance. In this case, <u>postdecisional dissonance</u> follows a choice and the person reduces the dissonance by developing a more favorable attitude toward the chosen alternative and a less favorable attitude toward the rejected alternative (see Wicklund & Brehm, 1976).

Before we consider an example of free-choice behavior we should note that not all postdecisional dissonance research shows that attitude change follows a free choice. Such factors as the relative attractiveness of the alternate choice has to be taken into account. That is, dissonance arousal is unlikely in situations where the alternatives are unequal in subjective value and the person choses the best alternative of two possible alternatives. For example, the choice between a boring job with low pay and an exciting position with relatively high pay would produce little if any dissonance, whereas the choice between two equally attractive jobs should lead to dissonance.

Another factor related to postdecisional dissonance is the similarity of the consequence of the chosen alternative to the unchosen alternative. If the choice results in similar consequences, choosing one of the alternatives does not necessarily suggest giving up the assumed attractiveness of the unchosen alternative. In this case little or no dissonance should follow. For example, Tim Brock (1963) asked children to state their preference for three toys and three different kinds of crackers. Then, the children were give the choice between two similar items or between two dissimilar items. Brock reports that more attitude change was found to occur when the choice was between two dissimilar rather than similar items.

The view that <u>choice</u> is a mediator of dissonance is important for the understanding of deviant behavior because when a person chooses to engage in discrepant or deviant behavior dissonance is likely to be aroused. And, to the degree that a person is able to foresee the consequences of her deviant actions the individual can either accept or deny responsibility for the deviant action. When the person denies responsibility dissonance reduction is unlikely. Hence, individuals most perceive a causal link between themselves and the deviant behavior (dissonance-arousing behavior) before dissonance reduction can take place (see Wicklund & Brehm, 1976).

Now what does dissonance theory have to say about __forced compliance__? First, forced compliance is said to exist when a person is induced to do or say something that does not agree with what the individual privately believes. For example, if an individual believes that his public statements or behaviors cannot be retracted, dissonance is said to exist and its reduction is likely to lead to a change in the person's private beliefs (internal justification), whereas when the person does not feel responsible for his bheavior or what he said, attitude change is unlikely. And, if the person's actions can be __externally justified__, dissonance reduction is not likely to occur. For example, logic would suggest that when a person is severely threatened for engaging in deviant behavior, the less likely the person would be to engage in the deviant behavior. On the other hand, dissonance theory predicts that where an individual is severely threatened with punishment for deviant actions, the activity itself remains attractive or indeed may become even more attractive. Later on, when the threat of punishment is removed, the person is even more likely to engage in "forbidden" behavior. What if the person is only mildly threatened with punishment? In this case punishment in itself does not provide "good reasons" for engaging in the deviant behavior. The person is likely to feel that the deviant behavior isn't really attractive afterall. In effect, then, an individual is likely to devalue the deviant activity and when the threat of mild punishment is no longer apparent the person is not likely to engage in the "forbidden action."

As can be seen, the utility of dissonance theory for deviant behavior seems obvious. Now that we have stated some general predictions from dissonance theory let us turn to the topic of forced compliance and see what happens when we attempt to predict deviant attitudes from deviant behavior.

DOES BEHAVIOR CAUSE ATTITUDES: THE FORCED COMPLIANCE PARADIGM?

Once agin, we ask the question: "Does deviant behavior cause deviant attitudes?" For example, what happens when an individual is induced by her peers to engage in deviant behavior--such as the use of dangerous drugs not consistent with the person's convictions about drugs--and then the individual subsequently changes her attitudes and future behavior so as to make them more or less consistent with the newly acquired drug-related behavior? In this case cognitive dissonance theory suggests that an active participation in public conformity is likely to facilitate private attitude change. Hence, according to dissonance theory when a person, who is enticed to engage in discrepant behavior, holds two very different cognitions or beliefs: (1) "I believe that drugs are dangerous and therefore should not be used," and (2) "I have used drugs," these two cognitions are obviously not consistent.

When the act of public conformity (e.g., drug use) has some important consequences for the person, there are a number of factors which may indeed lead the individual to feel responsible for his behavior. What then determines whether a person will feel personally responsible or feel that external factors have operated to cause the deviant behavior in question? People usually feel responsible if there is no clear cut external justification for their behavior. On the other hand, "public" behavior like drug use, undertaken without great inducement or pressure from others is more likely to produce feelings of personal responsibility especially if there are negative consequences for the actor. This very same reasoning was used to explain greater attitude change in the Festinger-Carlsmith (1959) experiment for those subjects paid $1.00 to tell a lie compared with those paid $20.00 to do so. Hence, people are more likely to feel responsible for those deviant behaviors about which they have had a choice to engage in rather than those actions perceived to be due to external pressures. And, of course, under these conditions the individual's behaviors and attitudes, at least for the moment, seem to be relatively consistent.

Given, then, that a person has somehow been enticed to engage in discrepant or norm-violating actions, can these actions in time become relatively consistent with the individual's newly formed deviant attitudes? The person who begins to deviate solely because it is suggested by others that he do so may in time seek reasons for engaging in the deviant behavior. Then, can the causes for this behavior be found in the individual or in the situation or both? Whatever the person's initial reasons for engaging in deviant behavior, the person may find herself "caught up" in the "new deviant experience," and the person may conclude that "deviance is fun."

Many situations, such as delinquent gangs, mental hospitals, and prisons, are able to exact conformity in its participating members. Then, an important question we need to ask is: "What if the conformity or private attitude change happens to violate the beliefs and attitudes of the greater society?" Before we attempt an answer to this question we need to know how deviant behavior can cause deviant attitudes. Since there have been a large number of studies which show that people's behavior does in fact influence their attitudes in important ways we will examine some of the research which seems to have the greatest relevance for deviant behavior.

First, it goes without saying that people do in fact engage in deviant behaviors, and it is understood that there are a number of reasons (causes) for these deviant actions. And we know according to labeling theory that deviant behavior is likely to get labeled, and as a result a new identity may emerge for the person. Then, if this is the case it is suggested here that a deviant identity may have its source in "new found" attitudes and beliefs which are relatively consistent with the person's public behavior (norm violating behavior).

However, before we hasten to conclude that deviant behavior causes deviant attitudes (including deviant self-regarding attitudes) let us take a closer look at some of the behavior-attitude research. Some years ago Leon Festinger and his associates published an interesting account of what happens when people find themselves holding unusual beliefs about the end of the world---When Prophecy Fails (Festinger, Riecken, & Schachter, 1956). The book deals with a religious sect whose founder (Mrs. Keech) claimed that she had received messages from ultra-terrestrial beings that most of the United States would be flooded on a specific day in the "near future." She also claimed that those who believed were to be spared and that the believers should assemble on a mountain top where a space ship would pick them up and whisp them off to safety. Mrs. Keech and her disciples had not attempted to "spread the word" to others nor did she attempt to recruit new members until after the group assembled and the doomsday prophecy had been disconfirmed. At this point she began an intensive campaign of proselytizing, especially through the mass media. Hence, proselytizing was explained by Festinger et al. as a mode of dissonance reduction resulting from disconfirmation of a rigidly held belief in doomsday by the "Lake City" group.

Festinger et al.'s study is informative because it demonstrates how the proselytizing of new members for a religious sect can serve to bolster the beliefs of the sect's members after such beliefs had been challenged by the disconfirmation of their doomsday prediction. And, the study has relevance for deviancy because it illustrates how deviant behavior (proselytizing) stems from disconfirmation of a deviant belief (a doomsday prediction). In addition, Festinger et al.'s (1956) study seems to have application to situations when people hold deviant political or religious beliefs. Especially where they are confronted with incontestable evidence of their beliefs invalidity. However, before the reader concludes that this is the whole story it should be pointed out that Robert A. Wicklund and Jack W. Brehm (1976) tell us that dissonance is dependent on the "foreseeability of the dissonance-producing event" (p. 297). In this regard Wicklund and Brehm suggest that the Lake City group did in fact come to anticipate disconfirmation of their beliefs. For example, "the Lake City group was exposed repeatedly to the taunts and sarcasms of nonbelievers, almost guaranteeing that every member foresaw the possibliity of disconfirmation" (p. 297). Then does Festinger et al.'s study lend itself to a dissonance interpretation? This is so claim Wicklund and Brehm (1976) because for one thing minimal social support seems to be a necessary condition to sustain a belief when the belief is disconfirmed. Too much rather than too little social support for a deviant belief produces only minimal dissonance, and consequently proselytizing is unlikely. If a group is already being ridiculed for its beliefs, one way to reduce dissonance would be to attempt to change the thinking of the community, but if the community voices no apparent adverse opinion there is no impetus to reduce dissonance by trying to proselyte. In short, the community under these conditions does not serve as a source of further dissonance.

DEVIANCE AS FUN: THE CASE OF SUFFICIENT JUSTIFICATION

As we have suggested earlier, one of the most widely used examples of induced attitude change is the forced compliance paradigm employed by cognitive dissonance researchers (see Wicklund and Brehm, 1976). And, forced compliance is said to exist when a person is induced to publicly say or do somethings that is inconsistent with a privately held belief. Since it is difficult to recant once the action becomes public knowledge dissonance is aroused and its reduction is likely to lead to a change in one's private beliefs. However, here is the punch line: The change is unlikely to occur unless the person is made to feel responsible for the attitude-discrepant behavior in the first place. And, as we have shown, if external justification is possible, the person is likely to feel that she has had little or no choice to engage in the discrepant behavior.

Folklore would have it that the more we threaten punishment for deviant behavior, the less likely a person is to engage in deviant behavior. "Not so," say Aronson and Carlsmith (1963). They had children rank order toys in terms of their attractiveness and then left the children alone with the toys and told them not to play with a "forbidden toy." Aronson and Carlsmith created a mild-threat condition by telling some of the children that they would be annoyed if indeed the child should play with the toy; in a severe-threat condition the experimenter told the child that if the toy was played with the researcher would become angry and as a result take away all of the toys. Then, after ten-minutes had passed, the child's preference for the forbidden toy was re-measured.

As Aronson and Carlsmith had predicted, children assigned to the mild-threat condition, where there was minimal justification for not playing with the "forbidden toy," the toy was ranked as less attractive. On the other hand, children assigned to the severe-threat condition, where avoidance of punishment was sufficiently justified for not playing with the toy, the toy did not change in its initial attractiveness for the children.

Before we discuss the implications for Aronson and Carlsmith's research, let us look at another related study. Mark R. Lepper (1973) threatened children for playing with a highly valued toy and then assessed the children's attitudes toward the "forbidden toy." Consistent with Aronson and Carlsmith's (1963) results, children given a mild threat devalued the toy more than those given a severe threat. Lepper also found that those children given a mild threat actually were subsequently more resistent to "temptation" when the toy was made more salient. And, children given the mild threat apparently changed their attitudes toward themselves: They were more likely to consider themselves honest than were children in the severe threat condition.

Then, it appears that research on "forbidden toys" has rediscovered the "original sin," forbidden fruit tastes better. Could it be that forbidden behavior (deviant or norm-violating behavior) becomes more attractive when engaged in under high threat of punishment? If this is the case, then threatening people for deviant actions could in effect make the deviant behavior much more positive. How do we explain this seemingly contradictory finding? To provide sufficient justification for not engaging in forbidden bebavior, one may end up convincing oneself that deviant behavior "isn't worth it," whereas where one finds insufficient justification for engaging in deviant actions under conditions of high threat one is likely to find out that forbidden behaviors are really very attractive after all.

SELF-PERCEPTION AND DISSONANCE THEORY

Then, cognitive dissonance theory predicts that people will, under conditions of pressure, bring their private attitudes in line with their public behavior. That is, one way to reduce dissonance is to change one's private beliefs so as to make them consistent with one's public behavior. Daryl J. Bem's (1967, 1972) self-perception theory provides yet another way to look at the behavior-causes-attitudes issue. For example, according to Bem's theory after a person has engaged in homosexual behavior for the first time, the individual may say to his partner "gee that was great, let's do it agin." Since the person is an observer of his own behavior, the individual may conclude that he really did enjoy the homosexual experience. Let us suppose, on the other hand, that an individual is forced to engage in deviant sexual behavior, for example in a prison setting, and observes himself resisting an attempt at "forced rape." The person has also observed that most young men also resist attempts at rape. Both the person and an outside observer in this case are unlikely to conclude that the rape was "fun for its victim."

According to Bem's (1967, 1972) <u>self-perception theory</u>, we are said to infer our own attitudes from our own behavior and the situation in which the behavior has taken place. In the case of attitude change in the forced compliance paradigm, after one engages in behavior at variance with one's initial position, one is said to be confronted with the fact that one has taken part in attitude-discrepant behavior and this seems to suggest that one's "true attitudes" are not really what one thought them to be prior to engaging in the deviant behavior. Then, in effect the actor reasons that: "I have violated a rule, and this is not really how I feel about the rule in question." And, the smaller the incentive (or the less reasons we have to engage in the counter-attitudinal behavior in the first place), the more likely we are to conclude that the counterattitudinal position was really not counterattitudinal after all. On the other hand, when large incentives follow discrepant behavior, the actor is likely to conclude that she engaged in the deviant behavior for what was gained in doing so. For example, the person may conclude that "I'm doing it for the money or rewards I anticipate from others." Hence, what Bem is telling us is that on the basis of observing our own behavior we make evaluations of our own attitudes much the same way that we make judgments about other people's attitudes on the basis of observing their behavior.

Then, how has Bem tested self-perception theory, and how is he able to offer his theory as an alternative to cognitive dissonance theory? First, Bem had subject-observers guess the attitudes of an actor on the basis of observing him. The reasoning here is that the observer might just be using the same kind of logic that he applies to himself when observing his own behavior. Hence, it is through what Bem labels "interpersonal simulations" of cognitive dissonance studies that he has produced findings that replicate dissonance results without subjects actually going through what dissonance theory labels "arousal and reduction of cognitive inconsistency."

Second, in order to put his theory to a hard test, Bem asked observer-subjects to read descriptions of the Festinger-Carlsmith (1959) experiment where it was obvious that subjects were paid either $1.00 or $20.00 for lying to another "subject" that they had had fun taking part in what otherwise was a boring task. The observer-subjects produced data not significantly different from that obtained by Festinger and Carlsmith "real subjects."

Bem went on to do other interpersonal simulations of dissonance studies and then concluded that self-perception theory accounts for the same results as obtained through the cognitive dissonance free-choice and forced-compliance experiments. However, these results did not silence dissonance researchers: They did studies that failed to confirm the self-perception hypothesis. For example, Jones, Linder, Kiesler, Zanna, and Brehm (1968) were quick to demonstrate that Bem's observer-subjects were not "aware" thet the discrepant act they were observing was indeed inconsistent with the real subject's original position. In addition, dissonance researchers noted that if the original subject's initial position was made salient to the observer, then indeed the observer might not infer correctly the person's attitudes merely on the basis of observing the discrepant act. Finally, Bem and McConnell (1970) claimed that subjects in the forced-compliance experiments aren't really able to remember their initial or premanipulation attitudes once they have engaged in the counterattitudinal act.

Now, where does the "truth" lie? According to self-perception theory, increasing the salience of the premanipulation attitude should in effect weaken or eliminate altogether attitude change following the discrepant act. This is so because it would short-circuit the self-perception process. On the other hand, dissonance researchers have claimed that by increasing the salience of subjects' initial attitudes this should in effect strengthen their attitude change due to the fact that additional dissonance should be aroused and reduced.

In summing up recent research on the self-perception-dissonance position for the salience of initial attitudes (e.g., Pallak, Sogin, & Cook, 1974),

Robert A. Wicklund and Jack W. Brehm conclude that:

> ...A blatant salience of initial attitudes does not systematically reduce the dissonance-reduction processes, as self-perception theory would assume. Further, the interpersonal replication paradigm does nothing to increase the tenability of Bem's assumption that "dissonance reduction" is merely a logical conclusion drawn from self-perception. With respect to this latter point, the evidence shows that a passive observer who is provided with a complete description of the original situation is incapable of accurately estimating involved subjects' attitudes (1976, Pp. 273-274).

Then, it appears, at least for the moment, that Bem's cutting edge for a self-perception theory account of dissonance theory findings must look to future research to settle the controversy. However, recent research has tended to support dissonance theory's position on the salience of initial attitudes for the forced-compliance paradigm (see Green, 1974; Ross & Shulman, 1973).

Before we leave the topic of self-perception theory, a fair question seems to be: "How might Bem's theory be used to account for deviancy?" First, we should say that self-perception theory has ties to B.F. Skinner's radical behaviorism and the theory is also consistent with the views of the soicologist George Herbert Mead. For example, the main proposition of self-perception theory is that internal events (private thoughts and feelings) are less important in the process of labeling behavior than are external or public factors. Meanwhile, Mead suggests that we evaluate our behavior by viewing the behavior from the perspective of significant others. Then, enters Bem, who is mainly concerned with how people explain the reasons or causes for their own behavior. For example, the person may ask: "Why did I just violate a traffic law when I know full well that I'll have to pay a large traffic fine and loose a days work in order to appear in traffic court?" The individual is likely to conclude that: "I was in a hurry to get home from work." At this point, Bem goes on to suggest that a person does not always know the "true reasons" or causes for his behavior. As a matter of fact Bem tells us that people apply the same rules when they explain their own behavior as they apply in explaining other people's behavior. Hence, a person observes her deviant behavior much like the outside observer and then asks: "What are the causes of my behavior?" What if we should observe that a friend has killed his spouse, we are likely to ask ourselves: "Was this action due to external or internal factors?" Then, according to Bem, if internal states are inferred, we are likely to rule out external explanations and infer that the individual has some negative trait which is linked to the deviant action. How about situations where a person attempts to explain their own behavior? Suppose that an individual observes himself mistreating animals. When the individual attempts to explain the "deviant" behavior he is likely to ask: "Why do I beat animals--I must dislike animals?" Then, it should be apparent that the observation of deviant behavior leads to the inferrence of deviant attitudes supportive of the deviant behavior.

DEVIANCE AND THE OVERLY SUFFICIENT JUSTIFICATION HYPOTHESIS

We have just found out that if a person finds too little reward for initially engaging in deviant behavior her attitudes toward that behavior are likely to become more positive (the dissonance effect). What if a person initially should find out that deviant behavior really "pays off?" In such cases we are introduced to an interesting idea known as the <u>overly sufficient justification hypothesis</u>. Overly sufficient justification deals with cases where a person's extrinsic rewards for doing something seem not to be necessary, hence the person would do the same thing without such rewards. And, in cases of overly sufficient justification, dissonance is unlikely because the person is rewarded for engaging in what is already enjoyable. On the other hand, what if we should over reward a person for engaging in deviant behavior and then without warning withdraw the reward? Although we don't have a ready answer to the above question, a study carried out at Horizon House (a psychiatric rehabilitation center in Philadelphia), seems to have relevance. For example, Bogart, Loeb, and Rittman (1969) decided to increase attendance at group therapy sessions. They instituted a reward system which entailed prizes for a "good" monthly attendance record. The value of the prizes was either $8.00 or $2.00. It was found that during the month in which the prizes were offered, attendance significantly increased.

After a month, the researchers withdrew the large reward and attendance dropped below the initial level, before prizes were given. In the small reward condition, attendance improved during the reward period and did not drop after the reward period was ended.

In other words, what Bogart *et al*. found out was that their subjects' interest in the group therapy sessions was undercut by the salience of a relatively high external reward. When in fact the reward was no longer forthcoming their attendance dropped. On the other hand, those who were not overly rewarded for attendance seemed to "find the group experience intricically rewarding."

Before we discuss the implications of overly sufficient justification for deviant behavior, we should note that Bem's self-perception theory has something important to say at this point. That is, as we have already indicated, overly sufficient justification should produce little or no dissonance because it is not dissonant to be reinforced for doing things that are fun. On the other hand, Bem's self-perception theory treats cases of overly sufficient justification much the same as insufficient justification. That is, the individual who finds that she is obtaining large external rewards for engaging in behavior initially less rewarding should come to evaluate her behavior and decide that the behavior is far from intricically interesting, but rather the reward is more important. At a later time should the external reward be taken away, the individual is likely to become less interested in the behavior than before the extrinic reward became available.

In line with this reasoning, Mark R. Lepper and his associates (Lepper, Greene, & Nisbett, 1973) tested the overjustification hypothesis with a sample of nursery school children. The children were asked to use a new type of drawing apparatus which was in itself very attractive. Some of the children were informed that they were taking part in order to obtain a "Good Player" award while other children were not offered an extrinsic reward. In one condition, the Good Player award was given at the end of the experiment and it had not been expected by the children (unexpected reward condition). Then, several days following the initial session, the children from all conditions were allowed once again to use the drawing apparatus or to play with other toys. At this juncture the experimenters hid behind a one-way mirror and found that as they had expected they noticed that the children who had initially expected and received an external reason for playing with the drawing apparatus actually played with it for about half as long as their counterparts: Their interest in the task had lessened by the liklihood of the Good Player award.

Then, the implications for the oversufficient justification hypothesis seems evident: Society should be cautious when rewarding people for non-deviant behaviors that seem to be enjoyable because nondeviant behaviors may lose some of their intrinsic interest and deviant behavior may come to take their place and consequently become difficult to inhibit.

DEFENSIVE PROJECTION: STILL ANOTHER CASE OF DISSONANCE

When people confront information suggesting to them that they have an undesirable "personality trait," or that their behavior is deviant, changes in their beliefs about other people may take place. For example, suppose that a person should find out that certain information implies that he has a negative "personality trait." Having found that this is "true" the individual could then reduce the inconsistnncy between his previous view of himself and the newly acquired information by attributing the negative characteristic to other people.

In this case, Dana Bramel has demonstrated how dissonance may be reduced through a process something akin to the psychoanalytic defensive mechanism projection defined as attributing unacceptable characteristics to others. Bramel (1962, 1969) predicted that males, whose self-esteem had been experimentally increased, would subsequently become more disturbed when told they had a "socially undesirable trait" (homosexuality) than would males whose self-esteem had been lowered.

Bramel gave male subjects a series of "personality tests" and then scheduled them to take part in a second session with another subject (an unacquainted male) where they were allegedly to take part in an impression formation task. Then, after the subjects met, they were separated and given false feedback about their personality tests. In each pair, one was given favorable and the other unfavorable information.

Subjects were then brought together again and they made ratings of each other and they were told that they would next estimate the degree of homosexual arousal of each other while viewing photos of men. Each of the subjects received false information from a meter which allegedly measured sexual reactions but in fact was controlled by the researcher. Each subject was given the task of recording his own meter reading and ask to estimate the other subject's meter reading for each of the male photographs. These reactions were used to measure <u>defensive projection</u>--the dependent variable.

Bramel found that high self-esteem subjects attributed (projected) significantly more homosexuality to their partner than did subjects with low self-esteem. Then, Bramel did additional analyses between the subjects initial attitude toward the subject's partner (i.e., the measure taken before the homosexual manipulation) and degree of homosexuality attributed to the subject's partner. Here it was found that more subjects in the low self-esteem condition liked their partner the less they attributed homosexuality to him. On the other hand, high self-esteem subjectd did not show this tendency. That is, when they did not like their partner, they attributed no more or less homosexuality to him, whereas when they had a partner they had initially liked, they attributed significantly more homosexuality than their counterpart low self-esteem subjects who had initially liked their partner equally well.

Then, on the basis of Bramel's research we have a fairly clear test of the idea that males with high self-esteem, who are made to feel deviant, can reduce their feelings of deviancy by "attributing these feelings" to another male they like rather than to a male they dislike. This projection seems to help reduce an unpleasant feeling of deviancy. Is it just possible, then, that the person who faces dissonant information about himself is able to reevaluate his feelings by looking for deviancy in others? If this is the case, then much of the anxiety associated with deviant feelings can be reduced. This suggests that unacceptable "deviant traits" attributed to others may actually have their origin in the process of attribution. We shall have more to say about this in a later chapter. But for the present discussion we have attempted to account for the attribution of a negative trait to others on the basis of self-esteem and defensive projection. On the other hand, suppose that a person is threatened, can the threat to a person's freedom to make choices produce deviance? We will consider this question next.

DEVIANCE AS REACTANCE

No doubt, most of us have at one time or another found ourselves confronted with the feeling that someone was trying to exert undue pressure on us to get us to do or say something we would rather not. In such cases some persons are likely to lean over backwards to do or say just the opposite of what is expected, if indeed they should feel that their freedom is threatened. The threatened reduction of a person's freedom to make decisions is the major source of arousal that Jack W. Brehm (1966, 1972) labels <u>psychological</u> <u>reactance</u>. Brehm indicates that:

> ...Whenever a person believes he has a freedom and finds that freedom threatened or eliminated, reactance is aroused. Furthermore, reactance results whether the threat to or elimination of freedom is social or nonsocial in origin. Finally, through reactance motivates a person to restore freedom and generally results in an increased tendency to express a threatened freedom, if excercise of the freedom is impossible, reactance results in an increased desire for the lost option (1972, p. 2).

What determines the amount of psychological reactance produced by a threat to a person's freedom? First, Brehm tells us that the magnitude of likely reactance depends on "how convinced the individual was that he had the freedom before it was threatened or eliminated" (1972, p. 2). Then, it follows that the more important the freedom is to the person the greater the reactance. In addition, if an individual should perceive a threat to her freedom, or actual elimination of a particular freedom, she may actually come to conclude that other freedoms are also subject to threat or elimination. However, greater reactance should in effect take place when the person feels that there are personal restrictions of many freedoms and that the future entails even more limits to the individual's ability to make free choices. For example, suppose that you decide to take a jet to New York (your preferred choice) and you cannot make flight arrangements, and then you decide to drive your car to New York (not your preferred choice because you are likely to have little time for a vacation). Then, after you are ready to leave by car for New York you are told that a flight is available. Inneffect you then may feel forced to take the jet. At this point your freedom to choose how to get to New York has been threatened. What follows is frustration and perhaps anger and/or aggression.

Stephen Worchel (1971) has studied aggression as a response to threatening his subjects under three different conditions: (1) the subject did not expect which of three objects, varying in attractiveness, would be forthcoming; (2) the subject was led to expect that he (male subjects were used) would get the most attractive of three objects; or (3) the subject expected to choose one of the three objects.

Worchel found that his subjects, who had expected one among three rewards (course credit for experimental participation, a bottle of after-shave lotion, or $4.00), whether they received the least or most attractive award, gave a more negative evaluation (aggression measure) of the experimenter's assistant more so than subjects in the other two conditions.

Then, what these results tell us is that when we eliminate a person's freedom, aggression is likely to result. What reactance theory also suggests is that the theory should be useful in understanding deviance.

First, since we know that reactance is an unpleasant state (motivational), directed toward restoring threatened or lost freedom, it seems tempting to stop here and generalize from reactance theory to deviance. Before we actually do this it should be made clear that the theory has not often been used to account for such phenomena as deviant behavior but the application seems obvious. For example, suppose that a person should discover that the majority of a group decides to introduce "hard drugs" at a group party as one way to increase their "kicks." At this point a member of the group is told that he could expect to either use drugs or drink beer (a perferred choice for the person), and when the party progresses the individual is then told that he cannot have his beer. What, then, should we expect? Of course, the person's freedom to drink beer has been elimited and he may attempt to restore his freedom by using an "excessive" amount of drugs. Then the person may actually convince himself that drugs are the "best way to turn on."

In our example we have shown that social pressure on a group member to choose one of two alternatives (beer or drugs) threatens the person's freedom to make the preferred choice (beer). The result is reactance and an attempt to restore a lost freedom culminates in "excessive" drug use. So far the person seems to be potentially "hooked" on drugs. However, this is not the whole story. If the group continues to insist that the person keep on using drugs, the individual's freedom has again been threatened. Then, if there is little or no possibility to restore the lost freedom, the desirability of the lost alternative (beer) should increase while the forced alternative's (drugs) attractiveness should decrease. By this time our person may become addicted to drugs and then find that he is "hooked" on drugs when he really does not like drugs and in fact would prefer to drink beer.

We have shown that people do indeed resist attempts to influence them when it threatens their freedom. In Chapter 2 we saw that a study carried out by James W. Pennebaker and Deborah Yates Sanders (1976) could be viewed from the perspective of reactance theory. As the reader will recall Pennebaker and Saunders threatened male subjects with either a high or low threat to their freedom to write on toilet stalls by attributing the threat to either a high or low authority source. Males who were threatened by the high authority source actually wrote more graffiti on the walls than those threatened by a low authority source. From the perspective of reactance theory why should this happen? According to reactance theory, the males' freedom to write on bathroom walls was threatened and they experienced arousal and subsequent attempts to restore that freedom took the form of "graffiti on the walls." The degree to which subjects wrote on the walls was a function of the magnitude of the threat. Where the threat to their freedom was high (high authority source), the males responded by failing to comply to the rule not to write on the walls. Finally, the same or similar analyses of anticonformity or deviance could be made for other instances of reactance and we may explain why some individuals, at least in certain situations, resist pressures to comply to the group's norms.

Finally, starting with the general notion of how deviant attitudes relate to deviant behavior, one can infer that a number of conclusions can be drawn. Attempts to understand deviant behavior have led researchers to examine the attitude-behavior question, and as we have just shown research on the effects of attitude-discrepant behavior suggests that deviant atttitudes can be shaped by deviant actions: Once a person has performed deviant actions, the individual may experience pressure to bring her attitudes into line with what has been said or done. On the other hand, the question of whether or not deviant attitudes also shape and determine deviant behavior is more difficult to ascertain. This is important because attempts to change deviant attitudes may have little or no impact on deviant behavior.

Another problem arises in the conception of deviancy: The conception of deviance in terms of stereotypes and social stigma. How are deviant behaviors and characteristics evaluated and what are the processes by which evaluation takes place? In the following section we will address these issues.

NEGATIVE STEREOTYPES AND IMPRESSIONS: HOW TO TELL A DEVIANT WHEN YOU SEE ONE

The study of deviancy has a clear interface with stereotype literature and research on <u>stigma</u>. Hence, stereotyping is a special case of person perception and relates to how people form negative or positive impressions of other people usually those who belong to racial and ethnic groups. It seems obvious, then, that an understanding of stereotyping has special relevance for the understanding of deviance. For example, when people claim that all homosexuals are "crazy," they are in effect attributing the "trait" <u>crazy</u> to all homosexuals.

While the stereotyping of racial, ethnic, and sexual categories has been widely researched, the stereotyping of specific kinds of deviancies has only received peripheral attention (see Secord & Backman, 1974), however, a recent study does show the dramatic effects of facial stereotyping of criminal deviants. This study was carried out by

Donald J. Shoemaker, Donald R. South, and Jay Lowe (1973). They asked whether or not people form positive or negative facial stereotypes of criminals on the basis of facial cues and further whether or not stereotypes are related to judgments of guilt or innocence when the evidence is unclear that the "criminal" was indeed the known perpetrator of a specific type of crime? The researchers classified facial photos of black and white middleaged males on the basis of four categories of "criminal deviance": homosexuality, murder, robbery, and treason. Each subject was asked to select from a set of twelve photos the persons that looked most and least likely to have perpetrated one of the four categories of crime. Subjects were also asked to evaluate the assumed degree of guilt or innocence of the men who allegedly committed each of the four types of crimes. Still a third group of subjects evaluated the guilt or innocence of one of the persons in the vignette setting, with four of the total twelve photos shown on slides, as the major person indicated in the vignette. This was done in order to rank the photos on a guilty-innocent continuum.

Shoemaker et al. found that there was a criminal-noncriminal stereotype and it was also found that a specific facial stereotype for each type of deviancy emerged. That is, negative and positive facial stereotypes were shown to exist for the "crimes" of homosexuality, murder, robbery, and treason. In addition, Shoemaker and his associates found that positive and negative facial stereotypes were positively related to subjects' judgments of guilt or innocence for the "deviant" actions of homosexuality, murder, robbery, and treason with the lowest correlation found for the "crime" of homosexuality. The relationship between negative and positive stereotypes and corresponding judgments for guilt and innocence were found to be significantly greater for males than for females for the "crimes" of homosexuality and for treason.

Generalizing from their findings, Shoemaker et al. suggest that:

> Practically, this study has implications for aspects of the system of criminal justice in the United States, particularly the "mug-shot" and the jury-trial procedures. Mug-shot pictures are usually much like the photographs

used in this study. On the basis of our findings, it would be plausible to assume that stereotype conceptions of what a particular subject "should" look like, or does not look like, could influence the selection of "the one who did it" by an eyewitness to a crime, particularly when that eyewitness did not have a good clear look at the offender (1973, p. 432).

What other kinds of stereotypes of deviants exist other than facial characteristics? Research on first impressions shows that voice inflection, body posture and movement, and style of dress can determine the impression we form of others especially deviant others (see Kleinke, 1975).

Before we discus additional forms of stereotyping it should be noted that Erving Goffman (1963) has suggested that physical characteristics of people, such as physical disability, are used to <u>disqualify</u> a person from social acceptance because of the <u>stigma</u> attached to these characteristics. Goffman defines stigma as a blemish or flaw which takes three different forms: physical disability; character defects like discrediting events in a person's past; and membership in a stigmatized group, such as homosexual or criminal group.

Then problems are said to arise when a nonstigmatized individual meets a stigmatized person in direct or face-to-face situations. If the stigma happens to be known or highly visiable, then the individual is likely to be discredited. Then, whenever possible a person might attempt to conceal socially unacceptable characteristics (see Freedman and Doob, 1968). And when this does occur, Goffman suggests that <u>information control</u> or <u>impression management</u> results. A problem arises if the person should disclose the stigma and in this case Goffman suggests the label, <u>tension control</u>. That is, when the stigma is disclosed others may evaluate the individual negatively. Taken in this sense, Goffman notes that a physical disability stigmatizes a person and that others tend to avoid the stigmatized person. Then, in effect physically disabled people are likely to become labeled as deviant (see Davis, 1961; Kelley <u>et al</u>., 1960; Kleck, 1966, 1968; Kleck, Ono, & Hastorf, 1966).

Social psychologists have carried out research

on Goffman's concept of stigma and have found out there is a "socially appropriate" distance maintained between stigmatized people and it has been noted that there are both situational as well as personal determinants involved. For example, whenever a norm for interaction distance is violated the person who is the "victim" of the violation is said to feel discomfort or even embarrassment (see Mehrabian, 1969, 1970; Sommer, 1967). Some additional evidence also shows that people do in fact tend to stand or sit closer to others when they like them and are unlikely to do so when they dislike others (Mehrabian, 1970). As a matter of fact, Robert Kleck and his associates report that subjects who interacted with a "stigmatized epileptic" (a confederate of the experimenters) moved their chairs six and one half feet from the "epileptic." On the other hand, control subjects placed their chairs at a distance of only five feet four inches from the person. Of course, this distance is significantly less than the distance found for the experimental subjects (Kleck, 1968).

Clearly, then, there is research which suggests that there seems to be a socially "appropriate distance" with which people place themselves from stigmatized persons. As a matter of fact Seltzer and his associates (Seltzer & Atchley, 1971; Atchley, 1972) suggest that old age and the condition of terminality act as sources of stigma. For elders their poverty, illnesses, and social isolation tend to be negatively labeled much the same way as social deviants are negatively labeled.

It has also been observed that there is a recent concern with so-called nonverbal deviant behavior. It also has been shown that this form of behavior is likely to have a potentially negative impact on peoples' social interaction patterns (see Birdwhistell, 1970; Hall, 1966; Kleck, 1968). More related to the problem at hand it has been shown that when people interact with a disabled person they are likely to distort their beliefs so as to render their beliefs more consistent with those of the disabled person. It has also been found that people in such interactions are likely to display greater <u>motoric inhibition</u> while they talk and listen to the disabled person (see Kleck, 1968).

There appears to be good reason to suspect that

in face-to-face interaction with deviant persons they tend to elicit from others behaviors which suggest that they (e.g., the disabled) are stigmatized. In this case it appears that the psysical appearance of being different has a distinct disadvantage vis-a-vis the negative reactions elicited from interacting others.

PHYSICAL APPEARENCE AS A SOURCE OF DEVIANCE

What about one's physical appearence does it have anything to do with the way people negatively or positively stereotype a person for better or worse? It should seem rather obvious that the more attractive a person, the more people are likely to overlook at least mild forms of deviancy or is this really the case?

Harold Sigall and Nancy Ostrove (1975) asked their subjects to judge a criminal case where it was made quite clear that the defendent was guilty of the crime she was charged with. Then, each subject was asked to "sentence the defendent" to what was felt would be an appropriate prison term. Sigall and Ostrove found that significantly more lenient sentences were given when the crime (burglary) was viewed as unrelated to the female's attractiveness, whereas when the crime was related to the female's attractiveness (she persuaded a middle-aged bachelor to invest money in a company that did not exist) her sentence was significantly longer than her physically unattractive counterpart.

Hence, it would appear that the status of a person's physical attractiveness has wide-ranging implications for deviancy (see Berscheid & Walster, 1974). That is, people who are extremely unattractive are likely to be unfavorably evaluated by others. As a matter of fact, Sigall and Landy (1973) suggest that the high visability of physical attractiveness and unattractiveness has either negative or positive effects. As a matter of fact they found that males were rated more positively when they had attractive girlfriends and less positively when they had unattractive girlfriends.

Then, given these findings for physical attractiveness it does seem that attractive persons who attempt suicide or in fact commit suicide are likely to be viewed as less justified in doing so than unattractive individuals. And, since those who attempt suicide are likely to receive considerable attention from others a question may be posed: "Do people who do not see justification for suicide also perceive the suicide attempter as emotionally unstable?"

In order to research the above question, Andrew J. Pavlos and James D. Newcomb (1974), presented male subjects with a description of an attractive or unattractive young female who either had been informed that she had treatable or terminal lung cancer. The authors predicted and found that where the medical prognosis for the female was one of treatable cancer, the patient's suicide attempt was perceived as more justifiable for the unattractive female than the attractive female. In addition, it was found that where the female's suicide attempt was viewed as unjustified, she was also more likely to be viewed as emotionally disturbed more so than where the suicide attempt was perceived as justified.

The findings for Pavlos and Newcomb's research suggest that people are more likely to view suicide as a form of deviancy (emotional disturbance) especially when they are unable to perceive justification for the suicide. In this regard, the unattractive female was less likely to be perceived as emotionally disturbed as the attractive female suicide attempter because the unattractive female was viewed as justified in her suicide attempt.

What happens when physically unattractive inmates get a "face lift?" Kurzberg and his associates (Kurtzberg, Safer, & Cavior, 1968) have suggested that research shows that there is a positive relationship between deviance and physical disfigurement. These researchers explored the hypothesis that cosmetic surgery might reduce the rate of recidivism in prisoners by increasing their likelihood of job success and personal adjustment. In order to test their hypothesis, Kurtzberg et al. screened a large number of disfigured inmates from the New York City jail and subsequently assigned these inmates to one of four different conditions: Surgery, Surgery and Social and Occupational Training, Social and Occupational Training, and No Surgery, and a Control Condition where there was no surgery and no attempt to provide social and occupational training. The inmates' disfigurements included such diverse physical characteristics as knife and burn scars, lop-ears, tattoos, needle tracks from drug usage and the like. In addition, the researchers used heroin and non-heroin addicts.

Kurtzberg et al. found that one year following their release from prison the recidivism rate for the non-heroin addicts, who received plastic surgery, was significantly less than that for the control subjects and for those who received only social and occupational training and no surgery. Hence, it was found that plastic surgery did not help the heroin addicts. In addition plastic surgery appeared to help those with facial disfigurements to a greater extent than those with disfigurements on other parts of their bodies (p. 650).

UGLY PEOPLE GET RIPPED OFF MORE THAN BEAUTIFUL PEOPLE

Are people more likely to behave in an honest way when interacting with a physically attractive person than when interacting with an unattractive individual? Or to put the question another way: "Do uglies get ripped off more than beautiful people?"

In order to answer this question Ralph Sroufe, Alan Charkin, Rita Cook, and Valerie Freeman (1977) carried out two studies to determine whether or not a female's physical attractiveness would affect how honest others were toward her. Sroufe reasoned that since honesty is a form of socially desirable behavior returning money ostensibly left in phone cubicles would be affected by the physical characteristics of the person asking for the return of the money. Subjects who had just left phone cubicles were asked by the experimenters' confederate (an attractive or unattractive female) if he had found money in the booth.

In both of two studies, the authors found that subjects asked by the attractive female, regardless of their sex, race, or age, were significantly more likely to return the money (honest response) than subjects who were asked by the unattractive girl.

Stroufe et al. (1977) suggest several possible explanations for their findings. For example, they suggest that people value attractive persons and are more honest with them in attempts to ingratiate themselves with them. Also, it has been shown that people tend to view attractive others as more kind, strong, poised, sociable, outgoing, modest, intelligent, sensitive, and more sexually responsive than unattractive others (see Berscheid & Walster, 1974). Still another explanation for the findings suggests that unattractive people are in effect bad and so deserve bad things like losing their money (just world). However, another possible alternative is that the subjects tended to like the pretty girl more than the ugly girl and returned the girl's money.

In an attempt to replicate and to extend Sroufe et al.'s (1978) research, in still a different setting, the author (Pavlos, 1978) carried out a field experiment. More particularily Pavlos sought to determine whether or not watch repairmen would respond in a more socially desirable manner (honest) when confronted with a physically attractive, as opposed to an unattractive female, who either expressed great or little concern over the cost for the cleaning and repair of her wrist watch.

A female confederate of the experimenter, who cosmetically arranged herself to appear physically attractive or unattractive, visited 80 different watch repair shops to obtain a cost estimate for the cleaning and repair of her wrist watch. In the Cost-Unimportant condition she told the repairman that "My watch is a present and the cost to have it repaired is really unimportant," whereas in the Cost-Important condition she told the repairman that "Although the watch is a gift I do not have much money to pay for its repair and cleaning." The confederate terminated her data collection for each subject upon receiving a cost estimate from the repairman and in no case did she leave the watch for repair.

Results showed that the mean cost estimate for the physically attractive condition was significantly lower ($p < .01$) than the cost estimate for the unattractive condition. In addition, the mean cost estimate for the cost-important condition was significantly lower than the cost estimate for the cost-unimportant condition ($p < .01$).

Based on the findings of Sroufe et al. and Pavlos' research it seems as though people are more likely to behave "honestly" with an attractive person than they are with an unattractive individual. In addition, consumer "ripoff" appears to be partly a function of the consumer herself suggesting that she can more or less afford excessive costs for a service.

We have examined the impact that physical attractiveness has on "honesty" and for the moment let us turn to obesity as a form of deviance.

OBESITY AND DEVIANCE: "I DON'T LOVE HER (HIM) SHE'S (HE'S) TOO FAT FOR ME"

It has been observed that being obese or "fat" in this society is a socially undesirable characteristic and it is likely to lead to a stigma much the same way as the stigmatization of racial and ethnic minorities (see Rodin, 1977).

There are enormous variations in the ways in which food takes on different meanings for people; especially obese and "normal" weight individuals. For example, Stanley Schachter (1968) has shown that food taste, gastric motility, the time food is eaten, the situation of eating, and food deprivation have different implications for obese than "normal" weight persons. Although most "normal" weighted people eat because they "experience" internal or physiological cues, these same cues seems to have little relevance for obese persons. Then, if internal cues (e.g., gastric motility) do not seem to control eating for obese people what other factors seem to? Schachter tells us that external cues mediate eating by obese individuals. Then, situations where food cues are made salient seem to induce eating in the obese. For instance, Schachter and Gross (1968) report that obese person eat significantly more than "normals" when they think they are eating after their usual dinner time. In addition, Schachter, Goldman, and Gordon (1968) have shown that "normal" and obese people show other differences in their eating patterns. For example, obese subjects, who had eaten roast beef sandwiches, subsequently ate as many crackers as those who had not eaten the sandwiches, whereas normal weight subjects, who had not eaten the roast beef, ate more than those who had eaten the sandwiches.

What Schachter's research shows us that both

the situation and internal cues are important for our eating behavior. However, external cues seem to govern eating patterns more for the obese, whereas internal cues seem to control eating patterns for people of normal weight.

Schachter's findings pose some interesting questions for deviancy. For example, in a recent review of literature on obesity, Judith Rodin (1977) has suggested that the problem of obesity entails the perception of self-control. And, obesity is an example of how stigma (deviance) affects behavior. "We in effect suggest to fat people that they should be ashamed of themselves for their seeming lack of self-control." Rodin concludes that people do indeed react with negative stereotypes to overweight persons: She notes that Bruch (1973):

> ...suggests, overweight people are thus caught in a real paradox. They have attained to a large extent the fulfillment of the great American dream, a life of ease and abundance for all, whose natural outcome is more ample nutrition. Yet at the same time Americans bend every effort to fight overweight, call it undesirable, and label it the "unsolved health problem of the nation." We have made excessive slimness the idea of health and beauty (1977, p. 335).

And Rodin goes on to tell us that even those persons only slightly overweight sometimes behave as deviants and consequently comply more to non-deviant "normal weight" individuals than to overweight persons, and in effect "share their deviance (see Rodin & Slochower, 1974). It seems that we are more severe with those we label deviant (at least those that are obese) when they do not attempt to control the source of their deviancy (e.g., overeating). A good example of the latter point comes from an experiment carried out by Andrew J. Pavlos and Julia C. Reynolds (1978). Pavlos and Reynolds had subjects evaluate an obese female who was said to have either initiated a diet for personal reasons or who was compelled to loose weight to keep her job as a receptionist in a dentist's office. Subjects read that after six months the dieter had lost either 15 percent or 30 percent of her pre-diet weight of 210 pounds. Results showed that the self-initiated dieter was rated as having more personal control over her life than the other induced dieter. And, the self-initiated dieter was rated as significantly more intelligent, energetic, secure, neat, and honest than the other-induced dieter.

Hence, the overall pattern of results for Pavlos and Reynolds' research suggests that when people perceive that an actor has gained personal control this tends to be translated into more positive characterizations of the actor. Where an actor displays self initiated behavior in an attempt to loose weight and fails to do so this attempt at personal control by itself is not a sufficient condition to elicit from others positive impressions. That is, even though an actor's behavior is viewed as self-initiated, if the action does not in fact produce a "desirable" effect (e.g., loss in weight), little if any change in negative stereotyping is likely. In other words, it may be no better to try and fail than not to try at all. The seeming failure of many obese persons to loose weight, even when they strive to do so seems relatively unimportant in changing people's negative stereotypes.

IF YOU SMELL BAD I DON'T LIKE YOU: BODY ODOR AND DEVIANCE

So far we have concentrated on physical characteristics of people subject to stereotyping and stigma. It is not surprising, then, that Freedman and Doob's (1968) difference theory, which postulates that people who are different are mistreated, would predict that physically disabled or obese persons are likely to be rejected. What about a seemingly insignificant characteristic of people--- their body odor? How might body odor be used to define a person as deviant? Is there a relationship between body odor unpleasantness and deviant traits attributed to those who produced the odor?

In order to answer this question Donald H. McBurney and his associates (McBurney, Levine, & Cavanaugh, 1977) had subjects rate the smell of twelve donor T-shirts worn for forty-eight hours on how "bad" each shirt smelled. Next, subjects were asked to rate the smell of each shirt and then to rate the assumed traits of the donor of the shirt by employing twenty 7-point bipolar semantic differential scales (e.g., dirty-clean, intelligent-unintelligent, industrious-lazy, good looking-bad looking). Finally, subjects were asked to smell each T-shirt and to try to identify their own shirt on the basis of its odor.

McBurney et al. found that persons whose odor was identified as unpleasant were perceived as: unsociable, dirty, unfriendly, unintelligent, nerous, unsophisticated, unpopular, bad looking, unhealthy, fat, poor, and unattractive to the opposite sex. It was also found that subjects tended to rank their own odor as less unpleasant than other raters. McBurney et al. suggest that:

> Donors' clear-cut tendency to overestimate the pleasantness of their own odor is consistent with the folk wisdom that "your own doesn't stink" (1977, p. 138).

Since McBurney et al.'s research on body odor (effluvia) was based on subjects' attributions to unknown persons, John M. Levine and Donald H. McBurney (1977) decided to carry out a study where subjects were, this time, given information about the "physical and psychological" characteristics of odor donors. That is, subjects were given booklets with descriptions of three different stimulus persons and they were asked to evaluate each by using twenty 7-point semantic differential scales (e.g., sociable-unsociable, industrious-lazy, strong-weak, good looking-bad looking). The stimulus person was presented as a male or a female, was depicted as either aware or unaware of the odor, and either capable or incapable of controlling the body odor.

Levine and McBurney predicted and found that odor awareness and odor controllability interacted. That is, both male and female subjects responded more favorably to a controllable same-sex than a controllable opposite-sex more so than an uncontrollable same-sex target.

Levine and McBurney suggest that:

> Although the variables that determine valence and intensity of reaction to various stigma have not been systematically investigated, available data suggest that "persons with characterological stigma are usually explicitly derogated ...,while persons with physical stigma are responded to with discomfort and avoidance but

not derogation...that is, characterological stigmata may elicit more derogation than physical stigmata because characterological stigmata are, in general, perceived as more controllable (and, hence, more intentional) than physical stigmata (1977, p. 445).

THE CASE OF BUMPER STICKERS AND THE COPS

Not only do members of the general community play a role in identifying deviance, the police in particular, are likely to play a major role in defining and controlling deviant behavior. In this respect, F.K. Heussenstamm (1971) suggests that the police detect and hence define who is deviant in their work of apprehending would-be criminals. He decided to test charges by Black Panthers that police selectively harass them while they go about their everyday business. Heussenstamm recruited subjects to participate in his research and carefully screened potential subjects until he obtained five blacks, five whites, and five Mexican Americans. All of those who took part in the study just happened to have been "exemplary" drivers. These fifteen drivers, with no record of traffic violations, were asked to display a "Black Panther" bumper sticker on their car.

It was found that the drivers received a total of 33 traffic citations over the seventeen day period of the study. They received traffic citations equally, regardless of their race, sex or ethnicity. In concluding his study Heussenstamm suggests that:

> It is possible, of course, that the subjects' bias influenced his driving, making it less circumspect than usual. But it is statistically unlikely that this number of previously "safe" drivers could amass such a collection of tickets without assuming real bias by police against drivers with Black Panther bumper stickers (1971, p. 33).

In addition to persons with low status in recent years it has become commonplace for the mass media to report crimes committed by persons with relatively high status. In the reporting of crimes and the failure to convict persons of high status not only does this raise serious questions about our criminal justice system of arrest, trial, conviction, and/or imprisonment, but it makes salient the fact that high-status offenders are less penalized by a criminal conviction or charge than are low-status offenders or would-be criminals.

Then, in order to assess the impact of social status on the likelihood of punishment, Richard D. Schwartz and Jerome H. Skolnick (1962), conducted two field-experiments. The researchers posed as an employment agent presenting information on an applicant for an unskilled job to prospective employers. Four employment folders were presented which were the same except for the criminal court record of each of the four applicants. The applicant was described as a thirty-two year old single male of "unspecified race, with high school training in mechanical trades, and a record of successive short term jobs as a kitchen helper, maintenance worker and handyman." The four folders differed only in the applicant's record of criminal court involvement. One of the folders stated that the applicant had been convicted and sentenced for an assault charge; one that he had been tried for assault and acquitted of that charge; another stated that the applicant was tried for assault and acquitted, but the judge had written a letter certifying the verdict of not guilty and reaffirming the innocence of the person. A final folder made no mention of any criminal record.

One hundred employers were randomly visited for their reactions to the applicants. Schwartz and Skolnick found that differences in employers' reactions to the applicant varied with the type of legal record of the applicant. When the applicant had been convicted, job losses corresponded with the punitive intent of the conviction. That is, less job opportunities existed for the convicted person. On the other hand, less job discrimination took place for the accused but acquitted and still less where the court made an attempt to stress the absence of a conviction and guilt.

In a second study, carried out by Schwartz, the extra-legal effects of medical malpractice suits were studied by obtaining records from a leading insurance company. Of fifty-seven malpractice cases studied, physicians clearly won thirty-eight; nineteen cases were dropped by the plantiff and nineteen were won by the defendant (the physician). Interviews with the physicians showed that of the fifty-eight, fifty-two reported that no negative effects of the legal suit on their medical practice had taken place. As a matter of fact, six specialists actually reported an improvement in their practice. No cases were found in which a physician's hospital privileges were affected following the malpractice suit.

From the standpoint of stigma, the major results of Schwartz, and Skolnick's research shows that high-status offenders (e.g., physicians) are less likely to be penalized by a civil or criminal conviction or charge than are low-status offenders (e.g., unskilled workers). That is, the status of physician seems not easily affected by criminal labeling, whereas unskilled workers suspected of a criminal offense are easily stigmatized and their job opportunities are markedly curtailed, and this takes place even when they have not been found guilty of any offense. Hence, Schwartz and Skolnick research suggests that the label of criminal denies the person employment even when little or no bases for the stigma exists. On the other hand, none of the medical doctors sued for malpractice suffered regardless of whether they won their case, lost, or settled out of court.

A major assumption following from the concept stigma is that decisions which are made to commit an individual to prison or to give the person a "second chance" are sometimes based on the race and past record of the defendant. In this respect the effect of a person's past behavior on expectations for future change has been researched from a number of perspectives. For example, research done on locus of control suggests that people do indeed use their own and others' past performance to predict future outcomes (see Phares, 1976). An alternative perspective---attribution theory---asks researchers to focus on the perceiver and suggests that perceivers do in fact infer that others will or will not change their behavior (see Shaver, 1975).

Then, following from attribution theory, Andrew J. Pavlos (1977) examined the expectations for a criminal defendant's rehabilitation within a simulated legal context. Subjects were asked to judge the rehabilitative change for a defendant based on information about his past behavior and his race. The author predicted and found that a defendant's past criminal record was given greater negative weighting for a black than a white defendant.

The subjects (males and females) were given one of six different case records describing a defendant charged with burglary and they were asked to imagine themselves as a judge making a decision to place the defendant on probation or in prison. The black and white defendant (a male) had either a past record of burglary or he was a first offender.

Subjects who judged the white first offender, as opposed to those who judged the white recidivist, expected greater probation success for the first offender. No such difference was found for the black first offender and recidivist. In addition, more subjects placed the black defendant in prison than the white defendant who was placed more often on probation.

Of course, Pavlos' research has implications when defendants are evaluated for probation or prison. In this case race seems to be a source of bias when judgments for possible change are considered.

In general, stigma has served as one reaction to deviancy. The whole concept of stigma might be dismissed if it were not for its importance in attempts to understand deviancy. For example, Darrell J. Steffensmeier and Robert M. Terry (1975) raise the issue of stigma by asking the question: "Given that someone has engaged in deviant behavior, how does this become translated into a deviant label? What factors lead to some acts being defined as deviant while still others are simply ignored?" (p. 234).

In an attempt to answer this pressing question, Steffensmeier and Terry set up a field experiment where shoplifting incidents were staged and customers could observe and react to the shoplifting incident. The shoplifter was either a male or female, a hippie or a straight person. The authors expected that the level of reporting of the shoplifting incident would be greater when a hippie stole merchandise than when the shoplifter was straight. The logic for this hypothesis suggests that "the shoplifter's appearance provides the potential reactor with information that enables her to locate the actor on a high-low evaluative continuum. That is, apparently a hippie-like appearance constitutes a negative identity which results in a greater willingness on the part of people to report the hippie over the straight shoplifter and by extension, a greater willingness to impute a deviant label to a hippie rather than a straight actor" (p. 244).

Results of the research showed that females were not any more likely to report the shoplifter than were males. In addition, sex of the shoplifter had little or no effect on levels of reporting. On the other hand, the appearance of the shoplifter did in fact produce a significant effect on reporting levels. That is, the hippie shoplifter was more likely to be reported than the straight shoplifter. This finding clearly demonstrates that the attribution *hippie* over *straight* constitutes a negative label or stigma.

Steffensmeier and Terry ask the question: "How to account for its appearance (i.e., hippie)?" They suggest that:

> The evidence presented clearly indicates that a hippie appearance constitutes a highly salient basis for social differentiation. From the perspective of "middle class" America, hippies and other beatnik types are viewed as basically unstable, as lacking in ambition and ability, and as marginal contributors to the social system. By the mere fad of being a hippie the perosn has demonstrated his lack of moral worth, his unrespectability, from the dominant cultural perspective. As such, a hippie label represents a stigma, an extreme negative identity (1975, p. 246).

SEEKING HELP FOR DEVIANT BEHAVIOR: STIGMA AND REJECTION

Social norms are likely to suggest that people who seek help for personal problems may be stigmatized much the same way that those with physical deformities and overweight individuals are when they are perceived as being different than most people. For example, Derek L. Phillips (1963) reports that "mental patients" who seek help are likely to be rejected by members of their community. In addition, when people discover that a person is deviant (e.g., a mental patient) and seeks outside help it makes a difference what kind of help is sought; a clergyman, a physician, a psychiatrist, or a mental hospital.

Phillips tells us that some people are better at identifying symptoms of "mental illness" than are others. Hence, for some persons only those individuals who have been in a mental hospital are considered "mentally ill." Phillips also predicted that people who show the same deviant behaviors (e.g., paranoid schizophmenia) would be increasingly rejected as they seek out the help of a clergyman, physician, psychiatrist or mental hospital.

In order to test his predictions, Phillips asked female subjects to respond to descriptions of "mental patients" who did not seek help, those who saw their clergyman, a physician, a psychiatrist, or those who had been in a mental hospital. For measures of rejection, Phillips used a modified social scale.

Phillips found that seeking help from a psychiatrist or a mental hospital led to the greatest rejection. He also found that those who did not seek help were rejected. This was especially true for those subjects who had experience with a "mentally ill" relative who did not seek help from a professional.

Results from this research seems to suggest that seeking help for "mental illness" somehow makes it easier for others to identify the individual as "mentally ill" or as a person who is unable to manage their own problems. Phillips tells us that:

> Mentally ill persons whose behavior does not deviate markedly from normal role-expectation may be assigned responsibility for their own behavior. If so, seeking any professional help is an admission of inability to meet their responsibility. An individual whose behavior is markedly abnormal (in this instance, the paranoid schizophrenic) may not, however, be considered responsible for his behavior or for his recovery, and is, therefore rejected less than other individuals when he seeks professional help (1963, p. 966).

WHAT ABOUT PEOPLE WHO TALK ABOUT THEIR DEVIANCY: SELF-DISCLOSURE AND DEVIANT BEHAVIOR?

Research shows that we tend to like people who tell us more about themselves than we do those who do not, however this depends on what people tell us about themselves (see Cozby, 1973). For example, Derlega, Harris, and Chaikin (1973) introduced subjects to a female (a confederate of the experimenter) who disclosed that she had been caught by her mother having sexual intercourse with someone who was either a male or a female. Derlega et al. found that the girl was liked significantly less when she disclosed the homosexual affair (deviant act) than when she disclosed having been caught engaging in a heterosexual act. Then, apparently telling a stranger about being caught making love to a person of the opposite sex is less offensive to a stranger than disclosing a deviant homosexual encounter.

What about people who tell "too much, too fast" about themselves? Does this condition counter the finding that people are willing to disclose more information about themselves to those who first disclose high rather than low amounts of intimate information (see Cozby, 1973)? That is, is it always true that reciporcity follows high self-disclosure? And, what impact does the timing of self-disclosure have on people's perceptions of deviancy?

Camille B. Wortman, Peter Adesman, Elliot Herman, and Richard Greenberg (1976) studied the effect on timing on disclosure and the responsibility for what was disclosed on subjects' attraction for the discloser. Subjects interacted with an experimenter's confederate who revealed personal information about himself ("his girlfriend had just become pregnant"). The disclosure either took place early or near the end of a 10-minute interaction. In addition, the confederate either acknowledged responsibility for the pregnancy or did not.

The results indicated that timing of a "negative" self-disclosure did indeed effect subjects' reactions to the discloser. The male who disclosed early in the relationship was perceived as signigicantly more inmature and maladjusted and more phoney and insecure than the late discloser. Overall, the late discloser was liked more than the early discloser. In addition, it was found that the late discloser was viewed as more open than the early discloser and subjects wanted to get to know only the late discloser more.

What do these results suggest? Obviously don't tell something negative about yourself unless you first become acquainted with the person you wish to disclose the information to. Also, as Wortman *et al*. found to their surprise, that the male who accepted responsibility for his girlfriends pregnancy received the least favorable reaction from the male subjects.

SUMMARY

We are left with an important question that begs an answer. That is, we have shown that basic to the study of deviancy are deviant attitudes and beliefs, which are said to underlie deviant behaviors, and since attitudes are considered relatively enduring dispositions, consistent or inconsistent with behavior, then to what extent does one's deviant attitudes relate to one's deviant behavior?

First, it does stand to reason that if one dislikes a group of people (e.g., criminal deviants), who are different, dissimilar or deviant, one will no doubt tend to avoid and stigmatize members of this group. And the attitudes and beliefs of those disliked, no doubt, have little if any impact on one's own attitudes and beliefs. Clearly, then when one holds negative attitudes toward others such attitudes sometimes are and sometimes are not translated into unfavorable treatment of those disliked.

Peoples' attitudes toward deviant issues are usually assessed by self-reports or questionnaires. Since studies dealing with attitude-behavior and belief-behavior consistency have not yielded encouraging results, what are we to conclude about the deviant attitude and belief issue as attitudes and beliefs are said to relate to deviant behavior? The research which shows the strongest evidence for an attitude-behavior or belief-behavior consistency comes from those studies dealing with the more specific kinds of attitudes and behaviors. Hence, when deviant behavior researchers attempt to predict deviant behavior from scales measuring highly specific attitudes (deviant) they are more likely to find higher correlations than when they attempt to predict deviant behavior from more general measures of attitudes. Nevertheless, with the present state of affairs we must conclude that attitude-behavior and belief-behavior consistency, as it relates to the study of deviancy, has not often been researched. And what research we do have shows that it is not necessarily true that those who possess deviant attitudes and beliefs will translate their attitudes and beliefs into correspondly deviant behaviors.

Cognitive-consistency theories postulate that people strive to maintain relative consistency between their attitudes, beliefs and behaviors. Inconsistent beliefs produce what cognitive dissonance theory labels <u>dissonance</u>---an unpleasant psychological state people try to reduce or eliminate. And in the process of reducing dissonance people who seem to have little or no perceived choice or who are forced to comply to the group's norms are likely to experience little or no responsibility for their behavior (deviant or non-deviant). On the other hand, those who do not feel great pressures to change may in fact change by making their attitudes more consistent with their discrepant behavior especially where others are perceived to hold similar attitudes or where social consensus is high (see Cook, Pallak, & Sogin, 1976). Hence, when a person perceives that she is not pressured by others, and finds social consensus for the deviant behavior, complying to the group's norms may in time lead to attitude change (conformity) consistent with the person's behavior (see Darley & Darley, 1973).

A viable alternative explanation for dissonance theory findings suggests that just as one infers what other peoples' beliefs are from what others do and say, so do individuals infer their own attitudes and beliefs from their own behavior. Hence, Bem's self-perception theory suggests that people infer deviant attitudes and beliefs from observing their own and others' deviant actions. Then, the generalization from self-perception theory to deviant behavior seems obvious: Deviant attitudes and beliefs are attributions made from observing deviant behavior and in turn deviant attitudes and beliefs reinforce deviant behavior.

Obviously, what seems clear from the self-perception proposition is that the perception of deviance in others (and self-perceptions) can have devastating affects on the labeling of deviance. That is, when the person deviates from normative expectations the individual may come to realize her attitudes are consistent with deviant behavior.

Although the assumed underlying processes for dissonance and self-perception theory are different the end result is that attitude-discrepant behavior (e.g., deviant behavior) can lead to deviant attitudes and beliefs. In addition, apparently freely choosing to engage in attitude-discrepant behavior for insufficient reasons is likely to imply a state of aversive arousal or dissonance leading to attitude change (see Fazio, Zanna, & Cooper, 1977).

Clearly, people tend to form impressions of others based on the information available to them and their own special biases. This is why an understanding of stereotypes for deviant persons has led social psychologists to locate the causes of stereotyping in the social influence processes and more particularily person perception. That is, we are told that our perceptions of others create our stereotypes. However, the way people stereotype and discriminate against deviant others functions in part on the basis of the perceived social consensus of stereotypes. And most social scientists seem to take the position that stereotyping of deviants is due to the seeming tendency for people to overestimate the between-group differences and to underestimate within-group variability implying, for example, that all male homosexuals are "neurotic" or "effeminate." And, according to Lee Ross and his associates (Ross, Greene, & House, 1977) people also assume that they are more or less accurate in their judgments of others behaviors when in point of fact research on probability estimates made by subjects demonstrates that they tend to perceive a "false consensus" or to view their own behavior as "relatively common and appropriate to existing circumstances while at the same time view alternative responses as uncommon, deviant or inappropriate" (p. 280). And, finally stereotypes often suggest that the group's deviant behaviors or characteristics are genetically or biologically determined or due to negative personality traits, for example, people are likely to think that homosexuals' behavior has its origin in sexual hormones or genetics or early childhood experiences when in point of fact the role that situational factors play is likely to be underestimated (see Campbell, 1967). And just as stereotyping of deviants has multiple causes, so to it has multiple effects? For example, deviants are likely to become the "victims" of non-deviants especially where self-fulfilling prophecies operate: They come to believe that the erroneous stereotype (attribute or label) attached to them is correct and behave according to the stereotype.

It should be noted in passing that it is not the existence of the stereotyped attribute but the consequence of the stereotype that seems to channel behavior so as to create its own social and personal reality: The stereotype functions as a self-fulfilling prophecy. And the self-fulfilling influences of social stereotypes of deviants can and do have serious societal consequences for stigmatized social groups who become "victims" of the erroneous tendencies of perceiver's who employ trait-defining characteristics in their attempt to understand and predict others' behavior (see Ryan, 1971; Snyder, Tanke, & Berscheid, 1977).

Finally, it has been noted that people seem to neglect "prior probabilities" or population parameters when they estimate and judge the "likelihood that an individual belongs to a given category" (see Ajzen, 1977; Kahneman & Tversky, 1973). Hence, people tend to overestimate the frequency of the existence of their trait stereotypes as an expression of social reality. Hence, the perception and interpretation of deviant actions constitute the underpinnings of self and other attribution. Then, to gain an insight into how attribution theory can help us understand deviancy, we will turn to an attribution perspective for deviant behavior.

CHAPTER 5: THE ATTRIBUTION PERSPECTIVE:
INFERRING DEVIANT TRAITS AND
MOTIVES

DEVIANCY: TRAITS OR SITUATIONS, OR BOTH?

When we ask questions about the causes of deviant behavior two very different explanations of deviancy are likely to be postulated; one that stresses internal or dispositional causes and the other external or situational determinants. And, if one takes a strict situational or environmental position it is claimed that personality researchers place far too much emphasis on the role of internal factors as the major determinants of deviancy (e.g., psychological traits, heredity, poor parent-child relationships etc.). In other words the situational view suggests that somehow people tend to overlook the role that social factors play in causing deviant actions (see Mischel, 1968, 1973). For example, sociologists and social psychologists generally agree with Mischel and stress the view that social factors tend to cause behavior and more particularily the situation the person happens to be in at the time is said to give rise to deviant behaviors.

Given that one postulates a strict situational view for deviancy the question still remains "how can differences be accounted for in the expression of nondeviant and deviant acts? In his attempt to confront this problem head on Walter Mischel (1973) argues that little evidence exists to show that traits per se cause observed differences in behavior. Mischel goes on to tell us that traits like honesty, persuasibility, and dependency really do not relate behaviorally across different settings (or situations) claimed to be reflective of a particular personality trait. And more particularily he claims that the trait view falls short of predicting specific behaviors from paper and pencil measures. For example, in a classic study carried out by Hartshorne and May (1928), the failure to predict a form of deviancy across situations illustrates the point. The researchers exposed young children to a number of situations (e.g., to tell a lie in order to save face, cheat on classroom tests, steal money) and found little intersituational reliability. That is, Hartshorne and May found correlations across different behaviors and different settings (situations) to be generally less than .30. What this shows is that if a child is "dishonest" in one situation one cannot be sure whether or not this very same child will be "dishonest" in still other situations. Hence, Hartshorne and May suggest that moral behavior is highly specific to the particular situation and does not generalize across situations.

Taking his lead from this earlier research, Mischel's (1968) work on delayed gratification does tend to show that there is little if any consistency between subjects' expressed desire to postpone smaller rewards for the "purpose" of getting larger ones and their actual postponement when in fact subjects are given the opportunity to do so. And, finally one of the most pointed criticisms of the psychological traits view is that of Edward E. Jones and Richard Nisbett who pose the question:

> How does it happen, then that students of personality have persistently embraced a trait construction of behavior? Why has it taken forty years of negative findings on the question for anyone to propose seriously in a textbook on personality that these trait dimensions may not exist? One answer is that the conclusion is based on inadequate data, another, that the traits have not been measured properly, or still a third, that the wrong traits have been examined. Another answer, and this is a conclusion that Mischel and the present writers prefer, is that traits exist more in the eyes of the beholder than in the psyche of the actor (1972, p. 89).

Of course, the above observation in no way rules out the likelihood that dispositional factors cause deviancy. What we really need to ask are such questions as "do both person and the situational variables interact to cause deviant behavior?" (see Buss, 1977).

Then, given that there are differences in the way researchers conceptualize the causes for deviancy one can expect different conclusions for deviant actions depending, of course, on whether researchers stress internal or external explanations or indeed both. Hence, on the basis of observing people act in deviant ways those who use personality trait measures to understand deviant behavior have suggested for example, that a person who is aggressive should display aggressive behaviors in a wide variety of situations. Hence, any dispositional view used to explain behavior must ask "are people who behave in similar ways in a great number of situations also different than people who behave in different ways in the same situations. That is, although a person may steal or lie still another individual may be inhibited and both kinds of behaviors are assumed to be due to internal factors like attitudes, habits or personality traits. On the other hand, situational views of deviancy attempt to explain why the same individuals tend to behave differently in a wide variety of situations. And, also situational views must attempt to explain why different people act in similar ways in the same situation.

Finally, as we have noted in an earlier chapter, sociologists have by and large avoided the problem of psychological traits as explanations for deviant behavior by viewing stable characteristics of the person as aspects of the person's roles. Then, whereas the concept role refers to uniformities in the behaviors of different persons occupying the same role, the concept personality traits refers to uniformities within the behavior of individuals.

THE MEDICAL MODEL: MYTH OR REALITY?

The psychological traits view of deviant behavior has a certain relationship to what has been variously labeled the "medical model," as evidenced by such concepts as "mental illness," "mental disease," "sick," and more generally trait models for "psychopathology." According to the "medical model," deviant behavior results from pathogenic factors generally assumed to have their origin in faulty parent-child relationships. Their traits are said to exist somewhere inside the person much like the locus of infection treated by a medical doctor. And, of course, "treatment" or therapy is a matter of changing the person so that the particular troublesome trait or characteristic no longer causes the deviant or pathological behavior.

The noted psychiatrist, Thomas Szasz (1961, 1970), has been quick to suggest that so-called pathogenic factors or negative personality traits, as explanations for most deviant behavior, oversimplifies the problem and more seriously has blinded researchers and therapists to the social determinants of deviancy. Hence, Szasz notes that deviant behavior and personality disorders may or may not co-exist with underlying feelings of anxiety, despair, lack of self-regard or other forms of "maladjustment." And, as a matter of fact, Szasz tells us that the mental health movement, and more particularly some forms of psychiatry, with its acceptance of the medical model, has attempted in the past to solve such problems by labeling people as troublemakers for whom no other social control system was available. That is, what Szasz is suggesting is that the labeling of people as mentally ill may in fact be a form of social control which has little or no relation to their assumed underlying deviant traits or personality trait characteristics.

Then, if deviant behavior is not a form of mental illness what in fact causes deviant behavior? Szasz tells us that deviancy stems from "problems of living" or problems of coping with the expression of socially unacceptable behavior. That is, deviancy is viewed as a problem having its origin in society not the individual actor.

ATTRIBUTION THEORY: HOW WE COME TO EXPLAIN DEVIANT BEHAVIOR

First, attributional theory suggests that deviancy or norm-violating behavior is primarily a matter of public behavior. And, the labeling of an individual's behavior as deviant (or disordered) is made on the basis of inferences about the cause or causes of the behavior in question. Hence, the reality of deviant behavior is explained in terms of the <u>causal attributions</u> people make for public behaviors that persistently violate the social norms and especially where it becomes more or less impossible for people to ignore the norm-violating behavior or to explain why the person violated the norms in the first place. Of course, most norm-violating behavior, if it is in fact merely transitory, is likely to be disregarded by the perceiver as a "true" representation of the person's behavior (see Shaver, 1975).

Now an attributional analysis of deviant behavior still leaves unanswered the question of why some people violate the social norms while still others do not, however, attribution theory find it unnecessary to postulate a special set of personal dispositions as explanations for deviant behavior. And, as we shall soon see, questions dealing with the actual causes of deviant behavior are said to lie in the situation vis-a-vis the determinants of social behavior. Hence, attribution theory focuses on the causal attributions that people formulate for their own as well as the actions of others. And, from the attributional perspective people are depicted as "intuitive psychologists" searching for the causes of human behavior, drawing inferences about "why people behave the way they do." And, attribution theory attempts to show how observers of deviant behavior come to understand other peoples' reasons for acting in a deviant manner by making interpersonal attributions for the causes of behavior. The deviant actor is said to search for the meaning of his own behavior (self-attribution) in the same way as others explain the behavior in question.

Now that we have discussed in rather general terms a psychological trait view of deviancy and have contrasted it with a situational view, let us now examine in greater detail how attribution theory can be successively employed to account for people's perception of the causes of deviant behavior.

First off it should be noted that attribution theory is in fact a cognitive approach to understanding the inferred causes made for behavior. And more specifically attribution theory bridges the area of person perception and the study of interpersonal behavior, and as such it is an important area of social psychology (see Shaver, 1975). Than, according to attribution theory, people tend to form impressions of others on the basis of the information available to them. And, since the "real" causes for behavior are not usually available to the individual, attribution theory treats the problem of causality as an attribution made by the perceiver for her own behavior and the behavior of other people. The perception of "why people behave the way they do" differs from the perception of nonperson objects because it involves inferences about internal states as the causes for people's behavior. Then, for the sake of simplicity, attributions are inferences that observers of behavior make about the reasons why people behave the way they do based on what is assumed by the perceiver to be true about the assumed internal causes for behavior. Hence, the particular perceiver always starts with what is observed and ends up searching for the meaning of the observed behavior. For example, consider a person who finds out that his neighbor is charged with the crime of robbery. In the language of attributions theory the observer of this behavior is likely to make attributions of causality: "Did my neighbor steal money because he is a "hardened criminal" (a personal disposition) or "were there circumstances which have provoked the crime such as is he a "hardened criminal" (a personal disposition) or "were there circumstances which have provoked the crime such as is he unable to obtain employment and does he have children who are without food and shelter (an environmental cause)?"

Then, it seems obvious that the way a perceiver evaluates another person's behavior depends at least in part on the attributions that are made for the cause of the person's behavior. If the perceiver makes a personal or dispositional attribution then she is likely to view someone who steals from others as a criminal. On the other hand, if an environmental attribution (e.g., the person stole in order to feed his family) is made the perceiver is unlikely to view the individual who apparently steals money out of necessity as a criminal. It also seems apparent that a judge or a jury will determine the person's (the defendant) fate partly on the basis of what kind of attributions are made for the cause(s) of the person's deviant behavior. So it appears that in most circumstances different people seem to make different kinds of inferences for the causes of the same behavior. And a personal attribution for the cause of a crime is more likely to culminate in a guilty verdict with a severe sentence, whereas an inferred evironmental cause may not actually lead to an acquital of the defendant, however, a lighter sentence seems more likely.

Historically, the original work on attribution theory is generally credited to Fritz Heider (1944, 1958). Heider focused on what he called <u>phenomenal causality</u> or how people conclude "what action was caused by what situation." He noted that the search for causal explanantions for behavior is a characteristic of all people not just psychologists or social scientists. In this case Heider considered the major problem faced by any perceiver to be the perception of "what caused what" or whether to attribute a given observed action to <u>internal states</u> or to <u>external</u> factors. That is, Heider tell us that a person is perceived by others as acting in a certain way either because of some internal motivation or because of some environmental or external pressure. However, Heider was quick to point out that behavior may be motivated in part by internal factors (e.g., needs, drives, etc.). however, he considered external factors to be far more important to the understanding of why people behave the way they do. For example, if a person is asking you for money it may be important for you to know whether the individual is motivated primarily by an "alcoholic habit" or by the necessity to get home because he has lost his wallet and money. In this case Heider tells us that:

> In common-sense psychology (as in scientific psychology) the result of an action is felt to depend on two sets of conditions, mainly factors within the person and factors within the environment (1958, p. 82).

And, as we should note Heider makes an important distinction between internal and external attributions for action; only actions that are viewed as "intentional" are attributed to internal factors (or personal dispositions), whereas expectations for future actions are said to depend on whether either of these two views of causality are used by the perceiver to explain a person's actions.

It should be noted here that Heider's theory had a limited data base, yet his theory has given rise to an important framework from which to account for deviant behavior. For example, Edward E. Jones and Keith Davis (1965) have expanded Heider's theory and have proposed that people examine overt acts and infer internal dispositions by paying "attention" to two very different aspects of the behavior in question: (1) those behaviors for which other people could have had only one or at best a few distinct reasons for behaving in contrast to those behaviors for which others could have had a great many reasons for doing what they did under the circumstances; and (2) people are said to focus on actions of other people which depart from the socially accepted norms. For example, suppose that all that you really know about a student is that the individual is a "good" student, is very competitive, and is married. Then, is this sufficient information to provide a basis for inferring much about the person's "general personality make-up?" Since all of these behaviors are more or less consistent with the existing social norms, we are unlikely to infer much about what kind of person this really is. On the other hand, suppose you find out that the student has in the recent past raped a young child, is known by others to be aggressive, and the student is a homosexual. Now you are in a better position to make all sorts of attributions about the person's personality. And, according to Jones and Davis' (1965) <u>correspondent inference theory</u> in this case the information reveals aspects of the person which show that he has departed markedly from the norms for "decent" behavior, and we began to find out that the individual's behavior is not entirely consistent with what is generally considered by most people as socially desirable behavior.

In addition, consistent with our example a person's public behavior seems to be more informative than the person's private behaviors. For example, we may find out that the "rapist" seems to respond to public questions about "proper" sexual behavior much like most people, and we may also find out that the individual claims to indulge in "conventional" sexual behavior but only where the conditions favor such behavior. Hence, from our example, we are likely to conclude that the inconsistency between the person's public and private behavior suggests that what is done in private is much more informative, or at least when people become "aware" of such behavior.

What we are suggesting here is that when a person observes other people's behavior he considers "noncommon effects" and then evaluate the <u>assumed social desirability</u> of these effects. And, in this way the perceiver is said to select a reference group to estimate the social desirability of the behavior in question. What if a perceiver concludes that most males do not engage in certain forms of sexual behavior? In such cases, Jones and Davis suggest that there is a certain likelihood or <u>prior probability</u> that the effect (e.g., rape) is viewed as socially undersirable by the person's reference group.

What, then, happens when a person employs a particular reference group to judge rape (who in fact consider rape undesirable and offensive)? The perceiver is highly likely to make personal dispositional attributions to the "rapist." When the person also finds out that the "rapist" could have obtained sexual satisfaction in more conventional ways (i.e., sex with a wife or girlfriend), rape under these circumstances is likely to be assumed by the perceiver to reflect a personal disposition. The "rapist" now is likely to be perceived as "sick," a criminal, etc. In other words the more the person's choice of sexual behavior deviates from the norms of the observer's reference group(s), the more the choice behavior (rape) will be attributed as a personal disposition.

Jones and Davis (1965) press on and suggest that a perceivers attributions may become distorted or biased where there is personal involvement with the individual being judged. This is so because the person's actions may have _hedonic relevance_ for the perceiver. That is, these actions can have either positive or negative outcomes for the perceiver. For example, if a person has insulted a friend of yours this action is likely to be negatively evaluated, whereas if the person has insulted someone you just happen not to like, this same action could be positively valued by yourself.

A second condition of personal involvement is noted by Jones and Davis where the perceiver comes to believe that the actions she observes are partly due to the perceiver's (her) presence in the situation. In this case, Jones and Davis suggest that the variable _personalism_ operates. To illustrate let us return to our earlier example. If you have attempted to persuade a person not to insult your friend and you later find out that she did in fact insult your friend, the personalistic attribution made is highly likely to be negative.

Then, what Jones and Davis suggest is that a perceiver of other peoples' actions (deviant or nondeviant) attempts to understand why these actions took place first by searching for dispositional causes for the person's intentions. Where the effects or outcomes resulting from the action are simple rather than complex, and where these effects are socially undesirable, more valuable information is available to the perceiver from which to make attributions for the causes of the action. It is in this sense that out-of-role behavior is more informative than in-role behavior.

Once again, what does Jones and Davis' correspondent inference theory tell us about deviant behavior? First, according to this theory, if a person acts in a "normal" way this does not tell us much about the person but merely reflects the individual's in-role behavior. We are likely to "discount" in-role behavior as nothing more or less than role-required behavior. That is, "normal" people act the way we expect them to act; we attribute their actions to external pressures and/or to role requirements. And Jones and Davis' perceiver is unlikely to always recognize external factors especially when the person's behavior just happens to be out-of-role, and especially where the out-of-role behavior does not meet the standards for social desirability. Of course, the same logic holds for making attributions about one's own behaviors. And, we are forced to amend our views when our behavior is consistent with our role requirements. When our behavior is inconsistent with our role requirements we are likely to attribute the behavior to personal characteristics (e.g., traits). In such cases labels (or attributions) are taken as "true representations" of our personality.

Once more, "what insights are provided by Jones and Davis that are directly relevant to the study of deviant behavior?" First, the major concern of Jones and Davis' theory are the attributions people make for other's attitudes, beliefs, motivations, and dispositions. And in order to provide predictability and meaningfulness for one's environment one is said to have a need to understand the causes for behavior. And, of course, the personal dispositions one assigns to other people depends on the special conditions surrounding the observed behavior in the first place.

Now for the sake of continuing our discussion suppose that you observe a fellow student engage in a deviant act (e.g., public nudity or heroin drug addiction), do you infer from these actions that the student is a deviant or in Jones and Davis' words "do you make a correspondent inference?" Whether you do or do not perceive the student as deviant, according to Jones and Davis' theory, depends upon the behavior and the situation in which the behavior takes place. When the circumstance seems to favor the behavior, one is unlikely to infer that the student is deviant. For example, a college fraternity that uses nudity as part of its initiation ritual is not likely to be labeled deviant by members of that fraternity or as a matter of fact the college at large. Actually, the students are unlikely to be perceived as having had a choice to go nude in public. In other words, as the circumstances seem to favor the behavior, people become less likely to make a personal or dispositional inference which is correspondent with deviant acts in question.

Jones and Davis do not tell us that a person makes the same inferences or goes through the same processes when observing his own behavior as he does about others' behavior. Why is this so? The person has more information about his own attitudes, beliefs and past history than others, whereas he is unlikely to have the very same kind of information about other people. And, interestingly enough, people do not always accept the reasons (causes) or attributions given by other people for their behavior. And, in some situations people do indeed seem to resist attributions of deviant. For example, Peter L. Berger suggests that in some cases people "replace a negative label with a positive one":

> Jewish reactions to antiSemitism furnish classic illustrations of this process with the Jewish counterdefinitions of their own identity simply reversing the signs attached to the antiSemitic categories without fundamentally challenging the categories themselves (1963, p. 158).

KELLEY'S ATTRIBUTION THEORY AND THE PROBLEM OF CAUSALITY

Harold H. Kelley (1967, 1971, 1973) has offered still another extention of Heider's theory. Kelley's theory attempts to explain how people attribute dispositions to others as the cause for others' behavior based on the proposition that perceivers are like "naive scientists." Again, as Jones and Davis tells us, people are said to look for the causes of behavior from what people do and what they say. That is, people attempt to reduce the variance from the many possible causes they infer for behavior and they try to locate the cause(s) either within a particular person (internal causality) or in the characteristics of the environment (external causality) or both. For example, suppose that you observe a student cheat on a classroom examination, you must then decide whether this action is unique to the person (the student cheats on exams and is dishonest) or that cheating is widespread on the college campus. If cheating is common behavior this merely tells us something about the college and not much about the particular student. In such cases as the above, Kelley tells us that we need to consider three basic sources of information before the action can really take on special meaning:

1. <u>Distinctiveness of the entity</u>. Does the student cheat in other situations or is his cheating behavior distinctive to the particular classroom setting? The more cheating is perceived as specific to a particular setting, the less the behavior tells us something unique about the student. That is, when there is <u>high</u> distinctiveness of the behavior we are likely to make an external attribution for the cause of the student's cheating behavior. That is, cheating in this case is likely to be viewed as provoked by the particular classroom setting. On the other hand where distinctiveness is <u>low</u> we are likely to view the student as a "cheater," which, of course, is a personal disposition.

2. <u>Consensus</u>. Do all persons react this very same way to the entity in question or in other words are students likely to cheat on college exams? If we should conclude that this is the case, then we are more likely to view the student's cheating as determined by the entity and not due to anything unique about the student. On the other hand, if the student is the only one or one of a few students who cheat on tests, in this case we can be more confident that the cheating tells us something unique about the student's behavior. And it is in this way that high consensus leads to external attributions and low consenus leads to personal or dispositional attributions for the cause of deviant behavior.

3. <u>Consistency</u>. The question here is "does the person often behave this way (cheat) over time and over different modalities? That is, is the student likely to cheat (time) and does the student cheat in different settings (modalities)? Hence, high consistency is a necessary condition to make either internal or external attributions for the student's cheating. What is important here is the source of cheating: We can be more confident that some stable characteristic (disposition) of the person was responsible (the student is dishonest) when we observe the

student cheat over time and in different settings. When there is low consistency this makes it difficult to make enduring attributions to either the student or to the environment.

Kelley's attributional model seems to provide us with an important approach to understanding deviant behavior. Now can we also apply the very *same* rules we used to make attributions for the cause of others' deviant behavior to an analysis of the causes of our own deviant actions. For example, if you are taking a classroom exam and observe yourself cheating you might ask yourself: "Why am I cheating?" "Am I dishonest or are most people likely to cheat in such situations?" As with the attributional process applied to other people, one is likely to make use of available information in terms of its distinctiveness, consensus, and seeming consistency relative to one's own behavior. More specifically, you might ask yourself: "Do I cheat on other examinations, of course, whenever this is possible?" The more distinctive the entity is (the particular classroom setting is conducive to cheating), the more likely one is to attribute dishonest behavior to the situation and not to one's self. On the other hand, the less distinctive one's behavior (the particular classroom setting was not conducive to cheating), the more likely one is to attribute one's cheating to characteristics of one's self (like dishonesty) and not to the situation.

What happens the next time you cheat or if you observe other students cheating on a classroom exam? When you observe this high-consensus behavior you are likely to assume that your dishonest behavior was due in part to the presence of others. On the other hand, if you do not observe others cheating, and you alone are "dishonest," this condition of low consensus may lead you to attribute cheating behavior to yourself perhaps as a unique aspect of your personality: For example, "I am a dishonest person."

Finally, one may speculate whether or not one's cheating behavior is consistent across various situations. That is, if one just happens to be in a different classroom, taking a different kind of test, would one cheat on the exam (time)? And, if one were filling out one's income tax return would one cheat the government (modality)? The less consistent one's behavior, the less likely one is to perceive cheating as a stable characteristic of one's self (or make an internal attribution). If this is the case then one is more likely to make an external attribution for the cause of one's behavior, and one's conception of cheating would be perceived as a transitory factor and not necessarily a stable disposition or characteristic of one's self.

As you no doubt suspect, Kelley's theory seems to be highly appropriate when we attempt to account for the perceived causality of deviant behavior. This is so because Kelley tells us how perceivers come to distinguish among the possible multiple causes for deviant behavior by first postulating the principle of <u>covariation,</u> which he defines as "an <u>effect</u> (that) <u>is attributed to one of its possible causes with which, over time, it covaries</u> (1973, p. 108). It is in this sense that Kelley's ideal perceiver is similar to the social scientist carrying out a number of studies in order to answer questions about cause and effect. That is, the perceiver attributes an effect (an outcome) to a particular cause when the cause is present, and, of course, preceeds the effect. In addition, there are three major dimensions---entities, persons, and time/modelity--which are said to serve the individual in making causal attributions on the bases of the covariation of each of these factors. The entities dimension represents attributionally distinct events in the perceiver's environment. For example, a person's reaction to a mental hospital is, of course, not the same as the individual's reaction to a college campus. The <u>persons</u> dimension represents the actor and other individuals who happen to have interacted with the particular entity (or distinct aspects of the environment), and in so doing have formed an opinion of the entity. And, the <u>time/modality</u> dimension depicts ways of interacting with the environment, and the different times this interaction has taken place.

Now that we have said something about attribution theory let us press on and suppose that an individual seems to enjoy that other people get punished and he especially enjoys seeing movies where a rapist kills his victim. What are we likely to conclude? First, in the language of H.H. Kelley this type of movie is an <u>entity</u> and other possible <u>entities</u> are, for example, TV rape-killings, and rape-killings in "real" life settings. Our special problem here is to account for the likely causal attribution for the person's seeming enjoyment of other peoples' pain and suffering, In this case, Kelley suggests that we are likely to employ the principle of covariation. First, we are likely to note that the person does not enjoy killings without accompaning rape. Hence, we are likely to conclude that the person's reaction to rape-killings is a distinctive reaction. Our perceiver next finds that the major enjoyment the individual seems to experience is rape-killings that take place in X-rated movies when the person is with friends. Now, the major problem facing our perceiver is whether the person's action is due to the entity (rape-killing) or to the context in which rape-killings take place (e.g., with friends in X-rated theaters). In order to ascertain these possibilities our perceiver is said to employ a <u>time/modality</u> dimension. And, if it is concluded that the person's seeming enjoyment of rape-murders takes place in different settings (e.g., X-rated films, TV programs, etc.), and further at different times our perceiver is likely to conclude that the person's enjoyment of rape-killings is consistent over different situations, and the perceiver may rule out different modalities (or context) as the major determiner of the person's apparent sadistic behavior (a personal disposition).

Now, an additional question is likely to be posed by our perceiver: "Do many other people seem to enjoy seeing rape-murders or is this indeed a characteristic of this individual case?" In other words, our perceiver is likely to ask: "Is this form of behavior characteristic of other people or unique to the individual in question?" In this case our perceiver employs the persons dimension.

Now suppose that our perceiver concludes that this characteristic is unique to the person who enjoys seeing rape killings. Then, finally, in Kelley's language: "Is there something about the stimulus (rape-killings) that caused the person to enjoy viewing rape-murders, something about the person (the individual is a sadist), or something about the circumstance (viewing X-rated films with friends)?

Now that we have applied Kelley's principle of covariation to a particular form of behavior, the question facing our perceiver is whether the person's behavior (enjoyment of rape-killings) reflects a stable personal disposition (e.g., sadism) or are situational factors of greater relevance? According to the covariation principle high consensus would suggest to the perceiver, that most other people also enjoy viewing rape-killings and, of course, a situational explanation is more likely than a personal or dispositional one.

A COMPARISON OF THE JONES-DAVIS AND KELLEY ATTRIBUTION THEORIES

Both Jones-Davis theory and Kelley theory derive from Heider's (1944, 1958) phenomenology. What then are the major differences between these two theories and how do they help us understand deviant behavior?

First, Kelley focuses on the inferences people make for the <u>intentionality</u> and <u>causality</u> of behavior: Kelley's perceiver must decide whether an action is deviant or nondeviant on the basis of some degree of consensus that other people would also somehow find the <u>same</u> action deviant. The perceiver must also decide whether or not her own perceptions of other people's actions are due to her own unique attitudes or motivations. That is, other people may or may not perceive the behavior in question the same way as the perceiver. Hence people's judgments of what is deviant is likely to vary because all people do not agree on what is and what is not deviant.

Kelley Shaver (1975) notes that Jones and Davis' (1965) ideal perceiver is an <u>information processor</u>. That is, the perceiver takes into account both what the actor has done and what in fact the actor might have done. And, the actor is perceived to have had a number of choices. Socially desirable actions that characterize most people's behavior have little or no attributional value to the observer. On the other hand, actions which have <u>noncommon effects</u> or are out-of-role or are undesirable or deviant are employed by the perceiver to make inferences for the actor's having made the particular choice of behavior as opposed to other possible choices of action. Hence, when an uncommon effect is undesirable the perceiver is likely to assume that the actor made the choice to engage in the particular behavior because he has a personal disposition to do. And, when there are noncommon effects for an actor's behavior and these effects are low in social desirability, Jones and Davis refer to the condition of

<u>correspondence of inference</u>, which means that the perceiver's inference about an actor's behavior corresponds to some personal disposition or trait assumed to have <u>caused</u> the actor to engage in the undesirable behavior in the first place. This is most likely to occur when the actor's behavior is unique or does not accord with what most other people would have done under the special circumstances.

In contrast to Jones and Davis, Kelley's perceiver is said to explain the perceived causes of behavior much like a social scientist, who goes about looking for cause and effect relationships for behavior. In general people are said to attribute the effect (the behavior) to a particular cause or causes perceived to co-vary with the effect. And, Kelley tells us that three kinds of information are used to provide different sources of covariation information: consistency, consensus, and distinctiveness of the deviant behavior in question.

DEVIANT BEHAVIOR AND THE ACTOR-OBSERVER HYPOTHESIS

If human life is at all organized it is because we are able to predict the behavior of others. Of course, not all behavior is equally predictable, but people do seem under most conditions to behave in more or less expected or "acceptable" ways. Then, off hand it would seem that we would predict our own behavior, as well as attempt to explain our own behavior, the very same way we do other peoples' behavior. Yet it should be clear by now that while deviance is behavior which departs from social norms, people do show a special bias when they attempt to explain the reasons for their own actions: How often do we say when we observe ourselves engaging in unexpected behavior: "Why did I do that?" And, although it may seem logical at the time for us to probe the reasons (causes) why other people act the way they do, it is not logical that we should attempt to understand our own behavior the same way we do other people's behavior. As a matter of fact Edward E. Jones and Richard Nisbett (1972) tell us that most people tend to overestimate the contribution of internal causes for the deviant actions of others, whereas in point of fact a person is more likely to assume that environmental or situational factors are more responsible than internal factors for his own deviant behavior. In this regard, Jones and Nisbett tell us that:

...The actor's perceptions of the causes of his behavior are at variance with those held by outside observers. The actor's view of his behavior emphasizes the role of environmental conditions at the moment of action. The observer's view emphasizes the causal role of stable dispositional properties of the actor: We wish to argue that there is a pervasive tendency for actors to attribute their actions to situational requirements, whereas observers tend to attribute the same actions to stable personal dispositions (1972, p. 80).

Then, to pose the question again, why do observers and actors seem to make divergent attributions for the causes of the very same behavior? First, although it is tempting to dismiss this question by suggesting that it depends on who is making the judgment about deviant behavior, Jones and Nisbett tell us that an actor generally has more information about her intentions, emotional state, and the events preceeding an action. Second, the actor's attention is more likely to be focused on the situation from which the actor derives cues to guide her behavior, whereas the observer's attention is focused on the actor and the actor's behavior. Hence, it follows from Jones and Nisbett's assertion that there is a tendency for the actor to attribute the causes of his behavior to the situation, whereas the observer is said to attribute other people's behavior to their personal dispositional characteristics.

In support of their contention, Jones and Nisbett reason that as people come to know an actor they are likely to conclude that the actor's behavior also varies across situations. This suggests that the observer's tendency to ascribe trait attributions (or personal dispositions) as causes for an actor's behavior should lessen as the observer comes to know an actor. However, Nisbett, Caputo, Legant, and Maracek (1973) asked subjects to rate whether a number of adjectives characterized more themselves or four different stimulus persons. They found support for the actor-observer hypothesis because their subjects used significantly less adjective traits to describe themselves than others. On the other hand, the four stimulus persons, who were varied in degree of acquaintanceship to the subjects, were all seen as possessing about the same number of personal traits regardless of the closeness of the relationship to the subject.

What this finding suggest is that it is not necessarily true that the closer we develop a relationship with another person, the more likely we are to ascribe situational causes for his behavior. Is this really the case? Shelley E. Taylor and Judith Hall Koivumaki (1976) carried out three studies to examine whether or not attributions for the causes of specific rather than global traits would be influenced by the degree of acquaintanceship with a stimulus person. The researchers employed both negative and positive behaviors and attempted to ascertain whether or not social desirability standards influence a persons causal attributions.

Taylor and Koivumaki found out that people are perceived to cause positive behaviors (e.g., paying a compliment, talking cheerfully, and having fun with other people), whereas situational factors were attributed as the causes for negative behaviors (e.g., having a heated argument , being rude, and forgetting to do something for another person). The latter finding was shown to operate for attributions made to intimate others (i.e., a spouse or a friend) and less so for strangers and liked and disliked acquaintances. Thus, Taylor and Koivumaki suggest that:

> The present studies found that people are generally regarded as causing good behaviors and that situational factors are generally regarded as causing bad behaviors (positivity effect). The addition of the valence factor all but eliminated the hypothesized actor-observer effect. The fact that this positivity effect increased with increasing degree of acquaintanceship suggests that in predicting how people perceive the behavior of others, motivational processes as well as cognitive ones must be taken into consideration. The implications of these data is that negative behaviors are easily dismissed as situationally produced, both for self and for others perhaps to avoid implications of fault or blame (1976, p. 407).

Since Taylor and Koivumaki (1976) found little support for Jones and Nisbett's (1972) actor-observer difference, an obvious area of concern now is with research testing this effect. And, since the evidence presented by Taylor and Koivumaki suggest that personal or dispositional attributions are made for positive behavior and situational attributions for negative behaviors by both the actor and observer let us now review some research which relates to this question and then suggest the relevance of such research for the study of deviant behavior.

MORE RESEARCH ON THE ACTOR-OBSERVER HYPOTHESIS

Birt L. Duncan (1976) has shown that differential social perceptions of intergroup violence can be accounted for through the application of Jones and Nisbett's (1972) actor-observer hypothesis. That is, Duncan expected that observers (white college students) of violent behavior would tend to attribute the violent behavior of the harmdoer to stable personal dispositions. In order to research this problem Duncan varied the race of the harmdoer (black-white) along with the race of the harmdoer's victim (black-white). Subjects viewed one of four videotape interactions, where a black person shoved a white, a white person shoved a black person, or where a black shoved a black, or a white shoved a white. Then, using scales, subjects were asked to assign blame to the harmdoer.

Results showed that when the harmdoer was black, the personal disposition "violent" was made, whereas when the harmdoer was white subjects viewed the act as situationally produced. Finally, Duncan asks: "How can this be explained," and he suggests that"

> ...the black man is imbued (stereotyped, categorized, etc.) with such salient personality properties (e.g., given to violence) that these traits tend to engulf the field rather than be confined to their position, the interpretation of which requires additional data about the situation. Dispositions then are treated as causal and are "packaged" (1976, p. 597).

In addition to Duncan's research (1976) some recent research has shown that people are likely to attribute a variety of negative characteristics or blame to rape victims (see Calhoun & Selby, 1976; Jones & Aronson, 1973; Selby, Calhoun & Brock, 1977). For example, in an attempt to extend Jones and Nisbett (1972) actor-observer hypothesis, James W. Selby, Lawrence G. Calhoun, and Thomas A. Brock (1977) predicted that female observers, who by virtue of being more similar to female rape victims than male perceivers, would in fact make more situational attributions for the cause of the victim's rape than would males. On the other hand, male perceivers, who are less similar to rape victims, were expected to view the same rape episode as the result of the female's personal characteristics.

In order to test these predictions, Selby et al. carried out two studies and found out that in both cases males did in fact perceive that rape is instigated by the victim's behavior immediately preceeding the rape and they felt that the rape was the fault of the victim more so than did the female subjects. In addition, Selby et al. report that males perceived that the victim's clothing and her general appearance contributed to her rape. The male subjects also assumed that the victim "unconsciously wanted to be raped." On the other hand, the female subjects concluded that the rape victim "had simply been at the wrong place at the wrong time."

Now what do these findings suggest for an actor-observer analysis of rape? Mainly that males tend to perceive a rape victim as playing a causal role in her own rape (a personal or dispostional attribution), whereas, females tend to view situational causes for rape. Of course, these findings are congruent with Jones and Nisbett's (1972) hypothesis. And, it seems that females perceive very different causes of rape not only because they are similar to rape victims, but also because "they may have a higher expectancy than males of someday having a similar experience" (1977, p. 415).

WATERGATE: OBSERVERS AND ACTORS' PERCEPTIONS

In order to test Jones and Nisbett's actor-observer effect, Stephen G. West, Steven P. Gunn, and Paul Chernicky (1975), carried out both laboratory and field research in an attempt to better understand crimes like the burglary of the Democratic party headquarters in the Watergate Hotel.

West et al. observed that the mass media (public observers) in general seemed to attribute the Watergate break-in to dispositional causes such as "Richard Nixon's paranoid view of those outside his administration" and the "amoral staff of workers on the

Committee to Re-elect the President." On the other hand, Nixon and members of his administration gave a very different version of the Watergate crimes. For example, the Watergate participates suggested that the break-in was their reaction to the plans of the radical left to take over the country, and that little or no alternative was available to them at the time but to re-elect President Nixon. And, of course, those involved in Watergate blamed the situation more than they did themselves.

West and his associates decided to create their own minature Watergate break-in (in a laboratory setting) as a way to test the actor-observer hypothesis. College students, from a southeastern university took part as subjects and they were asked by a local private investigator if they would like to take part in a project. The investigator suggested that the student could meet at his home or if the student wished at a local restaurant. An explanation of the project was to be given at the meeting. Fifty-six males and 24 females were asked and all of them made an appointment to meet with the private investigator.

During the meeting the investigator was accompanied by a confederate of the researchers who brought along a briefcase containing plans for carrying out a burglary at a local advertising agency. The experimental manipulation entailed giving subjects different reasons for the break-in. One group was told that the burglary was to be done for the Internal Revenue Service and it was being carried out for the purpose of microfilming illegal records as part of a front for a Miami investment firm, who was defrauding the IRS of over seven million dollars each year in federal and state taxes. Subjects were then told that the firm's records had to be microfilmed in order to obtain a warrant and subpoena to seize the firm's illegal records. Subjects were assured that the IRS would in fact guarantee them immunity from prosecution, if indeed they just happened to get caught.

A second group of subjects were given the same explanation except this time they were informed that the IRS could not offer them immunity from prosecution in the event they were found out. Subjects in a third condition were told that another local firm was willing to offer them $8000.00 for a copy of the first firm's records, and each subject was to be paid $2000.00 for his part in the crime. And, still a fourth group of subjects (control condition) were told that the break-in was planned merely to ascertain whether or not the burglary plans would in fact work. They were informed that although the break-in was illegal it would not require the subject to steal anything from the firm's office files.

In each case the subject was introduced to the confederate, who ostensively was to be the outside lookout on the would-be four-person burgulary team. And, the subject was given details of the break-in, which entailed aerial photos of the area of the crime, routes of the police, and a complete blueprint set of the "actual" site of the advertising firm. The subject's actual job was to serve as both an inside lookout and to microfilm the firm's records. Finally, each subject was asked to meet for a final planning of the burglary. If the subject did not agree to take part in the break-in, the experiment was concluded for the subject and she was told the "true purpose" of the experimenter's research. The major dependent variables entailed the subject's refusal or agreement to take part in the would-be break-in, and the reason given for the decision.

In still a second phase of the research 92 male and 146 female college students served as observer subjects. Each of the students was given a description of one of the above procedures used in the actor-subject conditions, and they were asked: "If 100 students were presented with this proposal, how many would you guess would agree to participate:" and "Would you do it?" Subjects were also asked to write their reactions to a student who either did or did not take part in the first part of the study.

Results of West *et al*.'s experiment tend to support the Jones and Nisbett's actor-observer hypothesis: actors attributed their own actions to situational or environmental factors, whereas observers attributed the actor's behavior to personal or dispositional characteristics of the actor. Hence, the observer subjects' attributions for the actor's agreement or refusal to take part in the burglary are consistent with Jones and Davis' (1965) correspondent inferences theory. This finding suggests that out-of-role or socially undersirable behavior (deviant behavior) is more likely to be attributed to a disposition of the actor than is socially desirable behavior. That is, people's attributions become increasingly more dispositional as they perceive that an actor's behavior is perceived to be out-of-role or negatively deviant.

One of the most intriguing implications for West et al.'s findings is, of course, how the attribution process can be used in understanding the Watergate crimes. Then, clearly attributional processes are at work when we attempt to answer questions about the perceived causes of complex behaviors. And, since most attempts to establish criteria for the accuracy of people's perceptions for the causes of deviant actions has been plagued by problems of measurement, an attributional analysis seems at least at the moment, to be a more productive way of viewing deviancy. Hence as you might guess, West et al.'s (1975) research suggests that when outside observers attempt to understand deviant behavior (especially society's official observers; the press), they are likely to give too much weight to dispositional explanations. In this regard, West et al. tell us that:

> ...observers seem to be relatively poor role players, so that in some cases, even attempting to put themselves in the role of the actor may not completely eliminate the attributional biases of the observer. Consequently, if an observer is to understand the causes of an actor's behavior, he should try to ascertain the precise situational pressures operating on the actor. In addition.....the observer should try to understand the past history of the events leading up to the action, the actor's emotional state, and the actor's intentions in choosing to pursue the particular course of action. To the extent that the observer can do these things, he should be able to increase his understanding of the causes of the actor's behavior (1975, p. 62).

Let us return now to an earlier question: "Can individual differences or personality variables account for the results obtained from West et al.'s research? For example, it could be argued that situations that create deviant behavior for one individual may in fact bring about nondeviant behavior for still another persons, and it is here that personality differences are likely to become important to the understanding of deviancy. On this note West et al. tell us that:

> While no personality measures were obtained on the subjects in the present experiment, based on the failures of personality measures to predict behavior in other situations in which strong situational pressures were placed on the subject,....it seems unlikely that personality variables would predict a significant portion of the variance in the present experimental situation (1975, p. 63).

Now, you might guess that an important question to ask about the above research is: "What really would have happened if indeed the authors would have employed personality variables in their research?" First, to this date attribution theory has not been concerned with personality factors: Only people's attributions for the perceived causality of deviant behavior has been researched from the attribution perspective (see Shaver, 1975).

It seems obvious that the attribution process is indeed complex. An appreciation of its complexity should require that we pose questions about the role that personality variables or attitude and belief factors might play in deviant behavior. As a matter of fact, Kelly G. Shaver (1977) tells us that enduring personal dispositions, such as authoritarianism, dogmatism, locus of control, and Machiavellianism are likely to produce "errors and distortions" in our perception of others and the causes of behavior.

Although the incidence of personality has not often been researched within the boundary conditions of social psychology, we will examine the role that personality variables play later on but for now let us point out that one of the most important conclusions gleamed from Webb _et al_.'s research is that we seem to explain the causes of deviant behaviors by first becoming "aware" of the deviant action and then by making either a situational or dispositional explanation for the cause of the behavior in question. Then, in a very real sense people attempt to explain public behavior on the basis of self and other attributions. And it is here that research lends support to the actor-observer hypothesis: Different attributions are made by actors and observers for the same deviant behavior. This observation is of concern for both students of deviant behavior and for questions of social policy. On this note Shaver suggests that:

...the sort of attribution chosen will to a large degree determine the solutions proposed. Personal attributions about the reasons for welfare lead to political speeches about "welfare chiselers," appeals for return to simpler days of the Protestant ethic, and laws designed to make needed financial assistance more difficult to obtain. Situational attributions, on the other hand, are likely to suggest that expanded government-supported employment, better job training, and increased educational opportunities for all will provide more lasting reductions in public assistance.

Unfortunately, especially for the people who happen to be in the problem groups, overemphasis on personal causes is as common with social problems as it is with other more individual behaviors. It is not simply that behavior engulfs the field, or even that personal attributions for social problems are more satisfying to the perceivers. Social conditions are less assessible to influence and more resistant to constructive change than are individual people. At the most elementary level, people are more easily identified than are conditions. If you violate a law, you are a criminal by definition; if you are physically dependent upon a drug, you are an addict; if your income is below an established level, you are officially poor. There are no problems of interpretation, no differences of opinion among experts to deal with, no necessity for determining relative weightings of possible causes. All that is necessary is knowledge of the defining characterteristic (1975, Pp. 133-134).

Then, the actor-observer hypothesis has proven useful in our understanding of how people come to explain other peoples' deviant behaviors. It has also provided us with a special insight into the actor's account of his own deviant actions. Then having attributed the cause of deviant behavior to either internal or external factors, the perceiver moves on to infer what kind of person the individual is who in point of fact has violated the social norms. And, of course, causal attributions can serve as a baseline from which people make attributions about their own or others' future behaviors. Once a person decides that an individual's deviant actions are caused by internal factors it then follows that deviant behavior will be more likely in the future whereas most situational explanations seem to imply that the deviant behavior is unlikely unless situational pressures operate.

Returning again to our earlier question: "Who is correct the actor or the observer?" That is, are situational or dispositional attributions more in line with the special causes for deviant behavior? In this context, Thomas C. Monson and Mark Snyder tell us that:

> Since actors are better informed about the temporal and situational organization of their own social behavior, they should more often make the "correct" situational attribution than observers who should more frequently "err" in making dispositional attributions.
>
> It is thus possible to derive the hypothesis of Jones and Nisbett (1972) from a consideration of differences in the ability of actors and observers to identify accurately the situational causes of the actor's behavior. Although we agree that actors are in a better position to generate accurate self-perceptions, we disagree that the correct answer is necessarily a situational attribution. Rather, we believe that attribution theorists themselves err when they regard dispositional attributions as incorrect attributions (1977, p. 95).

Monson and Snyder (1977) go on and tell us that research on the trait-situation issue seems to suggest that situational variables are "no better" than dispositional variables in accounting for behavior. These writers suggest that "this implies that although a situational attribution may sometimes be the 'right answer,' there are also many circumstances in which a dispositional attribution is correct" (p. 95).

Then, the research presented in this section leads one to speculate that the actor-observer hypothesis is in fact a misperception about the causes of deviant behavior. Hence, to the degree that one perceives another person's actions in a given situation as deviant from one's own actions, dispositional explanations are likely. On the other hand, situational factors, do doubt, are likely when little or no evidence can be found for dispositional determinants. In either case the question of who is correct the actor or the observer still remains to be answered by researchers.

ATTRIBUTIONS TO OTHERS FOR THE RESPONSIBLITY OR BLAME FOR THEIR DEVIANT ACTS

Thus far, the main concern here has been with perceptions for the causes of other people's deviant actions. And in spite of the importance of perceived causality in the attribution processes, people also make attributions for responsibility and blame. For example, if a person behaves in such a way as to cause injury or harm to others, will this person be held responsible? Of course, it depends on several factors not the least the person's intention to harm others.

Then, after one decides what causes produced what deviant behaviors one next is faced with the question of responsibility and blame. As a matter of fact the attributional process, as it operates in judicial matters, is mainly concerned with establishing legal responsibility for deviant criminal actions. However, there are indeed exceptions to the notion that people are always responsible for the effects that they cause (i.e., harm to others). Some defendent's are indeed judged legally insane or incompetent to stand trial, whereas they may still be held morally accountable for their behavior. This seems to be the case with several of the Watergate participants (see Shaver, 1975).

We should also note that whether or not we perceive that an actor <u>foresees</u> the consequences of her actions is related to whether or not she will be held responsible because her deviant behavior could have resulted from what Heider calls <u>environmental coercion</u>. That is, a person may not be held responsible even in cases where the action was intended due to the fact that strong coersive pressures were brought to bear. And, the outside observer is unlikely to explain this form of "deviant" behavior in terms of personal dispositions. As a matter of fact, Shaver (1975) tells us that <u>legal accountability</u> and <u>moral accountability</u> have two very different meanings when in point of fact one relates responsibility to the attribution process. And, of course, attributions of responsibility are influenced by dimensions of the person, the situation, and the person in the situation. For example, perceived intentionally produced deviant actions, as opposed to perceived unintentional or accidental behaviors, are more likely to be perceived as due to dispositions of the actor and hence in such cases more responsibility for the behavior is attributed to the actor. In addition, the more we assume that a deviant actor could have avoided the deviant behavior in the first place, the more we are likely to blame the actor. For example, a person who steals money from his employer when in fact the money could have been obtained from a bank loan is more likely to be held responsible for the criminal action than someone who has no other way to obtain money needed to feed his family.

DEFENSIVE ATTRIBUTION OR JUST WORLD?

Research interest in the topic of responsibility has derived from many sources most noteably research carried out by Elaine Walster (1966). She found that subjects held the owner of a parked car that rolled downhill more responsible for the damage when the outcome was serious than when it was not. And, she noted that people often make attributions of responsibility to protect themselves from the thought that a similar accident could in fact happen to them.

From Walster's research base it has been suggested that perceivers are likely to judge the results of a serious accident determined by internal dispositions or traits of the actor more so than less serious accidents. Subsequent research seemed to produce nonsupportive evidence for Walster's hypothesis (see Shaw & Skolnik, 1971; Walster, 1967), however Kelly G. Shaver (1970), tells us that people seem to avoid or reduce the threat that misfortune may befall them by attributing responsibility or blame to the actor only when they perceive the actor as dissimilar from themselves. In addition, Shaver (1970) notes that there must be a <u>situational possibility</u> or else the perceiver is unlikely to believe that she could in fact encounter a situation like the one faced by the victim. However, if the perceiver does in fact see himself as similar to the actor the negative outcome could be attributed to chance factors, for example, "being in the wrong place at the wrong time."

As a matter of fact, Chaikin and Darley (1973)

tested Shaver's (1970) <u>defensive attribution</u> theory, and found out that subjects did in fact tend to hold a victim of a severe accident more responsible than did subjects who were lead to believe that they themselves could in fact be victims.

We have, no doubt, heard many times that victims, who are harmed by the deviant actions of others actually "deserve their fate," for example, rape victims. In line with this logic Melvin J. Lerner (1966, 1970) has described what he labels a belief in a <u>just world</u>. That is, people seem to deny the possibility that negative things could in fact happen to them strickly on the basis of chance, and instead the person tends to believe that others' misfortunes or negative outcomes come about because they deserve them and hence caused their own negative outcomes either because of their personal characteristics, such as stupidity, or because they lack "just plain good judgment."

In order to test the just world hypothesis, Lerner and Simmons (1966) studied reactions to "innocent victims" by creating their own situation and by arranging so that their subjects viewed a victim (confederate of the experimenters) undergo electric shock ostensibly as part of a study of emotions. One group of subjects was told that the victim could not, even if he tried, avoid the electric shock; another group of subjects was told that they could intervene and hence prevent the victim from being shocked; and still another group was told that the victim had volunteered (martyr) to undergo additional shock for "the advancement of science." At this point all subjects were asked to rate the victim's attractiveness.

Results showed that the smallest degree of rejection of the victim took place when subjects were given the opportunity to stop the experiment, whereas the greatest rejection occurred where the victim took the role of a martyr. In other words, Lerner and Simmon's research shows that where there is nothing that can be done to help a victim, people derogate the victim.

Now what is likely to happen when you just happen to be the victim yourself? In this case Shaver asks:

> ...what happens if the innocent victim (who according to the just world should be devalued) happens to be <u>you</u>? Are you really likely to

assert that you deserved to suffer because of your bad moral character? It is more probable that under these circumstances you will defensively relinquish your belief in a just world, arguing that there are at least a few cases in which neqative outcomes are the result of bad luck. Whichever formulation eventually has the most explanatory value, the essential point remains: a perceiver's own self-protective motivation can sometimes distort his attributions of responsibility (1975, p. 110).

Then, what other limitations do you see for Lerner's hypothesis? First, Lerner's just world bypothesis suggests that after a harmdoer causes a victim to suffer he derogates the victim. In addition, Lerner clearly predicts that subjects will tend to derogate suffering victims in cases where someone else clearly harmed the victim. Meanwhile, Robert B. Cialdini and his associates (Cialdini, Kenrick, & Hoerig, 1976) claim that a belief in a just world may in fact be unnecessary to explain Lerner's findings. For example, they reasoned that subjects might just derogate a victim in an attempt to "justify their complicity in the victim's suffering" (p. 719). In other words subjects may "rationalize" their part in causing harm to others.

Cialdini et al. designed a study to test the likelihood that in point of fact victim derogation is unlikely to take place when the subject is clearly linked to the cause of the victim's suffereng or harm. The researchers predicted that in a typical or standard Lerner paradigm, where subjects are unambiguously told that they are not the cause of a victim's suffering, significant victim derogation should not take place. This prediction was confirmed. A second prediction---that there would be a significant derogation effect when subjects are given ambiguous or unclear information as to whether they were involved in the cause of the victim's suffering---was supported.

Apparently, Cialdini et al.'s findings suggest that "the mediator of the victim derogation phenomenon in the Lerner situation is not a tendency to behave in a just world but rather a tendency to justify one's complicity in the "harm-doing" (1976, p. 722). Then, could it just be that victim derogation is a form of dehumanization and that it results when one is confronted with the fact that one has caused harm to another person? In this case it is tempting to speculate that criminal deviancy, involving acts of harm inflicted on otherwise innocent victims, may be justified through derogation of the victim. And according to this reasoning criminal deviants are likely to derogate their victims and hence justify their crimes.

SELF-ATTRIBUTIONS: COMING TO FIND OUT THAT YOU'RE DEVIANT

So far we have focused primarily on how people come to attribute the causes for other people's deviant actions. Meanwhile the question of how the attribution process operates when one attempts to understand the reasons for one's own deviant feelings or behaviors still remains to be answered.

First we should note that Daryl J. Bem (1967, 1972) suggests that "individuals come to 'know' their own attitudes, emotions, and other internal states partially by inferring them from observations of their own overt behavior and/or the circumstances in which this behavior occurs" (1972, p. 2). In other words an actor comes to know her deviant feelings when she observes her own deviant behavior. For example, if one observes himself engaging in criminally deviant behavior one is likely to ask whether or not one does so by choice or because of social pressure to do so. And, if the individual just happens to observe himself behaving in an illegal manner, whenever the opportunity avails itself, it is highly likely that the person will infer that he has a positive attitude toward the enactment of criminal behavior. And, the person is likely to infer that his attitudes are in fact deviant. In other words what Bem is telling us is that, according to his self-perception theory, a person's deviant attitudes and beliefs follow from the observtaion of his deviant behaviors. What this suggests is that one comes to know one's own deviant attitudes by "inspecting" one's cognitions (beliefs) and affect (attitudes) in one's "consciousness," but by inferring them from one's own external behaviors. And, it is in this way that people are said to infer their own deviant attitudes much the same way that they infer other peoples' deviant attitudes: By examining the external cues which are available, and then by assigning what appears to be the appropriate causal attribution.

And Bem (as is the case with Kelley) not only is concerned with self-attributions, he suggests that the greater a person feels free to act, or the fewer restraints felt in behaving in a deviant way, the more likely the individual is to infer that his behavior reflects certain underlying deviant attitudes and beliefs. Then, according to Bem, self-observations do seem to have relevance for persons seeking to understand their own deviant behaviors especially where internal cues are ambiguous or just happen to be absent.

It has been observed that the labeling of one's physiological arousal is both the product of internal events and their accompaning environmental or situational cues (Schachter, 1964). And it seems clear that how a person labels his own arousal has important implications for his self-labeled deviant feelings. For example, Stanley Schachter and Jerome Singer (1962) did an experiment where they produced an arousal state in their subjects without providing any specific cues for the arousal. They did this by injecting subjects with epinephrine (a drug that produces arousal generally associated with emotions but not any particular emotion). Some of their subjects were informed that the drug would produce arousal while still others were not informed. In this way those who were informed could attribute their internal state to the drug and those not informed should be unable to do so. An additional group of subjects was not given epinephrine and as a consequence they were less aroused then the two other groups, who had been given the drug. Next, both aroused and unaroused subjects were placed in a situation where a confederate of the experimenters behaved euphorically or acted very angry.

Schachter and Singer found that subjects who did not expect the arousal, induced by the epinephrine injection, actually labeled their arousal state as either euphoria or anger depending, of course, on the cues provided by the behavior of the confederate.

What Schachter and Singer's findings indicates is that people tend to use cues in their immediate environment (external cues) to label their own internal state (arousal) when in fact the source of the arousal is ambiguous or unclear.

While the above discussion of emotional labeling

is provacative in its own right, perhaps research which bears more directly on the problem of self-labeled deviant feelings will be more informative. For this reason let us now turn to research suggesting that people do in fact under certain conditions label their arousal (or lack of arousal) as deviant. In this case Lykken (1957) suggests that one characteristic of the criminal sociopath is her relative deficit of anxiety. He indicates that this apparent lack of emotional arousal may in fact make it easier for the sociopath to engage in criminal activity. Meanwhile, Schachter and Latané (1964) have noted that "psychopaths" (and sociopaths) may in fact be much more sensitive to emotional arousing situations than their counterpart "normals" because they "have hibituated themselves to higher levels of arousal." Then, in order to test this prediction, Schachter and Latané (1964), injected criminal sociopaths with epinephrine (which arouses the sympathetic nervous system), and found out that subjects learned to avoid a mild level of electric shock quicker than those given a placebo, whereas, "normal" criminals did not show a significant change in arousal when injected with the drug.

What does this finding tell us about deviant behavior? Schachter and Latané note that criminal sociopaths do not have an inactive autonomic system, as a matter of fact they have an overactive sympathethic level and they have learned to label their arousal much the same way as Schachter and Singer's (1962) "informed subjects," whereas when sociopaths found out that they have been aroused without "good" reason they responded to the high arousal by showing anxiety and avoidance behaviors. On the other hand, "normal criminals" (i.e., those who experience anxiety associated with crime) learn to avoid pain even under placebo conditions. That is, normals learn to avoid pain even under placebo conditions. They have not had to learn to ignore their intense autonomic nervous systems reactions and hence they can attend to their arousal under most circumstances.

The research we have just described gives us some idea how differences in arousal relate to deviant behavior, but, is there perhaps some evidence which suggests that Schachter and Latané's (1964) results do not always hold? Thomas H. House and W.Lloyd Milligan (1976) tested these apparent conflicting views of arousal and responsivity in criminal psychopaths. They used young male subjects, obtained from a prison population, and divided the subjects according to their Pd scores (Psychopathic deviate scores on the Minnesota Multiphasic Personality Inventory) and on the basis of scores on the Welsh Anxiety Scale. Low and high scorers observed a person showing either mild or severe stress reactions to electric shock. Subjects' heart rate and skin conductance (measures of arousal) were obtained over a series of 15 trials.

House and Milligan found, as they had predicted, that low psychopathic deviates were significantly more aroused by the distress of the individual being shocked than were their high psychopathic-deviate counterparts. It was also found that high-anxious subjects were more responsive than low-anxious subjects, whereas the level of distress exhibited by the model did not have a significant effect on the subjects' level of arousal.

Then clearly, House and Milligan's findings do not support Schachter and Latané's (1964) paradoxical increase in arousal for psychopaths during mildly stressful stimulation. And, it now appears that Schachter and Latane's chronic-over-arousal-in-psychopaths hypothesis lacks support as evidenced by opposing research (e.g., House & Milligan, 1976).

MISATTRIBUTION AS SELF-LABELED DEVIANCY

In spite of research findings it does seem likely that anxiety (arousal) can in fact be generated by self-attributions or more particularly by what has been called misattribution of emotional arousal. For example, people no doubt experience adversive arousal when they are tempted to steal or cheat and consequently label their arousal as fear, or guilt or shame and, of course, it seems logical that such self-labeled arousal is likely to inhibit most persons from engaging in dishonest actions. In line with this reasoning, Dienstbier and Munter (1971) tested the hypothesis that people who are faced with a temptation to cheat are highly likely to show strong signs of autonomic arousal steming either from the fear of getting caught or being found out that they are indeed dishonest. Dienstbier and Munter reasoned that labeling of arousal in such cases could in fact deter some people from committing criminal acts.

The researchers gave their subjects a drug (actually a placebo) and told them that they were studying the effects of a vitamin supplement on vision. One group of subjects was led to believe that the side effects of the drug would arouse them (increased heart beat, hand tremor, warm or flushed face, sweating palms, etc.). In a control condition, subjects were led to expect a calm side effect. Then, as the subject waited for the drug to take its effect, she was administered a vocabulary test. The test was arranged so that all subjects would fail the test. Next, all subjects were permitted to check the correct answers to the test and then the experimenter left the room thus affording the subject an opportunity to cheat by changing her answers to the vocabulary test.

Dienstbier and Munter (1971) found that there was significantly more cheating when subjects believed that their arousal was a function of the drug they had taken (56.5 percent), whereas control subjects were less likely to cheat (17.4 percent). That is, control subjects labeled arousal as guilt, fear, or shame (internal attributions), and consequently they were less likely to cheat. On the other hand, subjects with an external label for their arousal (the drug) were less likely to attribute fear or guilt to themselves and as a result they were also less inhibited.

If we consider still another example of the self-labeling of internal states, then the marijuana smoker is a case in point. For example,,Howard Becker (1953) suggests that people have to learn what arousal state contitutes the "high" and in fact what is a pleasant and an unpleasant experience. In such cases, Becker tells us that marijuana effects are strongly influenced by the person's definition of the social situation in which marijuana is used. Those who just happen to be present are the source for one's cues and hence labeling of internal factors are associated with pot smoking.

As a matter of fact, Becker studied the reports of 50 marijuana smokers and he found out that the "typical" pot smoker has to learn the techniques for smoking pot. Next, the pot smoker learns to label her accompaning physiological symptoms as a "high." For example, Becker indicates that:

>...being high consists of two elements: the presence of symptoms caused by marijuana use and the recognition of the symptoms and their connection by the user with his use of the drug. It is not enough, that is, that the effects be present; they alone do not automatically provide the experience of being high. The user must be able to point them out to himself and consciously connect them with his having smoked marijuana before he can have this experience. Otherwise, regardless of the actual effects produced, he considers that the drug had no effect on him (1953, p. 20).

Becker's analysis of marijuana smoking suggests that the novice must learn to pay attention to and identify what is felt while smoking, must be taught to label a high, and the smoker must be taught that this arousal is indeed pleasant rather than unpleasant. That is, the marijuana-induced arousal takes its meaning and is labeled much the same way as any other cognitively determined label for emotional states.

The reader may question whether or not all people tend to label their internal states or indeed are there people who feel little or no pressure to label their emotions when observing their own behavior. Stuart Valins (1967) reports research showing that people who are unemotional (measured by scales) do not tend to label their internal states to the same degree as those who are emotional. Hence, some people seem to relie on their internal states more than do others and, no doubt, are more likely to label their feelings as deviant whenever their emotions and behavior are perceived as deviant or abnormal. Then, it seems that under certain conditions internal states serve as a way of evaluating deviant feelings and opinions and in still other conditions people are unlikely to label their feelings as deviant.

SELF-ATTRIBUTIONS FOR LONG STANDING DEVIANT BEHAVIORS

Since much of deviant behavior is long-standing perhaps we need to ask a fundamental question: "Is an individual more likely to attribute her recurrent deviant behavior to internal or external causes?" In other words, "Do people explain their long-standing and more serious deviant behaviors in terms of personal or situational causes?"

As a matter of fact H.H. Kelley (1967) does tell us that long-lasting or recurrent behavior tends to be attributed by the actor to internal or dispositional factors. In line with this reasoning, Calhoun, Peirce, and Dawes (1973) carried out a correlational study, where they studied a population of adult out-patients, who were obtained from a community mental health center. The male and female patients were interviewed and then they were given a five-item questionnaire and finally they were asked to rate their psychological problems on several six-point scales: for example, severity, uniqueness, duration, internal, and external cause.

Calhoun et al. found that the relationship between attributions to internal and external causes, and the scale responses of their subjects, were such that the more long-standing and severe problems were perceived by the patients as being more internally than externally caused.

Then, what are we to believe, or indeed understand, from the Calhoun's study? It seems as though people who observe that their deviancy is long-standing might just be more likely to resist change because they may assume that its cause is due to internal factors (e.g., psychological traits, heredity, early parent-child problem, etc.). On the other hand, those who observe that their deviancy is relatively short lived, or only very recent in its origin, should be more likely to change because its causes are inferred or assumed to be due to environmental or situational factors. Hence, the logic, "one can change the situation easier than the person," seems to hold.

NEGATIVE CONSEQUENCES OF MAKING ATTRIBUTIONS

On balance, it seems clear that there is ample evidence from attribution theory for the proposition that people are not dispassionate observers of their own and others' behavior. Hence, people do seem almost without exception to make attributions about the causes of behavior be it deviant or nondeviant. Interestingly enough, people's observations of their own behavior, no doubt, play an important role in determining their own behavior. And, as we have shown, just as we attribute causes for the behaviors of others, we also attribute internal or external causes for our own behaviors, sometimes with little or no accuracy in doing so. Then, suppose a dispositional attribution is not correct could there really be serious consequences for the individual? First, both labeling theory (following from sociological tradition) and attribution theory (having its origin in social psychology) attempt to show how the attributions (labels) people make influence the perceptions of those labeled, and in turn how the labeled person changes her self-perceptions. And, from the labeling perspective, it is further claimed that labels actually help create and sustain the attributes assigned to the individual. For example, Robert Rosenthal and Lemore Jacobson (1968) told elementary school teachers in California that they were in the process of doing research on intelligence testing. The teachers were given a list of students who supposedly had shown a great deal of potential success on a scale but who in point of fact had been selected at random. Then several months later they assessed the effects of teachers' expectations on the children's performance and on their intelligence tests scores. To do this, Rosenthal and Jacobson checked the childrens' IQ scores and grades in September and then again the following May.

Results of Rosenthal and Jacobson's findings at first seemed impressive; especially for first and second graders: Teachers who were led to believe that the children were "bloomers" gained in both grades and IQ scores significantly more than children labeled "nonbloomers." This happened even though teachers were not told to treat "bloomers" differently: All that was told the teachers was that they should expect children to "bloom by the end of the school year.

Rosenthal and Jacobson's research appears to have important implications for children especially when teachers hold negative beliefs about a child's ability based on how they label the child on the bases of test scores.

Before you hasten to conclude that Rosenthal and Jacobson's (1968) research can be generalized, it should be noted that this study does in fact suffer from some rather serious methodological problems. For example, a question may be raised about the use of repeated measures for the same IQ tests and the reliability coefficients obtained. That is, we might expect that under these conditions research findings may in fact be biased in the direction of producing greater change than really existed between the "bloomers" and the "nonbloomers." Hence, before we finally conclude that Rosenthal and Jacobson's "Pygmalion effect" operates in classroom settings we should say that not all attempts to replicate this effect has yielded similar findings as those obtained in the Rosenthal and Jacobson study. For example, a similar study has failed to yield a significant increase in students' IQ scores even after teachers were informed that a group of students would bloom, however, 61 percent of these teachers told the investigators that they had not expected that the children would bloom in spite of their "awareness" of the "bloomers" test scores (see Jose & Cody, 1971). On the other hand, classroom studies have confirmed and extended the "Pygmalion effect" (see Meichinbaum, Bowers, & Ross, 1969). And, as a matter of fact Burleight Seaver (1973) even found that a child's fate is determined not only by the teacher's perception of the child, but also by the teacher's information about a child's older brothers and sisters. That is, if a child just happened to have the same teacher as a brother or a sister, and the older sib did well, expectations for the younger child were that the child will also achieve, whereas if the older sib had performed at a low level, teachers' expected the younger child to do so.

By now you have probably guessed that the studies we have reported on the "Pygmalion effect" were not carefully controlled laboratory research and for this reason it might just be too difficult to assess the direction of causality. However, we do have indirect experimental evidence to support this effect. Jones and his associates (Jones, Rock, Shaver, Goethals, & Ward, 1968) had their subjects ostensibly observe a stimulus person perform a so-called test of intellectual ability which in fact was made to look like a college aptitude test that contained 30 items. In all conditions 15 of the 30 questions were answered correctly. In one of these conditions the stimulus person's correct answers took place in decending order (i.e., seven out of the first eight items were answered correctly). In a second condition the stimulus person answered the questions in ascending order from a poor start to an excellent finish. In still a third condition correct items were scattered ramdomly throughout the series.

Jones et al. found that their subjects predicted higher performance for the decending pattern and as a result they judged the stimulus person to be significantly more intelligent.

The Jones et al. study supports what is called a primacy effect and demonstrates its effect on peoples' judgments of others. That is, apparently an expectancy was established by the early success of the stimulus person. When subjects were asked to recall the number of correct items, they overestimated the number of correct items in the decending condition. Hence, just as Rosenthal and Jacobson (1968) found there is a decided advantage in being labeled an "early bloomer," Jones et al.'s study suggest that a child should avoid at all costs being labeled a "late bloomer." Hence, this would suggest that students who get off to a poor start at the beginning of a school year, may still be judged to be less intelligent than their counterparts who manage to acheive at the beginning of the school year.

Even more striking is a study reported by David L. Rosenhan (1973), who had eight "normal" persons admit themselves to psychiatric wards of different mental hospitals under peudonyms. These pseudo-patients told hospital staff that they had been hearing voices and admitted other obvious "psychotic symptoms." What Rosenhan wanted to see is whether or not the pseudopatients would be detected as "normals" instead of patients. In other words, he wanted to find out how the dispositional attribution (label) patient would influence the psychiatric staff's perceptions and reactions to the subjects.

Rosenhan's subjects were classified (labeled) schizophrenic by the hospital staff. Once the classification had taken place; they stopped hearing voices and resumed the role of the "normal person." They made copious notes of the reactions they observed from the hospital staff and patients. And, to their surprise the note taking itself was perceived by the staff as a schizophrenic symptom.

While the label schizophrenic was accepted by the psychiatric staff, fellow patients were not fooled. Actually some of the "real patients" detected the pseudopatients immediately and remarked: "you're checking up on the hospital" (p. 252), whereas the hospital staff never really detected the pseudopatients' masquerade.

Does this finding suggest that a certain number or percentage of "real patients" may in fact actually be pseudopatients after all? As a matter of fact, Rosenhan, at the conclusion of his study, did ask a psychiatric staff to "guess which of 193 patients admitted during a given time period were in fact "normals," and who among those admitted were passing?" In point of fact none of the pseudopatients were among this group, but the staff was unable to distinquish real patients from those assumed passing as patients. Rosenhan concludes that:

> A psychiatric label has a life and an influence of its own. Once the impression has been formed that the patient is schizophrenic, the expectation is that he will continue to be schizophrenic. When a sufficient amount of time has passed, during which the patient has done nothing bizarre, he is considered to be in remission and available for discharge. But the label endures beyond discharge, with the unconfirmed expectation that he will behave as a schizophrenic again (1973, p. 253).

Nothing that we have said about Rosenhan's study should be unfamiliar news to anyone reading Jones and Nisbett's (1972) actor-observer hypothesis. For example, the psychiatric staff's diagnosis tended to focus more on dispositional factors (e.g., schizophrenia), whereas the "real patients," who were closer to Rosenhan's pseudopatients, tended to attribute the pseudopatients' behavior more to situational factors (note taking as research). Thus, it is easy to guess the consequence; the patient's diagnosis tends to control and determine the hospital staff's interpretation of the patient's behavior.

Another striking observation has been made suggesting that patients are even skilled at <u>managing the impressions</u> they want hospital staff members to form of them (see Goffman, 1961). For example, in one of a series of studies, Benjamin Braginsky, Dorothea Braginsky, and Kenneth Ring (1969) have shown that long-term "mental" hospital patients found the hospital's hedonic accommodations and especially recreational aspects far more therapeutic than personal contacts with psychiatrists and psychologists. Hence, over 80 percent seem to know the location of the swimming pool, bowling alley, and gym, whereas only 26 percent knew the clinical psychologist or social worker on their ward.

Braginsky *et al*. brought long-term patients in for a personal interview and on the way to the interview the patient was informed of the ostensible purpose of the interview by a confederate of the experimenters. In one condition the patient was told that the purpose of the interview was to ascertain whether the patient should be placed on a closed or an open ward. Still other patients were told that its purpose was to check whether or not the patient was really ready for discharge.

Braginsky *et al*. expected that long-term patients did not really want to leave the hospital, however that they wanted to enjoy the freedom and hedonic aspects of the hospital. Hence, they predicted that these patients would present themselves as mentally ill when faced with the likelihood of discharge and as improved or well when confronted with the possibility of confinement to a closed ward.

Later on when the researchers played the taped interviews to three psychiatrists, without their knowledge of how the interviews were obtained, the psychiatrists diagnosed significantly more psychopathology among those patients told they were among those being considered for discharge than among those informed that they were being assessed for possible open or closed ward assignments.

This study demonstrates clearly that hospital patients do in fact seem to manage their impressions and that hospital staff tend to employ what patients do and tell them in order to make attributions (dispositional) relative to the patient's psychiatric status. Hence, far from being a passive victim of psychopathology, the mental hospital patient is likely to control her environment by telling the staff what they want them to know. Thus, it becomes increasingly evident that both patients and staff operate from clearly different perspectives: Psychiatrists, psychologists, and social workers, who deal with hospital patients, undoubtedly use their special training to diagnose patients, from what they observe their patients doing, whereas the patients, no doubt, have very different explanations for their own behavior. In short, then, the mental hospital setting is perhaps the clearest to demonstrate how dispositional attributions or labels determine peoples' outcomes. And finally we should go on to note that a fuller understanding of deviancy requires that we also consider criminal deviants incarcerated in our prisons, as another example of how attribution operates.

In Chapter three we noted that a prison staff is charged with the rssponsibility of managing its prisoners who, of course, have been involuntarily placed in their charge. And we noted that Craig Haney and his associates (Haney, Banks & Zimbardo, 1973) created a prison-like situation in order to study the guard-inmate relationship as well as to test what has come to be called the <u>dispositional</u> <u>hypothesis</u>. In the researchers' own words: "The deplorable condition of our penal system has a dehumanizing effect upon prisoners and guards due to the labeling of criminal behavior in terms of deviant traits" (p. 204).

Now, once again as the reader will recall a mock prison was created at Stanford University in which volunteer male students were randomly assigned to either a "guard" or a "prisoner" condition for a period of two weeks. The guards were not given specific details about how to treat the prisoners with the exception to keep order. Of course, what followed was a "chamber of horrors" causing some of the prisoners to "break down" and finally this forced the researchers to end the experiment after just a few days. That is, the prisoners experienced a loss of personal identity and the guards an increase in status and power and about a third of the guards did in fact show extreme forms of hostility; they dehumanized prisoners through their arbitrary control over them.

How do we account for the results of Haney <u>et al</u>'s mock prison study? Would the outside observer attribute the guards' behavior to stable dispositions or would he assume that the guard's behavior was due to the assigned role of guard and its situational role requirements? In this regard Haney <u>et al</u>. tell us that:

> Nevertheless, in less than a week their <u>behaviour</u> in this similated prison could be characterized

as pathological and anti-social. The negative anti-social reactions observed were not the product of an environment created by combining a collection of deviant personalities but rather, the result of an intrinsically pathological situation which should distort and rechannel the behaviour of essentially normal individuals. The abnormality here resided in the psychological nature of the situation and not in those who passed through it (1973, Pp. 81-82).

The results of this study, as well as other research, taken together, strongly suggest that in the prison environment, which establishes a guard-prisoner relationship, this situation does in fact bring about changes in the behavior of otherwise "normal" people. And, we are led to believe that explanations for this behavior are more in line with situational factors than dispositional factors. One wonders what would happen if indeed we were to ask "real" guards and "real" prisoners to explain their prison-related behaviors?

COMMUNITY-BASED ATTRIBUTIONS FOR DEVIANT BEHAVIOR

The analysis of deviant behavior thus far seems to provide us with clear evidence that attribution theory has far-reaching implications for the study of deviancy. Then, most people do seem to act like intuitive social scientists: they go about seeking the causes of deviant actions. And, we are told that the source of attributional bias seems to lie both in the actors and the observer's misperceptions. The presently reported research, however, also leads one to speculate that attributional differences may have their origin, at least to some degree, in the misconceptions that people hold for community-based deviant behavior. More particularily, it seems apparent that attributions can be distorted in consort by large numbers of people living in descriptive community settings when they react to "outsiders."

In line with this reasoning, Phillip Shaver, Robert Schurtman, and Thomas O. Blank (1975) have observed that in recent years false fire alarms have increased while at the same time actual structural fires have decreased, especially in our larger cities. Shaver and his associates trace this problem to the conflict between the urban poor and the predominantly white lower middle class who serve as fireman in ghettos. Hence, Shaver et al. tell us that:

> If fake alarms are a symptom of this conflict, it is doubtful that any of the commonly proposed solutions to the false alarm problem will work. These have included severe legal penalties; handcuff-and camera-equipped alarm boxes; invisible marking powder sprinkled on alarmbox handles; various kinds of noisemakers; and, most recently, voice-operated alarm systems....It is common for each such "solution" to be announced enthusiastically by city officials, only to have it quietly forgotten when the problem continues to increase in magnitude. It now seems quite likely that false alarms are a form of protest; if so, it is unlikely that they can be eliminated solely by technological means (1975, p. 242).

Shaver and his associates carried out two field studies in the greater New York City area. In the first study they found that for a random sample of fire alarm boxes, the number of false alarms was related to the number of vacant lots, schools, playgrounds, and abandoned buildings in the immediate area. In addition, false alarms were found to be related to "an open expressions of hostility toward firemen." On the other hand, false alarms were found to be negatively related to the residents' income level and to areas where greater surveillance such as busy streets and stores with windows overlooking fire alarm boxes.

Results of Shaver et al's second study showed that a large number of ghetto residents (i.e., the younger, non-white residents) tended to believe that firemen do "unnecessary damage, and that they are biased against nonwhites" (p. 259). And, here is the relevance of attribution theory: These young nonwhites tended to believe that the hostile actions against firemen were due to environmental factors, whereas whites and older nonwhites tended to blame false fire alarms on the perpetrators themselves (personal attribution).

Shaver and his associates suggest that their first study yields evidence in support of a nonwhite situational explanation were indeed the incidence of fake fire alarms is related to environmental factors. Hence, the observed expression of hostility between firemen and nonwhite (young) ghetto dwellers is viewed from a very different perspective. That is, it was observed that white firemen had often made negative racial comments about nonwhite ghetto residents, whereas the ghetto dwellers expressed their protest by harassing firemen.

Then, at the level of values, the difference seems to lie in where one places one's emphasis. Whether or not internal or external attributions are made for community-based deviant behavior we can gain an understanding for the ways people look at the source of their problems and, in doing so, people seem to act in accordance with their understanding of the causes of their problems. In this sense, Kelly G. Shaver asks a series of questions which bare on the relevance of attribution theory to community-based deviant behavior:

> Where does the responsiiility lie for the occurrence of crime? Is it the fault of individuals who commit single acts of criminal behavior? Or should some of the blame be shared by an economic and social system that induces high expectations in all of its people, regardless of their ability to obtain promised rewards through accepted channels? What about drug abuse? Are addicts personally responsible for their fate, or have the usually deplorable conditions of their daily lives led them to seek this sort of escape? When welfare rolls rise dramatically, is it because more and more individual people are refusing to work, or could it be that the advancing technology has less need for unskilled and marginal labor? (1975, p. 133).

ATTRIBUTION THEORY: UNIQUE OR JUST WARMEDOVER LABELING THEORY?

Now what about the claim made by labeling theory that deviance is "in the eye of the beholder or labeler?" Is it really so that deviant behavior can best be understood in terms of labels and/or causal attributions?

First, it seems quite clear that attribution theory (and labeling theory) relies on an explicit distinction made between dispositional and situational causes for deviant actions. Hence, deviant labeled behaviors, such as "criminal," "mental patient," or "homosexual," clearly have different meanings and consequences depending on whether dispositional or situational factors are inferred as the underlying causes. And we have observed that skepticism regarding the utility of personality traits as explanitory concepts for deviant actions has been raised (see Mischel, 1968). However, attribution theory (and labeling theory) does not attempt to deal with personality as the major cause of deviancy; only the perceptions of actors and observers. Hence, there is little or no attempt on the part of attribution theory to interpret trait concepts exclusively as labels or attributions. However, according to labeling theory, psychopathologies and the lesser forms of deviancy, are merely labels that psychologists and psychiatrists place on public behaviors that deviate from the social norms. However, labeling theory is more than that; the labels used to define (or describe) deviant actions are said to reflect the value judgments of the observers or labelers. And, there is a basic assumption made that the perception of deviancy is determined at least in part by the situation in which the action is observed (see Scheff, 1966).

Then, what we have alluded to as attribution theory in principle is very similar to <u>symbolic interactionism</u> and its by-product labeling theory. Now, this is why Hogan, DeSoto, and Solane (1977) suggest that attribution theory and labeling theory share some common characteristics. For example, both theories have attacked personality assessment for its stress on psychological traits as the major source of variance for deviant behavior. Hence, Hogan <u>et</u> <u>al</u>. indicate that:

> According to labeling theory, neurotic traits and psychotic symtoms are labels that mental health officials place on certain behaviors that deviate from societal norms. These labels reflect a priori value judgments on the part of the observers rather than aspects of the actor's personality (1977, p. 261).

Then, once again, "what seems to be the major differences between labeling and attribution theory perspectives? According to Kelly G. Shaver:

> Early interest in the relationship between self and other perceivers can be found in the sociological tradition that has come to be known as <u>symbolic interactionism</u> (beginning with Cooley,

1902). As compared to the psychological foundations of attribution theory, that focus on the individual perceiver, this more social view concentrates on interactions between two perceivers---self and other. Despite this difference in viewpoint, symbolic interactionism rests on many of the assumptions that also serve as support for attribution theory. For example, a basic presumption of symbolic interactionism is that people exist in a symbolic environment where even physical objects assume importance primarily because of their <u>social</u> meaning (1975, p. 77).

In other words, what Shaver is telling us is that the social interactionism perspective places its major stress on the social meaning of objects (including persons), found in the person's symbolic environment, which are said to take on either positive or negative value for the perceiver. And, symbolic communication takes place through <u>taking the role of the other person</u>. On the other hand, attribution theory focuses on how the individual perceiver assigns causes for behavior. Then, without questioning, for example, the proposition that deviant behavior needs to be predicted from the personal characteristics of deviant actors, symbolic interactionism suggests that deviant behavior is best understood by first examining the definition of the social interaction in which the behavior is observed.

Finally, social interactionism has been psychologically reinterpreted, and now in its simple and seemingly uncomplicated form it is known as <u>social comparison theory</u> (see Festinger, 1954). And according to social comparison theory, there exists a basic human drive to evaluate opinions and abilities. The way in which one finds evidence about the correctness or incorrectness of one's beliefs is said to vary with the physical evidence at hand. If one has a belief that the distance between Chicago and Detroit is about 280 miles, one can confirm or indeed disconfirm this belief by checking a road map, whereas if one holds a belief that abortion is morally wrong it then becomes such more difficult to evaluate this opinion. Hence, according to social comparison theory when we cannot use <u>physical reality</u> to evaluate our beliefs, we are forced to appeal to <u>social reality</u> or to evaluate our beliefs against the beliefs of others who are related to the issue at hand. And, in accord with symbolic interactionism, Festinger tells us that:

> Where the dependence upon physical reality is low, the dependence upon social reality is correspondingly high. An opinion, a belief, an attitude is "correct," "valid," and "proper" to the extent that it is anchored in a group of people with similar beliefs, opinions, and attitudes (1950, p. 272).

Now, we will return to our earlier point and suggest that labeling theory does not adequately provide us with the processes by which a norm violator becomes deviant. That is, an individual's behavior is said to get labeled deviant by those whose task it is to define and control deviant actions. Then, once the norm violator's role is labeled, whether it be "criminal," "mental patient," welfare recipient," or whatever, the role then is said to transform the person into what has been called "the initial entry into deviance." But contrary to labeling theory the process of role labeling does not always seem to work for all groups or all individuals. For example, Sampson notes that:

> Since the mid-1960s, we have seen an increasing number of instances in which populations of labelees have sought collectively to resist the implications of their label, by negotiating a new label, by rejecting the original label, by seeking self-determination of the entire labeling process. Women's groups, homosexual groups, radical groups, and especially ethnic groups have been actively involved in seeking to transform themselves and their collective identity by various political means, importantly including the whole role labeling and taking process (1976, p. 193).

Although these various observations help us to explain some of the discrepancies in labeling theory, it should also be realized that not every case of negative labeling or stigma eventually leads to an unfavorable evaluation. For example, Charles S. Carver and his associates (Carver, Glass, Snyder, & Katz, 1977) have demonstrated that the effect of the use of certain labels (black, physically handicapped) is to make the evaluation of those so labeled more favorable.

Carver et al., in a series of studies had their subjects evaluate a black, a Chicano, and a white stimulus person on the basis of bogus transcripts and interviews. The transcripts were arranged so as to make the stimulus person appear favorable (college student with an upper-middle class background, highly ambitions, varied interests, and many friends) or the stimulus person was protrayed unfavorably (a college student from a lower class background, with few friends, no particular interests, and no plans for the future). Finally, each subject rated one of the stimulus persons on a questionnaire used to obtain the dependent measure. It should also be noted that prior to the study, subjects were assessed on two measures (scales): prejudice against blacks and sympathy toward blacks.

Carver et al. found that the black stimulus person was rated more positively than the white, when in fact both were unfavorable portrayed (positivity effect). In addition, high prejudice-high-sympathy subjects rated the unfavorably-portrayed black more negatively than did low prejudice-high-sympathy subjects. And, no differences were found between the conditions for the white and Chicano stimulus persons.

What do these findings suggest? Since labeling theory tells us that negative labels are indeed causes of deviancy (identity), how is it that these labels for stigmatized others did not in fact lead to negative evaluations? The researchers suggest two very different reasons for their positivity effect:

> Subjects may have been attempting to behave in a socially desirable way....their normal reluctance to react negatively might have been exaggerated by their awareness of discrimination toward blacks, and a desire not to appear prejudice. The absence of the effect for Chicanos may reflect less salience of discrimination against Chicanos--thus less pressure to appear unbiased. Another interpretation derives from Kelley's (1971) "augmentation" principle of attribution, that observers credit actors for struggling against an environment that inhibits success. As the direct and indirect oppression of blacks has been publically recognized for some time, subjects may have given credit to the interviewees identified as black for having to contend with such obstacles. Constraints against

Chicanos may have been less apparent to our subjects, reducing the augmentation influence (1977, p. 234).

Then how about research which shows that telling people that they have certain attributes is likely to increase the likelihood that those characteristics will in fact emerge (see Rosenthal, 1966). It has long been believed, both by social psychologists and sociologists, that individuals engage in deviant behavior in order to fulfill label-based expectations that others seem to hold for them. For example, Kraut (1973) told some of his subjects, who had previously given to a charity, that they just happen to be charitable people, whereas others were not labeled charitable. Similarly, Kraut told subjects, who had just refused to contribute to the charity, that they were indeed uncharitable while he did not so label others. Then, at a later time he asked subjects to contribute to still another charity. Subjects who had contributed the first time were significantly more likely to do so the second time if in fact they were called charitable by the experimenter and not so if they were labeled uncharitable.

Still in another study Steele (1975) has shown that subjects who were called names by the researchers reacted to these negative labels with behavior inconsistent with the label. Housewives were called and berated for their seeming lack of concern in bettering their community. Later they were given the choice to help in a community project. Those negatively labeled complied more with the request than those who had not previously been derogated by the experimenter.

Clearly, then, research suggests that people do indeed reject negative labels. In this respect, Sharon B. Gurwitz and Bruce Topol (1978) suggests that an important difference exists between Kraut's and Steele's research in that in Kraut's study the label was directed toward the individual subject, whereas Steele directed the label to a person as a member of her community. This in effect made it much easier for Steele's subjects to reject the label as appropriate to them or personally.

In order to ascertain under what conditions people reject or accept negative labels, by confirming or disconfirming the label, Gurwitz and Topol (1978) carried out a field and a laboratory experiment where in the first case subjects were accused by the experimenter for not taking advantage of "cultural" opportunities in a nearby city. In a second study subjects were accused of having low self-regard. Some of the subjects were told that the negative label applied to other members of their group as well, whereas for other subjects the group identity factor was not mentioned.

The experimenter's reference to the group either increased or it decreased the subject's label-affirming behavior, of course, depending on whether or not the subject had been given evidence consistent with the negative label prior to the accusation. That is, when the investigator gave evidence, subjects tended to confirm the label more if the negative label was said to apply to many other group members than if it did not. And, where the researcher accused the subject without evidence subjects tended to disconfirm or reject the negative label more if the label was said to be characteristic of the subject's group than not.

The general conclusion to be drawn from the above research on labeling strongly suggests that negative labeling does not seem to have a uniform effect on the behavior of individuals as is suggested by the tradionally-oriented versions of labeling theory (.e.g., Becker, 1963; Schur, 1971). And additional research suggest that having labeled an individual as deviant tends to restrict the options open to the person. For example, Mark Snyder and William B. Swann (1978) noted that labeling theorist suggest that a person's negative perceptions of an actor can subsequently channel the actor's social interaction so as to <u>cause</u> the actor to provide "behavioral confirmation" of the perceiver's labels (and beliefs). However, labeling theorist have not offered research data to support this claim. Mainly for this reason, Snyder and Swann carried out an experiment where a male subject (the target) was introduced to two other male subjects (confederates of the experimenters playing the role of the "labeling perceiver" and the "naive perceiver") in a social context designed to allow the assessment of "open hostility." Just prior to this interaction, the "labeling perceiver" was told that the target was indeed either a hostile person (Hostile label condition) or a nonhostile individual (Nonhostile label condition). In addition, the target was told that either his actions were representative of a personal disposition (Dispositional attribution condition) or that the hostility was a reflection of the transitory influence of others (Situational attribution condition). Following this interaction, the target person interacted with a naive perceiver who, of course, had no prior informtion about the target.

Snyder and Swann found that those targets who interacted with the perceivers who expected hostile behavior showed greater hostility than did targets whose perceivers anticipated nonhostile partners. And, subsequently only when the target thought that his hostile behavior was caused by personal dispositions did this behavior persevere into the later interaction with the naive perceivers.

The research of Synder and Swann (1978) seems consistent with labeling theory which suggest that labelers may indeed initiate a chain of events that culminate in the labeled person's conformation of the labeler's beliefs. Hence, as a consequence of being negatively labeled, Snyder and Swann's subjects soon began to behave in a hostile manner. Clearly, then, as labeling theory suggests, people seem to behave in accord with the deviant labels with which they have been "tagged." Then true to the labels of the "prophets," individuals seem to go out of their way to prove them right. However, proponents of labeling theory have not given particular attention to the conditions under which negative and positive labeling occurs. That is, instead of investigating the conditions whereby the labeler comes to "tag" an individual as a "thief,"a "homosexual," or a "mental patient," labeling theorists focus on the consequences of labeling and leave the labeling process itself open to speculation. Hence, the question under what circumstances will the individual be labeled as deviant and under what conditions nondeviant is left an open question. Research carried out by the social psychologists Gurwitz and Topol (1978) and Synder and Swann (1978) go a long way toward our understanding of the labeling process. Of course, more research is needed to fully understand the process of labeling.

From our discussion one might just be tempted to conclude that both labeling theory and attribution theory do in fact make very similar predictions about how the actor and the observer formulate their explannations for the cause of deviancy. The basic question here is whether or not people really mean what they say or are they merely trying to mislead us or in fact deceive us and as a result we pay more attention to what they do rather than to what they say and we make causal attributions? In this case symbolic interactionism suggests that the misconception lies in the situation or social interaction, whereas attribution theory would have it that both the actor and the observer (in a social interaction) have special biases when they attempt to account for deviancy. For example, the actor-observer difference theory (from attribution theory), on closer inspection turns out to make very different predictions than labeling theory. That is, the individual who in labeling theory gets labeled as time goes by either more or less accepts or rejects the label, whereas in the framework of attribution theory the actor and the observer both are said to become motivated to search for the causes of the deviant action. However, the actor in attribution theory is likely to end up attributing the causes for her deviant behavior more to situations (not labels), whereas the observer is likely to conclude that the actor's deviant behavior had its origin in relatively enduring personal factors of the actor. On the other hand, labeling theory places the locus of the labeling process in the observer (or labeler) and goes on to suggest that in time both the person labeled and the labeler are likely to accept the label as a reflection of social reality. And, by contrast, attribution theory tells us that there are bias or distortions which lead to errors in the attribution processes. This is why attribution theory notes that actors and observers are said to systematically vary possible causes for deviant behavior in order to formulate the particular perceived cause(s) that covaries with the observed deviant action or the effect. And in this way attribution theory is based on the premise that people operate like social scientists (Kelley's theory) or information processors (Jones and Davis' theory) when they go out searching for an understanding of human behavior.

Since not all behavior (deviant or nondeviant) is predictable, errors are said to take place in peoples' perceptions of the causes of behavior. And attribution theory suggests how these attributional errors are likely to operate, whereas labeling theory starts with the label per se and traces the label as the cause of deviant behavior, attitudes, beliefs, and identity.

The causes for deviant behavior, according to attribution theory, are always treated as inferences made from the effects (deviant behavior), whereas labeling theory finds the causes for deviancy to lie in those who formulate and employ labels for norm-violating behaviors. And, finally both attribution theory and labeling theory do not tell us that personality attributes from childhood persist into adulthood and cause deviancy.

Thus far our discussion has centered on the role of person and interpersonal perception as the basis for understanding deviancy. As the reader has no doubt asked herself: "Can personality or individual difference variables serve as important determinants for a more general understanding and prediction of deviant behavior?" Then, after our summary of the present chapter, we will next examine the role of some personality constructs used as explanitory concepts for deviant behavior.

SUMMARY AND CONCLUSIONS

Unlike theories of deviant behavior formulated around so-called actual causes of behavior, attribution theory focuses not on the real causes per se of behavior but instead on how people come to perceive the causes of deviant behavior; both one's own and others' behavior. And the cause to which an individual attributes behavior, then, has important consequences for the deviant actor. For example, if a person attributes his obesity to negative personality characteristics or genetics, he is unlikely to go on a diet in order to loose weight. On the other hand if the person attributes her obesity to being with friends and relatives who just happen to overeat, she may attempt to avoid others who overeat in order to loose weight.

Then, attribution theories are different than trait theories because they employ the language of the everyday perceiver in explaining behavior, not necessarily the concepts that are part of the personologists technical or scientific vocabulary. There is also a heavy weighting placed on the role of cognition because people are said to have a "need" to explain and predict human events.

Jones and Davis (1965) describe the attribution process as an act-intention analysis. That is, the act or behavior and its effects are first observed and then the observer infers the actor's intention. For example, the perceiver who observes that a youth has taken a gun out of his pocket and has approached an elderly man is likely to conclude that the youth intends to rob the "old man." Finally the inference of intention results in the perceiver's attributing personal dispositions to the youth such as "he's a criminal; a psychopath." It is in this way that the observer proceeds from the deviant act to an intentional inference and finally, if intention is inferred, to a dispositional explanation of the deviant act.

Jones and Davis' theory of correspondent inferences suggests that when a person attributes a disposition to another individual, the dispositional explanation may or may not correspond to the actor's actual behavior. And further, the degree of correspondence between the behavior or act and the perceiver's causal attribution for the act is said to be influenced by the social desirability of the act. Highly correspondent attributions are more likely to be made for "out of role" behavior or behaviors that deviate from the social norms. Out of role behaviors are likely to be taken by observers to be socially undesirable because they are infrequent or in Kelley's terms low in consensus. In addition to out of role behaviors, the observer is said to consider the noncommon effects associated with an act. For example, suppose that a person has the choice of being released from prison or not and chooses to remain in prison. This choice is highly likely to lead to certain dispositions being made to the actor because it is unlikely that most people would refuse to leave prison. And still another variable, related to Jones and Davis' theory, is the personal involvement of the observer or whether or not the actor's behaviors are rewarding or indeed punishing to the observer.

Jones and Davis' theory of correspondent inferences has important implications for deviant behavior, however, one of its major shortcomings is its stress on causal attributions of other peoples' deviant actions and the relative neglect of self-attributions. It is for this reason that we considered Kelley's (1967) attribution theory, which extends Jones and Davis' (1965) analysis to account for self-attributions.

Kelley's major assumption is that peoples' causal attributions are the joint function of the perceived multiple causes for a given effect or act. The attributional processes involves selecting out from many possible causes the one or ones that best seems to explain the behavior. It is in this way that Kelley suggests that the attribution process applies to the observed actions of others as well as oneself.

In attempting to explain behavior, an attributor is said to use three kinds of information: <u>Distinctive</u>, <u>consensus</u>, and <u>consistency</u>. Hence, a college student may attempt to explain his cheating on exams by first examining the possiblity that he has cheated on different exams and concludes that he has. And, it appears that there is no <u>distinctive</u> stimulus responsible for his behavior. He then notes that other students on more than occasion cheat and our perceiver than concludes there is <u>consensus</u> for his cheating behavior. His self-attributions are not likely to be personal since others also cheat on exams. The student then considers whether of not his behavior is consistent and concludes that there is either consistency in his cheating behavior across situations or not. The student may conclude that he does not cheat on other exams, and if this is the case he concludes that his "dishonest" behavior is due to situational factors: Cheating is viewed as part of the college norm.

Kelley discusses the process of misattribution, and it should be noted that he was influenced by Jones and Nisbett's hypothesis that there exists a discrepancy between actors and observers where actors are said to attribute their own behavior to environmental causes and observers of the <u>same</u> behavior are said to attribute the behavior to internal causes such as personality traits or dispositons. Jones and Nisbett explain this discrepancy by noting that an actor is immersed in the situation and hence is more likely to use external causes.

In this chapter we have attempted to show how attribution theory has merit for understanding deviant behavior. And we have observed that attribution theory is a rational process where the cause for deviant behavior is "in the eye of the attributor" and there is little concern with postulating <u>actual</u> causes for deviant actions.

Finally, attribution theory, in general, has advantages and disadvantages. The constructs of causal attribution seem methodologically sound and have been operationally defined and researched in the laboratory setting. The disadvantages of attribution theory seem less obvious than its advantages. For example, do one's cognitions or attributions get translated into behavior, and if so, how? In particular, does an attributional analysis of deviant behavior necessarily explain deviant behavior? Making attributions about the cause of one's actions (or other peoples' actions) did not give rise to the action in the first place. Hence, people seem to act without first cognizing about the causes of their behavior. It is in this sense that attribution theory must finally recognize noncognitive sources of action (i.e., motivational factors). Nevertheless, attribution theory does indeed provide an interesting alternative to explaining deviant behavior over and above the more psychodynamic or behavioral models for divancy.

CHAPTER 6: PERSONALITY: THE SEARCH FOR THE DEVIANT INDIVIDUAL

DEVIANCE AND PERSONALITY: SOME PROBLEMS OF DEFINITION

Does deviant behavior have anything to do with personality? Before proceeding on to evaluate this question it seems necessary to first note that two sources of variation in personality have been considered by researchers: <u>Between-person variation and within-person variation.</u> For example, if we observe that a large number of people in the <u>same</u> situation behave differently this illustrates what is called between-person variation and what is of concern here is how people differ when situations are held relatively constant over time. On the other hand, if we should observe the <u>same</u> people in a number of different situations and find that their behavior varies from situation to situation the major concern in this case is within-person variation. And both sources of variation are important when we attempt to understand how personality factors are related to deviancy.

Even from this short glance at the two sources of variance it becomes rather clear that personality can have a very different meaning depending on where researchers place their emphasis. And, while recognizing that the sources of deviant behavior are far from simple one can make a case for the importance of ordering characteristics of individuals and then note how these personality characteristics influence how people react to different situations. And the central frame of reference taken for the study of between-person variation in deviant behavior suggest, for example, that people differ in their reactions to specific situational pressures due in part to personality differences among them such as self-esteem, dogmatism, need for social approval and the like.

An alternative approach, which focuses on within-person variation, requires that the researcher vary situations and hold personality characteristics constant in order to ascertain what effects situational pressures have on deviant behavior. Both approaches to the understanding of deviancy have been used. When consistency in deviant behavior is found researchers often suggest that there is a general tendency for people to behave in given ways in a wide variety of situations. Here personality appears to be the more important source of variance for deviant behavior.

In short, we will examine between-person variance and then attempt to make a case for personality characteristics as an important source (or cause) of deviant behavior. Here we rely primarily on distinguishable characteristics measured by personality scales. There is nothing implied here that the characteristics in question are changeable over time only that they can be measured.

To specify what is involved in the study of personality as a cause of deviancy is more complex than might at first be imagined: All people, of course, do not seem to react in the same way in similar circumstances. In Chapter 5 we considered in great detail the question of how people come to perceive the causes of deviant behavior without considering the problem of real or actual causes. We suggested that there is a sharp contrast between attribution theory and a personality-trait approach to deviancy. That is, a personality-trait view asserts that deviant behavior is best understood by identifying attributes of deviant individuals which seem to reflect underlying trait organization. The major stress is placed on relatively enduring behaviors and it is assumed that the deviant differs from nondeviant others. On the other hand, Jones (1976) argues from an attributional perspective and tells us that people (including trait theorists) are likely to misperceive the behavior required by social roles as an index of an actor's personality. That is, people are said to view the expected behaviors of others as cues to what they are really like. And, according to Jones, people apparently perceive the role-expected behaviors of others as indications of their "underlying" personality.

Then, in saying that the major source of the cause of deviancy is attributed to personality, we are in fact saying that when we attempt to explain deviant behavior we are likely to conclude that a major cause of deviancy is somewhere inside the deviant actor. That is, the cause of deviancy is said to have its origin in the personality characteristics of the individual and that these factors are direct or indirect causes of deviant behavior. And as a matter of fact anyone reading the literature on criminal behavior, drug-related deviancy, or "mental illness" soon discovers that researchers, who have been at the business of looking for relationships between psychogenic factors and deviancy, report that personality factors are in part determinants of deviant behavior. For example, trait views of deviancy attempt to explain extreme forms of deviancy (e.g, the behavior of criminals and psychotics) as characterized by distinguishable forms of behaviors from those of so-called normal behavior, traits, attitudes and beliefs (see Szasz, 1970).

Although traits are not generally viewed as direct causes of deviant behavior, they are in fact considered dispositions that indirectly determine behavior. And as a matter of fact it does seem logical that personality factors play an important role in determining deviant behavior. Also, it does seem quite obvious that one can easily recognize that many deviant individuals are markedly different from their counterparts who are not labeled deviant. Hence, people who deviate and subsequently become labeled as deviants seem to be characterized by a set of autonomous traits, attitudes, beliefs, and behaviors which are likely to be perceived by the observer as having their origin in the deviant actor's early life or personality makeup. And we should recognize that there does seem to be an advantage in postulating personality as an explanation for deviancy because personality factors are said to preceed deviant behavior. We should also emphasize that to claim that personality determines deviant behavior is in effect to force social psychologists interested in deviancy to examine what in fact is the relationship between personality and deviant behavior. And, unquestionably, any attempt to understand and predict deviancy must not overlook the fact that deviant behavior is likely to have multiple causes. Then, the serious student of deviant behavior should be alert to recognize that personality is indeed a real potential source of variance for deviancy.

Once again, why study personality factors within the boundary conditions we have set for the social psychology of deviant behavior? Most apparent is the observation that personality variables, at first blush, seem to contribute to deviant behavior. For example, personality factors are likely to be a potential source of predictive power for researchers who attempt to account for the seemingly great difference in behavior for persons classified in any one type of deviancy. Hence, personality variables are likely to turn out to be important covariates for deviancy; and could in fact account for a large portion of the error term for experimental findings. And, of course, it will be remembered that most of the research reported in previous chapters varied only non-personality variables. Then when there is a consistent trade off of personality variables for situational determinants, as seems to be the case in most social psychological research, researchers could in fact over look the possibility that a deviant action for one person could in fact be a reaction to situational pressures and still for another individual personality variables may in fact be the more important determinant of the deviant actor's behavior.

As a matter of fact David Marlowe and Kenneth J. Gergen tell us that the concept personality can indeed relate to or bridge internal (dispositional) factors with environmental factors in at least three very different ways:

> First one's personality development can be viewed as a product of the social behaviors of others; second, one's perception of the personality of others may effect the way he behaves toward those others; and third an individual's own personality may influence the way he perceives others (1970, p. 5).

Although these three views of personality all seem to suggest different roles that personality might play in the development of deviant behavior, there is good reason to suspect that there is more to personality as a cause of deviant behavior than first meets the eye. For example, when one claims that personality is the product of social learning this in turn implies that some degree of relative continuity exists in the individual's environment and suggests that there is relative stability and consistency in the person's behavior over time. And, of course, without some degree of stability and consistency over time we could not identify personality as a cause of behavior, nor in fact could we regard personality as an important determiner of deviant behavior.

Then the *sine qua non* of personality as a determiner of behavior requires that we examine the impact that personality has on deviant behavior as one of the many sources of causation. But when we evaluate personality as a cause of deviancy this is by no means a simple matter. That is, one's perception of others' behavior is a joint product of the person, the observer, and the situation giving rise to the behavior observed. So then perceptual processes seem to contribute to personality and in turn relate to the way one views their own and others' behavior. For example, once an individual has been labeled deviant selective perception intrudes and the observer is less likely to pay attention to nondeviant behaviors. Research on impression formation tends to bear out this observation. For example, research on how people form impressions of others shows the powerful effect of the order of information. For example, Solomon Asch (1952) illustrates how some attributes (trait adjectives) can be used to describe a person, and in fact lead to an entirely different impression depending, of course, upon the order of the information given about the person.

Then, in perceiving others, individuals seems to employ their own "implicit theory of personality," without, of course, realizing it, and they sometimes perceive others in ways more or less consistent with their perceptions of others. And in perceiving others, one's perception of others' intentions is an important factor. For example, one is likely to attribute deviant motives to a disliked person and benevolent motives to a liked individual. It is for this reason that some of the basic principles derived from the perception of nonsocial objects seems also to apply to the perception of persons.

Since studies of impression formation conclude that unfavorable information is given more weight than favorable, negative information is generally viewed as more informative. Why is this so? David E. Kanouse and L. Reid Hanson (1972) tell us that negative characteristics are more likely to be used to rule out positive ones than positive ones are to rule out negative ones for the perceiver. For example, an individual may be known as honest, however it is unlikely that you would trust this very same individual if indeed you also suspect that the person has embezzled money from a friend of yours.

Now, that we have observed that people weight different kinds of information about a person and integrate it from an overall impression of others we can see how perception enters into the process of personality because these factors also influence the attention people pay to perceptual cues.

TRAITS AND THEIR RELATIONSHIP TO BEHAVIOR

This, then, is clearly not the place to dispute whether personality variables are in point of fact the most or least important source of variance for deviant behavior. That is, it does not seem necessary for our purpose to defend unequivocally the view that between-person variation is the major source of deviancy. Rather than question the more general role of personality as a determiner of deviancy we will instead examine a few select personality variables in order to ascertain their relationship to deviancy.

Then, let us begin again and this time note that people attempt to account for their own and others' feelings or attitudes or personality in terms of the behavior they observe (see Bem, 1972). For example, when one becomes angry when provoked and does not harm the person who provoked him, and still another person who is provoked does in fact harm the individual who provoked her there is a clear difference in the behavior of these persons which might suggest that personality factors are important. However, although, no doubt, some individuals seem to have well-articulated verbal or self-report descriptions of their personality which seem to match their deviant behaviors while still other person's verbal descriptions or self-reports are in fact unrelated to their non-verbal behaviors. Then how do we account for this apparent discrepancy? We noted in Chapter 5 that attribution theory accounts for dispositional or personality consistency on the basis of behavioral consistency. And the attribution of consistency seems to apply more to others than to ourselves. For example, the reader will recall that Jones and Nisbett (1972) tell us that when we attempt to explain other people's behavior we tend to use dispositional factors assumed to have relative consistency: Joe is a neurotic who worries over trival matters; Mary is a clumsy individual who keeps hitting her toes on the edge of the table.

When we describe others (those we know the least) we seem to act like personality trait theorists, whereas when we attempt to explain our own actions we are said to act more like sociologists or social psychologists and to infer that our actions are due for the most part to the situation we just happen to be in at the time: Joe has a psychology test and is worried about his grade; Mary keeps hitting her toes on the edge of the table because the table legs are extended out too far. That is, some persons tend to view their behavior and attitudes or their personality dispositions as unrelated and according to Jones and Nisbett (1972) they tend to explain their behavior as if it were mostly determined by situational pressures rather than as a consequence of personal dispositions. Hence, personality characteristics in this case seem to be unimportant.

Then, as is the case with most behavior, research on deviant behavior seeks to establish a relationship between personality and deviant behavior. And an important question we should now ask is: "Are dispositional factors more important determiners of deviant behavior for some people than for others?" Although we don't have a direct answer to this question, Daryle Bem and Vernon L. Allen (1974), in attempting to answer this question, suggest that some people may in fact be consistent in at least some of their behavior and attitudes some of the time. This view, of course, is in marked contrast to the view which assumes that most traits characterize most people most of the time. That is, Bem and Allen tell us that some people indeed may be consistent on certain traits, however, they also note that nobody seems to be consistent on all traits all of the time. This suggests that students of deviant behavior should look for those people who show a relative consistency in their self-reported traits and their deviant behaviors. As a matter of fact, Bem and Allen (1974) did just that; they identified people who they thought would be consistent and those inconsistent on the traits of <u>friendliness</u> and <u>conscientionness</u>. They predicted that those who in fact identify themselves as consistent on a particular trait will in fact be more consistent in their behavior cross-situationally than persons who identify themselves as varient on the same trait. And, Bem and Allen did in fact find that those who identified themselves as consistent in level of friendliness showed a high level of consistency in friendliness across various measures (situations). Those who identified themselves as variable in friendliness tended to be variable in friendliness relative to the <u>same</u> situations.

What does Bem and Allen's (1974) research suggest for the study of deviant behavior? Some persons possessing deviant personality characteristics or attitudes may indeed show a high consistency between their perceived deviant personality traits (or attitudes) and their deviant behavior, whereas still other individuals possessing similar deviant personality traits may indeed be highly divergent in their behavior and perceived traits and in point of fact they may seldom display deviant behavior.

Then, it seems only logical that an important level of analysis requires that researchers classify not only persons as trait-consistent and trait-inconsistent but to also classify situations. Just such an attempt has been made to do this by Magnusson and Ekehammer (1973) and Rudoff H. Moos (1973, 1974). Their research has focused on individuals' perceptions of situations and peoples' similarity in classifying situations is taken as the basis for trait-like descriptions of situations such as "active," "passive," "negative," and "positive." For example, ratings of psychiatric wards and prisons have been classified in terms of decision-making and social support for its members (see Moos, 1974).

Thus, it is in terms of the classification of situations that social psychologists seem to have defined a central problem of deviancy: Situational factors are assumed to either facilitate or inhibit deviant behavior. And the stress on situational factors no doubt made it difficult for researchers to study only internal sources (e.g., personality factors) as causes of deviant behavior.

Then, deviancy implies relative continuity and in fact is build upon attributes of the individual which appear to have stability and consistency every time. When one notes that a person is deviant, for example, one does not generally attribute a deviant trait to the individual on the basis of a single observation but on the basis of several observations. And research does indeed show that people differ in the extent to which their behavior is relatively stable or relatively variable across a wide variety of situations (Bem & Allen, 1974). And, as we have indicated, it does appear that people whose deviant behavior is relatively invariant or stable across different situations also seem to possess certain personality traits, whereas individuals whose deviant behavior covaries with different social settings seem not to be driven to deviancy on the basis of personality traits

Why don't social psychologists generally take into account individual difference variables and more particularly why don't they do more research on person parameters in their attempts to account for deviant behavior? Paul F. Secord tells us that:

> It isn't that social psychologists never take person parameters into account. Sometimes we do, and often we don't. And we certainly do not regularly and systematically deal with them. It is easier to throw them into the error term by randomly assigning participants to treatments (1977, p. 45).

Secord's caveat seems clear: Individual difference variables (e.g., personality characteristics) may in fact interact with the researcher's treatment conditions or dependent variables, when subjects are randomly assigned to treatment conditions without taking into account these variables, and get in the way when the researcher attempts to generalize about social behavior. In other words Secord asks researchers to go beyond the main effects of a single dispositional variable (e.g., personality or attitude) and examine the interaction effects where two or more situational variables produce different affects on individuals with different personality characteristics. For example, it might turn out that highly Machiavellian individuals are more manipulative than those lower in Machiavellianism and only when they confront persons with low self-confidence and not high self-confidence.

Then, in most general sense the issue of transituational or cross-situational stability of personality traits is logically related to the question of whether or not specific traits reflect deviant behavior. Because, if indeed deviant behavior is determined by a given number of interacting variables, then to overlook personality as a possible determinant could indeed restrict the kinds of predictions and generalizations made for deviant behavior. In this regard, as we have observed, social psychologists have tradiionally attempted to establish the more general laws of social influence and they have seemingly shown little or no interest in person variables.

Then, in light of what we have observed, how are we to predict human behavior in general and deviant behavior in particular? In answering this question Henry A. Alker and David W. Owen (1977) give us a clue when they tell us that we should combine different assessment methods in order to predict performance on dependent measures: <u>trait-measures</u> or self-reports taking the form of questionnaires; <u>behavioral-sampling</u> or self-reports dealing with how individuals think they would behave in situations or in fact individuals' actual behaviors in a wide variety of situations; and <u>biographical variables</u> including demographic data collected over extensive periods of time.

Alker and Owen hypothesized and found that each of the above three assessment methods in fact best predict other similar categories of measurement. For example, traits best predict other traits, situationally defined behaviors best predict other situationally defined behaviors, and biographical data best predict changes in biographical status of subjects. And when all three methods are combined, they yield significantly higher portions of the variance then any of these approaches taken separately when applied to data collected in natural settings (e.g.. officers and enlisted men in the US Army Infantry School, Fort Benning, Georgia).

Given the results of Alker and Owen's research, the conclusion could be made that social psychologists, interested in deviant behavior, who seek relationships between single personality characteristics (e.g., authoritarianism) and deviancy and those that seek relationships for several characteristics and deviant behavior, no doubt, will find very different answers. For example, Marlowe and Gergen (1968, 1970) suggest that personality characteristics are likely to operate interactively not independently of each other in producing social behavior. That is, an attitude or trait may show significant effects upon certain behaviors and not others and in conjuction with other personality traits and not others. And, of course, most of the variance for an obtained relationship between personality and situational variables may in fact turn out to be due to interactions of these two sets of variables. And for our concern deviant behavior may be influenced by personality and in turn deviant behavior may inlfuence the personality of the deviant actor. Then, the question of why some individuals are more likely to violate the social norms and others not could turn out to be due (at least in part) to personality variables.

DEVIANT BEHAVIOR AND PERSONALITY: PROBLEMS OF MEASUREMENT

Our discussion, so far, clearly illustrates that there are a number of complexities one faces when seeking answers to seemingly simple questions about the causes of deviancy. For example, we suggested in an earlier chapter that conformity and deviation both share some common characteristics: They both are products of social interaction in groups. And now the question of whether or not there is a conforming or deviating personality seems like a fair question, however, personality factors have not often been employed and where researchers have used personality variables the results have been disappointing. For example, Charles A. Kiesler and Sara B. Kiesler (1969) are quick to point out that there are two pitfalls encountered when researchers set out to study the relationship between conformity and personality traits:

> ...by labeling people as "conformers" and "nonconformers" we may be encouraged to let value judgments intrude into our thinking;...the idea that conformity reflects an acquiescence or "conformer" personality is that this explanation is no explanation at all? All it really says is that conformers conform. But why do they conform? Do they conform in every situation? (1969, Pp. 11-12).

The Kieslers go on to tell us that conforming behavior does not reside in the person or situation alone. Conformity (also deviation) is, then, viewed as a product of the group who induces it and maintains it through committment to the group's norms. And the group opposes behavior not in accord with its norms.

While attribution theory researchers have been attempting to answer questions about how people come to perceive the causes of behavior, personality and social learning researchers have continued to raise questions about the actual causes of behavior. And we have shown questions raised by those who stress situational factors suggest that characteristics of the situation yield certain predictable behaviors, whereas dispositional factors or characteristics of the person are used by personality researchers to predict consistent behaviors over time (see Bower, 1973; Mischel, 1968; 1973). Still a third position suggests that people differ in the extent to which their behavior is invariant (or consistent) or variable (or inconsistent) across situations (see Bem & Allen, 1974; Snyder & Monson, 1975). People whose social behaviors are invariant across situations (i.e., transituational) seem to possess personality traits, whereas those whose social behavior depends more on situations don't seem to possess personality traits.

Then, the primary questions towards which this chapter is directed lie within the area of personality as cause of deviant behavior. And the intent here is to delineate parellels between deviant behavior and the characteristics of deviant actors. The specific questions towards which we will direct our attention are: Do characteristics of the deviant actor help explain his deviant behavior and are deviant personality factors uniquely related to deviant behavior?

First we should note that deviant personality factors are basically measured by psychological scales. However, when we employ scales, and use them as definitions of deviant personality, this immediately raises the question of reliability and validity for the scales employed. First, a <u>valid scale</u> reflects the theoretically defined dimension of a personality variable. And the major problem of validity arises because self-report measures, with very few exceptions, are far from perfect. Then, validity is concerned with the question: "Is the researcher measuring what she assumes she is measuring?" For example, is agreement with the statement "the best way to handle people is to tell them what they want to hear" an indication of the personality variable "Machiavellianism?" Operationally a Machiavellian is a person who agrees with items on the Mach scale. And there should be enough variation among respondents to the scale to characterize some as highly Machiavellian, some as moderate Machiavellian, and still others as strongly Machiavellian.

Then, the psychometric-trait approach to personality places great stress on the quantification of observations of behavioral characteristics usually in the form of rating scales. However, rating scales are only one of the many types of measures employed to assess personality traits. And as the label suggests, self-report methods rely on the individual's own appraisal of her psychological traits. Hence, self-rating scales provide the means whereby an individuals' impressions of his observed attributes are translated into personality measurement.

Then, how well does a particular scale measure the personality construct in question? Such questions have reference to validity and reliability. And it is essential that we note here that <u>reliability</u> is an indication of the extent to which a scale has variable error or errors that differs from individual to individual during an administration of a scale when the same scale is given on two different occasions. Hence, any scale has two components: A true component or measure of the variable in question and an error component. And reliability is defined as the ratio of the two components. Operationally, when the true component is statistically higher than the error component the scale is said to have a relative degree of reliability.

The first and most important consideration then concerns the decision with respect to what the test or scale measures (validity) and then our next concern is how reliable is the measure over time. For example, suppose one wanted to study the relationship between self-esteem and dishonesty. To test the hypothesis that self-esteem covaries with dishonesty we would have to study both of these variables. This task, however, requires that we have a more or less precise measure for these two variables. And this is why scales used to measure personality variables must be checked for their validity and reliability. And finally, the question of how we are to recognize deviant behavior goes from a consideration of personality traits to an understanding of how traits are translated into behavior.

Then, before we can begin to discuss the link between personality and deviant behavior, as well as its implications for a social psychology of deviant behavior, we need to make sure that we are not employing elusive personality concepts. To this extent the constructs we have chosen to include in our discussion of personality seem to meet the minimal criteria for validity and reliability.

An extensive discussion of personality is beyond the permissible limits of this chapter nevertheless we will discuss several personality trait characteristics which seem especially important to the social psychology of deviant behavior. Then, of interest in the present context is the theory of Machiavellianism or the manipulative personality, locus of control or the individual's tendency to perceive events or actions under his control (internal control) or to circumstances beyond his control (external control), need for social approval (assessed by the Social Desirability Scale and based on the assumption that those who score high are likely to engage in socially acceptable behavior to a greater degree than those who score low in self-esteem)authoritarianism, and finally dogmatism.

Finally, as we have suggested earlier, an understanding of personality variables per se has not for the most part yielded a strong relationship to behavior. That is, most social behaviors seems to result from the interaction of personality and situational variables. Here we will focus mainly on personality factors and then later on suggest how researchers can and should take into account both personality and situational factors.

Then, the reader should know that the way a person consistently behaves depends upon her perception of the situation within the limits of her past experiences. And what psychologists label traits are for our present purpose those relatively consistent or stable ways of behaving. Hence, traits are in effect consistent behaviors across situations. And it is from these consistent behaviors that personalogists infer a core or so-called inner dimension to the individual's personality. And, of course, personality traits are inferred from behavior.

In effect a personality view of deviancy attends to the dispositions (or traits) which are said to result in consistent or typical deviant behaviors. And as such the focus is not on the behavior per se. And up to this point we have observed that personality variables have not been shown to be acutely related to deviant behavior without taking into account situational variables. However over the years social psychologists have restricted their interests to situational factors. Hence, the literature on personality and deviant behavior and the research done by social psychologists on situational determinants is characterized by the study of seemingly unrelated variables which seem to be related to a general or to a specific theory of deviancy.

Finally at the very outset, it should be made clear that while the author will take certain interpretive liberties when employing personality variables to deviancy, it should be clear that findings derived from personality research have utility for the study of deviancy.

But we have said enough and we now turn to dispositions which have generally been studied by social psychologists such as authoritarianism, dogmatism, internal-external control, Machiavellianism, social desirability, and self-esteem. Each of these measures for personality will be discussed and then their role in determining deviant behavior will be assessed. And our approach to personality, as one form of cause for deviancy will not include the more traditional clinical trait approaches. That is, constructs such as manifest anxiety, introversion-extroversion, and neuroticism will not be discussed. Not because these constructs are unimportant for deviant behavior but because we have by definition limited our discussion to personality variables of interest to social psychologists.

ARE MACHIAVELLIANS DEVIANT?

We have just discussed some of the complexities of personality and behavior and now our first concern here will be with people who manipulate others. Hence, the question is can those who manipulate their fellow men be distinguished from those who do not seem to do so? And finally, since social interaction leads to social influence are those who successfully manipulate others or influence others for their own ends necessarily deviant? For example, imagine that a person has been lead to do something against his beliefs by someone who appeared at the time highly resistant to an appeal to honesty and fair play. That is, the person has been persuaded by a seemingly rational argument to do something dishonest (e.g., two business partners who cheat on their income tax) by someone who seemed at the time to be "cool" or emotionally detached. Not surprisingly, more often than not under these conditions both actors are likely to be considered deviant, however are we to use the same label for both actors (dishonest)? Probably not because the cheating was first conceived by one of the two actors. And even if the IRS does charge both actors with similar offenses the possible circumstances of the crime might be important to the disposition of the case unless, of course, the focus is on the crime and not the reasons for the crime.

Our example shows how one person can get carried away and go along with what another person suggests---in this case dishonesty, when in fact the individual's partner is characterized as highly Machiavellian. Why is this so? Christie and Geis (1970) tell us that high Machs show little concern with conventional morality: Dishonest behavior is seen as the consequence of affective detachment. However, lows are prone to accede to highs' cheating influences even though they are opposed to dishonesty in principle. Hence, lows can be persuaded by highs to cheat or lie or steal given a strong personal inducement to do so and especially in face-to-face situations.

Our example is not mere speculation because Christie and Geis have studied situations where in fact cheating or lying have taken place among high Machiavellians. That is, the search for the emotionally detached individual or the "manipulative personality" led Richard Christie and his associates (see Christie & Geis, 1970) to identify a pattern of behavior labeled Machiavellianism. And in order to measure this tactic, Christie and Geis (1970) operrationalized Machiavellianism by developing the Mach scales. These scales requires the individual to respond to such questions as "Never tell anyone the real reason you did something unless it is useful to do so," and "It is wise to flatter important people." Such statements as the above are contained in the Mach scales and were adopted from statements found in Machiavelli's The Prince and The Discourses.

Briefly, the type of philosophy espoused by the sixteenth century philosopher and Renaissance stateman, Niccole de Bernado Machiavelli was one of pragmatism in that he urged leaders to engage in behavior likely to be inconsistent with their private beliefs. Hence, Machiavelli suggested that leaders should not be concerned with means only with ends as long as the outcomes (ends) seem at the time to be advantageous to the leaders's long-range goals.

If we translate the cyniscism of Machavielli into present-day language we can see that he advocated telling others what they wish to hear. And it seems that Machavialli knew full well that people generally are unlikely to disclose to others their "true feelings," unless, of course, they can feel that they can trust others. Hence, we can see why it seemed logical to Machavielli that leaders should conceal their "true reasons" for making important political decisions.

What sort of individuals are modern-day Machiavellians or those whom Christie and Geis (1970) have identified? How are they different (or deviant) from those with less Machiavellian tendencies? Christie and Geis tell us that Machiavellians reject conventional ethics and morality, remain emotionally detached in their interpersonal relationships, and intend to and do in fact manipulate others for their own ends. They use deceit and believe that people are generally weak and subject to manipulation and exploitation.

Research done in a wide variety of conditions, and employing different kinds of subjects, has shown that those who score high on the Mach scales are indeed more convincing liars and look their experimenters in the eye while they purport their innocence of wrongdoing (Exline, Thibaut, Hickely, & Gunpert, 1970); they are more willing than low scorers to take a deceptive role when interacting with their peers (Geis, Christie, & Nelson, 1963); they violate instructions in an experimental setting more when it is to their advantage to do so (Miller & Minton, 1969); they expect to be rewarded for helping others in a crises (Pavlos, 1971); and they manage to keep their "cool" in an emotionally-toned bargaining game (Geis, Weinheimer, & Berger, 1970). In addition, they are more likely to be male than female; to come from urban than rural areas; to be young and as adults they are likely to be found in professions where the manipulation of people is part of "their game plan" (Christie & Geis, 1970). And, finally the Machiavellianism of mothers and fathers is positively related to their children's "deceitful" behaviors (Kraut & Price, 1976).

Research most immediately relevant to our question of how Machiavellianism is related to deviancy suggests that Machiavellianism may be an interpersonal tactic or personality style rather than a personality trait per se. For example, Exline, Thibaut, Hickey, and Gumpert (1970) arranged it so that a high Machiavellian and a low Machiavellian college student interacted while they were carrying out an experimental task. Then, in the middle of this task the experimenter was called out of the room to ostensibly answer a long-distance telephone call. And in the absence of the researcher the experimenter's confederate checked the answers for the uncompleted tasks and in so doing implicated the subject in cheating. Following this the experimenter returned and expressed amazement at the pair's early completion of the task. He first implied and later actually accused them both of cheating.

Exline et al. found that high Machiavellians resisted the influence attempt more than lows, however, during a second phase of the study (a post-experimental interview), when the experimenter accused each subject of cheating, high Machiavellian cheaters looked the experimenter in the eye and denied that they had cheated more so than their low Machiavellian counterpart felons. Also, highs tended to confess less and in fact lied more plausibly than did lows.

What this study suggests is that Machiavellianism may act as a disposition and the aspects of the situation afford the opportunity to manipulate others. And there appears to be a dispositional difference between low and high Machiavellians: Highs show greater emotional detachment than lows. For example, Florence Geis and her associates (Geis, Weinheimer, & Berger, 1970) asked whether or not highs are likely to win a "legislative log rolling game" over lows where the problem under discussion entailed emotionally-loaded issues (e.g., to revoke civil rights, to raise the minimum age for drinking to twenty-five, and universal military conscription).

Results of Geis' research supported her predictions; lows lost the emotionally-toned arguments in the bargaining game to highs even when they privately endorsed such issues. On the other hand, highs and lows did not differ when they argued over neutral issues. This shows that high Machiavellians are clearly able to take advantage of their relative emotional detachment in face-to-face situations and in doing so successfully manipulate others.

The evidence cited so far suggests an obvious answer to our earlier question: Persons who score high on the Mach scales apparently are more likely to remain "cool and detached" and they seem to have an advantage: They manipulate un-Machiavellian individuals at the expense of these lows by "bending the rules of social interaction" so that they take advantage of the situation even in the relative absense of ideological committment to or expressed interest in their own behavior. Then it should come as no surprise to find out that high Machiavellians are more likely to bargain in emotionally-toned situations, whereas lows are made "victims of the situation."

From the above observations one would expect that Machiavellians would bargain with a funeral director in a less emotional manner than un-Machiavellians when asked to arrange the "most financially equitable funeral" for a deceased friend or member of their family. Nevertheless, if we seek a more complete answer to our question we must also take into consideration the "sales pressure" a funeral director is likely to employ during the arrangement of a funeral. Hence, one would expect that a high Machiavellian would react strongly against a high pressure sales pitch as the funeral director attempts to move the high Mach client to consider an even more expensive funeral then she is willing to entertain. On the other hand when a funeral director uses little or no sales pressure, low and high Machs should not differ and they reach a financially comparable funeral arrangement.

Andrew J. Pavlos (1973), administered the Mach IV scale to students who at the time were enrolled in his death and dying classes. From these students thirty high and thirty low scorers (males) were identified and asked to take part in what was obstensibly a class project. That is, the subjects were told that a local funeral director (Mr. Johnson) would visit the campus and that as part of their course requirement they would be asked to role play a person who was asked to make funeral arrangements for a deceased member of their family.

When the subject arrived at an interview room he was introduced to the "funeral director" (actually a confederate of the experimenter). The subject was told that Mr. Johnson (the funeral director) would be on campus to talk to students and would explain to them how to make arrangements for a funeral. For one third of the subjects, from each of the two Mach conditions, the funeral director showed them information (a brochure) relative to the average costs for a funeral which included casket, vault, embalming and other such expenses. During the funeral director's "sales presentation" he did not attempt to pressure the subject relative to the cost for the funeral (low sales pressure condition). Another third of the subjects, from each of the Mach conditions, were strongly encouraged by the funeral director to spend 50 per cent more than they indicated that they wished to spend for the casket and vault (high sales pressure condition). The remaining third of the subjects merely checked items for the cost of the funeral without actually interacting with the funeral director, who at the time sat across the room from the subject (control condition).

Since the casket and vault are usually the funeral items most subject to bargaining during an arrangement for a funeral the total costs reached for these two items constituted the major dependent measure.

Results of an analysis of variance for the dependent measure yielded a significant main effect for Machiavellianism where low Machs arranged a more expensive funeral (M=$1870.70) than did high Machs (M=$1297.24) at the .01 level of significance. The main effect for the funeral director's sales pitch was also significant ($P<.05$). As expected the high sales pressure (M=$\overline{1623}$.81) resulted in a more costly funeral than did the low sales pressure (M=$1521.02).

What are we to make of these findings? Did these subjects view their task as unrealistic or did they take their assignment seriously? In order to assess these possibilities interviews were held immediately after each subject's research participation and it was discovered that subjects did in fact take their role-playing assignment as "serious business." Nonetheless, there remains the problem of relating these findings to the "real world." In this regard, the findings raises the question of what makes high Machiavellians bargain when, no doubt, most people are unlikely to do so? No matter what one thinks about funerals, the funeral ritual itself is likely to be considered sacred even though we have recently observed some rather serious criticisms of current mortuary practices (e.g., Harmer, 1963; Mitford, 1963). And we know that the funeral ritual itself calls for respect for the deceased and her family and any serious violation of the decease person's family expectations is likely to lead to strong disapproval. In this respect the highs, as expected, seemed to be less concerned with traditional morality.

WHAT ABOUT THE DEVELOPMENTAL ASPECTS OF MACHIAVELLIANISM?

Perhaps one of the best ways to underscore the importance of Machiavellianism for deviant behavior is to note its application to children. Then, based on the research with adults, Dorothea Braginsky (1966) modified the Mach IV scale for children by first studing a group of ten-year-old fifth graders. She then classified the children as low, middle, and high in Machiavellianism on the basis of the scores they obtained on her scale. After she had classified the children each child was paired with a middle-Mach target person and their high-or-low-Mach partner was given the task of persuading the target child to eat as many crackers (flavored with quinine in order to make the crackers taste bitter) as possible.

The researcher introduced herself as a home economist interested in the child's evaluation of "health crackers." And after the child had savored the crackers and drank some water he filled out a special questionnaire evaluating his liking for the "health crackers." At this point the subject was asked to induce a second child to eat "as many crackers as possible." In addition, the subject was told that she would receive five cents for each cracker the second child consumed.

Now, let's consider the results. High Mach children persuaded the target to consume an average 6.46 crackers, whereas low Mach children induced the target person to eat an average of 2.79 crackers. This difference is highly significant ($p<.003$), however there were no significant sex differences.

Braginsky then did a content analysis of tape recordings obtained from her subjects' "strategies" and found that the lies employed to increase the target person's cracker consumption could be classified as commissive or ommissive. And she reports that high-Mach subjects told more commissive lies (distortion of the truth) than did low-Mach boys, whereas high-Mach girls told more ommissive lies (withholding part of the truth) than low-Mach girls.

What do these findings suggest for deviant behavior, especially since children have not often been studied with respect to Machiavellianism? In particular, one wonders whether or not other forms of manipulative behavior are to be found in children? Certainly the finding that ten-year-olds are willing to lie directs our attention to the kind of family background from which high-Mach children emerge. In this regard Robert E. Kraut and J. Douglas Price (1976) studied the role that the family plays in the development of Machiavellianism. They researched high-and-low Mach sixth graders, who played a bluffing game, and then they had the parents of their subjects fill out Machiavellian scales.

Kraut and Price found that the childrens' fathers and mothers' scores were positively correlated with their child's "success" in deceiving other children. They also found that the children's Mach scores were positively related to their father's Mach scores. However, the investigators' unexpectedly found that their subjects' (the children) behavior and Mach scores were not significantly related. This, of course, suggests that children independently learn their Machiavellian beliefs and behaviors from their parents and as time passes their beliefs and their behavior become more consistent. This, no doubt, takes place some time before adulthood. Then, the existence of a positive relationship between parental and child Machiavellianism suggests that social modeling is likely to be responsible for the development of children's Machiavellian beliefs. As a matter of fact, Kraut and Price research supports this hypothesis.

The overall pattern of research results shown here suggest some provocative implications for deviant behavior. Perhaps the single most important observation made is that Machiavellians are deviant when the situation favors manipulation. This is taken to mean that Machiavellianism, as a personality variable, can influence interpersonal behavior especially when the situation is made ambiguous and especially when highly Machiavellian persons remain "cool and detached" as well as when they avoid conventional morality in their dealings with other people. Hence, the evidence seems compelling: Endorsement of Machiavellianism contributes to deviations from normative expectations. And an important clue as to how Machiavellianism develops comes from the finding that parents seem to have an impact on their children through social modeling. Clearly some children are more highly manipulative than their peers and we also know that their Mach scale scores are positively correlated with their fathers' Mach scores: Machiavellian fathers tend to have Machiavellian children.

THE NEED FOR SOCIAL APPROVAL AND SOCIAL DESIRABILITY

Personality factors are measured in several different ways. And we have suggested that the most common way to assess personality is through the use of self-ratings. As might be suspected personality scales may be subject to bias because individuals may attempt to present themselves in the most favorable light possible. This is most likely to happen when scales are used to evaluate socially sensitive areas. Then, in order to measure this potential source of bias a Social Desirability Scale has been developed. The scale has been shown to be related to a number of different psychological measures (see Edwards, 1957).

Douglas Crowne and David Marlowe (1964) have extended work on social desirability and they have developed a scale to measure peoples' need for social approval. That is, they studied peoples' motivation to gain social approval from others and they have labeled this personality variable the need _for_ social approval. That is, Crowne and Marlowe first noted that some people tend to respond to personality-scale items in terms of how they perceive socially desirable or acceptable behaviors. Crowne and Marlowe argue that people who tend to answer personality questionnaire items in a socially desirable way also tend to seek social approval from others. Hence, items on the Marlowe-Crowne Social Desirability Scale measure the individual's tendency to agree or disagree with socially desirable items (e.g., "I don't find it particularly difficult to get along with loud-mouth, obnoxious people," "I never hesitate to go out of my way to help someone in trouble") or socially undesirable statements such as, "I can remember 'playing sick' to get out of something."

Since most people seem to present themselves in the most positive light possible, it seems only logical that individuals who show a tendency toward social desirability should in effect be characterized by greater conformity to social influence attempts. In this respect it has been observed that people who conform more to group pressure also tend to conform more to social desirability standards (see Mann, 1959). And, as a matter of fact Crowne and Marlowe (1964) do indeed report that social desirability is positively related to conformity. And interestingly enough authoritarianism (F-scale) is both positively related to conformity and social desirability (see Weiner & McGinnies, 1961).

Then, if social desirability and social approval are personality characteristics it should appear in situations where socially sensitive issues are evident, however, one major problem in studying conformity and social desirability has been the lack of precise and clear-cut definitions of conformity. As we saw in an earlier chapter, conformity is clearly not the simple phenomenon it is often thought to be. Conformity can best be predicted from the knowledge of both the personality of the individual and the situation she interacts in when with other people. And it seems clear that in combination these two sets of variables must be studied before we can begin to know the answer to this questions.

THE AUTHORITARIAN PERSONALITY, DOGMATISM, AND DEVIANCY

The importance of authoritarianism to the understanding of conformity and deviation lies in its utility in predicting those likely to conform and those likely to deviate from the social norms. Hence, central to the concept authoritarianism is the view that there is a particular personality type prone to adopt a "Fascist political ideology."

Just as World War II was coming to an end a team of researchers, who felt strongly about Nazi atrocities, began to investigate the personality factors underlying Fascism and anti-Semitism. And researchers studied what they labeled the _authoritarian_ personality, persons denoted as fascistic, anti-Semitic, ethnocentric and highly conservative. And, Theodore Adorno, Else Frenkel-Brunswik, Daniel Levinson, and R. Nevitt Sanford (1950) developed four different attitude scales to measure this personality type: fascism, ethnocentrism, anti-Semitism, and political and economic conservatism. And it was subsequently found that individuals who scored high on one scale also tended to score high on other scales, hence the four scales are highly intercorrelated.

The scales consist of Likert-like items to which individuals express a degree of agreement or disagreement with such items as "Obedience and respect for authority are the most important virtues children should learn," and "Homosexuals are hardly better than criminals and ought to be severely punished." Those that agree with these kinds of statements are suppose to be characterized by a character structure assumed to have had its origin in early childhood experiences where the child is subjected to harse parental discipline and a lack of emotion warmth and love.

Once Adorno et al. (1950) identified what they labeled the authoritarian personality they then set out to construct the kinds of family and childhood backgrounds from which these individuals emerged. Data from subjects suggested that they had grown up in families with strict and punitive fathers who demanded obediance and loyalty. This was said to culminate in an adult personality that is hostile and prejudice toward minority groups, homosexuals, and criminal deviates. In addition, Adorno et al. found that authoritarianism is related to conservatism. Hence, those that score high on the F-scale tend to have conservative attitudes said to reflect an attitude that denys the rights of deviant others.

Since authoritarianism entails a high degree of conformity and obedience to authority figures, the tendency to conform to group pressure has been shown. For example, in Chapter 4 we noted that high F-scale scorers obeyed significantly more often than did low F-scale scorers when confronted with the Milgram experiment (see Elms & Milgram, 1966). And those who obeyed tended to have higher F-scale scores than those who defied the experimenter, however highs also tended to have less education than those who scored low on the F-scale. The finding that high F-scale scorers are more likely to come from groups who score low in intelligence, and who have little education, has suggested that authoritarianism is in effect a kind of "pseudoconservatism" reflecting a right-wing characteristic representing what Milton Rokeach (1960) labels the "closed mind." And it has been observed that if indeed the F-scale were to become devoid of its political ideology, left-wing adherrents, no doubt, would score as high as the right-wing authoritarians (Rokeach, 1960).

And we have observed that individual differences in subjects' F-scale scores have been found to be related to differences in education and acquiescence. That is, the items are worded in such a way as to suggest that answers indicate an acquiescent response set or a tendency to agree. Hence, it is not clear whether those who score high on the scale are authoritarians or acquiescent **persons** (see Wilson & Nies, 1972). In addition, education and F-scale scores show a significant negative correlation indicating that those with less education score higher than those with more education (see Kerscht & Dillehay, 1967). As a matter of fact Stuart Oskamp (1977) tells us that there are four major counts where research on the authoritarian personality can be faulted: (1) unrepresentative sampling where most of the subjects came from organizations such as labor groups, university campuses, and the like; (2) interviewer bias was not controlled; (3) an acquiescence response set due to the fact that the F-scale just happens to stress highly authoritarian questions; and (4) education and social economic class are highly negatively correlated with F-scale scores suggesting that lower social classes are in effect more likely to show higher F-scale scores than middle-or-upperclass individuals.

For these reasons, Milton Rokeach (1960) has developed a scale, which is related to authoritarianism, assumed to overcome some of these problems labeled the Dogmatism Scale. For example, agreement with items such as "It is only natural that a person would have a much better acquaintance with ideals he believes than with ideals he opposes" is an example of what Rokeach labels closed-mindedness. And a closed-mind or dogmatic person is highly likely to disgard beliefs that do not fit with his existing ones. And the dogmatic individual depends on authority guidelines not unlike Adorno et al.'s (1950) authoritarian personality.

And it is not surprising that research shows that the Dogmatism scale distinguishes between people who accept and do not accept "the official law enforcement explanation of the causes of riots in large cities." That is, highly dogmatic individuals agree more with the police that rioters are to blame than those with lower dogmatism scores (McCarthy & Johnson, 1962). In addition, highly dogmatic persons depend more on authority guidelines and conform more to authority figures than do their less dogmatic counterparts (Vidulich & Kaiman, 1961). And finally, it has been shown by Jacob Jacoby (1971) that low dogmatic subjects (open-minded persons) are more "accurate interpersonal perceivers" than highly dogmatic subjects (closed-minded persons).

Then, are high authoritarian or highly dogmatic persons likely to translate their authoritarian or dogmatic ideology into a variety of conforming or deviating behaviors? First we are told that those who score high on the F-scale also score high on the E-scale or ethnocentrism scale. And it has been shown that the ethnocentric and fasistic individual dislikes people or things that are different. As a matter of fact research has shown that high ethnocentrics and fascists are significantly less likely to purchase foreign-made cars (see Day & White, 1973). They are also likely to dislike minority groups, homosexuals, criminals, and in general a wide variety of deviants (see Christie & Cook, 1958; Kirscht & Dillehay, 1967; Stone, 1974).

In addition it has been shown that those who believed that Lieutenant Calley's actions during the My Lai massacre were "acceptable under the circumstances" were more authoritiarian than those who thought Calley should have been court martialed (Fink, 1973). In addition, Morton Deutsch (1960) studied the relationship between trusting behavior in a two-person non-zero-sum game and authoritarianism. He found that low F-scale scorers are more trusting and trustworthy, whereas high scorers tended to be more suspicious and exploitative with their game choices. Hence, the authoritarians displayed the kinds of behavior, vis-a-vis the interaction with other persons, one would predict from the theory of authoritarianism. And finally the dogmatic person, just as the authoritarian individual, has been shown to rely on authority guidlines (see Vidulich & Kaiman, 1961). That is, subjects who scored high or low on Rokeach's Dogmatism scale were put in a Sherif autokinetic situation, where each of the subjects privately judged the movement of a light over thirty trials. The subject then was told how other subjects had done and she was asked to judge the movement of the light for an additional thirty trials. In order to manipulate authority, half of the subjects in each dogmatism group were led to believe that the other individual was either a college professor (high authority or high status condition), whereas the other half were lead to believe that he was a high school student (low authority or low status condition).

Vidulich and Kaiman found that highly dogmatic individuals agreed significantly more with the college professor or high status person than with the high school student or low status individual. On the other hand, those low in dogmatism tended to agree more with the low status person than the high status individual.

What these results seem to suggest is that the personality dimension of dogmatism and willingness to accept high or low status influence are related. It has also been found that people who score high on dogmatism also tend to "care less about how they impress others" (Haiman & Duns, 1964). And it has been shown that female peers of highly dogmatic college students tend to like them less over time than their nondogmatic peers (Rosenfield & Nauman, 1969).

We have shown that a considerable amount of research evidence suggests that dogmatism and authorianism are related to deviant behavior. And despite the criticisms of the measures for dogmatism and authoritarianism it can be shown that the usefulness of these personality scales depend largely on the empirical evidence relating these measures to conformity and deviation. The question of what relationship exist between deviant behavior and dogmatic or authoritiarian attitudes is consistent with the proposition that personality and deviancy are often linked in meaningful ways. Then, without question the pioneering efforts of Adorno et al. (1950), and Rokeach (1960) cannot be ruled out as unimportant to the study of deviancy: The results are important for an understanding of deviant behavior even though measurement problems remain with these scales.

LOCUS OF CONTROL AND ITS RELATIONSHIP TO DEVIANCY

Another personality characteristic with especially significant implications for deviancy is the tendency for individuals to perceive a reinforcing event caused by internal or external factors (Rotter, 1966). Hence, there appears to be two very different ways that people have of perceiving their world: Some persons tend to attribute their reinforcements to their own actions, whereas still others are inclined to perceive their reinforcement beyond their control. And to measure this variable Julian Rotter (1966) has constructed a twenty-six item scale composed of external and internal statements. For example, the forced-choice I-E scale presents two alternatives (one scaled in the external direction and the other in the internal direction). And in general, then, the locus-of control personality scale represents the "expectancy between behavior and its outcomes." And expectancy is linked in a generalized way where people believe that they have personal control over their lives or that the control lies outside of their grasp. The more internally-oriented a person is, the more she is said to believe that events occur as a consequence of her actions and are in effect perceived of as under personal control; the more externally-oriented a person is the more the individual tends to believe that events seem to be unrelated to personal control.

The most widely-known of the locus-or-control scales is Rotter's Internal-External Control of Reinforcement Scale (see Rotter, 1966). And as we have noted, the subject is asked to make a choice between an external or an internal response and he chooses one of a pair ot items he agrees with and disregards the other statement. For example, two of the twenty-three pairs of statements scored in the scale are:

- a. In the long run people get the respect they deserve in the world (internal response).
- b. Unfortunately, an individual's worth often passes unrecognized no matter how hard he tries (external response).

- a. Many times I feel that I have little influence over the things that happen to me (external response).
- b. It is impossible for me to believe that chance or luck plays an important role in my life (internal response).

Items as above have been administered to a wide variety of groups and differences have generally been found in the predicted direction. And for our purpose, research shows that internally-controlled individuals differ from their externally-controlled counterparts, for example, some of the most immediately relevant applications of the locus of control dimension to deviancy shows that opiate addicts and alcoholics are more internal (Berzins, & Ross, 1973; Gross & Morosko, 1970). And externally-controlled federal reformatory inmates do not learn the kinds of information enabling them to cope with the "real world" effectively to the same degree that internals do (Seeman, 1963). Internally-oriented subjects are less sympathetic with welfare recipients than externally-oriented subjects (Phares & Lamiell, 1975). Internals have been found to be less helping and altruistic than externals (Phares & Wilson, 1972). And internals conform less than do externals (Crowne & Liverant, 1963; Tolor, 1971), whereas externally-controlled children cheat more than their counterpart internals (Johnson & Gormly, 1972), and finally, externals have been shown to display a greater unwillingness to blame Lt. William Calley for the My Lai incident (Hochreich, 1972).

Clearly, then, one would expect, at least from a common sense perspective, that externally-oriented persons would be found among alcoholics to a greater degree than internally-oriented individuals. As a matter of fact, Gross and Morosko (1970) predicted this, however interestingly enough they found that there were indeed significantly more internally controlled alcoholics in an out-patient population of 262 alcoholics than externally controlled alcoholics. Why is this so? Gross and Morosko tell us that internals tend to use alcohol to reduce their "fear and anxieties" and that drinking seems to be one way to allay these unpleasant feelings while at the same time the alcoholic tends to "gain control over these feelings." And interestingly enough, Berzins and Ross (1973) report similar results for opiate addicts. That is, they were found to be more internally controlled than a comparison group of non-addicts.

All of us have observed that some individuals usually seem to respond to their surroundings more so than others. In this respect, Seeman (1963) reasons that people who are internally-controlled tend to respond more than externally-oriented individuals to situational cues. He found that internally-oriented inmates in a federal reformatory setting tended to acquire more useful information about the general make up of the reformatory and parole regulations, and information necessary for survival after their release from the reformatory than externals.

On a different note, Charles Johnson and John Gormly (1972) studied the relationship between locus of control and resistance to temptation in fifth-grade boys and girls, who were classified as either cheaters or noncheaters. And it was found that students who had cheated more were also more external than their noncheating counterparts. On the other hand, males showed this general tendency much the same as did females, however the males' cheating behavior was less extreme than was the case with females.

The major importance of the above finding is that cheating is more an external thing than internal and, no doubt, it has something to do with how externals view their social environment. That is, because externals are supposed to be less sensitive to their social environment they may cheat when the situation favors it, whereas internals are less inclined to do so.

We may further ask whether or not those who observed or read about the My Lai court martial, and were immediately faced with the proposition of whether or not Lt. Calley should be convicted of murder, would be more likely to blame Calley and his men for My Lai than those who felt that Calley should not be convicted. Then, what does locus of control have to do with the My Lai incident? First, Dorothy J. Hochreich (1972) investigated the relationship between locus of control and the reactions of college students to the My Lai courts-martial. She hypothesized that externally-controlled students would be more likely than internally-controlled students to play down the responsibility of Lt. William Calley and his men and therefore to blame My Lai on the U.S. government and its military establishment.

Results showed that males and females did not differ in either their locus of control scores or a specially designed questionnaire about My Lai. And only males were found to support the hypothesized relationship between these measures. That is external males compared with internal males showed a greater unwillingness to assign responsibility to Lt. Calley and to blame My Lai on the U.S. government

What about self-esteem is it related to locus of control? First, E. Jerry Phares and his associates (Phares, Ritchie, & Davis, 1968) threatened internals and externals by having them take a series of personality tests and subsequently gave their subjects either positive or negative interpretations of their personalities. Subjects were then given an opportunity to seek "psychological help." Internals were more willing to engage (and actually did so) in remedial behavior as a way of coping with their "personality problems." More recently, Stuart J. Clayman and Richard M. Ryckman (1977) report a study where they varied their subjects' chronic self-esteem (high vs. low) and their locus of control (internal vs. externals) and found that more low than high self-esteem internals showed a greater willingness to visit a clinical psychologist's office in order to solve their problems, whereas no significant differences in such behavior were found between high and low self-esteem externals.

Obviously, these are interesting and important findings because there is good reason to believe that externality and psychopathology are positively correlated. For example, Phares tells us that:

> It may be concluded then that there is enough convergence of theoretical and empirical data to support the assumption of correlation between locus of control and psycholpathology. What is missing are the factual details that are needed to fill in the gaps related to specific questions of how and why (1976, p. 95).

As a matter of fact research does indeed support the view that persons with an external locus of control orientation tend to act more anti-socially than do individuals with an internal orientation. Is it just possible that these observed differences might be due to how externally-oriented persons explain the causes of their behavior. It has been shown that externals do tend to use personal or dispositional explanations for the behavior, whereas internals tend toward situational and/or environmental explaaations (see Midlarsky & Midlarsky, 1973). Finally, research does show that not only are psychiatric patients found to be more external or Rotter's I-E scale than nonpsychiatric patients, but they also are less competent than internals (see Palmer, 1971). Having said this we will next turn to a consideration of self-esteem, where both competence and self-esteem have been shown to be related to deviancy.

SELF-CONCEPT AND SELF-ESTEEM: THEIR DEVELOPMENT AND RELATIONSHIP TO DEVIANCY

As we have pointed out research correlating a single personality factor with behavior will generally yield less than impressive results and this is no less true for research carried out with the self-concept or self-esteem (see Marlowe & Gergen, 1970). Hence, before we detail what relationship exists between the self-concept (and self-esteem) and deviancy we will pose the following questions: "What is self-esteem (and the self-concept)?," and "Under what conditions is a person's self-concept formed and changed?"

First self-esteem is a complex concept; it is the evaluative component of the self-concept (see Gergen, 1971). And a useful definition must take into account its more or less enduring characteristics. For example, Stanley Coopersmith (1967) tells us that there are at least four determinants of self-esteem: power, virture, competence, and significance. <u>Power</u> is the person's ability to influence and to control other people; <u>virtue</u> is the degree to which an individual adheres to existing moral standards; <u>competence</u> refers to the meeting of performance standards for excellence; and <u>significance</u> is the acceptance and affection one receives from others.

Coopersmith (1967) tells us that a person's level of self-esteem is determeined by the above factors, however, he is quick to point out that <u>competence</u> and <u>significance</u> are by far the most important factors contributing to one's self-esteem. And Coopersmith's research with 10-to-12 year old boys shows that a boy's self-esteem is related to parental factors, obtained through ratings of the boy's self-esteem by mothers, evaluations of the boy's liking of himself (self-esteem scale), ratings from the child's teachers and school principal (behavior rating format), and related behavioral data.

Coopersmith found that a boys mother's self-esteem is related to the boy's estimate of his own self-esteem. In addition, the mother's stability or absence of anxiety was found to be related to the boy's level of self-esteem. That is, boys with low self-esteem tend to have mothers who are distant or not close to their sons, whereas the mothers of high self-esteem children report that they enforce rules more consistently than mothers of boys with low self-esteem.

High achievement in school is stressed by boys with high self-esteem and their mothers tend to "reason with their sons and to treat them as individuals." On the other hand low self-esteem boys tend to have arbritary limits set and their mothers tend to vacillate in their attempts to control their son's lives. Mothers of this group tend to perceives themselves as superior to their children and enforce rules without first reasoning with the boys. In addition, developmental data shows that low self-esteem children actually started to walk significantly later than higher self-esteem children.

Finally, it should be noted that Coopersmith's research is in effect based on correlational data and as such we cannot employ his data to establish cause and effect relationships. However, the importance of his research for the development of self-esteem suggests that mothers of his high self-esteem children also tend to have high self-esteem, are demanding of their sons, reason with them and show warmth and acceptance, whereas the fathers tend to set limits and are perceived as taking a great deal of interest in their sons more so than children with low self-esteem.

HOW STABLE IS ONE'S SELF-CONCEPT?

Returning to an earlier question, "under what conditions does a person's self-esteem change," we should first note from the outset that this is not a simple question. However, we cannot understand what is meant by change unless we indicate that an individual's self-concept (and self-esteem) changes at least for three very different reasons: (1) the perception of the reactions of others to one's behavior has changed; (2) one has compared his attitudes and opinions with those of similar others (social comparison); and (3) one has encountered discrepancies regarding the social appropriateness or desirability of one's self-image.

Of course, stability of one's self-concept is implied from the consistency of one's perceptions of other peoples' perceptions of one's self. And the fact that we are all at one time or another inconsistent cannot be gainsaid, but from what we have said it does not follow that we are tantamount to being inconsistent most of the time. Then, it is the position taking here that a person's self-concept is the result of social interaction. Nonetheless, one's self-concept does not remain static; it changes over time.

Perhaps the most formal statement about stability and change in self-concept is found in Paul F. Secord and Carl W. Backman's interpersonal congruence theory (Secord & Backman, 1965, 1974). That is, Secord and Backman postulate that when a person intereacts with other people the individual tends to maximize the consistency between her self-concept, her interpretation of her own behavior (B), and the behavior of others in relation to her own reactions to others (O).

Hence, Secord and Backman indicate that a person will interact with others in order to support his self-concept(s). And it is in this respect that congruity is said to exist. That is, when the person interprets his own behavior (B), in relation to how others define him (O), then the self-concept is said to be consistent. For example, if a person believes she is deviant, and behaves in a "deviant way," and is made to feel by others that she is deviant congruity is said exist between the three sources of congruity. On the other hand, incongruity is likely when others define the individual differently. And incongruity is said to lead to a reorganization of the self-concept (change) and as a matter of fact the person may deny or distort information from others and not change her self-concept after all.

We have just noted that one's self-concept changes as others come to perceive one differently. And, of course, the individual may finally come to see herself from a different perspective. We now turn from a focus on theoretical statements about the self-concept and self-esteem and turn to some specific considerations of self-esteem research which is related to deviancy in particular.

SELF-ESTEEM AND SOCIAL INFLUENCE

First, what about the view that there are some people who by the very nature of their personality characteristics seem to be more responsive to attitude change and conformity than others? Of particular interest here is the relationship between a person's self-esteem and persuasibility.

First we should note that early research tended to suggest a rather simple linear relationship between self-esteem and degree of attitude change. That is, it was assumed that the higher a person's self-esteem the less he seemed to change his attitudes (see Janis, 1954). However, more recent reviews of the attitude change literature show that self-esteem and attitude change has an inverted U relationship because comprehension of the message operates differently at different levels of self-esteem. For example, William McGuire (1969) suggests that self-esteem has little effect on the reception of a message when it is either too easy or too difficult to understand, whereas when a message is intermediate in level of difficulty, those with high self-esteem seem more receptive of the message than those with lower self-esteem. But people with higher self-esteem also have higher intelligence and they are more self-confident and yield less than low self-esteem subjects. Hence, it follows, from McGuire's reasoning that attitude change, which necessitates attention, comprehension, and yielding, shows a negative relationship with self-esteem in situations where the message is easy to understand. And, of course, the higher one's self-esteem, the less one experiences significant attitude change. In addition, as level of self-esteem increases more attitude change takes place up to a point and decreases as the message becomes extremely difficult to comprehend. Hence, McGuire (1968) suggests that personality characteristics (like self-esteem), having a positive relation to the reception of a counterattitudinal message, also tends to show a negative relationship to yielding.

Since McGuire (1969) tells us that personality variables (like self-esteem) affect the attention, comprehension, and yielding aspects of a communication, one would expect that McGuire's model has produced research in support of his hypothesis. This has not been the case because research on self-esteem has produced mixed results. However, research does show that individuals with low self-esteem (who no doubt, have low self-confidence) depend on others and in turn are more influenced by others.

Actually, then, early research did indeed show that subjects with low self-esteem changed their attitudes more than those with high self-esteem (see Cohen, 1958). However, more recently self-esteem has been studied by Gollob and Dittes (1965) and has yielded different results. They gave male students at Yale an ambiguous test on which one half of the subjects were led to believe their performance was well done (success manipulation), and the remaining half were told they had done poorly (failure manipulation). Following this subjects were asked to complete a questionnaire measuring their attitudes toward cancer research. Next, they read a short statement about cancer research and again answered the same questions about cancer experimentation.

Actually the three different statements about cancer research entailed different degrees of complexity. The first statement was a simple message and it was not threatening. The second was a fear inducing statement suggesting that cancer is unavoidable. And the third statement was a complex argument about how cancer research should be done.

Since Gollob and Dittes has obtained two measures on their subjects' self-esteem (a self-report measure and an acute or manipulated version) they compared these versions of self-esteem. And the researchers predicted that the success manipulation (high self-esteem condition) would indeed lead to greater resistance to the message only under the simple condition. Hence, an increase in a subject's self-esteem was expected to make him less resistant due to the fact that he could cope better with the message than those subjects who had their self-esteem experimentally lowered.

First, for the simple condition an inverse relationship was found between acute self-esteem and self-ratings of self-esteem and degree of persuasibility. On the other hand, for both the fear and complexity conditions the acute self-esteem condition showed that those with transiently high self-esteem held attitudes that were positively related to their level of self-esteem. And experimentally manipulated self-esteem was found to be an important determiner of attitude change more so than a chronic or self-report version of self-esteem. More recent research testing McGuire's model has shown that experimentally manipulated self-esteem is in fact more significantly related to persuasability than is chronic self-esteem (Zellner, 1970).

McGuire (1968) tells us that there are a number of different reasons why acute and chronic personality characteristics may yield different results. For one thing chronic personality attributes are generally correlated with other personality characteristics that may produce the results instead of the particular personality trait singled out for study. And temporary personality factors (i.e., acute or experimental manipulations of self-esteem) may be viewed by the subject as unauthentic and hence have a different impact depending on whether or not the manipulation is "successful."

The above arguments have implications for deviant behavior especially where research is done on both chronic and acute variables. And it should be noted that when a researcher employs a chronic version of an independent variable, in personality-based-deviant-behavior research, this generally entails the administration of scales (e.g., a self-esteem scale) to a large number of people. And then the investigator selects from those whose scores are either high or low samples of subjects who later are exposed to treatment conditions. On the other hand, an acute version or experimental manipulation of an independent variable requires that the experimenter create levels of the variable through a manipulation of a preestablished variable, of course, within a laboratory setting. For example, an experimenter may temporarily lower or increase her subjects' self-esteem through a false-feedback procedure and subsequently measure for changes in her subjects' behavior (dependent variable).

When a researcher uses a chronic version of an independent variable he is essentially using what is tantamount to a correlational design. In this respect Clyde Hendrick and Russell A. Jones (1972) have stressed the need for researchers to pit chronic and acute versions of independent variables against each other, whenever possible, within the same design and then to compare these effects on specific classes of dependent variables. And finally Hendrick and Jones suggest that if a variable can be manipulated that an acute manipulation is to be preferred over a chronic version due in part to the preciseness with which the manipulation reflects the independent variable in question.

Oddly enough, despite the fact that self-esteem seems pivotal to deviancy, research has not generally compared acute and chronic versions of individuals' self-esteem. And if deviant behavior is to a great extent determined by self-esteem or one's self-concept we would expect that research would bear this out. And similarly, with respect to self-esteem we would expect that a person who considers himself deviant would in fact act to confirm this self-image. This in fact would be the most fundamental requirement for the claim individuals with low self-esteem or self-concept are more likely to engage in deviant behavior than those with high self-esteem.

A number of reasons are suggested to account for this apparent lack of a strong relationship between self-esteem and deviancy. First, a major problem concerns itself with the way in which persons evaluate themselves. This has lead to various definitions of self-esteem by different authors and researchers. When we define self-esteem as an individual's self-evaluation or judgment of self-worth, self-esteem is understood as a relatively enduring characteristic of the person. And, of course, not all aspects of the person are given equal weight by the individual (see French & Kahn, 1962).

Given this conceptualization of self-esteem there is good reason to suspect that the link between self-esteem and conformity or deviation is indeed complex. And, indeed a positive or negative self-concept may operate quite differently in relation to conformity and deviation. This suggest that some of the more important determinants of self-esteem may covary with a deviant self-identity. Hence, there is reason to suspect that self-esteem is correlated with many of the causes of deviant behavior and both have some of the same antecedents. But self-esteem qua self-esteem seems to account for little of the variance in deviancy if in fact we limit deviancy to its social implications. That is, self-esteem by itself seems to make a relatively small contribution to deviant behavior (or nondeviant behavior).

Given the limitations stated above for self-esteem research, there seems to be little choice but to suggest that self-esteem taken singly seems not to explain a great of the variance for deviant behavior. Nonetheless, it seems only logical that low self-esteem can result in self-derogatory behavior.

From a different perspective social learning theory can be used to explain the function esteem plays in determining deviant behavior. That is, according to social learning theory a negative self-concept (or in fact low self-esteem) results when the individual devalues himself, whereas a positive self-concept results from favorable self-judgments. Hence, people seem to have different evaluative standards that produce different self-evaluations. For example, Albert Bandura notes that:

> Personality theories tend to attribute variations in behavior to differences in values, but they do not adequately explain how values regulate conduct. In the social learning analysis, one mode of operation is in terms of incentive preferences. People differ in the value they place on approval, money, material possessions, social status, exemption from restictions, and the like (1977, p. 139).

And, Bandura (1977) goes on to suggest that "personal misery can result from stringent standards for "self-appraisal" (p. 142). It is in this sense that "deviant standards" can create social as well as personal problems: For example, Bandura tells that:

> When a person's behavior is a source of self-criticism, defensive reactions that avert or lessen discomfort are thereby reinforced. Self-produced distress thus creates the conditions for the development of various forms of deviant behavior. Some people whose accomplishments bring them a sense of failure resort to alcoholic self-anesthetization; others escape into grandiose ideation where they achieve in fantasy what is unattainable in reality; many renounce pursuits having self-evaluative implications and gravitate to groups embracing anti-achievement norms; others protect themselves from self-condemnation for their self-alleged

faults by imputing persecutory schemes; and tragically still others are driven by relentless self-disparagement to suicide (1977, Pp. 141-142).

SELF-ESTEEM AND THE ACCEPTANCE OR REJECTION OF DEVIANT OTHERS

Clearly, as one would expect from self-concept theory, that the possibility exists that self-acceptance is related to the acceptance of others. As a matter of fact several writers have suggested that those who least accept themselves find it difficult to accept others (see Fromm, 1939; Rogers, 1959). And if we limit that part of the self-concept to the individual's self-esteem then self-esteem and esteem for others should in fact be correlated. As a matter of fact Carl Rogers (1959) is quick to tell us that esteem or regard from others depends on two factors: conditional or unconditional. Conditional esteem depends upon one meeting other's evaluation criteria and when this is the case one is accepted, whereas a failure to do so leads to rejection. Unconditional esteem is not contingent upon other peoples' evaluation criteria but depends instead on the value the person places on her own self. Rogers goes on to tell us that when esteem or self-regard is indeed conditional, the individual at this point evaluates himself conditionally and, of course, self-acceptance occurs when the person meets others' standards. And in fact the individual may come to distort his self-perception and in fact avoid others in order to avoid discredit from them. And finally the person is said to develop a generalized feeling toward others that may predispose the individual to behave in specific ways in response to the evaluations from others. And individuals should then be attracted to people who tend to evaluate them positively and reject those who evaluate them negatively. This is why Rogers (1959) suggests that those factors that increase one's self-esteem are indeed gratifying, whereas those circumstances that decrease one's self-esteem are dissatisfying and threatening. And it is in this sense that Rogers speaks of a "basic need for self-regard." And, one's "need for self-esteem" seems to have a direct bearing on one's reaction not only one's own but others' evaluations.

Recently Ayala Pines and Trudy Solomon (1977) have shown evidence which seemingly contradicts the widely held assumption of Rogers and others that persons who have high self-acceptance tend to possess positive perceptions and acceptance of others. As a matter of fact they carried out two field studies (one using mental health workers and the other elementary school children) and they have shown that those with low self-acceptance are indeed more empathetic than those with higher self-acceptance. And those high in self-regard tend to "dehumanize" and detach themselves from others.

Pines and Solomon's (1977) two field studies dealt with subjects' self attitudes and attitudes toward others assessed by a questionnaire. First, 76 mental health professionals (e.g., psychiatrists, psychologists, and psychiatric social workers), were given a questionnaire that assessed their attitudes toward the "average schizophrenic" patient, their work environment, their professional role, and mental health in general. The researchers also employed semantic differential scales to measure their subjects' self-perceptions. A second study employed 204 elementary school children who were obtained from the 4-6 grades. And a questionnaire asked each child to evaluate a case description of a hypothetical peer with serious personal problems. The children were given the same self-perception measures as were the adults with a slight linguistic modification to fit the children's level of understanding.

Pines and Soloman found that the mental health professionals, who had more negative self-perceptions, viewed themselves as significantly less "successful" in their respective professional role and were less satisfied with themselves, and less successful with their patients. Those with less positive self-perceptions saw themselves as more similar to the "average schizophrenic" than those with more positive self-perceptions.

The same pattern of results held true for the children. That is, they perceived the peer stimulus person much like themselves and they perceived the stimulus person as significantly more warm and normal than did their counterparts who possessed a more positive self-regard. Hence, children who like themselves more, and who are more self-confident, tend to perceive a stimulus peer as significantly more cold, negative and abnormal.

Could it be that those with positive self-perceptions are more rejecting and consequently dehumanize deviant others, whereas those with more negative self-perceptions tend to more or less accept deviant others and accord them "warmth and empathy." Unforturnately it is difficult to assess Pines and Solomon's (1977) findings because the clinical and personality-based assumption that high self-acceptance is linked to positive acceptance and Pine and Solomon's research do not make it clear whether self-acceptance or self-liking are involved in either case. Hence, self-regard (liking) and acceptance are two very different concepts and it is in this respect that Arthur W. Combs, Anne Cohen Richards, and Fred Richards tell us that:

> Acceptance of self should not be confused with "liking." Some experimenters, for example, have attempted to measure self-acceptance by asking subjects to indicate the degree to which they liked certain characteristics about themselves. But acceptance is no more related to liking than it is to resignation. It has to do with the admission of fact, the acknowledgement of existance, and has nothing to do with liking. An adequate personality may accept the fact, for example, that he is sometimes nasty to his children, but this hardly means that he likes himself so: Liking and disliking have to do with judgments about self, while acceptance is nonjudgmental. It has to do with the consideration of the evidence, not its evaluation. adequate personality neither overvalues nor undervalues self. He is able to examine himself like any other datumm (1976, p. 263).

Finally, in contrast to low self-esteem, high self-esteem seems to have a different impact on how individuals perceive themselves as deviant. This occurs when a person generally is uncertain about the boundaries of acceptable and unacceptable behavior. Hence, it follows from our discussion that the more positive one's self-appraisal the less one is attracted to deviant roles, however, more research is needed to firmly establish this relationship. Meanwhile there is good reason to suspect that one's self-esteem may be intrinsically related to perceptions of deviance. We have seen, for example, that those with high self-esteem do not necessarily accord deviant others high regard as is predicted from self-concept theory. We have also observed that events or persons boasting one's self-esteem have an impact on one's perception and acceptance of deviant others. And, of course, it seems clear that several different situational and personality variables are simultaneously at work in addition to self-esteem and influence one's self and other perceptions. We have seen that there is good reason to believe that those with low self-esteem are less likely to influence others and more likely to be influenced. And it is in this sense that the self-concept and more particularly self-esteem play a critical role in how people perceive deviant others.

Finally, is there good reason to suspect that externality and deviant behavior are positively related? Two recent texts on locus of control (E. Jerry Phares' *Locus of Control in Personality* and Herbert M. Lefcourt's *Locus of Control: Current Trends in Theory and Research*) have devoted a chapter each on the topic and conclude that externality and various forms of deviancy are positively related.

SUMMARY AND CONCLUSIONS

The social psychologist studing deviant behavior can start out with the hypothesis that some kind of fairly stable behavior characterizes deviancy. It is in this sense that psychologists usually refer to a stable tendency to engage in deviant behavior assumed to be caused wholly or in part by traits or dispositions. And when social psychologists posit traits or dispositions (attitudes etc.) as causes of deviant behavior they attempt to distinguish between those behaviors showing transituational characteristics and those that do not. Thus, the researcher would expect that persons with a high degree of a particular trait should behave rather consistently in many situations, whereas others with relatively low levels of this very same trait are expected to behave in ways that are inconsistent with those who are high on the deviant trait in question.

One problem that deviant behavior researchers face is that most deviant behavior appears to be influenced by several variables. Hence, multiply determined deviant behaviors seem to be the rule rather than the exception. And the question frequently comes up how can the deviant behavior investigator ever really be sure that a personality measure is tapping a particular cause of deviant behavior?

Most commonly, the deviant behaviors that social psychologists use to infer personality characteristics from consists of a set of questionnaire items. The person makes self-report statements by agreeing or disagreeing with the personality characteristic under investigation.

A difficult problem confronted by those studying personality variables which is related to deviancy is that several other variables other than the personality characteristics of interest can in fact systematically influence the individual's responses. This suggest that there is some probability that a particular subject's responses to one personality measure is correlated with several other personality variables not studied by the researcher.

Though we have suggested that personality-based views of deviant behavior, in general, have received some support, they by no means account for the greater portion of the variance for deviancy. It is for this reason that we have noted that social psychologists have by and large chosen to ignore personality differences---thinking that the impact of personality does not count nearly as much as do situational variables. Such reasoning, of course, is based on findings indicating that most personality characteristics generally show a weak relationship to most social behaviors studied by social psychologists.

From our rather limited sampling of personality variables we have attempted to demonstrate that personality research suggests, in general, that there is an influence of personality on the individual's susceptibility to deviant behavior.

First, in exploring the topic of Machiavellianism and its relationship to deviant behavior certain suggestions come to mind, and, no doubt, the reader has asked some of these very same questions. For example, whether highly Machiavellian individuals display norm-violating behavior to a greater degree than those low in Machiavellianism. And the obvious answer to this question seems to be that it depends on whether or not a Machiavellian form of manipulation is indeed considered to be deviant. On the other hand, we have shown that Machiavellians lie, cheat, and take advantage of their fellowmen. The "deviant behavior" in this case is not explained in terms of classical conceptions of psychopathology, but in terms of interpersonal opportunities to deviate from normatively derived social behaviors (see Christie & Geis, 1970).

Another kind of personality variable has been given much attention---authoritarianism and dogmatism. The authoritarian personality seems most secure in situations where there is a demand for the respect of authority. Hence, the application of the F-scale to a wide-range of populations shows that those who support right-wing groups and those who have conservative political beliefs have higher F-scores than do those of left-wing and liberal persuasion. Then, do these findings explain politically derived deviant behaviors? This is difficult to say because it has not been clearly demonstrated that one's authoritarianism translates into deviant behavior. Meanwhile, Milton Rokeach (1960) has developed a measure of authoritarianism, labeled the dogmatism scale and his scale appears to be free from political ideology, however it is difficult to establish just how dogmatism is translated into deviant behavior. In addition, Rotter's locus-of-control variable is treated as a personality characteristic by suggesting that there is a link between expectancy and behavior in a particular situation. And intuitively it does seem logical that people who believe that they control their lives should also be less likely to be influenced by other people than those who feel that external forces control their lives. The relatively modest correlations between psychopathology and externality suggests that externals are more likely to show deviations in personality related to schizophrenia and depression. Still there is the question of whether or not psychopathology or deviant behavior leads to external beliefs or does externality lead to deviant behavior or psychopathology? Or still do the same conditions that contribute to external beliefs also influence deviancy? These questions, and others, have not yet been answered by research on the locus of control varialbe (see Phares, 1976).

Since the role of self-esteem is assumed to be central in determining social behavior it seems only logical that self-esteem should be studied by social psychologists. Then, given the importance of self-esteem how do measures of self-esteem relate to deviant behavior? As with locus of control, social psychologists have attempted to demonstrate that self-esteem is related to the receptivity of social influence. Generally, research has shown mixed findings. That is, an inverted--U relationship holds between self-esteem and social influence where people with moderate degrees of self-esteem seem to be more subject to influence than those with low or high self-esteem.

Do those with low self-esteem possess negative feelings toward deviant others? Carl Rogers (1959) does indeed tell us that those with a positive self-regard are more likely to accept others. However, this clinically derived wisdom has not always been supported by social psychological research (e.g., Berschied & Walster, 1969; Pines & Solomon, 1977).

Finally, we must conclude that the relatively disappointing relationship between the more traditional personality variables studied by social psychologists and deviant behavior suggests the need for social psychologists to examine other possible personality variables; perhaps those used by clinical psychologists and personologists, particularily combining these measures with situational variables where interactions are of major interest.

CHAPTER 7: DEVIANT BEHAVIOR: RESEARCH METHODS AND PROBLEMS

INTRODUCTION: THE NATURE OF DEVIANT BEHAVIOR RESEARCH

The social psychologist who is interested in investigating deviancy cannot, of course, overlook the fact that value judgments intrude. Then, it appears that to a great extent a value-free social psychology of deviant behavior is more an ideal situation than an actuality. Then, what is in fact the main thrust of deviant behavior research is essentially the study of behaviors which differentiate deviant actions from nondeviant actions including behaviors as diverse and as general as criminal behaviors and drug addiction and as specific as nonconformity in small group settings. In either case the researcher is not entirely free from value judgments. It should also be noted that social psychologists who study deviancy seem to be in general agreement that the topic of deviant behavior is not the primary concern of most research efforts. Beyond this basic line of agreement, whenever researchers do carry out deviant behavior research their approach to the various topics of deviancy depends on their concern for research methodology And this is why there is more than one approach to the study of deviancy reported in the literature. A researcher's concern for choice of research methods can have an important impact on her approach to the study of deviancy. And whether deviancy is researched in the laboratory or in the "real world" it will depend largely on the specific research problems the investigator poses for herself. Then, the purpose of this chapter is quite simple: It is to focus on the kinds of research methods employed by social psychologists who study social behavior and more particularly on occasion those who study deviant behavior.

Greater knowledge of the research methods used to study deviant behavior and an "awareness" of the problems encountered in doing so should enhance one's knowledge of deviant behavior: It should broaden our understanding of deviance in general and especially should make it more meaningful when we attempt to evaluate the soundness of a piece of research. Hence, what seems to be needed here is an understanding of research which telescopes the single study or the limited research in a specific area of deviancy.

    First of all we do not even begin to have a general social psychological theory for deviance; our knowledge of its parameters are exceedingly limited at best. Even those few studies which exist, such as studies done in the area of conformity-deviation, have nowhere been systematically organized under a general set of principles that apply to specific or general patterns of deviant behavior. Possibly the most fruitful efforts toward a general understanding of deviant behavior are the social exchange and attribution perspectives. Yet basically, both of these views when applied to the study of deviancy have in common many research problems.

    Before we examine some of these problems it should be noted that common sense views of deviant behavior abound and obvious problems are associated with using such orientations, for example, that conformity and deviation are general characteristics of people or that deviancy can be explained essentually by appealing to general learning principles. However contemporary social psychology is a scientific endeavor and its problems represent a combination of scientific curiosity and values. The process of the accumulation of data is fundamental. For instance, suppose that the pressure a group exerts upon a member to act in a given way is observed this would require that one learn more about the possible relationships involved. We might create situations in which we systematically vary the degree of pressure exerted and then observe the degree of compliance or conformity (or lack of it) subjects display. Of course this hypothetical experiment will involve many factors, in addition to those studied, and the researcher's values will no doubt intrude in the experiment to an extent that they are difficult or impossible to assess. For example, the researcher (and her subjects) is likely to value conformity over deviant behavior and its occurrence in an experiment may be due in part to the way the problem is researched. In addition, it is not always possible to determine how an observed relationship holds. That is, no matter how precise we think our measurements and how well we design our studies, deviant behavior research is beset by problems sometimes labeled random error and sometimes labeled subject or experimenter bias. It is in this sense that the major criterion of science requires a stance of objectivity, however, this goal is never really fully attainable. Scientists are beset by some relative degree of subjectivity because they choose the variables they study within the social context of their environments.

Though the subject matter of deviant behavior is diverse, and often interdisciplinary, the researcher must first define a particular research problem where only a certain class of variables is studied. Sometimes this requires a more or less narrow focus on issues. And as a matter of fact, if indeed the research is too broad, much of the precision and possible application of the research is more than likely to be limited. Finally, the researcher must decide what research method to employ for a particular problem. This usually entails a choice among several available research methods, all of which may have certain obvious advantages and disadvantages. Hence, our intent here is to provide an evaluation of the several methods used to study deviant behavior. And we should note that no single method or technique has been able, at least at this time, to offer the "best" or "most adequate" method to study all of the many problems posed by deviant behavior researchers.

The investigation of a problem in deviancy usually starts with the question: "Why do some people show deviant behavior in certain situations while still others do not?" After formulating the question, the deviant behavior researcher must then decide what aspects of this very general question to formulate as a research hypothesis. Obviously, it would be impossible to try to consider all aspects of a research question whenever formulating a specific research hypothesis. This is so because, as we have noted, there is a great deal of inescapable complexity in any form of social behavior, and deviant behavior in particular is more than likely to have a multi-causal basis for it rather than a single variable cause-and-effect relationship. That is, many questions posed by researchers are far too general to find a siuuation in which to observe the phenomenon in question without taking into account the complexity of the situation in the first place.

LABORATORY EXPERIMENTS

Then, once having formulated a research question as a hypothesis, the researcher must next decide how to turn the hypothesis into a research method. For example, suppose that a researcher is interested in testing the effects of experimentally produced "feelings of deviancy" on behavior. In order to ascertain how these "feelings" influence the individual's behavior the method of choice used here would, of course, be an experimental method (see Freedman & Doob, 1968). And we should note here that laboratory experiments are carried out in highly controlled settings (labortories) where the experimenter is able to control the research situation in a sense that some variables are allowed to vary (independent) and other aspects of the situation are held constant. In our example, the investigator would control or hold constant those variables likely to influence the individual's deviant behavior. For this purpose random assignment of subjects to experimental and control groups is used to "control" for the effects of extraneous variables and to eliminate a major source of potential error.

We should note that relatively speaking there is a short history of experimentation in social psychology which bears on deviant behavior. For example, as we noted in an earlier chapter, in the 1930s Sherif (1935, 1936) carried out laboratory experiments on the emergence of social norms. Sherif used an ambiguous stimulus, the autokinetic effect, in order to increase his subjects' desire for social reality: A small spot of light was projected in a darkened room and was seen to move due to the fact that the confederates of the experimenter reported that the light had made continuous shifts.

The Sherif experiment was indeed a landmark in conformity and deviation research, which in fact encouraged additional experimentation dealing with the group's influence on the individual. This research, of course, lead to Asch's (1951) research on conformity. He used unambiguous stimuli to study conformity (or compliance) and his objective was much like that of Sherif: To induce individuals to either yield or to remain independent to the group judgments. And indeed Asch did find that in the presence of a single minority position this decreased the degree of conformity. In addition he found that his subjects were in effect showing compliance, that is, they made public responses different from their private responses.

Still one more extension of Sherif and Asch's laboratory work is Milgram's paradigm used to study obedience to authority (1964, 1974). The general purpose of Milgram's experiment was to determine when the subject refused to continue to shock the "learner," thereby showing when in fact disobedience to authority takes place.

The above examples of experimentation in social psychology are classical examples and they point toward the fact that in recent years, following these early examples, a high percentage of published research in social psychology has entailed the laboratory experiment as its choice method of research. There are good reasons for the heavy use of the laboratory-research method because more than any other method it allows the researcher to control the environment in which the data are collected. That is, the laboratory is arranged so that the experimenter manipulates independent variables and potentially irrelevant and confounding effects are for the most part eliminated or held constant so that they are unlikely to influence the relationship of independent and dependent variables (or variables that change in response to changes in the independent variable).

Because of the way data are collected in the laboratory-research design, and because of the more or less clear statements about causality for the relationships among variables, social psychologists have advocated its use and they have argued that it is one of the most adequate ways to carry out social psychological research (see Carlsmith, Ellsworth & Aronson, 1976; Crano & Brewer, 1973; Hendrick & Jones, 1972).

Then, since experiments seem to be the choice research method when researchers wish to maximize control we should also note that this is achieved by both the manipulation of independent variables in a laboratory setting and by random assignment of subjects to both treatment and control groups. For example, Craig Haney, W. Curtis Banks, and Philip G. Zimbardo (1973) illustrate the way in which an experiment is used to study deviant behavior. Haney *et al.*'s research entailed a more or less uncomplicated design in that they randomly assigned their subjects to one of two treatment conditions: either to a guard or a prisoner condition. This was done in order to study the possible impact of situational and dispositional variables. They screened out subjects who were judged to have relatively severe personality problems (and in effect they, no doubt, failed to adequately test for dispositional factors). And, hence, Haney *et al.*'s prison study can be classified as an experiment because of the nature of their research That is, they simulated a prison environment and they attempted to control extraneous variables while using what Aronson and Carlsmith (1968) call "mundane realism" in order to reduce the likelihood of demand characteristics.

We will next examine field experiments as an attempt to bridge the gap between the naturalness of the field or "real world" and the control that is part of the laboratory experiment.

GOING OUTSIDE THE LABORATORY: FIELD EXPERIMENTATION

In recent years, social psychological researchers, interested in deviant behavior, have decided to carry out investigations in the "real world." This has been done in order, as it were, to reduce the possibility that subjects may react differently in the laboratory than they do in the "outside world." In this sense it has been demonstrated that imaginative researchers can often employ the "real world" as a sort of laboratory. Experiments carried out in this way are usually called field experiments. For example, to return to our earlier case, suppose an investigator wishes to study how people react to a "deviant individual" and in general she observes that people generally mistreat deviants. Given the constraints of the "real world" how does the researcher go about investigating this problem? First, the researcher can take advantage of the more or less naturalness in which events take place. However, it is not always possible for the researcher to manipulate independent variables in natural settings. And in still other cases not only is it possible but it is advantageous to manipulate independent variables in a natural setting. For example, F.K. Henssenstamm (1971) varied the appearance of drivers who displayed bumper stickers depicting a large Black Panther sign. He found that students received citations from the police equally, regardless of race or sex or ethnicity.

The form of research cited above suffers from a lack of experimental control over extraneous variables; for example, the results could in fact be due to the increase or "crackdown" on traffic violators or as a matter of fact having a Black Panther bumper sticker on one's car could influence the way one drives and indeed culminate in greater traffic citations. Nevertheless, the data researchers obtain from field experiments may be more representative of the "real world" than are data obtained from well-controlled laboratory studies. This is so because subjects who participate in laboratory experiments may in fact be "aware" that they are being evaluated and in point of fact attempt to help the experimenter obtain results confirming or disconfirming the researcher's hypotheses. Of course, subjects in a field experiment generally are not "aware" that they are taking part in research. And as a result these subjects behave in more or less "natural" ways.

In light of what we have said about laboratory and field experiments we should ask "which method is the best for most deviant behavior research?" This question is difficult to answer because both methods have advantages and disadvantages. For example, the laboratory method is often faulted because it is said to be artificial by the standards of field experimentation, and its results may not generalize to more natural situations. Hence, the laboratory experiment can produce more precise results sometimes at the cost of generalization to the "real world."

Social psychologist have steadily increased their concern for studying social behavior in natural settings Perhaps this is so because many research ideas are untestable within a laboratory setting and because such ideas are likely to involve complex sets of social variables. Therefore, a challenging task for the social psychologist who is interested in deviant behavior is to design experiments which have some relative degree of "experimental control" while at the same time the researcher must increase the confidence he has between what is observed and the generalizations of the results obtained. However, as we have noted, where field experiments are carried out the researcher relinquishes the precision of experimental control. Some other shortcomings of field experimentation might be noted. For instance researchers have distinguished between field research done where the investigator does not intervene or does not directly interact with her subjects or <u>nonreactive</u> <u>research</u> and research which does indeed entail measures which are obtained in direct interaction with subjects labeled <u>reactive research</u> (see Webb, Campbell, Schwartz, & Sechrest, 1966).

At first blush there are several important points that should be considered when we evaluate <u>nonreactive</u> and <u>reactive</u> deviant-behavior research carried out in natural settings. First, one must consider the degree to which subjects are "aware" that they are being studied. Second, and as Paul G. Swingle (1973) has stressed, research done in natural settings may entail some of the same ethical problems as are noted for laboratory research. Hence, some rather serious ethical problems need to be considered. For instance, those observed in nonreactive research by definition are not likely to be "aware" that they are under the surveillance of the researcher. In this case, those who carry out field experimentation may have to resolve pressing ethical problems much like those who do laboratory research. For example, the researcher should consider whether or not she is in violation of her subjects right to privacy.

As we have pointed out earlier, the laboratory method, of course, cannot be applied to research most naturally occurring events such as riots or deindividuated behavior in real life settings because the researcher cannot randomly assign subjects to conditions nor can the experimenter vary independent variables in the same way as is done in the laboratory situation. In such cases the experimental approach can be used in only a limited degree For one thing the experimenter, at least in most cases, must deal with less extreme levels of independent variables than those that occur naturally in the "real world." For example, the investigator is unlikely to produce the extreme forms of deviant behavior as are likely to be observed under the desparate conditions often associated with the environmental or community conditions known to give raise to deviant behavior. For example, the painful experiences that drug addicts or criminals suffer are unlikely to be created in experiments; because these are experiences of only the "real world" not laboratory settings. We can see, then, how the deviant behavior experimenter has certain limitations imposed upon her.

We have continued to stress that deviant behavior research is complex as is also the case with any form of social behavior. Unlike much of animal research the use of human subjects is different because humans are often "aware" that they are being studied and this may affect their own behavior in many ways. This observation has lead some researchers to claim that social psychological researchers have to face some rather serious ethical problems. This observation is neither recent nor unknown---most researchers have had to cope with such problems for years. However, recently researchers have reacted to the limits placed on experimental research by attempting to show that research bias and so-called artifact do indeed set serious limits on experimental research. And it has been suggested that these limitations can indeed be circumvented, for example, Elliot Aronson and J. Merrill Carlsmith (1968) tell us that an artifactual claim for experimental work cannot be made or in fact refuted if in a particular research effort there is a general failure to replicate an existing study where the researcher does indeed modify the original investigator's research procedure. It would appear that in such cases it is necessary to employ the same or identical procedure and then when a replication attempt fails questions should be raised regarding the possible artifact of the experiment in question.

Of course, the suggestion being made by Aronson and Carlsmith (1968) is that if generalizations of research findings are to be made researchers must replicate essentially the same study (including the application of the same research design) with as many different kinds of populations as are available to the experimenter. And in this regard deviant behavior research, in general, does not receive a high mark. That is, the reproductibility of much of deviant behavior research, with the exception of the more classical forms of social psychological research on deviant behavior, seems to be limited in that the research is likely to be unique and the finding is likely to be based on the internal conditions of the particular research setting (see Back et al., 1977).

THE PROBLEM OF INTERNAL AND EXTERNAL VALIDITY

The question raised above leads us to a consideration of internal and external validity. And in this regard, Donald Campbell (see Campbell, 1957; Campbell & Stanley, 1966) has distinguished between two types of validity as it relates to psychological research: Internal and external. Internal validity is said to occur essentially where the researcher attempts to establish the causal relation between variables established within a specific research setting (e.g., a laboratory setting). The problem of establishing external validity takes place where the investigator attempts to demonstrate that a particular relationship holds in other than the initial research setting (e.g., the real world or in situations outside the laboratory).

In order to ascertain whether or not the particular research finding reported by the experimenter has comparable implications for research carried out within a different research context it may be necessary to do experiments in different research settings.

We have attempted to show that there are a number of different factors that may produce differences between the results of different studies especially where different research methods are used. Hence, data cannot always be obtained from subjects in situations where they are randomly assigned to experimental conditions, however, it does seem reasonable to expect that researchers should attempt to relate their research to the "real world" or in other words maximize external validity for their research. Nevertheless, we should hasten to add that researchers should guard against assuming that where experimental settings seem to be similar to the "real world" they are indeed correlates of the "real world." In other words what we are suggesting is that in particular the deviant behavior researcher must in most cases be highly tenative in his generalizations from a particular research setting to the "outside world."

What, then, is the real issue raised when we consider laboratory or field experimentation? In a few words the issue is whether research done in more or less controlled settings allows the researcher to generalize to what is observed in the "real world." Then, if this is the case it does seem that we can easily justify both research carried out in the "well-controlled" setting as well as field experimentation. Both types of research should relate to what is observed in the everyday world. Then the answer to our question is clearly yes, on both sides of the issue we need both laboratory and field experiments in deviant behavior. Indeed to deny this would be tantamount to denying that basic deviant behavior research is necessary.

Finally, it should be noted that generalizations which derive from deviant behavior research are limited by several important factors. Among these factors is the nature of the subjects studied. That is, much of the research cited in previous chapters entailed the use of college students as subjects, but we cannot always be certain that research findings obtained from college populations really apply to other groupings.

Before we proceed on to a consideration of some of the major sources of research bias it should be understood that many criticisms of social psychology have acrued over the years and indeed more recently some social psychologists have faulted social psychology on the grounds that it is not really an example of science afterall. For example, Kenneth Gergen (1973) contends that social psychology (and the social sciences in general) cannot produce the sort of laws and theories as are gleamed from the natural and physical sciences. That is, he suggests that hypotheses about human social behavior are constantly changing, whereas laws from the natural sciences are relatively fixed over time. Gergen believes that when people become "aware" of the "laws" of social behavior they in effect can and do change their everyday behaviors to disconfirm the particular law in question. For example, knowing that one is likely to obey an experimenter who orders one to shock a "victim" may lead one to disobey an order to harm others when this order is given by an experimenter.

Then, according to Gergen social psychologists only accummulate statements which describe social behavior which indeed are true at the time but which may change when people become "aware" of the implications of the researcher's findings. This is why Gergen contents that social psychology is in effect the study of history and not a science.

Before the reader hastens to agree with Gergen, it should be noted that Barry Schlenker (1974) tells us that there are several problems with the logic that social psychology is not a science. For example, data collected differs in kind from general scientific laws of behavior. The fact that an individual conforms or complies or does not to group pressure does not take into account the fact that an abstract statement, which attempts to explain the conditions under which conformity or nonconformity takes place, is indeed subsumed under a number of observations. That is, some individuals will conform and some will not and the reasons are likely to be complex, however a general law of social behavior should account for both cases. Hence, the question of whether or not people become "aware" of the general laws of social behavior and then attempt to disconfirm the laws, because they don't want to appear predictable seems to be itself an empirical question as yet not researched. Hence, what we've said about social psychology as science or as history in effect is simply a particular way of noting that the goals of science are different for some researchers than for others because being able to predict and understand social behavior depends on accounting for the laws of stability and change within the same set of laws.

Not only is the area of the social psychology of deviant behavior unable to predict what behaviors are likely to occur in particular situations in the present and future, they usually cannot foresee the overall effects deviant behaviors will have on the social life of particular kinds of persons. This is so because, since we cannot predict the exact form of future social behaviors, we cannot know what tomorrow's environments will be. Hence, according to the principle of determinism, all events have causes, not that all events lend themselves to prediction. The historical perspective suggests that past and present events are necessary to predict and explain future events. And in the same sense, the social scientist can only look for the causes of social behavior from an understanding of the effects that have already taken place.

Finally we should note that people do indeed formulate hypotheses about why they behave the way they do and at times attempt to understand the causes of their own and others' behavior.

SOURCES OF RESEARCH BIAS

People who interact in any given set of circumstances differentially influence others' behavior in countless ways. Deviant behavior is no exception. Hence, it makes sense to ask: "To what extend do deviant behavior researchers influence their subjects' behavior and conversely to what degree are experimenters influenced by their subjects?"

At first blush it does seem obvious that an answer to this question is likely to be found in an examination of the research situation. For example, Martin Orne (1962, 1969) argues that subjects are likely to view an experiment as a situation where the experimenter and the subject share a certain belief that science is a means to advance human welfare. Orne tells us that the experimental situation itself may get in the way and elicit demand characteristics or make cues for behavior that conforms to what the experimenter wants more likely.

How have social psychologists attempted to cope with demand characteristics? Of course, an answer to this question assumes that researchers must first identify the situational demands being placed on their subjects. To this extent Orne (1969) does come to our aid by suggesting that the researcher may employ what he calls the "nonexperiment technique." This requires that an experimenter ask her subjects how they might respond to the same situation as subjects who have actually been put through the research procedure without, of course, themselves having been subjected to the experimental treatment. The researcher then compares subjects from the "real experiment" with those from the "nonexperiment." If, indeed the same effects are shown for the "nonexperiment" as are shown for the "real experiment" the researcher then concludes that demand characteristics have probably operated and that the research has limitations in this respect.

Yet in still another context, Robert Rosenthal (1966, 1969) has been telling psychologists for some time that they have been unintentionally and systematically biasing their research findings. He and his associates have demonstrated that researchers do indeed influence their subjects' responses however, he has not been able, to date, to show just exactly how such influence operates. Nevertheless, Rosenthal has identified several factors which he considers likely sources of bias: The researcher's voice intonation, facial expression, and body cues.

The claim made by Rosenthal is that the experimenter somehow communicates expectancies for his research to his subjects and that in turn the subjects' responses are likely to change so that they tend to inadvertently support the researcher's hypotheses. However, Theodore X. Barber (see Barber & Silver, 1968; Barber, 1977) questions Rosenthal's claims from the standpoint of the soundness of Rosenthal's statistical analysis of his data. That is, Barber concludes that evidence for bias effects are not as robust as Rosenthal has claimed. However, in all fairness to Robert Rosenthal we should point out that he has more recently shown that experimenter and subject bias does indeed operate and that it is incumbant upon the researcher to consider potential sources of bias.

Although we cannot go into the details of Rosenthal's work here the reader is urged to consult this research. Meanwhile, the deviant behavior researcher should attempt to formulate research which is relatively free from bias. In this respect, it is proposed here that social psychological research on deviant behavior affords several solutions for avoiding researcher and subject bias. For example, subjects' naieveté can be maintained through the application of a "cover story" or through a deception technique. However, unfortunately deception entails serious ethical problems. We will discuss some of these problems shortly, however, it should be noted first that role playing has been offered as an alternative to deception and, of course, a role-playing technique is used to reduce some of the serious ethical problems (see Kelman, 1967). Nevertheless, John G. Adair (1973) argues that studies are needed in order to establish role-playing as a viable alternative to deception. And Adair suggests that naturalistic research is another alternative to deception especially when it is used in conjunction with laboratory research.

Perhaps one important solution to research bias is to employ converging research methods where the same problem is researched in a number of different settings by applying a number of different research designs including deception and role-playing techniques. In this way we are likely to learn what the effects of the particular research setting are as well as the most appropriate research design that can be used for the problem of interest to the researcher (see Carlsmith, Ellsworth & Aronson, 1976).

RESEARCH ETHICS FOR DEVIANT BEHAVIOR EXPERIMENTATION

Social psychologists---along with other behavioral scientists---who do deviant behavior research must, of course, consider the potential impact that their research is likely to have on those who are employed as subjects. What we have in mind here is the nagging question whether or not the researcher has violated the subject's right of privacy. In order to prevent the occurrance of an invasion of the subject's privacy the subject's consent should first be obtained when one gathers data from subjects under conditions that potentially arouse intense emotional feelings. In this respect it may be highly inappropriate to expose subjects to treatment conditions likely to produce intense negative reactions. It is also essential that subjects be given feedback about the purpose of the research especially where they have been exposed to deceptive research techniques. This is important because a large percentage of social psychological research does indeed involve the use of deception.

It should be noted that the use of deception has been both a blessing and a source of serious ethical problems for social psychological researchers (see Kelman, 1967). For example, Dana Bramel (1962) and Stanley Milgram's (1963, 1974) research are examples of experimental situations where perhaps excessive deception was used. In the case of Bramel's research it could be argued that males who are led to believe that they have latent homosexual tendencies may subsequently harbor negative self-feelings. And in the Milgram experiment, no doubt, a great deal of stress was induced in subjects who obeyed the experimenter and shocked the "learner." And finally, more recently the research carried out by West, Gunn, and Chernicky (1975), no doubt, produced negative feelings in the conditions where subjects agreed to take part in an illegal break-in for either money or where complete immunity from legal prosecution was offered subjects. One can only wonder how one would react to having agreed to take part in a type of action strongly condemned by society and clearly a criminal violation. On the other hand it should be recognized that while some social psychologists do in fact clearly support the use of deception, because at least at the moment there appears to be no real alternative, not all researchers are so inclined. Nevertheless, Elliot Aronson and J. Merrell Carlsmith (1968) believe that subjects can be "successfully" debriefed and they claim that deception is unlikely to result in "undue harmful side effects."

Of course, the reader should be alert to the fact that not all researchers agree with Aronson and Carlsmith (e.g., Katz, 1967; Kelman, 1967), however, the reader should also note that the social psychological researcher is likely to do research entailing ethical problems especially those problems peculiar to deviant behavior research. For example, the deviant behavior researcher may offend or perhaps even challenge subjects' moral beliefs unless she uses the utmost caution. In addition, the investigator who does research with individuals who are "emotionally unstable" may create situations that are likely to produce undue anxiety and apprehension, and of course, this should be avoided at all costs.

The deviant behavior researcher should work closely with his subjects and attempt to make them feel that an important contribution can be made to social psychology and to society in general through their participation in deviant behavior research. This may be accomplished by first obtaining consent from subjects. And finally at all times the person should feel that she is free to curtail participation in the researcher's work. What we are suggesting here is that _informed consent_ be used and that subjects be made aware of the possible risks or harm before they agree to participate in an experimenter's research. In addition, once the research is concluded, the researcher should debrief her subjects, especially where deception is used. This generally requires telling one's subjects the _real_ reasons for doing the study and the need to use a "cover story" in the first place.

On a more positive note it should be stressed that where deception is used, as seems to be the case with most social psychological research, it need not have a detrimental impact on subjects. For example, Phillip G. Zimbardo (1974) tells us that in his studies, for example, the Stanford Prison experiment, debriefing tended to elimate possible negative reactions, no doubt, having their origin in the deception process (see Glasgow & Davis, 1977).

And as we have already suggested, an alternative to deception has been proposed--_role playing_. For example, Schultz (1969) tells us that researchers can provide their subjects with complete information about a study and subsequently have them take the role of a would-be naive subject. This suggestion implies that data obtained from role-playing subjects would in effect approximate data obtained from _actual_ subjects who, of course, have been deceived or not told the real purpose of the research. However, Jonathan L. Freedman (1969) and Arthur G. Miller (1972) are quick to point out that data obtained from role players is in point of truth nothing more than guesses about how _real_ subjects would in fact respond. Supporting this argument Holmes and Bennett (1974) have demonstrated that role players and actual subjects produce different data. That is, subjects who were told that they were about to receive electric shocks (informed subjects), as opposed to those asked to make believe that they were about to be shocked (role players), differed. Contrary to the role-playing hypothesis, role players were unable to reproduce the responses of real subjects.

More recently C.D. Spencer tells us that there are two forms of role playing:

> When employed as a method of research, role-playing has been viewed as a threat to both the internal and external validity of an experiment. Two frequently employed types of role playing are defined...with respect to the type of threat each poses to valid inference. Empirical role playing exists when the role has been prescribed and independently monitored by the experimenter. Hypothe-

tical role playing exists when the role-playing response is not or cannot be independently and reliably monitored. Empirical role playing poses a threat to the external validity of a study, while hypothetical role playing threatens both internal and external validity. It is concluded that if a researcher must use role playing, empirical role playing is the only defensible substitute for in vivo research (1978, p. 265).

ARE THOSE WHO STUDY DEVIANTS, DEVIANT?

What happens when researchers study deviant behavior? Anyone who investigates deviancy sooner or later is likely to ask: "Do people who study deviant behavior exempt themselves from the label deviant or is it just possible that some scholars of deviancy engage in deviant behavior in the process of researching the social psychology of deviant behavior?

As a matter of fact, David W. Wilson and Edward Donnerstein (1976) raise the question whether or not social psychologists who conduct nonreactive research in natural settings are not themselves in violation of the public's trust? Wilson and Donnerstein attempted to answer this question by assessing a random sample of subjects' reactions to nonreactive research methods. And the subjects were encouraged to "express their views without a feeling of obligation or pressure." Hence, after presenting a variety of examples of nonreactive research methods to college subjects and older adults, who were obtained in several natural settings, Wilson and Donnerstein carried out interviews and asked their subjects to assess four different field studies relative to the question of ethics, personal harm to subjects, and the legal implications of the particular study.

It is of interest here to note that a small number of subjects viewed the experiments as unjustified, whereas most of the subjects felt that the field experiments did not "erode the public's trust in social scientific research." However, a sizable minority of subjects (as high as 32% for one of the studies assessed by the subjects) indeed said that they would consult a lawyer if they had taken part in the research.

Wilson and Donnerstein note that "apparently. there is still some feeling among the public that anything done for the sake of science is legitimate" (p. 771). On the other hand the authors suggest that: "More than one in three of our subjects felt that social scientists should stop deceiving the public and that a public protest should be mounted" (p. 771). Actually Wilson and Donnerstein indicate that a researcher (Silverman, 1975) did in fact put the question of legality to a hard test:

> He gave two lawyers descriptions of 10 nonreactive methods that have recently been reported in social psychological literature and asked them to consider whether any of the actions were in violation of any civil or criminal laws. In short, the two lawyers disagreed considerably. One believed that all the methods were outside the purview of criminal law, with only one possibly susceptible on civil grounds. The second lawyer felt that several of the methods were in violation of laws regarding trespass while all were criminally actionable for harassment, disorderly conduct, or both. An interesting point is that the lawyers seemed to agree that an injunction against the psychologist could be obtained if just one subject reported the incident to a justice of the peace (Wilson & Donnerstein, 1976, p. 776).

Overall, then, researchers have shown an interest in how the general public feels about psychological experimentation. However, as we have suggested, only recently have social psychologists gone out into the "real world" and actually asked people for their reactions to procedures involving potential harrassment and deception. And as we just saw, Wilson and Donnerstein (1976) did in fact find that the general public's reaction to eight different nonreactive field studies was by and large a feeling that researchers had not invaded their subjects' "rights to privacy" nor were the studies considered unethical.

Is it just conceivable that research showing negative human behavior is judged more innocuous than where the outcomes of research is less negative? In order to provide an answer to this question, Leonard Bickman and Matthew Zarantonello (1978) had subjects, found in front of a civic center and riders of a rapid transit line (in a large midwestern city) read one of four versions of the Milgram (1964) obedience experiment. The researchers varied both the degree of obedience obtained from subjects in the Milgram experiment (high versus low) and whether or not the subjects in the experiment had been exposed to a deception procedure (deception versus no deception).

Results of Bickman and Zarantonello's research showed that subjects rated those who participated in the Milgram study more on the basis of the outcome of the Milgram obedience experiment than on the basis of the deception procedure employed. That is, subjects assigned to the high obedience condition viewed the results of the study more unfavorably than did subjects in the low obedience condition. Subjects also thought that those who had volunteered in the high obedience condition "harmed" the "victim" significantly more than did volunteers in the low obedience condition. In addition, high-obedience subjects felt that the volunteers had acted significantly more irresponsibly than subjects asked to judge those in the low obedience condition. On the other hand, subjects in the low obedience condition felt that the volunteers were more uncomfortable in disobeying the experimenter's orders. Finally, Bickman and Zarantonello indicate that:

> One may wonder if the Milgram study would have been the subject of public outrage if the results had turned out differently. These data suggest that if most of Milgram's subjects had disobeyed, his experiment would have not received as much condemation....Critics may be responding to the unflattering portrayal of human nature discovered using deceptive methodologies rather than the act of deception itself (1978, Pp. 84-85).

As we have suggested earlier social psychologists doing research related to deviant behavior sometimes do not make their presense known to their subjects and as such ethical problems may arise. For example, Dennis Middlemist, Eric Knowels and Charles Matter (1976) researched "bathroom behavior" where they set up a hidden periscope in a public lavatory and observed males peeing, of course, without the males' knowing they were being observed. The researchers' confederate went into the lavatory where the subject was micturating and noted how quickly the subject finished peeing and how much volume of urine was released. In addition, the researchers were interested in what happens when the subject is alone or whether all three urinals are busy. When all three of the urinals were occupied little "personal space" resulted and the subjects delayed their micturition.

Then along came Gerald Koocher (1977) and protested to the editors of the _Journal of Personality and Social Psychology_ on the grounds that it is unethical to observe people without telling them and especially when this takes place in public lavatories. Koocher notes that:

> One must also consider the role of the journal editors and consultants who reviewed this manuscript. There are those who believe that all journal aricles using human subjects ought to include the basis for informed consent as part of the Method section. Indeed, a number of medical journals currently refuse to review manuscripts submitted without such data. I subscribe to the belief that when a potential problem of a subject's rights is at issue, a discussion of the cost/benefit rationale is imperative. Certainly the fact that a study was or was not approved by an institutional or peer review panel ought to be noted. By not insisting on this data, the editors of the journal in question appear to condone the practices, or at the very least tacitly suggest that the methods used represent the acceptable practices of researchers in the field (1977, p. 121).

In all fairness to Dennis Middlemist and his associates it should be noted that subsequent to the reporting of their original research they did report an "assessment and cost/benefit ration information" as well as an account of possible ethical problems entailed in their research (see Middlemist et al., 1977). Meanwhile, William B. Saunders tells us that:

> While sociologists are not ethically required to announce their research intentions in public places, in some situations it may be difficult to differentiate between private and public settings; some very private business takes place in public. An excellent example is the research by L. Humphreys,(1970) in which Humphreys, in the role of a "watch queen," or voyeur, observed impersonal sex between men in public toilets. On the one hand, Humphreys was not invading a private space, and that criterion alone justified his presence without announcing that he was a sociologist engaging in research. On the other hand, the sexual activity was private, and it was not the type of behavior with which most of the participants would want their names associated; therefore, in this sense the research can be taken as an invasion of privacy. The resolution of where the invasion of privacy begins and where the public domain ends

must be in terms of the general standards of public and private places. Thus, since no one needs special permission to enter a public toilet as one would need for entering a private home, it can be argued that observation of such domains should not be forbidden to the unannounced researcher (1976, Pp. 9-10).

CORRELATIONAL METHODS

Our discussion thus far is intended to sensitize the reader to a critical perspective and to point out that deviant behavior research depends on the kind of research design employed. And more importantly it suggests that a better picture of deviant behavior is gained by understanding how researchers go about investigating deviancy.

As we stressed earlier it makes sense to consider a variety of research methods because a critical view demands that one employ more than a single method in order to increase the validity and generalizations of one's findings. This is true even though many researchers have continued to stress that laboratory experimental methods are the "best" examples of the scientific model. This does not, however, exclude the recent stress on field experiments. By analyzing what people do in the "real world," for example, much has been gained in understanding deviant behavior.

For testing propositions social psychologists have a number of methods from which to choose. The choice of method depends on the researcher's problem and what resources are available for gathering information. For example, if a researcher wishes to find out peoples' reactions to a particular class of deviants she can in fact decide to interview deviant individuals and observe whether or not people are mistreated or she could carry out well-controlled laboratory experiments (e.g., Freedman & Doob, 1968). Then, in the course of their research, social psychologists must first gather and then analyze data and in doing so they must first consider the "best" research method for the particular problem.

Correlational research is undertaken when the social psychologist observes a negative or a positive relationship between or among two or more variables. The question posed is whether one variable is related to another variable and if so when the researcher finds that indeed one variable is high (e.g., self-esteem) and another is also high (e.g., cheating behavior) a positive relationship is said to exist. On the other hand, when one variable is high (e.g., locus of control) and another low (e.g., cheating behavior) a negative relationship holds. Still when two variables are unrelated no correlation exist between the variables being investigated. And it should be noted that correlations obtained between or among variables are of interest especially in cases where a positive relationship holds between two variables such as when attitudes reported by subjects about their feelings toward drug use increases and also their use of drugs increases. On the other end, if one variable is negatively related to another variable in this case as one's attitude toward drugs increases one's drug use decreases.

Up to this point the situation seems more or less straightforward, however, one of the major problems with correlational research is that when one studies naturally occurring events or obtains self-report measures from subjects these variables may have several covariates which are likely to make it more or less difficult to interpret the research findings. For example, if a deviant behavior researcher wishes to study the relationship between subjects' attitudes toward law enforcement and their "law abiding behavior," even if the investigator does obtain a positive relationship between these two variables, other covariates, such as self-esteem or locus of control, could provide alternative explanations for the researcher's findings. That is, an obtained relationship between any two of a given population of variables may be due to a third, to a forth, and so on, source of variation which may or may not be causally linked to one or both of the variables under study.

Of course, one of the obvious advantages in using a correlational approach to study deviant behavior is that it is a highly efficient way to collect large amounts of research data in relatively short periods of time. For example, a researcher can obtain self-report measures from many subjects at the same time and from this data the deviant behavior researcher can ascertain whether or not there is a relationship between or among particular variables.

In addition to describing the relationship between certain variables---for example, between attitudes about crime and social status---a researcher may wish to keep the value of one variable unchanged and examine the value of the other variables in relation to the variable held constant. For example, in comparing individuals' attitudes toward homosexuality, the investigator may first determine attitudes for and against homosexuality and hold social economic class constant. The researcher then can ascertain if more people who are middle class are positive toward homosexuality then those who are working or lower class. Research done in this manner allows one to see if a relationship just happens to exist between social economic class and attitudes toward homosexuality. Nevertheless, the investigator may not accept the obtained relationship. For example, religious affiliation may in fact be more important than social economic class and to make this analysis the researcher may employ both social economic class and religion toward homosexuality. If the researcher just happens to find that there is a relationship between social economic class and religion then do both of these variables seem to account for subjects' attitudes toward homosexuality? In this case the researcher will want to see if religion or social class best explain subjects' attitudes. It is in this sense that researchers attempt to determine whether or not an obtained relationship holds between two variables or in fact is spurious.

Finally, social psychologists generally agree that the lack of control and possible effects of extraneous variables create special problems for reserachers who employ correlational methods especially in attempting to establish the direction of causality and functional relationship among or between variables. However, not all is so dismal because more recent correlational procedures have made it possible to carry out multivariate correlational analyses that allow for the testing of functional relationships for social psychological variables (see McGuire, 1973).

OBSERVATIONAL METHODS: A BASIC RESEARCH PARADIGM

As we have noted earlier, once a researcher has decided what research problem she is interested in she is then faced with what research design seems most appropriate for her study. And if the investigator decides to observe deviant behavior first hand, she does not have to ask deviants about their own actions she can merely observe what they do. Of course, this enables the investigator to obtain data without having the data contaminated by problems of recall and the like. Moreover, data obtained this way is collected in "natural settings" and the artificality of the laboratory is unlikely to intrude. And, of course, observational methods can indeed be used to study behaviors usually not verbalized.

Observation can take place in many forms from the most unstructured to the most sophisticated laboratory form (e.g., video cameras, one-way screens, etc). However, the first step concerns the decision of what is to be observed. For example, suppose a researcher is interested in studing the relation between deindividuation and aggression and hypothesizes that aggression increases as subjects' identity decreases. In order to research this hypothesis, subjects are observed in conditions where their personal identity is manipulated (e.g., see Zimbardo, 1970) and the researcher then observes subjects levels of aggression. Of course, dependent measures for aggression can take many forms, for example, nonverbal or verbal.

A factor of interest to those who do observational research is the kinds of inferences employed. Hence, an investigator observes a certain form of deviant action and then makes an inference that the behavior describes a given dependent measure or variable. Of concern here is the level of inference. For example, suppose the researcher observes people harm a victim, an inference then must be made by the researcher, for example, whether this action represents a form of deviant behavior or not and if so what form. The suggestion here is that researchers must operationize their concepts.

Observational research can be carried out in either a laboratory settings or in the field. In either event causality is "best" established when the researcher maximizes control over possible confounding variables either in the laboratory or the field setting. It may be recalled that Lawrence Wrightsman (1969) carried out naturalistic observations (during the 1968 presidential election) of people who he identified as committed to either one of the three major political candidates. Since Alabama's Governor George Wallace was thought to be the law-and-order candidate, Wrightsman decided to take advantage of a then recent law that required drivers to obtain and display a tax sticker on their car. He had researcher assistants check cars in parking lots for bumper stickers and automobile tax stickers. Wrightsman found that Wallace supporters were significantly less-law-abiding than supporters of Richard Nixon or Hubert Humphrey. That is, those with Wallace bumper stickers were less likely to have automobile tax stickers than either those with Nixon or Humphrey stickers.

We should note that naturalistic observation, such as Wrightsmans' study, is limited to the unlikelihood that such phenomena as observed by Wrightsman occurs only rarely. This has led researchers to create their own situations and then observe the frequency of occurrence of certain classes of deviant behavior.

It should also be pointed out that naturalistic observations do not provide the kinds of control over extraneous variables as laboratory experiments do. And it is difficult to obtain unbiased samples in order to secure dependent measures. As a matter of fact extraneous variables are difficult to identify in natural settings, however, the reader must realize that there are several kinds of deviant behaviors which cannot be investigated in the "well-controlled" laboratory setting. And, of course, nautralistic observations should, when possible, be checked by using experimental methods. Nevertheless, naturalistic observations seem to be highly valued because they take place in the "real world" and they do not generally entail serious ethical problems as seems to be the case with much of laboratory experimentation. Hence, naturalistic studies seem to have appeal to deviant behavior researchers because they are much more difficult than field or laboratory experiments to fault on the basis of ethics and, of course, deception procedures are not generally used to collect data.

Since there is no single research methodology characteristically used by all social psychologists who study deviancy the investigator must become "aware" of different methods used to study deviant behavior including observational methods. In general, as we have suggested, observational methods poses questions of what one observes and who is to do the observing? This is important because several different observers who independently describe even the simplest form of social behavior are highly likely to select different characteristics of the behavior to observe. Of course, a common solution to the problem of selectivity and subjectivity in observation is to insist that common factors be abstracted from the descriptions of several different observers of the *same* set of events. This should help reduce the seemingly arbitrary nature of observational techniques because the variability in between-observer focus is on what is observed and this is largely determined by the observer's interest or research goals. For example, if an observer has a special interest in the relationship of personality and deviant behavior, she is likely to "pay attention" to personality characteristics when making observations of individuals when she attempts to assess deviant behavior. On the other hand, a second observer, who has a special interest in the relationship of group pressure on deviant behavior, is likely to be attentive to this kind of information. This is why we have suggested that a considerable amount of variability in description and observation can in fact be accounted for by considering the goals and interests of observers. Briefly, then, we should note that the observer contributes to the process when he observe events.

From our general discussion of observational methods questions may be posed. For a given observer and a given situation how can we ever be sure that what is observed and reported is relatively free from bias? When different observers agree (high inter-observer agreement) on what is observed are we to take these descriptions as an index of social reality? Finally, is it really necessary that different observers agree on what is observed and described?

First, we can never be absolutely sure that bias does not operate when observers go about their business of describing social events like deviant behavior, however, people can be trained to more or less objectively report what is observed. Second, since science must depend on consensus, when different observers agree on the meaning of social phenomena this broadens our knowledge and tends to give us confidence in our empirical statements. This view should not be taken to mean that several individuals cannot be collectively in error on what they report as consensus data.

Finally, methods of natural observation, used to study events in the "real world," are typically employed by social psychologists who cannot experimentally manipulated variables without destroying the phenomena in question. Hence, the social psychologist does the next best thing by noting the variables he wishes to observe, and he attempts to reach the most sound conclusions, of course, in the absence of the control achieved in laboratory experimentation.

SURVEY RESEARCH

    Surveys are often used to systematically collect data through personal interviews or mailed questionnaires. Personal interviews, of course, take place <u>vis-a-vis</u> interpersonal situations, and are subject to their own special biases. This is so because the interviewer sometimes asks respondents socially sensitive questions.

    Interviews can be <u>structured</u> or <u>nonstructured</u>. That is, the researcher can give little or no direction to the interview and respondents are then encouraged to respond to open-ended questions or respondents are asked highly specific questions. For example, respondents may be asked about their involvement in deviant acts such as drug addiction or homosexuality. In such cases the interviewer can, in the nonstructed interview, probe areas of interest as well as raise specific questions about the special meaning the respondent places on her verbal statements. As an example, David and Chava Nachmias (1976) allude to Becker's research on marijuana smokers as deviant behavior research employing a nonstructured interview technique. As the reader will recall, Becker (1953) interviewed respondents and followed up the initial interviews with subsequent interviews in order to ascertain the "correctness" of the information gleamed from the earlier interview.

    Surveys have often been used to assess the general opinions of large segments of the general population. The results of surveys have yielded considerable valuable demographic data relative to deviant behavior. However, in order to adequately infer characteristics of a population the survey investigator must first obtain representative samples from a given population and then obtain interview data or mailed questionnaire data. In this sense it is supposed that the distribution of sample characteristics are representative of those found in the population from which the samples are drawn. If in fact they are not, the samples are, no doubt, biased hence invalidating the survey results. For example, when samples do not accurately represent the total population of people from which the samples are drawn or where the size of the sample is under or overrepresented in the characteristic(s) studied problems of sample bias are said to occur. In addition, there are special problems with constructing questionnaire items which are reliable and valid, problems of training interviewers, and/or problems of developing or structuring the interview format and these are potential sources of survey research bias (see Selltiz, Wrightsman, & Cook, 1976).

Then, since questionnaires are frequently used to obtain large amounts of data, because they usually save time and money, it should be stressed that there are several disadvantages over other research methods we have discussed. For example, questionnaires generally show a low rate of return (sometimes as low as 30 per cent); respondents must be able to read and understand the questions; and respondents generally do not entirely complete lengthy questionnaires which restricts the number of questions that can be used.

Suppose that a chain of department stores wishes to ascertain why some customers seem not to observe the "no smoking rule" of the department store. Of course, the amount of smoking will vary from day to day and from store to store, however, the population characteristics of interest are those of people who violate the no smoking rule. One simple way to determine what people say are the reasons for smoking violations is to obtain a random sample of store customers perhaps from the records of those who have charge accounts and also from those who seem to make frequent purchases from the store. In other words, we are interested in estimating the population characteristics from a sample(s) of the store's customers.

After we have constructed our questionnaire we will then want to know how large our sample(s) size should be, of course, this is done to avoid errors in our estimation of the population characteristics (parameters). Finally, we should follow up those subjects who do not return their questionnaires until we seem to have a sizable return rate.

Since surveys are designed to collect information from samples, they are often compared to the more mental methods. For example, since control is frequently impossible when doing surveys, as opposed to experiments, social scientists must be more concerned with the characteristics of sampling and the kinds of inferences made. This is so because the major objective of sampling surveys is to estimate population parameters (e.g., the population means and standard deviations) from information gleamed from samples of the target population. Also, it should be noted that the survey researcher controls the kind of information obtained from his sample by the number and kinds of sampling units employed and the kind of questionnaire responses sought from respondents.

Now let us return to our example of the department store who wishes to survey smoking violators. It should be noted that the investigator conducting the survey is highly likely to be interested in estimating the proportion of the population studied which possesses a negative attitude toward the no smoking rule. For example, the researcher may find out that those under thirty years of age might think the no smoking rule more restrictive of their personal freedom than those over fifty years of age. In this sense, the investigator might be interested in the proportion of the total population which he can attribute negative characteristics to more so than those who do not seem to show these same characteristics. These negative attitudes are likely to be found in a higher proportion of the customers who are smokers than nonsmokers, of course, by first estimating those proportions of the population who are smokers and nonsmokers.

Finally, after the survey researcher has designed his study, there are various methods of collecting sample data open to him such as mailed questionnaires, personal interviews, telephone interviews, and the like. The interested reader should consult one of several of the recent texts detailing the advantages and disadvantages of each of these survey methods (e.g., Mendenhall, Ott, & Scheaffer, 1971; Selltiz, Wrightsman, & Cook, 1976).

MEASUREMENT: SOCIAL PSYCHOLOGISTS ASSESS DEVIANT BEHAVIOR

The scaling techniques used to measure deviant behavior range from the more or less simple nominal scaling techniques to the more complex interval scales. And when researchers use _nominal_ measurement they essentially label observed events and place them in qualitatively different categories. Hence, it is relatively easy to construct nominal classification measures since most people have at least some tendency to classify people in terms of categories. For example, one may classify people as criminals or noncriminals on the basis of criminal conviction. And most deviant behavior researchers find it important to be able to determine the number of people who are placed in the different categories of deviant behavior, however, it should be remembered that categorical measurement is qualitative, not quantitative.

When researchers use an ordinal scaling technique this requires that they use statements like "more than" or "less than," however, we do not always know how much "more than" or "less than" one thing is compared to another. Hence, sometimes a single continuum underlies a classification system. For example, when one observes that a continuum or a degree of deviant behavior underlies a given classification category, then, it is generally useful to rank the categories and then treat them as ordinal rather than nominal. That is, a researcher may rank order the seriousness of a particular type of deviant behavior and then give each rank a score, for example, 0, 1, and 2, respectively. And, of course, these numbers indicate relative degrees of deviancy. Then, when numbers are employed to indicate the amount of a given characteristic and the differences between successive units of measurement are not equal, ordinal data are involved.

Finally, when interval scaling is used we do in fact know how much more or less the property being measured is, for example, when equal---appearing interval scales are used to measure attitudes. In this case, the units represent a quanitative difference and the intervals between successive units are assumed, for the sake of measurement, to be equal. For example, the difference between an IQ score of 100 and 120 is assumed, to be the same as the difference between 60 and 80. Yet an interval scale is in no way the same as a ratio scale because the "ratio" obtained does not allow one to claim that an IQ of 100 is twice as great as an IQ of 50. That is, a ratio scale does indeed have equal intervals between successive units and an absolute zero. Weight is an example of a ratio scale because weight has an absolute zero and equal intervals between successive units.

SELF-REPORT MEASURES

What, then, is the best way to measure deviant attitudes, beliefs, and behavior? First we should note that there are several kinds of measurement and usually measurement is likely to take the form of scales. Then, for better or for worse, deviancy has been operationalized in several ways. For example, countless self-report measures have been developed to measure people's attitudes or beliefs (for example, criminal behavior, drug use, alcoholism, attitudes toward mental patients, and the like), however, among the most commonly used measures to study deviancy are <u>Likert</u> and <u>Thurstone scales</u>.

No doubt, the most popular way to measure deviant attitudes and beliefs is to use a Likert scale, for example, to measure such variables as attitudes toward criminals and disabled persons. The typical Likert format contains questions something like the following: "Criminals are less intelligent than law-abiding citizens." The respondent answers by checking one of generally five different categories: Strongly approve (5); Approve (4); Undecided (3); Disapprove (2); Strongly disapprove (1). The individual respondent's attitude score is the sum of his ratings on all scale items.

Even though Likert scales are by far the most common way to measure deviant attitudes and beliefs, occasionally the Thurstone Method of Equal-appearing Intervals is employed by deviant behavior researchers.

First, it should be noted that attitude and belief scales are generally regarded as examples of interval scales. For example, Thurstone (1928) offered a proceduce for developing "equal" interval scales. The researcher collects a large number of items or statements that seem to be related to the attitude domain of interest. And then several people are asked to take the role of a judge: They sort the items into eleven evenly spaced piles where the number one represents those items judged to be most favorable to the attitude issue and eleven those most unfavorable.

Subsequent to this initial task, the researcher selects about 20 of the "best" items and these statements then constitute the attitude scale. Finally, the scale is given to respondents who in effect are asked to "Agree" or "Disagree" with each statement. And the more favorable the statement the respondent is willing to endorse, the higher is the person's score.

The <u>semantic differential</u> is yet another widely used format to study attitudes. It was developed by Osgood, Suci, and Tannenbaum (1957) to assess the connotative meaning of concepts and is taken as an indication of one's attitudes toward the particular concept of interest to the researcher.

Semantic differential scales are appliable to any concept of interest to deviant behavior researchers and it should be stressed that it is unnecessary to construct special sets of statements to measure a person's attitudes as is the case with Likert and Thurstone scales. That is, sets of bipolar adjectives are presented to the subject, who in turn rates a particular concept (e.g., mental patient) on a given series of seven-point scales such as the following scales: Good-Bad, Clean-Dirty, Cold-Warm, and Honest-Dishonest. The subject who happens to dislike "mental patients" will check the blanks closest to "Bad," "Dirty," "Cold," and "Dishonest," whereas those who feel more positive toward "mental patients" will check the blanks closest to "Good," "Clean," "Warm," and "Honest."

Because the semantic differential is less obvious in its intention than most self-rating scales, researchers are likely to find it can provide a "good" measure for their subjects' attitudes. Nevertheless, the researcher should be careful to check that "appropriate" bipolar adjectives are selected, for example, those adjectives that seem correlated with concepts to be evaluated.

SOME PROBLEMS WITH SELF-REPORT MEASURES

The three self-report measures we have discussed, as well as self-report measures in general, of course, are not without their special problems. For example, an individual's response to a particular set of questions is likely to be determined by several factors in addition to the variable of interest to the researcher. The subject may be motivated to impress the experimenter by creating a favorable image of himself or in other words give socially desirable answers to the questions. Hence, when the subject is asked a particular question for which a certain response seems more desirable than another there could in fact be subtle pressures placed on the subject to give the desirable answer when in fact this is not an "honest" response. This is why researchers should provide the kinds of situations and self-report format most likely to produce "honest" answers from subjects (see Weber & Cook, 1972).

Carlsmith, Ellsworth, and Aronson (1976) tell us there are at least three major problems with verbal reports: (a) such measures in effect tap what subjects tell us about themselves and this may not in fact correspond to the variable of interest to the researcher;

(b) subjects generally "know" that they are being assessed or evaluated by the experimenter and they may not "tell the truth" about themselves; and (c) self-report measures seem not to involve the subject in the task at hand allowing her to reflect on non-related factors which could in fact contribute to distortion of the questions and responses.

THEN WHY NOT DO LONGITUDINAL RESEARCH?

The number of research methods presented in this chapter immediately brings into focus a number of questions, for example, the problem of assessing deviant behavior over time. One would expect that clearly the problem of long-range developmental aspects of deviant behavior should be considered. Then, when attention is turned to collecting <u>longitudinal</u> data (or data obtained from the same individuals taken at different points in their lives) stability and change in personality characteristics and behavior can be noted. In this way researchers are likely to get a better understanding of how a person's "life experiences" contribute to deviancy. And when one does indeed trace the development of deviant behavior one is likely to find its "roots." Such questions as "will characteristics like aggressive behavior and delinquency observed in childhood persist into adulthood?," seems most adequately investigated when researchers use repeated measures obtained from the same subjects over relatively long periods of time.

Before one concludes that the longitudinal approach to deviancy is without problems it should be noted that this method has been plagued by some rather serious problems. For example, the cost of such research is sometimes staggering and there is the nagging problem of sample constancy. Hence, those subjects the researcher is unable to follow or the so-called dropouts may in fact distort or change the findings for longitudinal research. And when one administers the <u>same</u> measures several times subjects may become "wise" to the researcher's hypothesis. Hence, it follows that if one wishes to do longitudinal deviant behavior research a high degree of planning is necessary.

SUMMARY AND CONCLUSIONS

For the beginning a student in social psychology the task of linking research methodology to research findings is a crucial test of their understanding of the implications for the particular research. Hence, one of the problems in examining research methods is that students may consider it to be nothing more than an abstract enterprise separate and distinct from the "real problems" of deviant behavior. Sometimes there is a thread of truth in this claim. However, research methods define the kinds of data and observations that are likely to direct the researcher's efforts. And sometimes the student's seeming inability to appreciate research methods derives from the distinct "need" to relate empirical facts to "day to day living experiences" sometimes labeled "problems of relevance." This is not altogether surprising, since it is not always an easy task to understand a researcher's central purpose in carrying out particular experiments or studies. And while a particular research effort seems to have little bearing on the individual student's personal life this hardly invalidates the particular concern the researcher has with research methodology; at its very best research methodology makes it an easier task to understand and appreciate how deviant behavior researchers go about investigating the causes of deviant behavior.

There are several important points about research methods made in this chapter. First, no particular method is free of difficulty when it comes to the "hard test." The danger of carrying out deviant behavior research with a single research method is well known. Aside from this problem, even when a method is used to study problems apparently well suited to the method, results are not always easy to replicate. For example, suppose an investigator wishes to discover whether a relationship exists between deviant behavior and a certain personality pattern, the researcher may not be able to select a random sample of subjects and administer personality scales to each, and hence systematically assign them to conditions likely to produce deviant behavior. Aside from the ethical considerations the possible design of the research limits the study of this problem in this manner. Instead, the researcher must turn to already existing deviant behavior and then look for certain patterns of personality characteristics assumed to cause the behavior in question. This does not mean that using different subjects will yield similar results unless the researcher can show that certain personality characteristics "cause" deviant behavior in the first place.

In most respects, then, when researchers use correlational methods or natural observational methods they are unable to claim cause and effect relationships. If they are willing to create a controlled situation, in which to manipulate variables, if all of the important extraneous variables have in fact been controlled, the experimenter can in fact claim cause and effect relationships. This is so because the social psychologists who creates situations in which she can control and manipulate variables in fact sets up the conditions that determine changes in her dependent variables. However, the problem arises where there are phenomena in the "real" world that cannot be experimentally manipulated without distroying the phenomena in question or where ethical problem intrude.

Sometimes subjects become suspicious when taking part in research and then become motivated to distort their "true feelings." Such "suspicious" behavior can lead to biasing of research results. And as a consequence it is now customary to check for the possibility of demand characteristics. And in most cases, outright "lying" to subjects seems necessary. Hence, social psychologists often use deception in order to conceal the "true purpose" of their research.

One solution offered for the problem of telling lies to subjects is to use role playing techniques, however, research has shown that role playing yields different data than data obtained from subjects who are not told the "real" reasons for the research. Another solution to the problem of deception has been suggested---nonreactive research. This form of research usually means that subjects are "unaware" that they are participating in a study. Typically such research is conducted in natural settings rather than the psychological laboratory. And unfortunately the obvious restriction placed on nonreactive research is that it becomes difficult if not impossible to assign subjects to conditions on a random basis. In this respect, again, the problem of establishing cause and effect relationships seems obvious. And even here serious ethical and moral questions relative to the invasion of privacy have been raised.

Since designing and planning deviant behavior research involves choosing subjects to study a specific form of deviant behavior certain research strategies and methods seem more fruitful than others for accomplishing this purpose. Then, the criteria for using a particular research design suggests that there are some obvious factors the investigator should consider.

Then, in order to ascertain which of the many research methods is the most appropriate its relative advantages and disadvantages should be assessed. Nevertheless certain general criteria seem to be suggested by deviant behavior researchers, for example, control, representativeness, and the generalizability of the findings.

Laboratory experiments, field experiments, and natural observation are characterized by decreasing degrees of control over would-be extraneous factors. Field experiments and natural observations increases representativeness and generalizability of research finding at the cost of experimental control. And the relative non-reactivity of field experiments and natural observation is a decided advantage over the "well-controlled" laboratory experiment. However, of the alternative research methods, laboratory and field experiments seem to have the greatest merit. And, of course, field experiments relative to laboratory experiments, come closest to approximating "real life." Hence, when a researcher is considering testing a research hypothesis, if control is desired or of paramount importance whenever possible the researcher should consider a laboratory experiment. When the deviant behavior in question seems inappropriate to study in contrived settings the researcher should consider the advantages of field experiments because they are less likely to entail reactivity and they permit greater generalizability of the findings. Nevertheless, random assignment is not always possible in field experiments and the effects of many extraneous factors are not always possible to eliminate as a sources of error.

Finally, it should be noted that the most obvious limitations of the laboratory experiment are its relatively artificial nature and reactivity or the extent to which subjects' "awareness" of their research activities intrude on the situation or behavior being researched.

Before a research problem has been formulated in terms of a particular research design, the researcher should select the appropriate statistical analyses. The choice of a particular statistical analysis is important and should not be an after thought in the research. This is why the investigator should ultimately decide what level of data are to be collected and what statistical analyses will yield the most scientifically sound results from which to generalize the reseach findings.

Finally, ethical considerations can enter the research at any stage and should be considered. The recent development of research guidelines for the protection of human subjects needs to be consulted. For example, the American Psychological Association has adopted standards for research and has published these in the January, 1973, issue of the <u>American</u> <u>Psychologist</u>. Informed consent seems to be the most basic consideration embodied in these standards. Hence, the researcher has an obligation to her subjects to inform them of the potential risks of taking part in the research. And if there are serious questions about whether a particular procedure is in fact in violation of the ethical standards, the investigator can seek advice whether or not to abandon the research or to carry out the investigation.

REFERENCES

Abelson, R.P., Aronson, E., McGuire, W.J., Newcomb, T.M., Rosenberg, M.J., & Tannenbaum, P.H. (Eds.), *Theories of Cognitive Consistency: A sourcebook*. New York: Rand McNally, 1968.

Adair, J.G. *The human subject: The social psychology of the psychological experiment*. Boston: Little Brown, 1973.

Adorno, T.W., Frenkel-Brumswik, E., Levinson, D.J., & Sanford, R.N. *The authoritarian personality*. New York: Harper & Row, 1950.

Alker, H.A. & Owen, D.W. Biographical, trait, and behavioral-sampling predictions of performance in a stressful life setting. *Journal of Personality and Social Psychology*, 1977, 35, 717-723.

Akers, R.L. *Deviant behavior: A social learning approach*. Belmont, Cal.: Wadsworth, 1973.

Akers, R.L. *Deviant behavior: A social learning approach* (Sec. ed.) Belmont, Cal.: Wadsworth, 1977.

Allen, V.L. Conformity and the role of deviate. *Journal of Personality*. 1965a, 33, 584-597

Allen, V.L. Situational factors in conformity. In L. Berkowitz (Ed.), *Advances in experimental social psychology*. Vol. 2. New York: Academic Press, 1965b.

Allen, V.L. Personality correlates of conformity pressure at different degrees of extremeness of the group norm. Unpublished manuscript, 1966.

Allen, V.L. Social support for nonconformity. In L. Berkowitz (Ed.), *Advances in experimental social psychology*. Vol. 8. New York: Academic Press, 1975.

Allen, V.L., & Levine, J.M. Social support, dissent, and conformity. *Sociometry*, 1968, 31, 138-149.

Allen, V.L., & Levine, J.M. Consensus and conformity. Journal of Experimental Social Psychology, 1969, 5, 389-399.

Allen, V.L., & Levine, J.M. Social support and conformity: The role of independent assessment of reality. Journal of Experimental Social Psychology, 1971, 7, 48-58.

Alvarez, R. Informal reactions to deviance in simulated work organizations: A laboratory experiment. American Sociological Review, 1968, 33, 895-912.

Aronson, E., & Carlsmith, J.M. Experimentation in social psychology. In G. Lindzey & E. Aronson (Eds.), Handbook of social psychology. Vol. 2. Reading, Mass.: Addison-Wesley, 1968.

Aronson, E., & Carlsmith, J.M. The effect of the severity of threat on the devaluation of forbidden behavior. Journal of Abnormal and Social Psychology, 1963, 66, 584-588.

Asch, S. Social psychology. Englewood Cliffs, N.J.: Prentice-Hall, 1952.

Asch, S. Studies of independence and conformity: 1. A minority of one against a unanimous majority. Psychological Monographs, 1956, 70.

Asch, S.E. Effects of group pressure upon the modification and distortion of judgments. In H. Guetzkow (Ed.), Groups, leadership, and men. Pittsbury, Pa.: Carnegie Press, 1951.

Atchley, R.A. The social forces in later life: An introduction to social gerontology. Belmont, Cal.: Wadsworth, 1972.

Ajzen, I. Intuitive theories of events and the effects of base-rate information and prediction. Journal of Personality and Social Psychology, 1977, 35, 303-314.

Back, K.W. (Ed.), Social psychology. New York: Wiley, 1977.

Bandura, A. Influence of model's reinforcement contingencies on the acquisition of imitative responses. Journal of Personality and Social Psychology,

1965a, 61, 589-595.

Bandura, A. Influence of models' reinforcement contingencies on the acquisition of imitative response. *Journal of Personality and Social Psychology*, 1965b, 1, 589-595.

Bandura, A. *Aggression: A social learning analysis.* Englewood Cliffs, N.J.: Prentice-Hall, 1973.

Bandura, A. *Principles of behavior modification.* New York: Holt, Rinehart, and Winston, 1969.

Bandura, A. Vicarious processes: A case of no-trail learning. In L. Berkowitz (Ed.), *Advances in experimental social psychology.* Vol. 2. New York: Academic Press, 1965c.

Bandura, A. *Social learning theory.* Englewood Cliffs, Prentice-Hall, 1977.

Bandura, A., & McDonald, F.J. The influence of social reinforcement and the behavior of models in shaping children's moral judgments. *Journal of Abnormal and Social Psychology*, 1963, 67, 271-284.

Bandura, A., & Mischel, W. Modification of self-imposed delay of reward through exposure to live and symbolic models. *Journal of Personality and Social Psychology*, 1965, 2, 698-705.

Bandura, A., Ross, D., & Ross, S.A. Imitation of film-mediated aggressive models. *Journal of Abnormal and Social Psychology*, 1963, 66, 3-11.

Bandura, A., & Walters, R.H. *Social learning and personality development.* New York: Holt, Rinehart and Winston, 1963.

Banuarzizi, A., & Movahedi, S. Interpersonal dynamics in a simulated prison: A methodological analysis. *American Psychologist*, 1975, 30, 152-160.

Baron, R.A., & Bryne, D. Social psychology: *Understanding human interaction* (Sec. ed.). Boston, Mass.: Allyn and Bacon, 1977.

Barber, T.X. *Pitfalls in human research: Ten pivotal points*, New York: Pergamon Press, 1976.

Barber, T.X., & Silver, M.J. Fact, fiction and the experimenter bias effect. *Psychological Bulletin*, 1968, 70, 1-29.

Becker, H.S. Becoming a marijuana user. *American Journal of Sociology*, 1953, 59, 235-242.

Becker, H.S. *Outsiders: Studies in the sociology of of deviance.* New York: The Free Press, 1963.

Bem, D.J. Constructing cross-situational consistencies in behavior: Some thoughts on Alker's critique of Mischel. *Journal of Personality*, 1972, 40, 17-26.

Bem, D.J. Self-perception theory. In L. Berkowitz (Ed.), *Advances in experimental social psychology* Vol. 6. New York: Academic Press, 1972.

Bem, D.J. Self-perception: An alternative interpretation of cognitive dissonance phenomena. *Psychological Review*, 1967, 74, 183-200.

Bem, D.J., Allen, A. On predicting some of the people some of the time: The research for cross-situational consistencies in behavior. *Psychological Review*, 1974, 81, 506-520.

Bem, D.J., & McConnell, H.K. Testing the self-perception explanation of dissonance phenomena: On the salience of premanipulation attitudes. *Journal of Personality and Social Psychology*, 1970, 14, 23-31.

Berg, I.A. Deviant responses and deviant people: The formulation of the deviation hypothesis. *Journal of Conseling Psychology*, 1957, 4, 154-161.

Berg, I.A. Measuring deviant behavior by means of deviant behavior by means of deviant response sets. In I.A. Berg & B.M. Bass (Eds.), *Conformity and deviation.* New York: Harper, 1961.

Berg, I.A., & Bass, B.M. (Eds.), *Conformity and deviation.* New York: Harper & Brothers, 1961.

Berg, I.A. Response bias and personality: The deviation hypothesis. *Journal of Psychology*, 1955, 40, 60-71.

Berger, P.L. *Invitation to sociology: A humanistic perspective*. Garden City, N.Y.: Doubleday, 1963.

Berscheid, E., & Walster, E. *Interpersonal attraction* (Sec. ed.). Reading, Mass.: Addison-Wesley, 1978.

Berscheid, E., & Walster, E. Physical attractiveness. In L. Berkowitz (Ed.), *Advances in experimental social psychology*. Vol. 7. New York: Academic Press, 1974.

Berzins, J.I., & Ross, W.F. Locus of control among opiate addicts. *Journal of Consulting and Clinical Psychology*, 1973, *40*, 84-91.

Bickman, L., & Zarantonello, M. The effects of deception and level of obedience on subjects' ratings of the Milgram study. *Personality and Social Psychology Bulletin*, 1978, *4*, 81-85.

Biddle, B.J., & Thomas, E.J. *Role theory; concepts and research*. New York: Wiley, 1966.

Birdwhistell, R.L. *Kinesis and context: Essays on body motion and communication*. Philadelphia: University of Pennsylvania Press, 1970.

Bogart, K., Loeb, A., & Rittman, J.D. *Behavioral consequences of cognitive dissonance*. Paper presented at the Eastern Psychological Association, 1969.

Borden, R.J. Influence of an observer's sex and value on aggressive responding. *Journal of Personality and Social Psychology*, 1975, *31*, 567-573.

Bowers, K.S. Situationism in psychology: An analysis and a critique. *Psychological Review*, 1973, *80*, 307-336.

Braginsky, B.M., Braginsky, D.D., & Ring, K. *Methods of Madness: The mental hospital as a last resort*. New York: Holt, Rinehart & Winston, 1969.

Braginsky, D.D. Machiavellianism and manipulative interpersonal behavior in children: Two explorative studies. Unpublished doctoral dissertation. University of Connecticut, 1966.

Bramel, D. A dissonance theory approach to defensive projection. *Journal of Abnormal and Social Psycho-*

logy, 1962, 64, 121-129.

Bramel, D. Interpersonal attraction, hostility, and perception. In J. Mills (Ed.), Experimental social psychology. Toronto, Ontario: Collier-MacMillan, 1969.

Brehm, J.W. A theory of psychological reactance. New York: Academic Press, 1966.

Brehm, J.W. Responses to loss of freedom: A theory of psychological reactance. Morristown, N.J.: General Learning Press, 1972.

Brehm, J.W., & Cohen, A.R. Explorations in cognitive dissonance. New York: Wiley, 1962.

Briar, S., & Piliavin, I.M. Delinquency, situational inducements, and commitment to conformity. Social Problems, 1965, 12, 35-45.

Brock, T.C. Effects of prior dishonesty on post-decision dissonance. Journal of Abnormal and Social Psychology, 1963, 66, 325-332.

Bruch, H. Eating disorders. New York: Basic Books, 1973.

Burgess, R.L., & Akers, R.L. A differential association-reinforcement theory of criminal behavior. Social Problems, 1966, 14, 128-147.

Buss, A.R. The trait-situation controversy and the concept interaction. Personality and Social Psychology Bulletin, 1977, 3, 196-201.

Calder, B.J., & Ross, M. Attitudes and behavior. Morristown, N.J.: General Learning Press, 1973.

Calhoun, L.G., Peirce, J.R., & Dawes, A.S. Attribution theory concepts and outpatients' perceptions of the causal locus of their psychological problems. Journal of Community Psychology, 1973, 1, 37-39.

Calhoun, L.G., Selby, J.W., & Warring, L.J. Social perception of the victim's causal role in rape. Human Relations, 1976, 29, 517-526.

Campbell, D. Stereotypes and the perception of group differences. American Psychologist, 1967, 22, 817-829.

Campbell, D.T. Factors relevant to the validity of experiments in social settings. *Psychological Bulletin*, 1957, *54*, 297-312.

Campbell, D.T., & Stanley, J. *Experimental and quasi-experimental designs for research*. Chicago: Rand McNally, 1963.

Carlsmith, J.M., Ellsworth, P.C., & Aronson, E. *Methods of research in social psychology*. Reading, Mass.: Addison-Wesley, 1976.

Carver, C.S., Glass, D.C., Snyder, M.L., & Katz, I. Favorable evaluations of stigmatized others. *Personality and Social Psychology Bulletin*, 1977, *3*, 232-235.

Chaikin, A.L., & Darley, J.M. Victim or perpetrator: Defensive attribution of responsibility and the need for order and justice. *Journal of Personality and Social Psychology*, 1973, *25*, 268-275.

Chiricos, T.G., & Waldo, G.P. Socioeconomic status and criminal sentencing: An empirical assessment of a conflict proposition. *American Sociological Review*, 1975, *40*, 753-772.

Christie, R., & Cook, P. A guide to the published literature relating to the authoritarian personality through 1956. *Journal of Psychology*, 1958, *45*, 171-199.

Christie, R., & Geis, F.L. *Studies in machiavellianism*. New York: Academic Press, 1970.

Cialdini, B., Kenrick, T., & Hoerig, J.H. Victim derogation in the Lerner paradigm: Just world or just justification. *Journal of Personality and Social Psychology*, 1976, *33*, 719-724.

Clayman, S.J., & Ryckman, R.M. Locus of control and chronic self-esteem as determinants of acceptance of positive and negative self-evaluative feedback. *Personality and Social Psychology Bulletin*, 1977, *3*, 236-239.

Clinard, M.B. *Sociology of deviant behavior*. New York: 'Holt, Rinehart & Winston, 1963.

Cohen, A.R. Upward communication in experimentally created hierarchies. *Human Relations*, 1958, *11*, 41-54.

Combs, A.W., Richards, A.C., & Richards, F. *Perceptual psychology: A humanistic approach to the study of persons.* New York: Harper & Row, 1976.

Cook, D.A., Pallak, M.S., & Sogin, S.R. The effect of consensus on attitude change and attribution of causality. *Personality and Social Psychology Bulletin*, 1976, *2*, 248-251.

Cooper, J., & Worchel, S. Role of undesired consequences in arousing cognitive dissonance. *Journal of Personality and Social Psychology*. 1970, *16* 199-206.

Coopersmith, S. *The antecedents of self-esteem.* San Francisco: Freeman, 1967.

Cozby, P.C. Self-disclosure: A literature review. *Psychological Bulletin*, 1973, *79*, 73-91.

Crano, W.D., & Brewer, M.B. *Principles of research in social psychology.* New York: McGraw-Hill, 1973.

Crowne, D.P., & Liverant, S. Conformity under varying conditions of personal commitment. *Journal of Abnormal and Social Psychology*, 1963, *66*, 547-555.

Darley, J., & Darley, S.A. *Conformity and deviation.* Morristown, N.J.: General Learning Press, 1973.

Darley, J., Moriarty, T., Darley, S.A., & Berscheid, E. Increased conformity to a fellow deviant as a function of prior deviation. *Journal of Experimental Social Psychology,* 1974, *10*, 211-223.

Davis, F. Deviance disavowel: The management of strained interaction by the visibly handicapped. *Social Problems*, 1961, *9*, 120-132.

Davison, G.C., & Neale, J.M. *Abnormal Psychology: An experimental clinical approach* (Sec. ed.). New York: Wiley, 1978.

Day, H.R., & White, C. *International prejudice as a factor in domestic versus foreign car ownership and preferences.* Paper presented at the 20th

Internation Congress of Psychology, Tokyo, Japan, 1973.

Derlega, V.J., Harris, M.S., & Chaikin, A.L. Self-disclosure reciprocity, liking and the deviant. *Journal of Experimental Social Psychology*, 1973, 9, 277-284.

Deutsch, M. Trust, trustworthiness, and the F scale. *Journal of Abnormal and Social Psychology*, 1960, 61, 138-140.

Deutsch, M., & Gerard, H.B. A study of normative and informational social influences upon individual judgment. *Journal of Abnormal and Social Psychology*, 1955, 51, 629-636.

Diener, E. Effects of prior destructive behavior, anonymity, and group presence on deindividuation and aggression. *Journal of Personality and Social Psychology*, 1976, 33, 497-507.

Diener, E., Dineen, J., Endresen, K., Beaman, A.L., & Fraser, S.C. Effects of altered responsibility, cognitive set, and modeling on physical aggression and deindividuation. *Journal of Personality and Social Psychology*, 1975, 31, 328-337.

Diener, E., Westford, K.L., Dineen, J., & Fraser, S.C. Beat the pacifist: The deindividuating effects of anonymity and group presence. *Proceedings of the 81st. Annual Convention of the American Psychological Association*, 1973, 8, 221-222.

Dienstbier, R.A., & Munter, P.O. Cheating as a function of labeling of natural arousal. *Journal of Personality and Social Psychology*, 1971, 17, 208-213.

Dillehay, R.C. On the irrelevance of the classical negative evidence concerning the effect of attitudes on behavior. *American Psychologist*, 1973, 28, 887-891.

Dittes, J.E., & Kelley, H.H. Effects of different conditions of acceptance on conformity to group norms. *Journal of Abnormal and Social Psychology*, 1956, 53, 100-107.

Doob, A.N. Deviance: Society's side show. In D.J. Steffensmeier & R.M. Terry (Eds.), *Examining deviance experimentally: Selected readings*. Port Washington, N.Y.: Alfred, 1975.

Doob, A.N., & Ecker, B.P. Stigma and compliance. *Journal of Personality and Social Psychology*, 1970, *14*, 302-304.

Duncan, B.L. Differential social perception and attribution of intergroup violence: Testing the lower limits of stereotyping of blacks. *Journal of Personality and Social Psychology*, 1976, *34*, 590-598.

Duval, S. Conformity on a task as a function of personal novelty on attitudinal dimensions and being reminded of the object status of self. *Journal of Experimental Social Psychology*, 1976, *12*, 87-98.

Duval, S., & Wicklund, R.A. *A theory of objective self awareness*. New York: Academic Press, 1972.

Edgerton, R.B. *Deviance: A cross-cultural perspective*. Menlo Park, Cal.: Cummings, 1976.

Edgerton, R.B. Pokot intersexuality: An east african example of the resolution of sexual incongruity. *American Anthropologist*, 1964, *66*, 1288-1298.

Edwards, A.L. *The social desirability variable in personality assessment and research*. New York: Dryden, 1957.

Elms, A.C., & Milgram, S. Personality characteristics associated with obedience and defiance toward authoritative command. *Journal of Experimental Research in Personality*, 1966, *1*, 282-289.

Exline, R.V., Thibaut, J., Hickey, C.O., & Gumpert, P. Visual interaction in relation to Machiavellianism and an unethical act. In R. Christie & F.L. Geis (Eds.), *Studies in Machiavellianism*. New York: Academic Press, 1970.

Fazio, R.H., Zanna, M.P., & Cooper, J. Dissonance and self-perception: An integrative view of each theory's proper domain of application. *Journal of Experimental Social Psychology*, 1977, *13*, 464-479.

Festinger, L. *A theory of cognitive dissonance*. New York: Harper & Row, 1957.

Festinger, L. A theory of social comparison processes. Human Relations, 1954, 7, 117-140.

Festinger, L. Informal social communication. Psychological Review, 1950, 57, 271-282.

Festinger, L., & Carlsmith, J.M. Cognitive consequences of forced compliance. Journal of Abnormal and Social Psychology, 1959, 58, 203-210.

Festinger, L., Riechen, H., & Schachter, S. When prophecy fails. Minneapolis: University of Minnesota Press, 1956.

Filter, T.A., & Gross, A.E. Effects of public and private deviancy on compliance with a request. Journal of Experimental Social Psychology, 1975, 11, 553-559.

Fink, H.C. Attitudes toward the Calley-My Lai case, authoritarianism, and political beliefs. Paper presented at the meeting of the Eastern Psychological Association, Washington, D.C., 1973.

Fishbein, M. Attitude and the prediction of behavior. In M. Fishbein (Ed.), Readings in attitude theory and measurement. New York: Wiley, 1967.

Fishbein, M. The prediction of behavior from attitudinal variables. In K.K. Sereno & C.C. Mortensen (Eds.), Advances in communication research. New York: Harper & Row, 1972.

Fishbein, M., & Ajzen, I. Belief, attitude, intentions, and behavior.: An introduction to theory and research. Reading, Mass.: Addison-Wesley, 1975.

Flowers, M.L. A laboratory test of some implications of Janis' group think hypothesis. Journal of Personality and Social Psychology, 1977, 35, 888-896.

Fraser, S.C., Keiem, R.T., Diener, E., & Beaman, A.L. The Halloween caper: The effects of deindividuation variables on stealing. Paper presented at the meeting of the Western Psychological Association, Portland, Ore. May, 1972.

Freedman, J.L. Role playing: Psychology by consensus. Journal of Personality and Social Psychology, 1969, 13, 107-114.

Freedman, J.L., & Doob, A.N. Deviancy: The psychology of being different. New York: Academic Press, 1968.

French, J.R.P. Jr., & Kahn, R.L. A progammatic approach to studing the industrial environment and mental health. Journal of Social Issues, 1962, 18, 1-47.

Fromm, E. Selfishness and self love. Psychiatry, 1939, 2, 507-523.

Geis, F.L., Christie, R., & Nelson, C. In search of the Machiavel. Unpublished Mimeo, Columbia University, 1963.

Geis, F.L., Weinheimer, S., & Berger, D. Playing legislature: Cool heads and hot issues. In R. Christie & F.L. Geis (Eds.), Studies in Machiavellianism. New York: Academic Press, 1970.

Gerard, H.B., & Rotter, G.S. Time perspective, consistency of attitude and social influence. Journal of Abnormal and Social Psychology, 1961, 62, 565-572.

Gergen, K.J. The concept of self. New York: Holt, Rinehart, & Winston, 1971.

Gergen, K.J. Social psychology as history. Journal of Personality and Social Psychology, 1973, 26, 309-320.

Gergen, K.J., Gergen, M.M., & Barton, W.H. Deviance in the dark. Psychology Today, 1973, 7, 129-130.

Gerrard, N.L. The serpent-handling religions of West Virginia, Transaction, 1968, 5, 60-63.

Gibbons, D.C., & Jones, J.F. The study of deviance: Perspectives and problems. Englewood Cliffs, N.J.: Prentice-Hall, 1975.

Gibbs, J.P. Conceptions of deviant behavior: The old and the new. Pacific Sociological Review, 1960, 9, 9-14.

Gleasgow, D.R., & Davis, S.F. The project must count: Subject attitude toward experimental deception. Paper presented to the Southern Society for Philosophy and Psychology, Nashville, Tenn., 1977.

Goffman, E. Asylums. Garden City, N.Y.: Doubleday, 1961.

Goffman, E. Stigma. Englewood Cliffs, N.J.: Prentice-Hall, 1963.

Gollob, H.F., & Dittes, J.E. Effects of manipulated self-esteem on persuasibility depending on threat and complexity of communication. Journal of Personality and Social Psychology, 1965, 2, 195-201.

Goss, A., & Morosko, I.E. Relations between a dimension of internal-external control and the MMPI with an alcoholic population. Journal of Consulting and Clinical Psychology, 1970, 34, 189-192.

Gouldner, A.W. The sociologist as partisan: Sociology and the welfare state. American Sociologists, 1968, 3, 103-116.

Gove, W.R. Societal reaction as an explanation of mental illness: An evaluation. American Sociological Review. 1970, 35, 873-884.

Gove, W.R., & Howell, P. Individual resources and mental hospitalization: A comparison and evaluation of the societal reaction and psychiatric perspectives. American Sociological Review, 1974, 39, 86-100.

Green, D. Dissonance and self-perception analyses of "forced compliance": When two theories make competing predictions, Journal of Personality and Social Psychology, 1974, 29, 814-824.

Gurwitz, S.B., & Topol, B. Determinants of confirming and disconfirming responses to negative social labels. Journal of Experimental Social Psychology, 1978, 14, 31-42.

Guten, S. Deviant identity formation: A social psychogical synthesis. In S.D. Feldman (Ed.), Deciphering deviance. Boston, Mass.: Little Brown, 1978.

Haiman, F.S., & Duns, D.F. Validation in communication behavior of attitude scale measures of dogmatism. Journal of Social Psychology, 1964, 64, 287-297.

Hall, E.T. The hidden dimension. Garden City, N.Y.: Doubleday, 1966.

Haney, C., Banks, C., & Zimbardo, P. Interpersonal dynamics in a simulated prison. International Journal of Criminology and Penology, 1973, 1, 69-97.

Harner, R.M. The high cost of dying. New York: Macmillan, 1963.

Harris, F.R., Wolf, M.M., & Baer, D.M. Effects of adult social reinforcement on child behavior. Young Children, 1964, 20, 8-17.

Harris, F.R., Wolf, M.M., & Baer, D.M. Effects of adult social reinforcement on child behavior. Young Children, 1964, 20, 8-17.

Harshorne, H., & May, M.A. Studies in the nature of character. Vol. 1. Studies in deceit. New York: Macmillan, 1928.

Heider, F. Social perception and phenomenal causality. Psychological Review, 1944, 51, 358-374.

Heider, F. The psychology of interpersonal relations. New York: Wiley, 1958.

Heine, P.J. Personality in social theory. Chicago, Aldine, 1971.

Hendrick, C., & Jones, R.A. The nature of theory and research in social psychology. New York: Academic Press, 1972.

Heussenstamm, F.K. Bumper stickers and the cops. Transaction, 1971, 8, 32-33.

Hochreich, D.J. Internal-external control and reaction to the My Lai court martial. Journal of Applied Social Psychology, 1972, 2, 319-325.

Hogan, R., DeSoto, C.B., & Solano, C. Traits, tests, and personality research. American Psychologist, 1977, 32, 255-264.

Hollander, E.P. Conformity, status, and idiosyncrasy credit. Psychological Review, 1958, 65, 117-127.

Hollander, E.P. Leaders, groups and influence. New York: Oxford University Press, 1964.

Holmes, D.S., & Bennett, D.H. Experiments to answer questions raised by the use of deception in psychological research. *Journal of Personality and Social Psychology*, 1974, *29*, 358-367.

Homans, G.C. *Social behavior: Its elementary forms*. New York: Harcourt Brace Jovanovich, 1961.

Homans, G.C. *Social behavior: Its elementary forms* (Revised Ed.). New York: Harcourt Brace Jovanovich, 1974.

House, T.H., & Milligan, W.L. Autonomic responses to modeled distress in prison psychopaths. *Journal of Personality and Social Psychology*, 1976, *34*, 556-560.

Humphreys, L. *Tearoom trade: Inpersonal sex in public places*. Chicago: Aldine, 1970.

Jacobs, P.A., Brunton, M., & Melville, M.M. Aggressive behavior, mental subnormality and the XYY male. *Nature*, 1965, *208*, 1351-1352.

Jacoby, J. Interpersonal perceptual accuracy as a function of dogmatism. *Journal of Experimental Social Psychology*, 1971, *7*, 221-236.

Janis, I.L. Personality correlates of susceptibility to persuasion. *Journal of Personality*, 1954, *22*, 504-518.

Janis, I.L. *Victims of groupthink*. Boston: Houghton-Mifflin, 1972.

Jarvis, L., Klodin, V., & Matsuyama, S.S. Human aggression and the extra Y chromosome. Fact or fantasy? *American Psychologist*, 1973, *28*, 674-682.

Johnson, C.D., & Gormly, J. Academic cheating: The contribution of sex, personality, and situational variables. *Developmental Psychology*, 1972, *6*, 320-325.

Jones, E.E. How do people perceive the causes of behavior? *American Scientist*, 1976, *64*, 300-305.

Jones, C., & Aronson, E. Attributions of fault to a rape victim as a function of respectability of the victim. *Journal of Personality and Social*

Psychology, 1973, 26, 415-419.

Jones, E.E., & Davis, K.E. From acts to dispositions: The attribution process in person perception. In L. Berkowitz (Ed.), Advances in experimental social psychology. Vol. 2. New York: Academic Press, 1965.

Jones, E.E., Davis, K.E., & Gergen, K.J. Role-playing variations and their information value for person perception. Journal of Abnormal and Social Psychology, 1961, 63, 302-310.

Jones, E.E., & Gerard, H.D. Foundations of social psychology. New York: Wiley, 1967.

Jones, E.E., Gergen, K.J., & Jones, R.G. Tactics of ingratiation among leaders and subordinates in a status hierarchy. Psychological Monographs, 1963, 77, 566.

Jones, E.E., & Nisbett, R.E. The actor and the observer: Divergent perceptions of the causes of behavior. In E.E. Jones, D.E. Kanouse, H.H. Kelley, R.E. Nisbett, S. Valins, & B. Weiner (Eds.), Attribution: Perceiving the causes of behavior. Morristown, N.J.: General Learning Press, 1972.

Jones, E.E., Rock, L., Shaver, K.G., Goethals, G.R., & Ward, L.M Pattern of performance and ability attribution: An unexpected primacy effect. Journal of Personality and Social Psychology, 1968, 10, 317-340.

Jones, R.A., Linder, D., Kiesler, C., Zanna, M., & Brehm, J. Internal states or external stimuli: Observers' attitude judgments and the dissonance theory-self-persuasion controversy. Journal of Experimental Social Psychology, 1968, 4, 247-269.

Jorgenson, D.O., & Dukes, F.O. Deindividuation as a function of density and group membership. Journal of Personality and Social Psychology, 1976, 34, 24-29.

Jose, J., & Cody, J.J. Teacher-pupil interaction as it relates to attempted changes in teacher expectancy of academic ability and achievement. American Educational Research Journal, 1971, 8, 39-49.

Kahneman, D., & Tversky, A. On the psychology of prediction. *Psychological Review*, 1973, *80*, 237-251.

Kanouse, D.E., & Hanson, L.R. Negativity in evaluations. In E.E. Jones, D.E. Kanouse, H.H. Kelley, R.E. Nisbett, S. Valins, & B. Weiner, *Attribution: Perceiving the causes of behavior*. Morristown, N.J.: General Learning Press, 1972.

Katz, M.E. Ethical issues in the use of human subjects in psychopharmacologic research. *American Psychologist*, 1967, *22*, 360-363.

Kelley, H.H. Two functions of reference groups. In G.E. Swanson, T.M. Newcomb, & E.L. Hartley (Eds.), *Readings in social psychology*, 2nd ed., New York: Holt, Rinehart & Winston, 1952.

Kelley, H.H. Attribution theory in social psychology. In D. Levine (Ed.), *Nebraska Symposium on Motivation*, 1967, *15*, 192-238.

Kelley, H.H. Attribution in social interaction. In E.E. Jones et. al. (Eds.), *Attribution: Perceiving the causes of behavior*. New Jersey: General Learning Press, 1971.

Kelley, H.H. The processes of causal attribution. *American Psychologist*, 1973, *28*, 107-128.

Kelley, H.H., Hostorf, A.H., Jones, E.E., Thibaut, J.W., & Usdane, W. Some implication of social-psychological theory for research on the handicapped. In *Psychological Research and Rehabilitation*. Miami Conf. Report: American Psychological Association, 1960.

Kelman, H.C. Compliance, identification, and internalization: Three processes of attitude change. *Journal of Conflict Resolution*, 1958, *2*, 51-60.

Kelman, H.C. Human use of human subjects: The problem of deception in social psychological experiments. *Psychological Bulletin*, 1967, *67*, 1-11.

Kelman, H., & Lawrence, L. Violent man: American responses to the trial of Lt. William L. Calley. *Psychology Today*, 1972, *6*, 41-45, 78-82.

Kiesler, C.A. Group pressure and conformity. In J. Mills *Experimental social psychology*. New York: Macmillan, 1969.

Kiesler, C.A., & Kiesler, S.B. *Conformity*, Reading, Mass.: Addison-Wesley, 1969.

Kilham, W., & Mann, L. Level of destructive obedience as a function of transmitter and executant roles in the Milgram obedience paradigm. *Journal of Personality and Social Psychology*, 1974, *29*, 696-702.

Kimbrell, D., & Blake, R. Motivational factors in the violation of a prohibition. *Journal of Abnormal and Social Psychology*, 1958, *56*, 132-137.

Kinch, J.W. *Social psychology*. New York: McGraw-Hill, 1973.

Kirscht, J.P. & Dillehay, R.C. *Dimensions of authoritarianism, A review of research and theory*. Lexington, Ky.: University of Kentucky Press, 1967.

Kleck, R. Emotional arousal in interactions with stigmatized persons. *Psychological Reports*, 1966, *19*, 1226.

Kleck, R. Physical stigma and nonverbal cues emitted in face-to-face interactions. *Human Relations*, 1968, *21*, 19-28.

Kleck, R., Ono, H., & Hostrof, A.H. The effects of physical deviance upon face-to-face interaction. *Human Relations*, 1966, *19*, 425-436.

Kleinke, C., *First impressions: The psychology of encountering others*. Englewood Cliffs, N.J.: Prentice-Hall, 1975.

Kohlberg, L. Education for justice: A modern statement of the platonic view. In N.F. Sizer & T.R. Sizer (Eds.), *Moral education*. Cambridge Mass.: Harvard University Press, 1970.

Koocher, G.P. Bathroom behavior and human dignity. *Journal of Personality and Social Psychology*, 1977, *35*, 120-121.

Kraut, R.E. Effects of social labeling on giving to charity. *Journal of Experimental Social Psychology*, 1973, *9*, 551-562.

Kraut, R.E., Price, J.D. Machiavellianism in parents and their children. *Journal of Personality and Social Psychology*, 1976, *33*, 782-786.

Kuhn, T. *The structure of scientific revolutions*. Chicago: University of Chicago Press, 1962.

Kurtzberg, R.L., Safar, H., & Cavior, N. Surgical and social rehabilitation of adult offenders. *Proceedings of the 76th Annual Convention of the American Psychological Association,* 1968, *3*, 649-650.

LaPiere, R.T. Attitudes vs. actions. *Social Forces*. 1934, *13*, 230-237.

Latané, B., & Darley, J.M. *The unresponsive bystander: Why doesn't he help?* New York: Appleton-Century-Crofts, 1970.

Lerner, M.J. *The unjust consequences of the need to believe in a just world*. Paper presented at the meeting of the American Psychological Association, 1966.

LeBon, G. *The crowd*. London; Unwin, 1896.

Lefcourt, H.M. *Locus of control: Current trends in theory and research*. New York: John Wiley, 1976.

Lefkowitz, M., Blake, R., & Mouton, J. Status factors in pedestrian violation of traffic signals. *Journal of Abnormal and Social Psychology*, 1955, *51*, 704-706.

Lemert, E.M. *Human deviance, social problems, and social control*. Englewood Cliffs, N.J.: Prentice-Hall, 1967.

Lemert, E.M. *Human deviation, social problems, and social control*. (2nd ed.). Englewood Cliffs, N.J.: Prentice-Hall, 1972.

Lepper, M.R. Dissonance, self-perception, and honesty in children. *Journal of Personality and Social Psychology*, 1973, *25*, 65-74.

Lepper, M.R., Greene, D., & Nisbett, R.E. Undermining children's intrinsic interest with extrinsic reward: A test of the overjustification hypothesis. *Journal of Personality and Social Psychology*, 1973, *28*, 129-137.

Lerner, M. The desire for justice and reaction to victims. In J. Macaulay & L. Berkowitz (Eds.), *Altruism and helping behavior: Social psychological studies of some antecedents and consequences*. New York: Academic Press, 1970.

Lerner, M.J., & Simmon, C. Observer's reaction to the innocent victim: compassion or rejection? *Journal of Personality and Social Psychology*, 1966, *4*, 203-210.

Levine, J.M., & McBurney, D.H. Causes and consequences of effluvia body odor awareness and controllability as determinants of interpersonal evaluation. *Personality and Social Psychology Bulletin*, 1977, *3*, 412-415.

Levine, J.M., Saxe, L., & Ranetti, C.J. Extreme dissent, conformity reduction, and the bases of social influence. Unpublished manuscript, University of Pittsburg, 1974.

Liebert, R.M., & Baron, R.A. Some immediate effects of televised violence on childrens' behavior. *Developmental Psychology*, 1972, *6*, 469-475.

Lykken, D.T. A study of anxiety in the sociopathic personality. *Journal of Abnormal and Social Psychology*, 1957, *55*, 6-10.

MacDonald, A.P., & Majumder, R.K. On the resolution and tolerance of cognitive inconsistency in another naturally occurring event: Attitudes and beliefs following the Senator Eagleton incident. *Journal of Applied Social Psychology*, 1973, *3*, 132-143.

Mack, R. *Transforming America: Patterns of social change*. New York: Random House, 1967.

Magnusson, D. & Ekehammar, B. An analysis of situational dimensions: A replication. *Multivariate Behavioral Research*, 1973, *8*, 331-339.

Mann, R.D. A review of the relationships between personality and performance in small groups, Psychological Bulletin, 1959, 56, 241-270.

Mantell, D.M. The potential of violence in Germany. Journal of Social Issues, 1971, 27, 101-112.

Marlowe, D., & Gergen, K.J. Personality and social interaction. In G. Lindzey & E. Aronson (Eds.), Handbook of social psychology. Vol. 3. (2nd ed.), Reading, Mass.: Addison-Wesley, 1968.

Marlowe, D., & Gergen, K.J. Personality and behavior. In K.J. Gergen & D. Marlowe (Eds.), Personality and social behavior. Reading, Mass.: Addison-Wesley, 1970.

Marlowe, L. Social psychology: An interdisciplinary approach to human behavior (Sec. ed.). Boston, Mass.: Holbrook Press, 1975.

Matza, D. Becoming deviant. Englewood Cliffs, N.J.: Prentice-Hall, 1969.

McBurney, D.H., Levine, J.M., & Cavanaugh, P.H. Psychophysical and social ratings of human body odor. Personality and Social Psychology Bulletin, 1977, 3, 135-138.

McCarthy, J., & Johnson, R.C. Interpretation of the "city hall riots" as a function of general dogmatism. Psychological Reports, 1962, 11, 243-345.

McGuire, W.J. Personality and susceptibility to social influence. In E.F. Borgatta & W.W. Lambert (Eds.), Handbook of personality theory and research, Chicago: Rand-McNally, 1968.

McGuire, W.J. The nature of attitudes and attitude change. In G. Lindzey & E. Aronson (Eds.), The handbook of social psychology. Cambridge, Mass.: Addison-Wesley, 1969.

McGuire, W.J. The yin and yang of progress in social psychology: seven koan. Journal of Personality and Social Psychology, 1973, 26, 446-456.

Mehrabian, A. Significance of posture and position in the communications of attitude and status relationships. Psychological Bulletin, 1969, 71, 359-372.

Mehrabian, A. A semantic space for nonverbal behavior. *Journal of Consulting and Clinical Psychology*, 1970, *35*, 248-257.

Meichinbaum, D.H., Bowers, K., & Ross, R.R. A behavioral analysis of teacher expectancy effect. *Journal of Personality and Social Psychology*, 1969, *13*, 306-316.

Mendenhall, W., Ott, L., & Scheaffer, R.L. *Elementary survey sampling*. Belmont, Cal.: Duxbury Press, 1971.

Michael, D.E., Penner, L.A., & Brookmire, D.A. *The commission of a pro or anti social behavior as a function of the estimates of the costs involved in the behavior*. Paper presented at the Southeastern Psychological Association annual meeting. Atlanta, Ga., March, 1978.

Middlemist, D.R., Knowles, E.S., & Matter, C.F. Personal space invasions in the lavatory: Suggestive evidence for arousal. *Journal of Personality and Social Psychology*, 1976, *33*, 541-546.

Midlarsky, E., & Midlarsky, M. Some determinants of aiding under experimentally induced stress. *Journal of Personality*, 1973, *41*, 305-327.

Milgram, S. Behavioral study of obedience. *Journal of Abnormal and Social Psychology*, 1963, *67*, 317-378.

Milgram, S. Some conditions of obedience and disobedience to authority. *Human Relations*, 1965, *18*, 57-76.

Milgram, S. *Obedience to authority: An experimental view*. New York: Harper & Row, 1974.

Miller, A.G. Role playing: An alternative to deception?: A review of the evidence. *American Psychologist*, 1972, *27*, 623-636.

Miller, N.W., & Dollard, J.C. *Social learning and imitation*. New Haven: Yale University Press, 1941.

Miller, A.G., & Minton, H.L. Machiavellianism, internal-external control, and the violation of experimental instructions. *The Psychological Record*, 1969, *19*, 369-380.

Mischel, W. Preference for delayed reinforcement and social responsibility. Journal of Abnormal and Social Psychology, 1961, 62, 1-7.

Mischel, W. Personality and assessment. New York: Wiley, 1968.

Mischel, W. Toward a cognitive social learning reconceptualization of personality. Psychological Review, 1973, 80, 252-283.

Mischel, W. Introduction to personality. New York: Holt, Rinehart, & Winston, 1976.

Mitford, J. The American way of death. New York: Simon & Schuster, 1963.

Monson, T.C., & Snyder, M. Actors, observers, and the attribution process: Toward a reconceptualization. Journal of Experimental Social Psychology, 1977, 13, 89-111.

Montanino, F., & Sagarin, E. Deviants: Voluntarism and responsibility. In F. Montanino & E. Sagarin (Eds.), Deviants: Voluntary actors in a hostile world. Morristown, N.J.: General Learning Press, 1977.

Moos, R.H. Conceptualizations of human environments. American Psychologist, 1973, 28, 652-665.

Moos, R.H. Systems for the assessment and classification of human evvironments. In R.H. Moos, & P.M. Insel (Eds.), Issues in social ecology. Palo Alto, Cal.: National Press Books, 1974.

Moriarty, T. Role of stigma in the experience of deviance. Journal of Personality and Social Psychology, 1974, 29, 849-855.

Morris, W.M., & Miller, R.S. The effects of consensus-breaking and consensus-preempting partners on reduction of conformity. Journal of Experimental Social Psychology, 1975, 11, 215-223.

Murphy, J.M. Psychiatric labeling in cross-cultural perspective. Science, 1976, 191, 1019-1028.

Nachnias, D., & Nachnias, C. Research methods in the social sciences. New York: St. Martin's Press, 1976.

Nisbett, R.E., Caputo, C., Legant, Pl, & Maracek, J. Behavior as seen by the actor and as seen by the observer. *Journal of Personality and Social Psychology*, 1973, *27*, 154-164.

O'Leary, C.J., Willis, F.N., & Tomich, E. Conformity under deceptive and non-deceptive techniques. *Sociological Quarterly*, 1969, Winter, 87-93.

Orne, M.T. On the social psychology of the psychological experiment: With a particular reference to demand characteristics and their implication. *American Psychologist*, 1962, *17*, 776-783.

Orne, M.T. Demand characteristics and the concept of design controls. In R. Rosenthal & R.L. Rosnow (Eds.), *Artifact in behavioral research*. New York: Academic Press, 1969.

Orne, M.T., & Holland, C.H. On the ecological validity of laboratory deceptions. *Journal of Psychiatry*, 1968, *6*, 16-27.

Osgood, C.E., Suci, G.J., & Tannenbaum, P.H. *The measurement of meaning*. Urbana: University of Illinois Press, 1957.

Oskamp, S. *Attitudes and opinions*. Englewood Cliffs, N.J.: Prentice-Hall, 1977.

Pallak, M.S., Sogin, S.R., & Cook, D. Dissonance and self-perception: Attitude change and belief inference for actors and observers. Unpublished manuscript, University of Iowa, 1974.

Palmer, R.D. Parental perception and perceived locus of control in psychopathology. *Journal of Personality*, 1971, *3*, 420-431.

Parke, R.D. The role of punishment in the socialization process. In R.A. Hoppe, G.A. Milton, & E.C. Simmel (Eds.), *Early experiences and the processes of socialization*. New York: Academic Press, 1970, Pp. 81-108.

Pavlos, A.J. *Effects of machiavellianism on helping behavior with or without a model present and with or without an expected reward*. Southeastern Psychological Association, Miami, Fla., 1971.

Pavlos, A.J., & Newcomb, J.D. Effects of physical attractiveness and severity of physical illness on justification seen for attempting suicide. *Personality and Social Psychology Bulletin*, 1974, *1*, 36-39.

Pavlos, A.J. *Consumer ripoff: Effects of physical attractiveness and financial status on cost estimate for a service*. Paper presented at the Southeastern Psychological Association annual meeting, Atlanta, Ga., March, 1978.

Pavlos, A.J., & Reynolds, J.C. Perceived control, diet, and the fading of obesity stereotypes. Unpublished manuscript, George Williams College, 1978.

Pennebaker, J.W., & Sanders, D.Y. American graffiti: Effects of authority and reactance arousal. *Personality and Social Psychology Bulletin*, 1976, *2*, 264-267.

Phares, E.J. *Locus of control in personality*. Morristown, N.J.: General Learning Press, 1976.

Phares, E.J., & Lamiell, J.T. Internal-external control interpersonal judgments of others in need, and attribution of responsibility. *Journal of Personality*, 1975, *43*, 23-38.

Phares, E.J., Ritchie, D.E., & Davis, W.L. Internal-external control and reaction to threat. *Journal of Personality and Social Psychology*, 1968, *10*, 402-405.

Phares, E.J., & Wilson, K.G. Responsibility attribution: Role of outcome severity, situational ambiguity, and internal-external control. *Journal of Personality*, 1972, *40*, 392-406.

Phillips, D.L. Rejection: A possible consequence of seeking help for mental disorders. *American Sociological Review*, 1963, *28*, 963-972.

Piliavin, I.M., Hardyck, J.A., & Vadum, A.C. Constraining effects on personal costs on the trangressions of juveniles. *Journal of Personality and Social Psychology*, 1968, *10*, 227-231.

Piliavin, I.M., Vadum, A.C., & Hardyck, J.A. Delinquency, personal costs, and parental treatment:

A test of a cost-reward model. *Journal of Criminal Law, Criminology, and Police Science,* 1969, *6*, 116-122.

Pines, A., & Solomon, T. Perception of self as a mediator in the dehumanization process. *Personality and Social Psychology Bulletin,* 1977, *3*, 219-223.

Price, W.H., & Whatmore, P.B. Behavior disorders and patterns of crime among XYY males identified at a maximum security hospital. *British Medical Journal,* 1967, *1*, 533-536.

Rodin, J. Research on eating behavior and obesity: Where does it fit in personality and social psychology? *Personality and Social Psychology Bulletin,* 1977, *3*, 333-355.

Rodin, J., & Slochower, J. Fat chance for a favor: Obese normal differences in compliance and incidental learning. *Journal of Personality and Social Psychology,* 1974, *29*, 557-765.

Rogers, C. Therapy, personality and interpersonal relationship. In S. Koch (Ed.), *Psychology: A study of a science.* Vol. III. New York: McGraw-Hill, 1959.

Rohrer, J.H., Baron, S.H., Hoffman, E.L., & Swander, D.V. The stability of autokinetic judgments. *Journal of Abnormal and Social Psychology,* 1954, *49*, 595-597.

Rokeach, M. *The open and closed mind.* New York: Basic Books, 1960.

Rokeach, M., Kliejunas, P. Behavior as a function of attitude-toward object and attitude-toward situation. *Journal of Personality and Social Psychology,* 1972, *22*, 194-201.

Rosenfeld, H.M., & Nauman, D. Effects of dogmatism on the development of informal relationships among women. *Journal of Personality,* 1969, *37*, 497-511.

Rosenhan, D.L. On being sane in insane places. *Science,* 1973, *179*, 250-258.

Rosenthal, R. *Experimenter effects in behavioral research.* New York: Appleton-Century-Crofts, 1966.

Rosenthal, R. Interpersonal expectations: Effects of the experimenter's hypothesis. In R. Rosenthal & R.L. Rosnow (Eds.), Artifact in behavioral research. New York: Academic Press, 1969.

Rosenthal, R., & Jacobson, L. Pygmalion in the classroom: Teacher expectations and pupils' intellectual development. New York: Holt, Rinehart & Winston, 1968.

Ross, L., Bierbrauer, G., & Hoffman, S. The role of attribution processes in conformity and dissent: Revisiting the Asch situation. American Psychologist, 1976, 31, 148-157.

Ross, L., Greene, D., & House, P. The "false consensus effect": An egocentric bias in social perception and attribution processes. Journal of Experimental Social Psychology, 1977, 13, 279-301.

Ross, M., & Shulman, R.F. Increasing the salience of initial attitudes: Dissonance versus self-perception theory. Journal of Personality and Social Psychology, 1973, 28, 138-144.

Rothbart, M. Perceiving social injustice: Observations on the relationship between liberal attitudes and proximity to social problems. Journal of Applied Social Psychology, 1973, 3, 291-302.

Rotter, J.B. Generalized expectancies for internal versus external control of reinforcement. Psychological Monographs, 1966, 80, (1, Whole No. 609).

Ryan, W. Blaming the victim. New York: Vintage Books, 1971.

Sampson, E.E. Social psychology and contemporary society, (2nd ed.), New York: Wiley, 1976.

Sarbin, T. Role enactment. In B.J. Biddle & E.J. Thomas (Eds.), Role Theory: Concepts and research. New York: Wiley, 1966.

Saunders, W.B. The methods and evidence of detectives and sociologists. In W.B. Saunders (Ed.), The sociologist as detective: An introduction to research methods. New York: Praeger, 1976.

Scarpitti, F.R., & McFarlane, P.T. (Eds.), Deviance:

Action, reaction, interaction: Studies in positive and negative deviance. Reading, Mass.: Addison-Wesley, 1975.

Schachter, S. Deviation, rejection and communication. Journal of Abnormal and Social Psychology, 1951, 46, 190-207.

Schachter, S. The interaction of cognitive and physiological determinants of emotional states. In L. Berkowitz (Ed.), Advances in experimental social psychology. Vol. 1., New York: Academic Press, 1964.

Schachter, S. Obesity and eating. Science, 1968, 161, 751-756.

Schachter, S., Goldman, S., & Gordon, A. Effects of fear, food deprivation, and obesity on eating. Journal of Personality and Social Psychology, 1968, 10, 91-97.

Schachter, S., & Gross, L. Manipulated time and eating behavior. Journal of Personality and Social Psychology, 1968, 10, 98-106.

Schachter, S., & Latane, B. Crime, cognition, and the autonomic nervous system. In D. Levine (Ed.), Nebraska Symposium on Motivation. (Vol. 12), Lincoln: University of Nebraska Press, 1964.

Schachter, S., Nuttin, J., DeMonchaux, C., Mancorps, P.H., Osmer, O., Duijker, H., Rommetveit, R., & Israel, J. Cross-cultural experiments on threat and rejection. Human Relations, 1954, 7, 405-440.

Schachter, S., & Singer, J. Cognitive, social and physiological determinents of emotional state. Psychological Review, 1962, 69, 379-399.

Scheff, T.J. Being mentally ill: A sociological theory. Chicago: Aldine, 1966.

Schlenker, B.R. Social psychology and science. Journal of Personality and Social Psychology, 1974, 29, 1-15.

Schultz, D.P. The human subject in psychological research. Psychological Bulletin, 1969, 72, 214-228.

Schur, E.M. *Crimes without victims*. Englewood Cliffs, N.J.: Prentice-Hall, 1965.

Schur, E.M. *Labeling deviant behavior*. New York: Harper & Row, 1971.

Schwartz, R.D., & Skolnik, J.H. Two studies of legal stigma. *Social Problems*, 1962, 10, 133-138.

Scott, R.A. Deviance. In K.W. Back (Ed.), *Social psychology*. New York: Wiley, 1977, Pp. 200-237.

Seaver, B. Effects of naturally induced teacher expectations. *Journal of Personality and Social Psychology*, 1973, 28, 333-342.

Secord, P.F. Social psychology in search of a paradigm. *Personality and Social Psychology Bulletin*, 1977, 3, 41-50.

Secord, P.F., & Backman, C.W. An interpersonal approach to personality. In B.A. Maher (Ed.), *Progress in experimental personality research*. Vol. 2. New York: Academic Press, 1965.

Secord, P.F. & Backman, C.W. *Social Psychology* (Sec. Ed.), New York: McGraw-Hill, 1974.

Seeman, M. Alienation and social learning in a reformatory. *American Journal of Sociology*, 1963, 69, 270-284.

Selby, J.W., Calhoun, L.G., & Brock, T.A. Sex differences in the social perception of rape victims. *Personality and Social Psychology Bulletin*, 1977, 3, 412-415.

Selltiz, C., Wrightsman, L.S., & Cook, S.W. *Research methods in social relations* (3rd. ed.)., New York: Holt, Rinehart & Winston, 1976.

Seltzer, M.M., & Atchley, R.A. The concept of old: Changing attitudes and stereotypes. *Gerontologist*, 1971, 11, 226-230.

Shanab, M.I., & Yahya, K.A. A behavioral study of obedience in children. *Journal of Personality and Social Psychology*, 1977, 35, 530-536.

Shaw, M.E., & Costanzo, P.R. *Theories of social*

psychology. New York: McGraw-Hill, 1970.

Shaw, J.I., & Skolnick, P. Attribution of responsibility for a happy accident. Journal of Personality and Social Psychology, 1971, 18, 380-383.

Shaver, K.G. Defensive attribution: Effects of severity and relevance of the responsibility assigned for an accident. Journal of Personality and Social Psychology, 1970, 14, 101-113.

Shaver, K.G. An introduction to attribution processes. Cambridge, Mass.: Winthrop, 1975.

Shaver, K.G. Principles of social psychology. Cambridge, Mass.: Winthrop, 1977.

Shaver, P., Schurtman, R., & Blank, T.O. Conflict between fireman and ghetto dwellers: Environmental and attitudinal factors. Journal of Applied Social Psychology, 1975, 5, 240-261.

Sheridan, C.L., & Kling, R.G. Obedience to authority with an authentic victim. Proceedings, 80th Annual Convention of the American Psychological Association, 1972, 7, 165-166.

Sherif, M. A study of some social factors in perception. Archives in Psychology, 1935, 27, No. 187.

Sherif, M. The psychology of social norms, New York: Harper, 1936.

Shoemaker, D.J., South, D.R., & Lowe, J. Facial stereotypes of deviants and judgments of guilt or innocence. Social Forces, 1973, 51, 427-433.

Sigall, H., & Landy, D. Radiating beauty: Effects of having a physically attractive partner on person perception. Journal of Personality and Social Psychology, 1973, 28, 218-224.

Sigall, H., & Ostrove, N. Beautiful but dangerous: Effects of offender attractiveness and nature of the crime on juridic judgment. Journal of Personality and Social Psychology, 1975, 31, 410-414.

Silverman, I. On the resolution and tolerance of cognitive inconsistency in a natural-occurring event: Attitudes and beliefs following the Senator

Edward M. Kennedy incident. *Journal of Personality and Social Psychology*, 1971, *17*, 171-178.

Snyder, M., & Monson, T.C. Persons, situations, and the control of social behavior. *Journal of Personality and Social Psychology*, 1975, *32*, 637-644.

Snyder, M., & Swann, W.B. Jr. Behavioral confirmation in social interaction: From social perception to social reality. *Journal of Experimental Social Psychology*, 1978, *14*, 148-162.

Snyder, M., Tanke, E.D., & Berscheid, E. Social perception and interpersonal behavior: On the selffullfilling nature of social stereotypes. *Journal of Personality and Social Psychology*, 1977, *35*, 656-666.

Spencer, C.D. Two types of role playing: Threats to internal and external validity. *American Psychologist*, 1978, *33*, 265-268.

Spielberger, C.D., O'Hagen, S.E., & Kling, J.K. Diminsions of the psychopathic personality: Anxiety and sociopathy. In R. Hare & D. Schalling (Eds.), *Psychopathy and Behavior*, New York: John Wiley, 1977.

Sommer, R. Small group ecology. *Psychological Bulletin*, 1967, *67*, 145-152.

Sroufe, R., Chaikin, A., Cook, R., & Freeman, V. The effects of physical attractiveness on honesty: A socially desirable response. Personality and *Social Psychology Bulletin*, 1977, *3*, 59-62.

Stang, D.J. Conformity, ability, and self-esteem. *Representative Research in Social Psychology*, 1972, *3*, 97-103.

Steele, C.M. Name-calling and compliance. *Journal of Personality and Social Psychology*, 1975, *31*, 361-369.

Steffensmeier, D.J., & Terry, R.M. *Examining deviance experimentally: Selected readings.* Port Washington, N.Y.: Alfred, 1975.

Steffensmeier, D.J., & Terry, R.M. Deviance and respectability: An observational study of reactions to shoplifting. In D.J. Steffensmeier & R.M. Terry (Eds.), *Examining deviance experimentally: Selected readings*. Port Washington, N.Y.: Alfred, 1975.

Stevens, S.S. *Psychophysics and social scaling*. Morristown, N.J.: General Learning Press, 1972.

Stone, W.F. *The psychology of politics*. New York: Free Press, 1974.

Stumphauzer, J.S. Increased delay of gratification in young prison inmates through imitating of high-delay peer models. *Journal of Personality and Social Psychology*, 1972, *21*, 10-17.

Swingle, P.G. (Ed.), *Social psychology in natural settings: A reader in field experimentation*. Chicago: Aldine, 1973.

Szasz, T. *The myth of mental illness*. New York: Paul B. Hoeber, 1961.

Szasz, T. *The manufacture of madness*. New York: Harper & Row, 1970.

Taylor, S.E., & Koivumake, J.H. The perception of self and others: Acquaintanceship, affect, and actor-observer differences. *Journal of Personality and Social Psychology*, 1976, *33*, 403-408.

Thibaut, J.W., & Kelley, H.H. *The social psychology of groups*. New York: Wiley, 1959.

Thurstone, L.L. Attitudes can be measured. *American Journal of Sociology*, 1928, *33*, 529-554.

Tilker, H.A. Socially responsible behavior as a function of observer responsibility and victim feedback. *Journal of Personality and Social Psychology*, 1970, *14*, 95-100.

Tolor, A. Are the alienated more suggestible? *Journal of Clinical Psychology*, 1971, *27*, 441-442.

Turner, R.H. Deviance avowal as neutralization of commitment. *Social Problems*, 1972, *19*, 308-321.

Valins, S. Cognitive effects of false heart-rate feedback. *Journal of Personality and Social Psychology*,

1967, _4_, 400-408.

Valins, S., & Nisbett, R.E. Attribution processes in the development and treatment of emotional disorder. In E.E. Jones et al. Attribution: Perceiving the causes of behavior. Morristown, N.J.: General Learning Press, 1972.

Vidulich, R.N., & Kaiman, I.P. The effects of information source, status and dogmatism upon conformity behavior. Journal of Abnormal and Social Psychology, 1961, _63_, 639-642.

Walker, N., & Argyle, M. Does the law affect moral judgments? British Journal of Criminology, 1964, (October), 570-581.

Walker, E.L., & Heyns, R.W. An anatomy of conformity. Belmont, Cal.: Brooks/Cole, 1967.

Walster, E. Attribution of responsibility for an accident. Journal of Personality and Social Psychology, 1966, _3_, 73-79.

Walster, E. "Second guessing" important events. Human Relations, 1967, _20_, 239-250.

Walters, R.H., Leat, M., & Mezei, L. Inhibition and disinhibition of responses through empathetic learning. Canadian Journal of Psychology, 1963, _17_, 235-243.

Walters, R.H., & Parke, R.D. Influence of the response consequence to a social model on resistance to deviation. Journal of Experimental Child Psychology, 1964, _1_, 269-280.

Webb, E.J., Campbell, D.T., Schwartz, R.D., & Sechrest, L. Unobtrusive measures: Nonreactive research in the social sciences. Chicago: Rand McNally, 1966.

Weber, S.J., & Cook, T.D. Subject effects in laboratory research: An examination of subject roles, demand characteristics, and valid inference. Psychological Bulletin, 1972, _77_, 273-295.

Weiner, H., & McGinnies, E. Authoritarianism, conformity, and confidence in a perceptual judgment situation. Journal of Social Psychology, 1961, _55_, 77-84.

Wellford, C. Labeling theory and criminology: An assessment. *Social Problems*, 1975, *22*, 332-345.

West, S.G., Gunn, S.P., & Chernicky, P. Ubiquitous Watergate: An attributional analysis. *Journal of Personality and Social Psychology*, 1975, *32*, 55-65.

Wheeler, L. Toward a theory of behavioral contagion. *Psychological Review*, 1966, *73*, 179-192.

Wicker, A.W. Attitudes versus actions: The relationship of verbal and overt behavioral responses to attitude objects. *Journal of Social Issues*, 1969, *25*, 41-78.

Wicker, A.W. An examination of the "other variables" explanation of attitude-behavior inconsistency. *Journal of Personality and Social Psychology*, 1971, *19*, 18-30.

Wicklund, R.A. Objective self-awareness. In L. Berkowitz (Ed.), *Advances in experimental social psychology*. Vol. 7., New York: Academic Press, 1975.

Wicklund, R.A., & Brehm, J.W. *Perspectives on cognitive dissonance*. Hillsdale, N.J.: Lawrence Erlbaum Associates, 1976.

Wilson, D.W., & Donnerstein, E. Legal and ethical aspects of nonreactive social psychological research: An excursion into the public mind. *American Psychologist*, 1976, *31*, 765-773.

Wilson, L., & Rogers, R.W. The fire this time: Effects of race of target, insult, and potential retaliation on black aggression. *Journal of Personality and Social Psychology*, 1975, *32*, 857-864.

Wilson, G.D., & Nias, D.K.B. Measurement of social attitudes: A new approach. *Perceptual and Motor Skills*, 1972, *35*, 827-834.

Worchel, S. *The effect of reactance, violated expectancy and simple frustration on the instigation of aggression*. Doctoral dissertation, Duke University, 1971.

Worchel, S., & Cooper, J. *Understanding social psychology*. Homewood, Ill.: The Dorsey Press, 1976.

Wortman, C.B., Adesman, P., Herman, E., & Greenberg, R. Self-disclosure: An attributional perspective. *Journal of Personality and Social Psychology*, 1976, *33*, 184-191.

Wrightsman, L. Wallace supporters and adherence to "law and order." *Journal of Personality and Social Psychology*, 1969, *13*, 17-22.

Yankelovich, D. *The new morality: A profile of American youth in the 70's.* New York: McGraw-Hill, 1974.

Zellner, M. Self-esteem, reception and influentiability. *Journal of Personality and Social Psychology*, 1970, *15*, 87-93.

Zimbardo, P.G. The human choice: Individuation, reason, and order versus deindividuation, impulse and chaos. In W.J. Arnold & D. Levine (Eds.), *Nebraska Symposium on Motivation*, Lincoln: University of Nebraska Press, 1970.

Zimbardo, P.G. On the ethics of intervention in human psychological research: With special reference to the Stanford prison experiment. *Cognition*, 1974, *2*, 243-256.

AUTHOR INDEX

Abelson, R.P., 92
Aaair, J.G., 283
Adesman, P., 159-160
Adorno, T.W., 246-247, 248 250
Ajzen, I., 120, 163
Akers, R.L., 12, 31, 53-56 58
Alker, H.A., 232
Allen, A. 229, 230, 234
Allen, V.L., 18, 79-80, 81
Alvarez, R., 85-86
Argyle, M., 29-30
Aronson, E., 92, 129-130 183, 274, 277-278, 283, 284, 301-302
Asch, S., 76-77, 227, 273
Atchley, R.A., 144

Back, K.W., 278
Backman, C.W., 7-8, 141, 257
Baer, D.M., 56
Bandura, A., 40, 41, 42, 43, 44, 46, 47-49, 52, 56, 68, 162-163
Banks, C., 109-110, 207-208, 274
Banuarzizi, A., 110
Barber, T.X., 282-283
Baron, R.A., 1, 46, 117
Barton, W.H., 114
Bass, B.M., 26
Beaman, A.L., 50-51, 111-112
Becker, H.S., 6, 10-11, 13, 15, 87, 199-200, 216, 296
Bem, D.J., 130-132, 133, 134, 195-196, 228, 229, 230, 234
Bennett, D.H., 285
Berg, I.A. 25, 26
Berger, D., 240
Berger, P.L., 174

Berscheid, E., 145, 163, 269
Berzins, J.I., 252
Bickman, L., 287-288
Biddle, B.J., 19
Bierbrauer, G., 81-82
Birdwhistell, R.L., 144
Blake, R., 86
Blank, T.O., 208-209
Bogart, K., 134-135
Borden, R.J., 51
Bowers, K.S., 203, 234
Braginski, B.M., 205-206
Braginski, D.D., 205-206, 243-244
Bramel, D., 136-138, 283
Brehm, J.W., 123-124, 128, 129, 132, 133, 138
Brewer, M.B., 274
Briar, S., 63, 64
Brock, T.A. 124, 183-184
Brookmire, D.A., 65
Bruch, H., 150
Bryne, D., 1, 117
Buss, A.R., 165-166
Calder, B.J., 118
Calhoun, L.G., 183-184, 201
Calley, W. Lt., 101, 105, 249, 252, 253, 254
Campbell, D.T. 163, 276, 278
Caputo, C., 181-182
Carlsmith, J.M., 74-75, 126, 129-130, 132, 274, 277-278, 283, 284
Carver, C.S., 213-216
Cavanaugh, P.H., 151-153
Cavior, N., 146-147
Chaikin, A.L., 159, 192-193
Charkin, A., 147-148
Chernicky, P., 184-191, 284
Chiricos, T.G., 14

Christie, R., 238-239, 249, 268
Cialdini, R.B., 194
Clayman, S.J., 254
Clinard, S.J., 254
Cody, J.J., 203
Cohen, A.R. 259
Combs, A.W., 265
Cook, D.A., 101, 132
Cook, P., 249
Cook, R., 147-148
Cook, S.W., 297, 298
Cook, T.D., 301
Cooper, J., 72, 75, 77-78, 162
Coopersmith, S., 255-256
Costanzo, P.R., 19-20, 44-45
Cozby, P.C., 159
Crano, W.D., 274
Crowne, D.P., 245-246, 252

Darley, J.M., 28-29, 73-74, 96, 112-113, 161, 192-193
Darley, S.A., 28-29, 73-74, 96, 161
Davis, F., 143
Davis, K.E., 4, 91-92, 170-174, 179-180, 182, 186, 218, 220
Davis, S.F., 285
Davis, W.L., 254
Davison, G.C., 27
Dawes, A.S., 201
Day, H.R., 249
DeMouchaux, C., 90
Derlega, V.J., 139
DeSoto, C.B., 17, 211
Deutsch, M., 78, 248, 249
Diener, E., 50-51, 107-108, 109, 111-112
Dienstbiar, R.A., 198-199
Dillehay, R.C., 119, 249
Dineen, J., 50-51, 107-108
Dittes, J.E., 91, 259-260
Dollard, J.C., 39
Donnerstein, E., 286-287
Doob, A.N., 27-28, 31, 73, 79, 87-88, 89, 90, 143, 151, 273, 290
Duijker, H., 90

Dukes, F.O., 108
Duncan, B.L., 183
Duns, D.F., 250
Duval, S., 96, 97

Eagleton, T., 93-94
Ecker, B.P., 89
Edgerton, R.B., 23, 24
Edwards, A.L., 245
Eichman, A., 101
Ekehammer, B., 230
Ellsworth, P.C., 274, 283, 301-302
Elms, A.C., 247
Endresen, K., 50-51
Exline, R.V., 239, 240

Fazio, R.H., 162
Festinger, L., 74-75, 100-101, 122-123, 126, 127-128, 132, 212-213
Filter, T.A., 95-96
Fink, H.C., 249
Fishbein, M., 118, 120
Flowers, M.L., 99
Frankel-Brunswik, E., 246-247
Fraser, S.C., 50-51, 111-112
Freedman, J.L., 27-28, 31, 73, 79, 87-88, 90, 143, 151, 273, 285, 290
Freeman, V., 147-148
French, J.R.P. Jr., 261
Fromm, E., 263

Geis, F.L., 238-239, 240, 268
Gerard, H.B., 9, 65, 78, 79, 87
Gergen, K.J., 78-79, 91-92, 114, 226, 232, 255, 279-280
Gergen, M.M., 114
Gerrard, N.L., 121
Gibbons, D.C., 30
Gibbs, J.P., 15
Glass, D.C., 213-216
Gleasgow, D.R., 285

Goethals, G.R., 203
Goffman, E., 87, 143, 144, 205
Goldman, S., 149-150
Gollob, H.F., 259-260
Gordon, A., 149-150
Gormly, J., 252, 253
Green, D., 133
Greenberg, R., 159-160
Greene, D., 135-136, 162
Gross, A.E., 149, 252
Gross, L., 95-96
Gumpert, P., 239, 240
Gunn, S.P., 184-191, 284
Gurwitz, S.B., 215-216
Guten, S., 15

Haiman, F.S., 250
Hall, E.T., 144
Haney, C., 109-110, 207-208, 274
Hanson, L.R., 227
Hardyck, J.A., 63-65
Harner, R.M., 243
Harshorne, H., 164-165
Harris, F.R., 56
Harris, M.S., 159
Hartley, E.L.
Harvey, J.H., 97
Heider, F., 169-170, 179
Heine, P.J., 29
Hendrick, C., 260-261, 274
Herman, E., 159-160
Henssenstamm, F.K., 153-154, 275
Heyns, R.W., 99-100
Hickey, C.O., 239, 240
Hitler, A., 101
Hochreich, D.J., 252, 253
Hoerig, J.H., 194-195
Hoffman, S., 81-82
Hogan, R., 17, 211
Holland, C.H., 101
Hollander, E.P., 85
Holmes, D.S., 285
Homans, G.C., 60-62
Hostorf, A.H., 143
House, T.H., 162, 197-198
Humphrey, H.H., 294
Humphreys, L., 289-290

Israel, J., 91

Jacobs, P.A., 40
Jacobson, L., 202-204
Janis, I.L., 78-79, 258
Jarvic, L., 40
Johnson, C.D., 252, 253
Johnson, R.C., 249
Jones, E.E., 4, 9, 30, 65, 78-79, 91-92, 165, 170-174, 179-180, 181, 182, 183-184, 186, 190, 203, 205, 218, 220, 221, 224, 228-229,
Jones, R.A., 78-79, 132, 260-261, 274
Jorgenson, D.O., 108
Jose, J., 203

Kahn, R.L., 261
Kahneman, D., 163
Kaiman, I.P., 249-250
Kanouse, D.E., 227
Katz, I., 213-216, 284
Keech, Mrs. 127
Keiem, R.T., 112-113
Kelley, H.H., 8, 18, 58-60, 66, 69, 91, 143, 174-179, 196, 201, 214, 218, 220, 221
Kelman, H.C., 71, 105, 283, 284
Kennedy, E., 92-94
Kenrick, T., 194-195
Kiesler, C.A., 71-72, 132, 233
Kiester, S.B., 71-72, 233
Kilham, W., 103
Kimbrell, D., 86
Kinch, J.W., 6, 22
King, R.G., 103
Kiracht, J.P., 248, 249
Kleck, R., 143-144
Kleinke, C., 143
Kliejunas, P., 120
Kling, J.K., 65
Klodin, V., 40
Kohlberg, L., 104-105
Koivumski, J.H., 182-183

Koocher, G.P., 288-290
Knowles, E.S., 288-290
Kraut, R.E., 215, 239, 244
Kuhn, T., 3
Kurtzberg, R.L., 146-147

Landy, D., 145
LaPiere, R.T., 118-119
Latane, B., 112-113, 197
Lawrence, L., 105
Lamiell, J.T., 254
Leat, M., 45
LeBon, G., 106
Lefcourt, H.M., 266
Lefkowitz, M., 86
Legant, P., 181-182
Lemert, E.M., 6, 10, 20
Lepper, M.R., 130, 135-136
Lerner, M.R., 193-194
Levine, D.,
LeVine, J.M., 79-80, 81, 151-153
Levinson, D.J., 246-247
Liebert, R.M., 46
Linder, D., 132
Linerant, S., 252
Loeb, A., 134-135
Lykken, D.T., 197

MacDonald, A.P., 93, 94
Machiavelli, N., 238-239
Mack, R., 22-23
Magnusson, D., 230
Majumder, R.K., 93, 94
Mann, L., 246
Mann, R.D. 103
Mancorps, P.H., 90
Mantell, D.M., 103
Maracek, J., 181-182
Marlowe, D., 226, 232, 245-246, 255
Marlowe, L., 11-12
Matter, C.F., 288-290
Matsuysma, S.S., 40
Matza, D., 10
May, M.A., 164-165
McBurney, D.H., 151-153
McCarthy, J., 249
McConnell, H.K., 132

McDonald, F.J., 47-49
McDougall, W., 39
McFarlane, P.T., 32
McGinnes, E., 246
McGuire, W.J., 92, 258-259, 260, 292

Mehrabian, A., 144
Meichinbaum, D.H., 203
Melville, M.M., 40
Mendenhall, W., 298
Mezei, L., 45
Michael, D.E., 65
Middlemist, D.R., 288-290
Midlarsky, E., 254-255
Midlarsky, M., 254-255
Milgram, S., 101-103, 104, 247, 273, 283, 287
Miller, A.G., 239, 285
Miller, N.W., 39
Milligan, W.L., 197-198
Minton, H.L., 239
Mischel, W., 26, 51, 53, 164-165, 211, 234
Mitford, J. 243
Monson, T.C., 190-191, 234
Montanino, F., 32-33
Moos, R.H., 230
Moriarty, T., 83-85, 96
Morosko, I.E., 252
Morris, W.M., 83
Mouton, J., 86
Movahedi, S., 110
Munter, P.O., 198-199
Murphy, J.M., 17

Nachnias, C., 296
Nachmias, D., 296
Nauman, D., 250
Neale, J.M., 27
Nelson, C., 239
Newcomb, J.D., 146
Newcomb, T.M., 92, 146
Nias, D.K.B., 248
Nisbett, R.E., 15, 135-136, 165, 180-181, 183-184, 190, 205, 221, 228-229

Nixon, R.M., 294
Nuttin, J., 90

O'Hagen, S.E., 65
O'Leary, C.J., 101
Ono, H., 143
Orne, M.T., 101, 110, 281-282
Osgood, C.E., 300
Oskamp, S., 248
Osmer, O., 90
Ostrove, N., 145
Ott, L., 298
Owen, D.W., 232

Pallak, M.S., 132, 161
Palmer, R.D., 255
Parke, R.D., 42, 43, 44, 49
Pavlos, A.J., 146, 148-149, 150-151, 155-156, 239, 241-242
Peirce, J.R., 201
Pennebaker, J.W., 113-114, 140-141
Penner, L.A., 65
Phares, E.J., 155, 252, 254, 266, 268
Phillips, D.L., 157-158
Piliavin, I.M., 63-65
Piliavin, J.A., 63-65
Pines, A., 263-264, 269
Price, J.D., 239, 244
Price, W.H., 40

Ranetti, C.J., 80
Reynolds, J.C., 150-151
Richards, A.C., 265
Richards, F., 265
Riechen, H., 127-128
Ring, K., 205-206
Ritchie, D.E., 254
Rittman, J.D., 134
Rock, L., 203
Rodin, J., 149-150
Rogers, C., 263-264, 269
Rogers, R.W., 56
Rokeach, M., 120, 247-248, 250, 268
Rommetveit, R., 91
Rosenberg, M.J., 92

Rosenfield, H.M., 250
Rosenhan, D.L., 204-205
Rosenthal, R., 202, 204, 215, 282
Ross, D., 41, 43, 49
Ross, L., 162
Ross, M., 118, 133
Ross, R.R., 203
Ross, S.A., 41, 43, 49
Ross, W.F., 252
Rothbart, M., 121-122
Rotter, G.S., 80
Rotter, J.B., 79, 87, 251-252
Ryan, W., 163
Ryckman, R.M., 254

Safer, H., 146
Sagarin, E., 32-33
Sampson, E.E., 213
Sanders, D.Y., 113-114, 140-141
Sanford, R.N., 246-247
Saxe, L., 80
Scarpitti, F.R., 31-32
Schachter, S., 79, 87, 90, 127-128, 149-150, 196-197
Scheaffer, R.L., 298
Scheff, T.J., 11, 211
Schlenker, B.R., 280
Schultz, D.P., 285
Schur, E.M., 10, 15, 21, 216
Schurtman, R., 208-209
Schwartz, R.D., 154-155, 276
Scott, R.A., 23, 24
Seaver, B., 203
Sechrest, L., 276
Secord, P.F., 7-8, 141, 231, 257
Seeman, M., 252-253
Selby, J.W., 183-184
Selltiz, C., 297-298
Seltzer, M.M., 144
Shanab, M.I., 103-104
Shaver, K.G., 155, 167-168, 179, 187-189, 191-193, 210, 211-212

Shaver, P., 208-209
Shaw, J.I., 192
Shaw, M.E., 19-20, 44-45
Sheridan, C.L., 103
Sherif, M., 75-76, 273
Shoemaker, D.J., 142-143
Shulman, R.F., 133
Sigall, H., 145
Silver, M.J., 282
Silverman, I., 92-94
Simmon, C., 193-194
Singer, J., 195-196
Skinner, B.F., 53, 133
Skolnik, J.H., 154-155
Skolnik, P., 92
Slochower, J., 150
Smith, D.R., 142-143
Smith, W.P., 97
Snyder, M., 163, 190-191, 213-216, 217, 234
Sogin, S.R., 132, 161
Solano, C., 17, 211
Solomon, T., 263-264, 269
Sommer, R., 144
Spencer, C.D., 285-286
Spielberger, C.D., 65
Sroufe, R., 147-148
Stang, D.J., 95
Stanley, J., 278
Steele, C.M., 95, 215
Steffensmeier, D.J., 156-157
Stevens, S.S., 8
Stone, W.F., 249
Stumphauzer, J.S., 51, 52
Suci, G.J., 300
Sutherland, E.H., 53
Swann, W.B. Jr., 216-217
Swingle, P.G., 276
Szasz, T., 11, 166-167, 225

Tanke, E.G., 163
Tannenbaum, P.H., 92, 300
Taylor, S.E., 182-183
Terry, R.M., 7, 156-157
Thibaut, J.W., 8, 18, 58-60, 66, 69, 239, 240
Thomas, E.J., 19
Thurstone, L.L., 300
Tilker, H.A., 105
Tolor, A., 252

Tomich, E., 101
Topol, B., 215-216
Turner, R.H., 18
Tversky, A., 163

Valins, S., 200
Vidulich, R.N., 249-250

Waldo, G.P., 14
Wallace, G., 293-294
Walker, E.L., 99-100
Walker, N., 29-30
Walster, E., 145, 192, 269
Walters, R.H., 43, 44, 45, 49
Ward, L.M., 203
Webb, E.J., 276
Weber, S.J., 301
Weiner, H., 246
Weinheimer, S., 239, 240
Welford, C., 14
West, S.G., 184-191, 284
Westford, K.L., 107-108
Whatmore, P.B., 40
White, C., 249
Wicker, A.W., 118
Wicklund, R.A., 96, 123-124, 128, 129, 133
Willis, F.M., 101
Wilson, D.W., 56, 286-287
Wilson, G.D., 248
Wilson, K.G., 252
Wilson, L., 49-50
Wolf, M.M., 56
Worchel, S., 72, 75, 77-78, 139
Wortman, C.B., 159-160
Wrightsman, L.S., 119, 293, 297, 298

Yahya, K.A., 103-104
Yankelovich, D., 30

Zanna, M.P., 132-162
Zarantonello, M., 287-288
Zellner, M., 260
Zimbardo, P., 106-107, 108, 109-110, 111, 115, 116, 207-208, 274, 285, 293

SUBJECT INDEX

Actor-observer hypothesis, 180-183
Acute self-esteem, 260-261
Asch line judgment task, 76-78
Aggression, 49-51 and modeling, 49-51
Attitudes, defined, 117 as cause of behavior, 118-122, consistency with behavior, 117-122, importance, 120
Attribution, negative, 201-208, and labeling theory compared, 210
Authoritarianism, 246-248, methological problems, 248
Autokinetic phenonenon, 75-76

Behavior as cause of attitudes, 125-128
Behavioral contagion, 50
Behavioral control, 66
Behavioral intentions, 120
Behavioral sampling, 232
Between-person variance, 223
Biographical variables, 232
Body odor and deviance, 151-152
Bystander effects and deviance, 112-114

Causal attributions and "actual" causes of behavior, 167-168
Chronic self-esteem, 260-261
Cognitive consistency and attitude change, 92, 95
Cognitive dissonance theory, 73-75, choice, 124-125, external justification, 73-75, postdecisional aspects, 123-124
Common-sense psychology, 170
Community-based attributions, 208-210

Comparison level, 59
Comparison level for alternatives, 59, 66
Conformity, defined, 71, 72, choice points, 28-29, commitment, 233, early research. 75, group pressure, 72, groupthink, 98-100
Compliance, defined, 71, group pressure, 72
Consensus, defined, 175
Consistency, defined 175-176
Correlational research, 290-292, and cause and effect, 291
Correspondent inference theory, 171-174, and assumed social desirability, 171, out of role behavior, 171
Covariation principle, 177
Credit theory, 85-86
Criminal behavior and perceived rehabilitation success, 155
Cross-situational stability of personality and deviant behavior, 231-232

Defensive attribution, 192-195, just world hypothesis, 192-195, situational possibility, 192-195
Deception paradigm, 283-285, 286-289
Defensive projection, 136-138, and dissonance, 137-138
Deindividuation, 100, and the dark, 114-115
Delay of gratification

and modeling, 51-53
Demand characteristics, 103, 281-282
Dependent variable, defined, 274
Deviant behavior, defined, 3-6, 30, research and value judgments, 270-272
Deviant identity, 15
Deviation hypothesis, 24-26
Difference theory, 27, 87-90
Disinhibition, 43-44
Dispositional hypothesis, 207
Distinctiveness, defined, 175
Distributive justice, 62-63
Dogmatism, 248-250

Employment and criminal record, 154-155
Environmental coercion, 191
Ethnocentrism, 249
Exchange theory, 58-67, behavioral control, 66, fate control, 66, residual outcomes, 59-66
Expectancies, 202-204, and grades, 203-204 and IQ, 202
Experimental control, 273
Experimenter bias, 282-283
External justification, 125
External validity, 278-279

Fate control, 66
Field research, 275-278, and experimental control, 275
Forbidden behavior and dissonance, 129-130
Forced compliance, 125-127
Funeral arrangements, 241-242

Genetics and deviance, 39
Group pressure and conformity, 72
Groupthink and conformity, 98-100

Hedonic relevance, 172
Honesty and deviant behavior, 164-165

Idiosyncrasy credits, 85-86
I-E Scale, 251-252, alcoholism, 252, My Lai, 253-254, self help, 254-255
Impression management, 143
Independent variable, defined, 274
Information control, 143
Informed consent, 284-285
Inhibition, 43-44
Intentionality and causality, 179
Internal-external causality, 169-170
Internal validity, 278-279
Interval measurement, 299
Involuntary deviance, 33

Jones-Davis attribution theory, 218-220, and Kelley's attribution theory, 179-180
Just world hypothesis, 192-195, and defensive attribution, 192

Kelley's attribution theory, 174-179, 218 and Jones-Davis attribution theory, 179-180

Labeling theory, 9-16, and mental hospital patients, 204-207
Laboratory research, 272-275, dependent variables, 274, experimental control, 274, independent variable, 274
Likert scales, 300
Locus of control, 250-255
Longitudinal research, 302

Machiavellianism, 237, developmental aspects, 243-245

Managing impressions, 205-206
Marijuana, 199-200, and labeling of arousal, 199-200
Measurement, 298-302, interval, 299, Likert scales, 300, nominal, 298, ordinal, 298, problems, 301-302, ratio, 299, self-report, 299-302, semantic differential, 300-301, Thurstone scales, 300
Medical model, 166-167
Misattribution, 198-200
Modeling, 49-51, and aggression, 49-51
Moral accountability, 191
Moral development, 47-48, 104-105, and social learning, 98
Mortoric inhibition, 144

Nominal measurement, 298
Nonreactive research, 276
Nonverbal behavior, 144
Normative influence, 78
Norm-sending and comformity, 90
Norm violation and deviancy, 3, 6-8

Obediance and deviance, 101, moral development, 104-105, responsibility, 105-106
Obesity and deviance, 149, stigma, 150
Objective self-awareness and deviance, 96
Observational learning, 42
Observational research, 292-296, field, 293, laboratory, 293
Ordinal measurement, 299
Overly sufficient justification hypothesis, 134-136

Perceiver as an information processor, 179
Personality, defined, 223 cause of behavior, 223, measurement, 233-236 person perception, 227-228, versus situational cause, 223-226
Personal involvement of observer, 220
Personalism, 172
Phenomenal causality, 169
Physical attractiveness, 145-146, and deviance, 145-146, 156-157
Primary deviance, 6
Prior probability, 171
Private acceptance, 71
Prophecy and attitude change, 127-128
Psychological perspective of deviance, 13, 24-26
Psychological reactance, 138-141, as a motivational state, 139

Radical behaviorism, 133
Ratio measurement, 299
Reactive research, 276
"Real" causes for behavior, 219
Rejection and deviancy, 79-85
Reliability, defined, 234-235
Research ethics, 283-286, and right of privacy, 287-290
Research hypotheses, 272-273
Residual outcomes, 59, 66
Reward-cost model, 63
Role-playing technique, 285-286
Role theory and deviance, 17, and conformity, 20
Responsibility attributions, 191-192, and foreseeability, 191

Secondary deviance, 6

Seeking help for deviant behavior, 157-158
Self-attributions, 195-198 deviant behavior, 200-201, long standing behavior, 200-201, self-labeled arousal, 196-198, self-labeled emotions, 196-198
Self-concept, defined, 255
Self-disclosure and deviance, 159-160
Self-esteem, defined, 255, acceptance of others, 263-266, acute, 260, 261, chronic, 260, 261, conformity and deviation, 95-96 developmental aspects, 255-256, rejection of others, 263-266, social influence, 258, social learning theory, 262-263, stability over time, 256-257
Self-perception theory, 130-134, 195
Self-report scales, 299-302
Semantic differential scales, 300-301
Significant others, 133
Situations as cause of deviant behavior, 164-166, versus personality variables, 230-231
Social approval, 245-246
Social comparison theory, 100, 212-213, physical reality, 100, 212-213, social reality, 100, 212-213
Social control, 7-8
Social desirability, 220, 245, 246
Social influence, 78, informational, 78, normative, 78
Social learning, 40, 57-58, reinforcement theory, 53-58, 57-58, vicarious conditioning, 41-42, 44-45
Social psychology of deviant behavior, 1-2, 26

Social psychology as history or science, 279-281
Stanford Prison study, 109-112, 207-208, and the dispositional hypothesis, 109
Status and conformity, 85
Stereotypes of deviants, 141-145
Stigma, 141-143, and obesity, 150
Subculture and deviance, 22-24
Subject bias, 282-283
Sufficient justification hypothesis, 129-130
Suicide attempter and justification, 145
Survey research, 296-298, sample size, 296, structured, 296, unstructured, 296
Symbolic interactionism, 5-6, 211-212

Tension control, 143
Thurstone scales, 300
Traits as cause of behavior, 164-166, 228-233, measures, 232

Unattractive persons and consumer rip off, 147-149

Validity, 234-235
Vicarious conditioning, 41-42, 44-45
Voluntary deviance, 33

Watergate, 184-189, actor-observer effect, 180-183, 183-191
Within-person variables, 223

XYY chronosome male and deviancy, 39

LIBRARY OF DAVIDSON COLLEGE